Metaphrastes,
or,
Gained in translation

BELFAST BYZANTINE TEXTS AND TRANSLATIONS

General Editor: Professor M.E. Mullett

Editorial Assistant: C. McColgan

Editorial Board: Dr R.H. Jordan
Professor M.J. McGann
Dr E.A.M. Haan

Advisory Board: Professor M.J. Angold
Professor A.A.M. Bryer
Professor R. Cormack
Professor J. Herrin

Published titles

BBTT1	The Life of Michael the Synkellos
BBTT4.1	Alexios I Komnenos
BBTT6.1	The Theotokos Evergetis and eleventh-century monasticism
BBTT6.2	Work and worship at the Theotokos Evergetis
BBTT6.5	The Synaxarion of the monastery of the Theotokos Evergetis
BBTT8	One hundred practical texts of perception and spiritual discernment from Diadochos of Photike

Titles in preparation

BBTT2	The XL Martyrs of Sebasteia
BBTT3	The Lives of Meletios of Myoupolis
BBTT4.2	Alexios I Komnenos II
BBTT5.1	Ubertino Pusculo, Constantinopolis
BBTT6.3	Founders and refounders of Byzantine monasteries

Metaphrastes, or, Gained in translation

Essays and translations in honour of Robert H. Jordan

edited by Margaret Mullett

BELFAST BYZANTINE TEXTS AND TRANSLATIONS, 9

2004

First published in 2004
by Belfast Byzantine Enterprises
Institute of Byzantine Studies
Queen's University Belfast

© Belfast Byzantine Enterprises 2004

All rights reserved. No part of this publication may be reproduced,
stored in a retrieval system, or transmitted, in any form or by any means, electronic, mechanical, photocopying, recording or otherwise,
without the prior permission of the publisher.

ISBN: 085389-871-5
ISSN: 0960-9997

British Library Cataloguing-in-Publication Data

A catalogue record for this book
is available from the British Library

Printed and bound in Northern Ireland
by Priory Press, Holywood, Co Down.

Contents

Contributors — ix
Editor's note — xii
Dr Robert Jordan — xiii
Bibliography — xiv

INTRODUCTION

1. The other side of a tapestry
   Margaret Mullett — 3

ESSAYS

2. Baldrick and Blackadder revive an ancient exegetical question relating to Ruth
   Derek Beattie — 15

3. Hurdles in Greek
   Joseph Munitiz — 22

4. The Letter and the Spirit: some problems in transmitting patristic texts to a modern audience
   Mary Cunningham — 28

5. Bishops, monks and holy men: military defence and the shedding of blood
   Stephen McCotter — 39

6. Cutting the tusk
   Lyn Rodley — 51

7. The limits of translation: multiple meanings in a Byzantine religious poem
   Dirk Krausmüller — 57

8. Constantine's Constantinople
   Liz James — 62

9	*Stephanites kai Ichnelates* and the tale of the swindler, the simpleton and the buried treasure *Alison Noble*	66
10	Byzantine marriages and classical transmission in the *Cliges* of Chrétien de Troyes *Evelyn Mullally*	72
11	*Urbs parva, sed loco munita*: translation, culture and the institution *David Johnston*	83
12	Translating cultures: suggestions from the Middle English Prose *Brut* *Stephen Kelly*	91
13	A Virgin 'lost in translation'?: another fine mess for Geoffrey Chaucer, John Lydgate and English literary history *John Thompson*	103
14	'The adorning of my native tongue': linguistic metamorphosis in Milton *Estelle Haan*	111
15	Richard Mant's translations from the Roman breviary *George Woodman*	128

TRANSLATIONS

16	Verse translation of Horace, *Odes* I.5 *Estelle Haan*	141
17	Romanos's *kontakion On Elijah* *James Peden*	143
18	Alexander the Monk, *Discovery of the True Cross* *Roger Scott*	157
19	Paul of Monembasia, *Historia animae utilis:* text and commentary BHG 1449d *Alastair Carroll*	185

20	The tale of Daniel's sister: text, translation and commentary *BHG* 1438hb *Evangeli Skaka and John Wortley*	194
21	Ælfric of Eynsham's *Letter to Sigeweard* (Treatise on the Old and New Testaments) *Hugh Magennis*	210
22	Symeon the New Theologian, ep. 2 *John Turner*	236
23	The liturgy of the Minor Blessing of the Water according to Cod. Paris. Coisl. 213 *Jeffrey Anderson and John Nesbitt*	240
24	A feast for the senses *Patricia Finlay*	248
25	Philip of Oxford, on preaching the Holy Cross in England *Edward Moss*	249
26	Two catecheses on the office of monastic tonsure *Angela Constantinides Hero*	267
27	The liturgical *typikon* of Symeon of Sinai *Nancy Ševčenko*	274
28	Politian's ode to Horace *Michael McGann*	287
29	Alexandros Papadiamandis, *Love in the snow* *Kathryn Baird*	289
30	C.P. Cavafy: fourteen Byzantine texts and translations *Anthony Hirst*	296
31	From the *Holy Mountain Journal* of Angelos Sikelianos *Anastasia Psoni*	314
32	Five imitations of Jenny Mastoraki *Sarah Ekdawi Brandt*	332

ENVOI

33 'Use the middle – passive not used in Attic prose':
    a master's stimulus to a life of translation trials
    Paul Tuffin   339

Abbreviations   342
Index   343

Contributors

Jeffrey C. Anderson is Professor of Art History at George Washington University and former Leverhulme Professor of Byzantine Studies, QUB.

Kathryn Baird is an MA student of the Institute of Byzantine Studies, QUB.

Derek Beattie is Senior Lecturer in Semitic Languages at the Institute of Byzantine Studies, QUB.

Alastair Carroll is a PhD student of the Institute of Byzantine Studies, QUB.

Angela Constantinides Hero was Adjunct Professor of Byzantine and Balkan History at Queen's College, City University of New York, from 1978 to 1992, and co-editor of the Dumbarton Oaks Typikon Project.

Mary Cunningham is AHRB Research Fellow at the Centre for Byzantine, Ottoman and Modern Greek Studies, University of Birmingham, and a translator and member of the Spirituality team of the British Academy's Evergetis Project.

Sarah Ekdawi Brandt is Director of Studies at the Oxford English Centre and a Faculty Research Fellow at the University of Oxford; she was also a Visiting and Honorary Research Fellow at the Institute of Byzantine Studies, QUB.

Patricia Finlay is a PhD student of the Institute of Byzantine Studies, QUB.

Estelle Haan (Sheehan) is a Reader in English in the School of English, and an Associate of the Institute of Byzantine Studies, QUB.

Anthony Hirst is a Leverhulme Special Research Fellow and Head of Modern Greek at the Institute of Byzantine Studies, QUB.

Liz James is Reader in the History of Art, University of Sussex and Associate Director of the AHRB Centre for Byzantine Cultural History.

David Johnston is Professor of Hispanic Studies in the School of Languages, Literatures and Arts, and an Associate of the Institute of Byzantine Studies, QUB.

Stephen Kelly is a post-doctoral Research Fellow to the AHRB Imagining History Project, and an Associate of the Institute of Byzantine Studies, QUB.

Dirk Krausmüller has held various research and teaching posts at Dumbarton Oaks and the AHRB Centre for Byzantine Cultural History; he is currently a Visiting Research Fellow at the Institute of Byzantine Studies, QUB.

Hugh Magennis is Professor of Old English Literature at Queen's University Belfast, and an Associate of the Institute of Byzantine Studies, QUB.

Edward Moss has recently completed his PhD in Byzantine Studies and Medieval English, QUB.

Evelyn Mullally is a former Senior Lecturer in Medieval French, and an Associate of the Institute of Byzantine Studies, QUB.

Margaret Mullett is Professor of Byzantine Studies and Director of the Institute of Byzantine Studies, QUB, and Director of the AHRB Centre for Byzantine Cultural History.

Joseph A. Munitiz SJ is editor of texts (Corpus Christianorum), Research Fellow of the Centre for Byzantine, Ottoman and Modern Greek Studies, University of Birmingham, and adviser to the Spirituality team of the British Academy's Evergetis Project.

Stephen McCotter is a former student of Bob Jordan's and a Teaching Fellow at the Institute of Byzantine Studies, QUB.

Michael McGann is Professor Emeritus of Latin at the Institute of Byzantine Studies, QUB.

John W. Nesbitt is Research Associate, Byzantine Sigillography, at Dumbarton Oaks.

Alison Noble was an MA and PhD student and is now a Visiting Research Fellow at the Institute of Byzantine Studies, QUB.

James Peden was an MA student, and is now a Teaching Assistant in Byzantine Greek at the Institute of Byzantine Studies, QUB.

Anastasia Psoni is a Teaching Assistant in Modern Greek at the Institute of Byzantine Studies, QUB.

Lyn Rodley is a Helen Waddell Visiting Professor at the Institute of Byzantine Studies, QUB, and adviser for Art History and Archaeology to the British Academy's Evergetis Project.

Roger Scott is Associate Professor and Reader at the Centre for Classics and Archaeology at the University of Melbourne, and a member of the AHRB Centre's Skylitzes Project; he was a Visiting Professor at the Institute of Byzantine Studies, QUB, from 2000–2003.

Nancy Ševčenko is an independent scholar, South Woodstock, Vermont and is a member of the Liturgy team of the British Academy's Evergetis Project.

Evangeli Skaka is a DPhil student at Oxford and British Academy Research Fellow to the Evergetis Project.

John Thompson is Professor of English Textual Cultures and an Associate of the Institute of Byzantine Studies, QUB.

Paul Tuffin is an Honorary Visiting Research Fellow of the Centre for European Studies and General Linguistics at the University of Adelaide, and a member of the AHRB Centre's Skylitzes Project.

John Turner is the author of *St Symeon the New Theologian and spiritual fatherhood* (Leiden and New York, 1990) and a translator and member of the Spirituality team of the British Academy's Evergetis Project.

George Woodman is a librarian on the staff of the Northern Ireland Assembly Library. A graduate in classics of Dublin University, he is Belfast branch secretary of the Fellowship of St Alban and St Sergius, and Honorary Librarian to the AHRB Centre's Benefactors' Library at the Institute of Byzantine Studies, QUB.

John Wortley is Professor Emeritus of Medieval History at the University of Manitoba (Canada), and International Fellow (previously Leverhulme Visiting Professor) a the Institute of Byzantine Studies, QUB.

Editor's note

This volume came together very quickly, from the germ of an idea in Dumbarton Oaks to its presentation on the thirtieth anniversary of Byzantine Studies at Queen's. We are very grateful to the AHRB and to Queen's University Belfast for making it possible. What we expected to be a slim volume became something more extensive, since no-one wished to be excluded; many more potential contributors simply conceded defeat when faced with the deadline, and so send their wishes instead. Editing over a summer spent partly in India and Australia has meant that I am more than usually indebted to the editorial assistance of learned colleagues and friends. Anthony Hirst took on the Modern Greek contributions; Dirk Krausmüller helped with many Byzantine ones; Michael McGann and Estelle Sheehan lent their sharp eyes unstintingly at the end. For all of us the work was eased by the professionalism and commitment of Catherine McColgan. I should like to thank the contributors for their helpfulness and their tolerance: they have received fewer sets of proofs than we are accustomed to offer, and not every editorial standardisation at the end could be cleared with every contributor, who might have excellent reason for wishing to be allowed an exception. Finally, it would have been a better book had we had at our disposal (as for every other book in the series) the eyes of Robert Jordan – but in all its imperfections we offer it to him now.

Margaret Mullett
1.ix.04

Front cover: Paul of Evergetis: detail, Colin McGookin, *The Feast of Wisdom*, mural in the Institute of Byzantine Studies, QUB, May 2003.

Back cover: the beginning of the *Hypotyposis* of Evergetis, Athon. gr. 788, fol. 180r.

Robert Hamilton Jordan

Robert Hamilton Jordan

BIBLIOGRAPHY

Classical

Iliad, I: *introduction, notes and vocabulary* (with J.A. Harrison) (Bristol Classical Press, 1983), xv + 88pp

Iliad, VI: *introduction, notes and vocabulary* (with J.A. Harrison) (Bristol Classical Press, 1985), 106pp

Aeneid, X: *introduction, notes and vocabulary* (Bristol Classical Press, 1990), xviii + 123pp

Aeneid, II: *introduction, notes and vocabulary* (Bristol Classical Press, 1999), xvi + 105pp

Byzantine

'The monastery of the Theotokos Evergetis, its children and grandchildren', *The Theotokos Evergetis and eleventh-century monasticism*, ed. M. Mullett and A. Kirby (BBTT, 6.1, Belfast, 1994), 215–245

'The *Hypotyposis* of Evergetis: a unitary text?', *Work and worship at the Evergetis Theotokos*, ed. M. Mullett and A. Kirby (BBTT, 6.2, Belfast, 1997), 230–249

'John of Phoberou: a voice crying in the wilderness', *Strangers to themselves: the Byzantine outsider*, ed. D.C. Smythe (SPBS, 7, Aldershot, 2000), 61–73

English translations of the *typika* of the monasteries of Evergetis, Pakourianos, Kecharitomene, Pantokrator and Phoberou, *Byzantine monastic foundation documents*, ed. J.P. Thomas and A. Constantinides Hero, 5 vols (DOS, 35, Washington, DC, 2000), II, 454–506; 507–563; 649–724; 724–781; III, 872–953

The Synaxarion of the Theotokos Evergetis, I (September–February): text and English translation (BBTT, 6.4, Belfast, 2000) xv + 572pp

'Choice and change in the writing of monastic typika', *Omagiu Virgil Cândea*, ed. P.H. Stahl (Bucharest, 2002), I, 337–349

In press or progress

'Founders and second founders: Paul and Timothy', *Founders and refounders of Byzantine monasteries,* ed. M. Mullett (BBTT, 6.3, Belfast, 2004), forthcoming

The Synaxarion of the Theotokos Evergetis, II (March–August and the movable feasts): text and English translation (BBTT, 6.5, Belfast, 2004)

The Synaxarion of the Theotokos Evergetis, III (Indexes) (BBTT, 6.6, Belfast, 2005)

The Hypotyposis of Timothy for the monastery of the Theotokos Evergetis: English translation and commentary (with R. Morris) (BBTT, 6.7, Belfast)

The Synagoge of Paul Evergetinos: I: English translation (BBTT, 6.11, Belfast)

Constantine the Rhodian (with V. Dimitropoulou and L. James) (BBTT, 5.3, Belfast, 2004), forthcoming

Beginners' reading course in Byzantine Greek

INTRODUCTION

1

The other side of a tapestry

Margaret Mullett

This volume is concerned with the role of translation in Byzantine cultural history. It comprises translations and essays on translation by members of the Institute of Byzantine Studies and the AHRB Centre for Byzantine Cultural History and their constituent projects, written at the point when their first Assistant Director is retiring. While there is no question of him being lost to the Byzantine community, it is an appropriate moment to ask rather what is and what has been gained in translation.

Robert Hamilton Jordan
Bob Jordan, as his colleagues and students (though not his wife) know him, was born in Dublin, off the South Circular Rd, where his father was an Anglican minister. The family (he has a younger brother and sister) moved to England when he was a baby, to St Helen's in Lancashire, then to Wolverhampton, Bristol and London. He attended Bristol Grammar School from 1950 to 1957 and went up to Jesus College Cambridge with a Rustat Exhibition. There he was taught by Moses Finlay and Shackleton Bailey, who induced in him a love respectively of ancient history and textual criticism. Neither could have suspected that the area of academic study where he was to bring these two interests together was in Byzantine monasticism. After Cambridge, where he left with a Second and a Certificate in Education, together with a driving licence gained in Yorkshire while on teaching practice, he went to Sevenoaks in Kent as assistant master in classics. While there he married the future Margaret Jordan, whom he met at the Young People's Guild in Northwood. She was to give him a son and a daughter and three grandchildren, and to keep him excellent company in between her commitments to the Women's Institute and Scottish dancing. After five years at Sevenoaks he was interviewed by the then headmaster of Methodist College Belfast, Dr Stanley Worrall, at Heathrow Airport, and was on his way to a thirty-year career at Methody.

For his time at Sevenoaks Paul Tuffin, an early student and fine translator, has offered a sketch;[1] for the Methody years (and he is still archivist there) others of

---

[1] See below, 339–341.

our contributors can vouch.[2] The awe in which he was held[3] as (successively) master in charge of public examinations, head of classics, senior resident master, senior master with responsibility for the junior school, vice-principal with responsibility for day-to-day running and senior vice-principal was somehow consistent with a reputation sans pareil for playing the pantomime dame Sadie the cleaner in a series of brilliant pantomimes which he wrote with Michael Harrison over a period of about twenty years.[4] Bob was delighted to be back in Ireland where he had spent happy childhood holidays and took full advantage of life in Belfast as well as in school: he produced plays and coached hockey at Methody, and sang in the Philharmonic choir until very recently. He is the ultimate 'good citizen', serving on bodies as diverse as the Northern Ireland branch committee of the Joint Association of Classical Teachers, convenor of the classics panel at QUB Teachers' Centre, secretary and chairman of the ancient history subject panel of Northern Ireland GCE Examinations Board; coauthor and moderator of the Northern Ireland GCE 'O' level syllabus in classical studies, member of subject panels of the northern Ireland GCE, then GCSE examinations board; teachers' representative on various advisory committees.

The pantomimes offered him relief from all this: they offered audiences, as well as pyrotechnics from the chemistry department, a satirical view of school life based on years of observation of pupils – and the vagaries of an academic community. Only a senior master who toured the staff-rooms every day to check that everyone was happy could have such a detailed and caustic view of life at ground level. This concern for the happiness of an academic community was evident in the years before and during the establishment of the Institute of Byzantine Studies at Queen's: a troubled research fellow is whisked off to walk along the towpath; a despondent group of postgraduates find themselves admiring the goldfish (and Bob and Margaret's wonderful garden) at Drumbeg. The high point of every project meeting was always the Drumbeg dinner – after which we sometimes worked.

But this is to get ahead of the story. Somehow it became clear to Bob that he did not want to be a career teacher in the sense of moving higher and higher away from the classroom and into the boardroom. He missed scholarship, so he embarked with James Harrison, another legendary Hellenist of Methody, on a series of classical editions.[5] But he also missed the ancient history of the Finlay seminars. He fell into the charismatic hands of George Huxley, enrolled for an MA and

---

[2] See below, 289–294. Other prominent Byzantinists taught by him there include Dion Smythe (Queen's) Shaun Tougher (Cardiff) and Judith Waring (Cambridge).

[3] A prospective research student fell silent when his name was mentioned as one of the other people registered for a PhD. 'Would that be **the** Mr Jordan?' she asked.

[4] Cinder Hoo; Snow Hoo; Al Hoo; Who's Robin Hoom? The What Files.

[5] *Iliad,* I, VI, *Aeneid,* II, X, See the Bibliography above, xiv.

wrote about early Greek migration in the Peloponnese.[6] He regularly attended George's bi-annual meetings at the Ballymascanlon Hotel, the Hibernian Hellenists, and in 1976 started to teach in ancient history. The next year he began teaching classical Greek to beginners in the department of Greek and then in the merged department of Greek and Latin. He also taught classical Latin from time to time. In 1987 after the growth of the Byzantine Studies programme, whose students had joined his classes at Queen's, he realised that they and the classicists had different needs. He asked for reading matter, to see what was available which could be used by beginners. From this stemmed his highly successful *Beginners' reading course in Byzantine Greek,* but also a whole new career, which explains why this volume is entitled not *Grammatikos* but *Metaphrastes.*

The Metaphrast

What other people find difficult to understand about Bob is his thoroughness. No-one could have suspected that when given a bundle of text which included a foundation charter (*typikon*) of an eleventh-century monastery he would come back with both a plan for the teaching of the course and a complete translation of the text. And wanted more. So when Dumbarton Oaks in Washington DC planned a project to translate all extant documents of this kind, and the then external examiner at Belfast, Anthony Bryer, who was enjoying a period as fellow in Washington mentioned his name, it was entirely understandable that he should have agreed to translate for them five of the most important, and take a full part in the discussions among translators which were a notable part of that most splendid early collaborative project.[7] He then discovered that one of the monasteries assigned to him was the Theotokos Evergetis, and when a fellow-translator pointed out to him that it had a liturgical typikon as well he started to translate that also. He also discovered that a research student at Queen's, Earl Collins, now Gregory Collins, OSB, director of the Monastic Institute at the Anselmiano in Rome, was interested in the same monastery because of its ascetic collection, which he saw as offering a different model of monastic spirituality from that of Symeon the New Theologian. Bob then translated the first volume of the ascetic collection.

This interesting conjuncture had further results. Bob was now translating from 4 am to arrive in school at 8 am and he (and Margaret on an Olivetti typewriter) had been through many versions of his Dumbarton Oaks translations. It seemed a good idea to try to make sense of the total output of this apparently modest monastery. Professor Robert Taft SJ had heard of this phenomenally accurate and en-

---

[6] *Studies in early Peloponnesian migrations* (unpublished MA, Queen's University Belfast, 1970).
[7] See below Angela Hero's account. It was also told at the launch colloquium for the Byzantine Monastic Foundation Documents which he attended along with Rosemary Morris and Margaret Mullett from Evergetis, who gave papers.

thusiastic translator form the *typikon* project and had a student of his own, Andreas Thiermeyer, whom he wanted to put to work on the liturgical typikon, the *Synaxarion*. From these origins grew the British Academy's Evergetis Project, first funded in 1990, adopted as an Academy Research Project in 1996, and due to produce fifteen volumes by 2010.

Bob was essential to Evergetis. He instantly became moderator of the translators and imposed his own exacting standards on a seminar which met in Byzantine Studies on Friday afternoons to agree his own translations of book I. At the first Evergetis colloquium in 1991 his authority was very clear in a discussion of translation practice in ascetic texts attended among others by such notable translators as Joe Munitiz, John Wortley and Mary Cunningham, who are all represented in this volume.[8] Arguments about translation were central to the work of Evergetis: do we transliterate γέρων to show that it has nothing to do with actual age? How do we render the irrational externality of λογισμοί? In all cruces Bob's good sense prevailed. Bob is a natural collaborator: he worked with John Klentos on the liturgy, Rosemary Morris on the foundation charter and still found time to get his PhD[9] – as well as enabling the running of one of the largest grammar schools in the United Kingdom. Sometimes school and university came together: we were approached by Professor Cândea,[10] who was producing a Romanian translation of Evergetis, and with whom Bob collaborated happily, while also entering into guardianship of a Romanian student at Methody. Both daughters were present at his PhD graduation.

Bob contributed to other Belfast research projects as well, producing with Charlotte Roueché a translation of the *Mousai* of Alexios Komnenos, and serving nobly on the editorial board of Belfast Byzantine Texts and Translations. He made the transition from schoolmaster to academic very smoothly: he first held a Dr M. Aylwin Cotton Foundation Fellowship to release him from teaching. He trod the boards for the last time in a pantomime the day before he gave his first conference paper at the Spring Symposium of Byzantine Studies, edited, appropriately, by a former pupil.[11] And increasingly he became drawn into the teaching of Greek in Byzantine Studies as his beginners advanced into their own research. By 1995 he was finding it hard to balance the ascetic regime he had taken on: a diet of translation plus teaching plus administration plus research makes for heavy days. So when

---

[8] See below, 22–27, 194–209, 28–38.
[9] R.H. Jordan, *The hypotyposis of the Theotokos Evergetis and the making of a monastic typikon* (Unpublished PhD, Queen's University Belfast, 1997).
[10] See his article for the Festschift, 'Choice and change in the writing of monastic typika', *Omagiu Virgil Cândea,* ed. P.H. Stahl (Bucharest, 2002), I, 337–349.
[11] 'John of Phoberou, a voice crying in the wilderness', *Strangers to themselves: the Byzantine outsider*, ed. D.C. Smythe (SPBS, 7, Aldershot, 2000), 61–73.

the chance of early retirement from Methody came up he leapt at the opportunity. By then there was talk of an institute of Byzantine Studies at Queen's, and the possibility of a major grant from the Arts and Humanities Research Board to make it happen. Bob was the natural assistant director of both: maintaining communications, keeping people happy, ensuring that things ran smoothly, signalling crises before they happened. He memorably persuaded the future director to consider this delegation of duties, on the eve of the AHRB interview and after a particularly trying faculty meeting, by driving her to the airport laying down very clearly how things would run in the new institute.

It is his creation as much as hers. He has taught Greek at all levels, acted as postgraduate tutor, driven Evergetis as more large projects came on the scene, proofread volumes, chaired the house committee where everyone has their say. He is drawn into translation issues at every level: the authors of a volume under consideration by the press visit to have their translation checked; postgraduates run translations past him, in a weekly Greek 'surgery' for PhD students which is a model of good practice. He spearheaded the drive for a Byzantine Greek beginners' summer school (the only one in the world), housing the first cohort in his own home, and submitting to queries about vocabulary over dinner. He took on the hated directorship for a semester to allow the director a blissful Dumbarton Oaks stay – appropriately spent translating as well as writing.

Byzantine imperial rhetoric of the twelfth century, particularly imperial verse, and the annual speech to the emperor of the *maistor ton rhetoron* on 6 January, makes great play of Jordan imagery.[12] It was then appropriate, since that was the feast of the Baptism, but how much more appropriate it would now be to use it to praise our present honorand. For it is impossible for anyone who has once been immersed in that stream of eloquence and learning to ignore the power of language or of Bob's teaching, as will be apparent from the contributions from students in this volume.

It is equally impossible to imagine the institute without him, as in future he gives more time to growing vegetables, a skill he learned while helping his father. It would be impossible, that is, except that he will still be in the institute as researcher and translator. But then, when all is said and done, Bob is above all a translator. He has that very rare gift of lucidity combined with transparent mapping of the source text, rigorous consistency combined with imaginative understanding which comes

---

[12] E.g Eustathios of Thessalonike, or. 3 to Manuel I Komnenos, ed. W.E. Regel, *Fontes rerum byzantinarum: rhetorum saeculi XII orationes politicae*, I (Leipzig, 1892, repr. 1982), 25, 45, 56, 57; Michael *ho tou Thessalonikes*, or. 8 to Manuel I Komnenos, ed. Regel, 131, 146; or. 10, ed. Regel, 165; John Kamateros, or. 14, ed. Regel, 250; George Tornikes, or. 15 to Isaac Angelos, ed. Regel, 255; Theodore Prodromos, poems 10, 33, 40, ed. W. Hörandner, *Theodoros Prodromos, Historische Gedichte* (WByzSt, 11, Vienna, 1974), 249, 369, 391.

only with a deep knowledge of the workings of Greek, and the ability to write clear and elegant English.

Gained in translation
The importance of these skills at the present time is underlined by Mary Cunningham below.[13] But translation has a wider importance in the study of Byzantium. The empire was multilingual and multicultural through most of its history, housing substantial minorities and exporting cultural achievements to the surrounding world. Gone are the days when those achievements were thought of simply as preserving the classical Greek heritage for the renaissance to rediscover it: the Byzantines were not just the librarians of the middle ages. The desert heritage on which Bob has spent so much scholarly time shows at its beginning the interplay between Coptic and Greek, and the stories of that tradition quickly found their way into Latin, Arabic and Church Slavonic.[14] Syriac verse-forms and poetics underly the achievements of the greatest of the hymnographers,[15] and after the early Byzantine Greek monopoly of historiography[16] grinds to a halt under Heraclius, the story is taken up in Coptic and Syriac. Greek texts like Sophronios's hagiography and Gregory Dialogos influenced writing in Anglo-Saxon England[17] and were to continue to resonate through Renaissance Europe, and into the hymnody of the nineteenth century.[18]

Nor was Byzantine culture a closed system: in the eleventh century, narrative, medical and oneirocritical texts from the Sanskrit and Arabic were imported into Byzantium and translated through imperial commission, a tendency which has been seen to have a direct effect on the revival of fiction in the Byzantine twelfth century. Meanwhile, the late antique translation of ancient Greek scientific and philosophical texts into Syriac and Arabic would soon find its way into western Europe and the opening up of study in the twelfth-century Renaissance.[19] In twelfth-century Sicily, as in twelfth-century Toledo, a particular multicultural society produced particular kinds of texts: the same text, whose translation from Arabic to Greek Alexios I Komnenos had commissioned from the court doctor Symeon Seth, was in the possession of the admiral Eugenios of Sicily in a new and extended Greek recension, and was soon to be available in Latin as well.[20] Not that facility in language-exchange always promoted the peaceful coexistence of com-

---

[13] 28–38.
[14] See Skaka and Wortley below, 194–209.
[15] See Peden below, 143–156.
[16] Characterised by Scott, 157–184 below.
[17] Such as the writings of Ælfric, highlighted below in Magennis's contribution, 210–235.
[18] See the contributions below of McGann, 287–288 and Woodman, 128–137.
[19] See Johnston below, 83–90.
[20] See Noble below, 66–71.

munities; increasingly we see this was so in Sicily, still more in the relations of east Mediterranean states in the age of the crusades when language was put at the service of warfare.[21]

Byzantine Greek itself was a complex linguistic entity: skilled writers moved with apparent effortlessness between registers of the language, to translate, metaphrasise, texts from high-style to low, or in the opposite direction. To some extent this is a matter of the interplay of different periods of Greek culture: this is not simply a matter of transmission but a far more interactive relationship which characterises the interplay of classical, Byzantine and contemporary Greek, not just in Byzantium but in Modern Greek as well.[22] And its practitioners appear to us supremely self-confident in their grasp and manipulation of their readership in their rhetorical facility, their measured ambiguities.[23]

Translation is not of course a purely linguistic concept: bishops and relics were also translated in Byzantium, and during the middle ages Byzantium was the society where precious materials came from the ends of the earth to the *omphalos* of the *oikoumene*: murex and silkworms, lapis lazuli and ivory.[24] Spheres were transgressed also and culture-wide distances travelled: monks step into the shoes of soldiers,[25] and diplomatic marriages act as catalysts for innovatory texts.[26] Texts of course travel in even stranger ways and stranger directions; cultures and religions follow after.

It is surprising that this rich carpet-weave has not before attracted studies of translation. Unlike seventeenth- and eighteenth-century schoolmasters[27] the Byzantines were themselves innocent of translation theory. Modern debates over the proper translation of certain kinds of text have surfaced in the workings of large projects and spill over into contributions here,[28] as well as in discussions planned for elsewhere. This is not the first volume of translations to be put together to honour a Byzantinist, and we are honoured to have with us in this volume the editor of that one.[29] But it is the first time that questions have begun to be asked about the role of translation in Byzantium and of Byzantium. That they are not

---

[21] See Moss below, 249–266.
[22] See Baird below, 289–294 on Romanos in Papadiamandis, and Hirst below, 296–313 on Cavafy's Byzantium.
[23] See Krausmüller below, 57–61.
[24] See Rodley below, 51–56.
[25] See McCotter below, 39–50.
[26] See Mullally below, 72–82.
[27] See Haan below, 111–127 and 141.
[28] For example Costantinides Hero, Cunningham below, 267–273 and 28–38.
[29] *Byzantine authors: literary activities and preoccupations: texts and translations dedicated to the memory of Nicolas Oikonomides*, ed. J. W. Nesbitt (The Medieval Mediterranean, 49, Leiden, 2003); for John Nesbitt's contribution to this volume, see Anderson and Nesbitt below, 240–247.

more systematically addressed in this volume is a result of its function as gift: each giftgiver gives what he or she hopes will please. But one gift we hope will be received (and not only by our laudandus) is a sense of the value of translation, its potential for opening portals into other cultures, pumping oxygen into a curriculum, realigning and rejuvenating the study of cultures.

And it comes at a time when translation studies in the academy at large are felt to have come of age,[30] and when Brian Friel and Sylvia Coppola have lifted academic concerns to a universal (as well as memorably localised) plane. Both *Translations* and *Lost in translation* indicate the power of translation, and the vulnerability of those caught in the liminal places of transculturality. But they also indicate what is preserved, or gained, as well as lost, for it has long been observed that the translation process benefits both source and target culture. It would be hard now to find a commentator who sees translation as a direct transmission from source-text to target-text, rather than a creative process, and for this there is good medieval justification.[31] *Translatio imperii* and *translatio studii* are generally seen less as a non-stop journey from the ancient world to the renaissance, more as a stopping train with interesting interactions with local communities. Translation now implies the crossing of boundaries, a mechanism for change in a culture and across cultures.

In this volume all kinds of theorists are evoked: George Steiner and Walter Benjamin, I.A. Richards and Jacques Derrida, Lawrence Venuti and Wolfgang Iser. No single approach unites the papers, let alone the translations. Some contributors magnify the achievement of the honorand by stressing the difficulties of translating certain texts:[32] the difficulties of vocabulary without proper lexica, or of conveying multiple meanings, or of reconstructing a source-text. Others trace the history of translation from the Septuagint and the targums to the Church of Ireland in the nineteenth century and beyond:[33] others deal with process: concepts like polyglot and bilingual, and John Dryden's categories of metaphrase/paraphrase/imitation are explored. This in turn makes possible selfconscious versions which aim at a particular mode of translation.[34] Spotlights are shone on particular translators, and apparently familiar authors are seen in a new light like Chaucer the 'grant translateur'. Translation is seen as performance, and the translator as social actor and cultural enabler.

---

[30] See the Preface to the third edition of George Steiner's *After Babel* (Oxford, 1975, rev.ed.1998) in which he simultaneously argues there is no such thing as translation theory and (quite rightly) claims paternity. For an efficient assessment of the state of play in 1991 see S. Bassnett–McGuire, *Translation studies* (London, 1980, rev.ed.1991).
[31] See Kelly below, 98, referring to Rita Copeland.
[32] See Munitiz and Krausmüller below, 22–27, 57–61.
[33] See Beattie, Haan and Woodman below, 15–21; 111–127; 128–137.
[34] See Haan, below, 111–127, 141–142; Ekdawi Brandt, below, 332–335.

Some papers make significant contributions outside their specific areas. Stephen Kelly brilliantly explores the role of the English Prose *Brut* in defining English identity, and its ultimate failure in 'the *Brut*'s colonial project'. He sees clearly the destabilising and undercutting, subversive function of translation. His charting of the transmission from (questionable) Welsh to Latin to French to English shows a continuous reinterpretation and reassimilation of a classical foundation-myth, in contrast to Evelyn Mullally's rooting of a similar tale in a diachronic journey which meets a synchronic – but Mediterranean-wide – network.[35] John Thompson maps the reception history of a less than canonical text on to the reinvention of writers in the Reformation: just as Chaucer becomes more Protestant, his most Catholic writing is reunited to his oeuvre, as a piece of juvenilia and a curious product of the old religion: no Mant-like reticence here about Marian texts. There are implications here above all for the canon, but also for translation as crossing religious loyalties and devotional practices.[36] David Johnston eloquently uses the work of the Toledo School of Translators, a happier example perhaps than Palermo, as a metaphor for cultural and curricular change: he ranges widely in the theory and practice of translation, seeking the imaginative leaps which set new courses for the disciplines of the future.[37]

His persuasive plea for openness must find a note of resonance in Byzantinists, who of all scholars cannot afford to retreat to a ghetto. To look at Byzantium without studying the classical world, the world of the Jewish diaspora, the western middle ages and the realms of Islam is a nonsense. But to fail to see where Byzantium is echoed in the worlds of the Renaissance, the Ottoman empire and the modern Greek state is also a great danger. We are proud in the Institute and Centre to be able to offer these contexts to students and colleagues, and to allude to them in the present volume.

Translations gained and given
This is a present of translations, and reflections on translation, for a great translator. Byzantine diplomatic gifts favoured the small, and perfect and richly ornate: enamels and ivories and precious books, but also the large and showy: waterclocks and gilt beds and multiples of eunuchs. So this volume offers tiny translations of well-chosen poems,[38] and a single crux in Ruth,[39] but also a rich study of translation practice from the renaissance to the eighteenth century,[40] and substantial transla-

---

[35] See Kelly below, 91–102; ct Mullally below, 72–82.
[36] See Thompson below, 103–110; ct Woodman, below, 133–136.
[37] See Johnston below, 83–90; ct Noble, below, 66–71.
[38] See Finlay, McGann below, 248; 249–250.
[39] See Beattie below, 15–21.
[40] See Haan below, 111–127.

tions of whole historiographical and hagiographical texts. It includes an essay by a translator whose work is regularly performed on the metropolitan stage,[41] and MA translation work from students of the institute.[42] It involves discussions of works in Latin, Hebrew, Arabic, Old English, Old French and Middle English as well as in Greek; it spans the period from the book of Ruth to the poems of Jenny Mastoraki. Even the art historians and archaeologists of the Centre have been able to contribute: ' "any fule kno" ', says Liz James, 'that art historians don't translate', but she offers a foretaste of a translated text, not in the form of a translation for that would be to return without interest the gift of Bob Jordan's labours, but a study of the way in which Byzantium in this text translates identities across the centuries.[43] Lyn Rodley trenchantly castigates any attempt to justify her contribution through the cultural interchange that is however clearly implied by her chosen subject of ivory.[44] Patricia Finlay offers a small feast of a poem in the margins of her manuscript.[45] And Jeffrey Anderson[46] and Nancy Ševčenko[47] have produced an edition and a translation respectively of liturgical texts particularly appropriate to Bob Jordan. George Woodman takes up the liturgical theme,[48] and monastic themes are found in other offerings as well. Contributors have been generous with the significance of what they have to offer: the firstfruits of John Turner's English edition of the letters of Symeon the New Theologian;[49] a new psychophelitic tale from John Wortley the Répétoiriste, with Evangeli Skaka's text,[50] new catecheses by Neophytos of Cyprus,[51] Sikelianos's Athos diary.[52] Roger Scott and Anthony Hirst have also offered firstfruits of important work in progress.[53] These offerings are multisensual: the sound of Romanos's verse, the sight of the ivory diptychs, the astounding smells of the Paul of Monembasia story. We very much hope, Bob, that you will enjoy them.

---

[41] See Johnston below, 15–21.
[42] The contributions of Baird, Carroll, Moss and Peden, 289–294, 185–193, 249–266, 143–156, were all undertaken as part of MA study, at Queen's or in Moss's case at Leeds.
[43] See James below, 62–65.
[44] See Rodley below, 51.
[45] See Finlay below, 248.
[46] See Anderson and Nesbitt below, 240–247.
[47] See Ševčenko, below, 274–286.
[48] See Woodman below, 128–137.
[49] See Turner below, 236–239.
[50] See Skaka and Wortley below, 194–209.
[51] See Hero below, 267–273.
[52] See Psoni below, 314–331.
[53] See Scott and Hirst below, 157–184, 296–313.

ESSAYS

2

Baldrick and Blackadder revive an ancient exegetical question relating to Ruth

Derek Beattie

You may recall the incident, in an episode of the *Blackadder II* series of television programmes, in which Baldrick, faithful servant of the eponymous hero, prepared a dish called turnip surprise in readiness for a visit by the vegetarian aunt Lady Whiteadder, and was in turn surprised to be told that, in that lady's theology, cooking is an abomination and turnips should be eaten raw. This incident, encapsulating neatly, as it does, the question whether the primary connotation of the word turnip is of something firm and hard or of something soft and mushy, illustrates nicely the problem faced in ancient times by exegetes of the biblical book of Ruth.[1]

You may be wondering where turnip occurs in Ruth. Could it be, you may be asking, that Keats was mistaken when he visualised Ruth standing 'in tears amid the alien corn'? No, Keats certainly misunderstood Ruth, but his crop-identification was not at fault. The turnip, though well-rooted in the story, is not immediately apparent in most translations, or in the Hebrew text. Some explanation is clearly required.

In the scene at the threshing-floor in Ruth chapter three, we read that, in the middle of the night 'the man' (Boaz) did two things immediately prior to finding a woman lying in his proximity. In other words, there is a sentence containing two verbs with 'the man' as subject of both. The first verb וַיֶּחֱרַד presents no difficulty other than, perhaps, that of choosing the most satisfying English word for the context. The verb חרד is well known as meaning 'to tremble; be anxious, be worried'. One might be tempted to suggest 'to quake' on account of its application in Hebrew usage to denote religious folk, but in the present context I am inclined

---

[1] This is a revised version of a paper read to the Research Seminar of the School of Greek, Roman and Byzantine Studies in April 2000. In offering it now as a modest tribute to Bob Jordan it is not intended to imply that any resemblance may be discerned between him and either of the characters named in the title.

myself to translate 'the man stirred', or 'was startled'. I think the idea of slight movement as in 'trembling' is of greater importance than that of fright or anxiety.

The second verb וַיִּלָּפֵת, however, is one that occurs in only three places in the Hebrew bible. In Judges 16:29 it describes what Samson did to the pillars of the Philistine temple in preparation for pulling the structure down, i.e. he grasped them, or caught hold of them. In Ruth the verb has a *niph`al* or passive form and, accordingly, I think it means something like 'he was caught'. So did Rashi in the eleventh century and David Kimchi, or whoever it was that wrote the commentary attributed to him, in the thirteenth, but almost everybody else thinks or has thought differently. Why this should be so calls for a short excursion to Job 6:18 where we find the third occurrence of the verb in question. In that passage Job is berating his friends, his so-called comforters, for being as useless as *wadis* in the desert that dry up just when they are needed. Verse 18 is commonly understood to say something about caravans turning aside from their routes. In achieving this translation, the verb, which is the plural form of the one in Ruth, is understood on the basis of an Arabic cognate, which means 'to twist, turn' (transitively, if I am not mistaken), but there is something wrong with the Hebrew text. The word 'caravans' is there, but the verb is passive and the word translated 'their routes' must be either the object, which it cannot be since the verb is passive, or a kind of joint-subject with 'caravans'. The solution, I suggest, is either to treat 'caravans' as an accidental intrusion from the following verse or to read instead 'paths of', which involves a very small change in the vocalisation of the word. The verse may then be translated '(the paths of) their ways [i.e. of the *wadis*] are caught (or, perhaps, trapped)'; all three occurrences of the verb are intelligible on the basis of the case in Judges.

But the proper, correct or best explanation of the word is for our present purpose immaterial. In ancient times this verb – at least so far as its occurrence in Ruth was concerned – was explained on the basis of a presumed relationship with the noun לֶפֶת which has the same three consonants and means turnip in both Hebrew and Aramaic. The verb, as has already been observed, has a *niph`al* or passive form, so the question to be addressed becomes 'what does "he was turnipped" mean?' To construe it as 'he became like a turnip (or, like turnip)' offers some small advance but leads immediately to the further question of what precise similitude is envisaged. The targum opted for turnip in its boiled and mashed state and so interpreted the verb in Ruth as symbolising something soft and mushy and attributed to Boaz a state induced through alarm. This may be seen in the opening words of my translation:

> In the middle of the night the man was startled, and he was afraid, *and his flesh became soft like turnip from fear. He saw,* and behold, a woman was lying at his feet, *but he restrained his desire and did not approach her, just as Joseph the Righteous did, who refused to approach the Egyptian woman, the wife of his master, just as Paltiel bar Laish the Pious did, who*

placed a sword between himself and Michal daughter of Saul, wife of David, whom he refused to approach.

At this point a brief digression on the subject of targums (or, *targumim*) may be appropriate. Originally the Aramaic word for translation, and adopted into Hebrew with the same meaning, a targum could be simply a translation of anything from any language into any other. But, although this usage continues in Hebrew, the word has been used since ancient times to refer specifically to Aramaic translations of the books of the Hebrew bible. Many questions exist in relation to the origin of these translations. This is especially the case in relation to the targums of the Writings, the third section of the Jewish bible canon. There is a measure of consensus that the extant targums of the Pentateuch, and of the Prophets, originated in the early centuries of the Christian era, and reached their final form by the time of the Muslim conquest of Babylonia. In relation to the targums of the Writings, the received wisdom is, or used to be, that they originated only at a very late date. This perhaps owes something to the statement of Rashi that there is no targum of the writings. Perhaps a brief comment about Rashi is called for, at this his second mention. Living in northern France in the eleventh century (1040–1105 to be precise), he wrote commentaries on all the books of the Hebrew bible, and on the talmud, and is renowned chiefly for being a champion of *peshat*, or simple, straightforward, common-sense interpretation. We shall probably hear more of him, but for now his statement that there is no targum of the writings has to be reconciled with the fact that Rashi's contemporary Nathan ben Jehiel of Rome (1035–c.1110) cited texts from this work in his talmudic dictionary, the *Arukh*. More commonly, the idea that the targum of Ruth (to be specific) should be assigned to a late date is based on the belief that it draws on the talmud and other rabbinic writings for its material. On the other hand, the existence within the text of elements that must be assigned to an early date has been suggested, by me[2] amongst others, too. It is against this background that the question under review today may be of some importance. Let us now return to the text of the targum of Ruth.

The first thing to note is the length of the verse in comparison with the original. In my translation, given above, the portion in roman type is the Aramaic translation of the Hebrew and it is for that part only that I have given the Aramaic, which is useful for comparison with the other versions, in the table which follows; the part printed in italic represents additional material, not found in the bible. Let us deal first with this part.

---

[2] D.R.G. Beattie, 'Ancient elements in the targum of Ruth', *Proceedings of the Ninth World Congress of Jewish Studies Division A: The Period of the Bible* (Jerusalem, 1986), 159–165.

The story of Joseph's refusal to sleep with Potiphar's wife is well known. You may like to know more about Paltiel. During David's outlaw period Saul gave his daughter Michal, who had already been married to David when he was in favour with Saul, to Palti ben Laish, as he is called in 1 Sam 25:44. When David came to power he demanded the return of Michal and she was taken away from Paltiel ben Laish in 2 Sam 3:15. The change of name provided the rabbis with an opportunity to exonerate Michal from any accusation of adultery. While she was with Palti, they said, the couple had slept with a sword between them and it was for this meritorious conduct that Palti acquired the suffix 'el' (God) for his name. The details are recorded in the talmud (*b.Sanh.19b*), where Boaz is said to have done better, by spending a whole night with Ruth, than Joseph, who resisted the woman's advances on only one occasion, but not so well as Palti(el) who slept chastely for many nights with Michal. Perhaps the most interesting feature of the talmudic story is its attribution to R. Yohanan, who lived in the third century CE, since this means it is the earliest-dated account of the sword-motif that might be thought to belong properly to Tristan and Iseut.

Returning now to the biblical text, I discovered when I began to prepare this paper a very old note, written by me when I was a research student, about a matter of which I had completely lost sight. According to this note, the ancient versions treated the second verb in Ruth 3:8 as a synonym of the first, so I have checked these sources and assembled their translations below. The synonymity is illustrated nicely by Payne Smith's *Thesaurus* when it explains the second verb of the Syriac version ܐܬܠ as meaning *pavit*, the meaning given to the first by the Vulgate, saying it translates חרד (the first verb) in Ruth 3:8. The Syriac verb just mentioned (i.e. the second one) is, by a switch of alphabet, the first one in the targum. So, at first sight it would appear that the targum does the same thing as the other ancient versions, adding a midrashic explanation for its translation of the second verb.

Ruth 3:8 in the Ancient Versions

Hebrew Bible:
ויהי בחצי הלילה ויחרד האיש וילפת והנה אשה שכבת מרגלתיו:
In the middle of the night the man ויחרד and וילפת and behold, a woman was lying at his 'footplace'.

Septuagint:
ἐγένετο δὲ ἐν τῷ μεσονυκτίῳ καὶ ἐξέστη ὁ ἀνὴρ καὶ ἰδοὺ γυνὴ κοιμᾶται πρὸς ποδῶν αὐτοῦ.

Vulgate:
Et ecce, nocte jam media expavit homo, et conturbatus est: viditq; mulierem jacentem ad pedes suos.

Peshitto:
ܘܗܘܐ ܒܦܠܓܗ ܕܠܠܝܐ ܘܕܚܠ ܓܒܪܐ ܘܐܬܬܙܝܥ ܘܚܙܐ ܐܢܬܬܐ ܕܕܡܟܐ ܠܘܬ ܪܓܠܘܗܝ

Targum:
והוה בפלגות ליליא ותהווה גבר ורתת ... וחמא והא איתתא דמכא כל קבל רגלוי

But is that really what is happening? Is it really likely that different translators would choose to treat an unusual word as synonymous with another word in its vicinity, especially when that word has a perfectly clear meaning in another place? And should the question of the chronological relation between the targum's single word translation and its midrashic explanation be prejudged? I would suggest that the extended comment came first, for we should remember that 'turnip' is firmly rooted in the Hebrew, with the one-word translation being added at a secondary stage by someone concerned to ensure that every word of the Hebrew should be represented by one in Aramaic. There is a single manuscript that has the reading that I envisage as original, but I do not attach great importance to this, for that manuscript is a very late one. However, there is some evidence that in other cases of double translations the literal translation is later than the non-literal, and sometimes double translations occur at a very late stage as the result of variant readings being incorporated in a single manuscript. If it is correct to suggest, as I did in my earlier treatment of this topic, that 'there is no way of getting from [the Hebrew] וילפת to 'fear' or 'trembling' except *via* 'turnip' (boiled, and probably mashed, turnip, at that)',[3] then it must seem strange that the same meaning is given by other versions too. Did they follow the lead of the targum, and have we found another argument in favour of a relatively (at least) early date for the targum's composition? If there is anything of value in what has just been said, this may prove to be the most important element in the present study.

Thus far we have focused on what may be called the Baldrick exegesis and you will doubtless recall that my title appears to promise a second one. The Blackadder (or perhaps it should be Whiteadder) interpretation appears in the talmud. In *B. Sanh.* 19b Rab explains וילפת as meaning 'his flesh became like turnip-heads'. For the benefit of anyone who is unclear about the significance of this, Rashi is ready

---

[3] D.R.G. Beattie, 'Towards dating the targum of Ruth', *A word in season: essays in honour of William McKane*, ed. J.D. Martin and P.R. Davies (Journal for the Study of the Old Testament Supplement Series, 42, Sheffield, 1986), 216.

with the explanation 'his member became hard'. This will doubtless also be of assistance to anyone who was uncertain about the precise meaning of the other explanation. Rashi's comment continues: 'but nevertheless he suppressed his desire, although she was unmarried and in bed with him'. In saying 'he suppressed his desire' Rashi uses the same two words as the targum, but that is probably of no significance. Rashi cannot have quoted from a document whose existence he has denied. While it is not impossible that the additional material, which forms the bulk of the targum's verse, was added after Rashi's time, stronger evidence would be needed to suggest that material which had been available for several centuries had not been added earlier.

On that previous occasion when I considered the possibility that there might be a connection between the two explanations I concluded 'that the two conclusions as to the application of "turnip" to Ruth 3:8 are so diametrically opposed that neither conclusion can have been known to the proponents of the other'.[4] The matter may bear reconsideration. Clearly, we have no simple case of borrowing by the targum from the talmud (which is, as it seems, the kind of argument that was once put forward). Might the targum be bowdlerising for its more innocent clientele, the general public of the synagogue, the adult treatment by the men of the Beth Midrash? Or is the converse at all arguable? This is the position from which I reached my earlier conclusion but now I would express it differently. Drawing on an argument that has been used in another area,[5] I think it can be said that it is impossible that the targum's contradictory interpretation could have originated after the talmud had achieved its authoritative status. This might then be offered as supplementary evidence in favour of a relatively early date for the targum's reading.

On the occasion of the revival of my interest I find other, new, questions arising. The starting-point for my re-examination of the matter was my realisation that there is an inconsistency within the targum's text. For Boaz, in the circumstances in which we are told he has just found himself, to have restrained his carnal appetite is hardly remarkable, let alone praiseworthy. So it could be said that the text, in continuing as it does, indicates *either* that once it referred to 'hardening' not 'softening' *or* that the passage about Boaz's commendable restraint is a secondary addition? The latter possibility would imply the insertion, with complete disregard to the context into which it was being inserted, of at least one block of material derived from another source. In other words, we may have evidence for what has often been asserted without real evidence or argument.

---

[4] Beattie, 'Towards dating the targum of Ruth'.
[5] J. Heinemann, 'The targum of Exodus 22:4 and the Ancient Halachah' (Hebrew), *Tarbiz*, 38 (1968–1969), 294–296.

But one other question must also be considered. Did Boaz really 'subdue' his desire? All extant manuscripts save one agree in reading וכבש; the exception, which happens to be the earliest manuscript, reads ותקף, which has the same meaning in the *pa'el* form but in the *p^e'al* means 'grow strong'. Read in the latter way, the text provides for Boaz to experience a transition from the unfortunate state in which he found himself as the result of his sudden awakening to one in which he was able to practise his meritorious restraint, and there is no longer any need to conclude that there is an inconsistency in the text.

Reflecting on the existence of this variant reading, I find that, while I can see some reason why the reading תקף should have been suppressed in favour of כבש, I can think of no plausible explanation for substituting תקף for כבש. Does it follow that תקף must have been an earlier reading that has been successfully suppressed? Does it also follow that its original meaning must have been 'grew strong'? I put the matter in the form of questions because I feel some hesitation about making such a radical suggestion, however rational it may appear. Perhaps I also feel I should be content with having made one small advance that I did not expect. To have found that the targum's interpretation of Ruth 3:8 is at the root of the readings of all the ancient versions might indeed be described as a turnip surprise.

3

Hurdles in Greek

Joseph A. Munitiz

The Greek language must surely be one of the sturdiest and longest-lived among all languages: it can be recognised as such in linear-B tablets dating from nearly two millennia BC and can be heard in the streets of Athens today. An age of four thousand years – admirable though this must be – does create some hurdles for a reader's understanding of written texts, as any modern Greek trying to read Homer will readily admit, and our honorand has had to overcome quite a few as he unravelled the complicated liturgical text that he bravely undertook to translate and comment. It may amuse him to see an attempt to categorise, at least in general terms, some of these hurdles. The remarks that follow will be restricted to the Byzantine period where his interests have mainly focused, and to a few of the problems encountered.

Difficulties with the words

It may seem paradoxical, but the first of the hurdles that meets any translator of Greek is usually not the most serious: individual words that are not immediately understood. Fortunately there is now an impressive array of dictionaries to help one here, the earliest being the remarkable work of Du Cange,[1] and the latest *Lexikon zur byzantinischen Gräzität* still being published in Vienna by Erich Trapp.[2] But from the first – and already during the period in question (witness the lexicon attributed to Photios and, probably later, that entitled the *Souda*) – lexicographers were busy tracking down unusual words and offering equivalents or explanations. The difficulty arises when experts disagree: good examples are to be found in the fourteenth-century Pseudo-Kodinos[3] text with its list of ceremonial robes, many

---

[1] C. Du Cange, *Glossarium ad scriptores mediae et infimae graecitatis* (Lyon, 1688).
[2] Published under the auspices of the Österreichische Akademie der Wissenschaften (Philosophisch-historische Klass) by the Kommission für Byzantinistik, Band VI/1–4 with the title *Lexikon zür byzantinischen Gräzitáat besonders des 9.–12. Jahrhunderts* (Vienna, 2001). Only vol. I (Band A-K) has appeared so far.
[3] *Pseudo-Kodinos, Traité des Offices. Introduction, texte et traduction*, ed. J. Verpeaux (†) (Le Monde Byzantin, 1, Paris, 1966). This text is now the subject of a research seminar organised by Dimiter Angelov and Ruth Macrides at the Centre for Byzantine, Ottoman and Modern Greek Studies, University of Birmingham, 2003–2004.

elaborately decorated: e.g. the word ἀήρ may mean a 'veil' (hanging behind the headgear to protect the neck) but the text states that the owner's name was embroidered on it, which seems unlikely for a veil; was it rather some sort of visor or peak? Again, βλάτιον is generally said to have been a 'purple silk', but in this text it is described at times as 'white'. The word καββάδιον can mean a 'mantle' (as can the word ταμπάριον), but at other times it stands for the Arab-style 'caftan' (while ταμπάριον seems to be a sort of 'jerkin', called at times a 'chlamys'). When the text mentions the decorations of the robes, with words like κλαπωτός, μαργέλλιον, ῥιζαί, and σεῖα cropping up (probably meaning 'corded knobs', 'gold braid', 'knotted stitches', and 'pendants') one feels the need for a course in needle-work. So often, the English equivalent may be equally *ignotum*. Each specialised text – whether dealing with liturgical rites or gastronomic delicacies – presents its particular verbal problems.

Difficulties with the text

All too frequently a reader can be misled by an incorrectly written (or printed) text: here the lack of an accent or a single incorrect letter can be crucial: e.g. the text that is given as: ἄγεσθαί μου ἐπέρχεται αὖθις ἐρωτομανῶς ἀνακυκλῶν τινος ἕνεκεν οὗτος ὁ ἱστορικός οὔπω τοῖς φιλέλλησιν προεξενήθη will puzzle some readers, but once the μου is changed to μοι, and an acute accent placed on τίνος, it becomes clear that what is meant is: 'I am led to ask once more in puzzlement why this historian has not yet been presented to lovers of Greek'.[4] Very often it is enough to consult the apparatus criticus for variants, or to ask oneself if certain corrections need to be made (more tricky!). A curious example of possible confusion simply because of the lay-out of the text occurs in *Vallicellianus graecus* 74 (E55), a fifteenth-century manuscript which contains a poem of Makarios Makres on the Emperor Manuel II Palaeologos (f. 130v): the poem is written in two columns, but if read one column at a time, they make no sense; they have to be read across the columns.[5] The importance of accents is clearly shown by the confusion that can arise if οὗ is taken to be the same as οὐ.

Difficulties with idioms

It is when a competent Greek writer begins to play with idioms that more serious difficulties arise. Many idioms are difficult because they leave out words which are

---

[4] The example comes from a sixteenth-century Greek dedicatory letter to a copy of Procopius (*Salamantinus* 2750) written by Antonios Kalosynas: Gregorio de Andrés, *Helenistas del Renacimiento en Toledo, El Copista Cretense Antonio Calosinás* (Toledo, 1999), cf. 135: in this case the errors in the Greek are probably due to the scribe rather than to the editor.

[5] This example was found thanks to the thesis of Sophia Kapetanaki (an edition of some of the works of Makarios Makres) successfully defended in London in 2002.

implied: e.g. (i) τὸ τοῦ Δαυΐδ meaning 'as <in the case of> David' or '<to use an expression> of David' (depending on the context); (ii) μέχρι μὲν καὶ ἐς τόδε ἡμέρας, meaning, 'until this <point, moment, hour> of the day'. It is not uncommon for writers to omit the copulative ἐστί. In other cases the use of the double negative can be confusing, e.g. οὐδὲ γὰρ οὐδ' αὐτοὶ μὴ οὐ συλλαλεῖν ἡμῖν ἀνέξονται meaning that 'neither will these bear not to speak together with us', or a sophisticated order of words – so that ἡ τῆς βασιλικῆς θερμότης πίστεως cannot mean 'the heat of <the speaker's> faith in the emperor', but rather 'the warmth of the emperor's faith'.[6] The combination of conjunctions can also be difficult: e.g. εἰ καὶ 'even if' and εἰ δ' οὖν 'if not' (*si minus*); also the subtle use of καὶ can mislead, as in οἷος καὶ ('whoever'), or καὶ μάλιστα ('especially'), or ἔνθα καὶ ('wherever'), and of course the agglomeration of genitives – absolute or otherwise – can be confusing. A helpful overview of the grammatical peculiarities to be found in the letters of Theodore II Laskaris is given by the Italian scholar, Nicolao Festa,[7] but they can help one to understand other authors as well.

Difficulties with the thought

George Steiner has written of the fascination that certain writers have for 'the difficult'.[8] It is fairly obvious that in some cases the aim of the writer is to impress readers by his own verbal dexterity and learning: Nikephoros Blemmydes can be found indulging in this trick when he thinks the occasion requires.[9] At other times there can be a deliberate cultivation of obscurity as in the famous 'Oracles' falsely attributed to Leo the Wise, which have been described as 'the most obscure text in Byzantine prophetic literature'. The Flemish scholar, Dr Jeannine Vereecken,

---

[6] These examples are taken from Eustathios of Thessalonike, *Eustathii Opera Minora*, ed. P. Wirth (Berlin, 2000), 211.6; 202.5; 218.28; 209.58–59. Another good example occurs in the recent edition of the works of Theodore Dexios (CCSG, 55) where the very competent editor, Ioannis D. Polemis hesitates over the repeated μὴ; (15: 23).

[7] *Theodori Ducae Lascaris Epistulae CCXVII* (Florence, 1898), Indiculus grammaticus, 411–414.

[8] G. Steiner, *On difficulty* (Oxford, 1972). Being a polyglot scholar, Steiner can range over a vast array of poetic literature; unfortunately he does not comment in detail on any Greek writers.

[9] The opening paragraph of the elaborate letter written to defend himself before patriarch Manuel II (1243–1254) is a case in point: J.A. Munitiz, 'Blemmydes revisited: the letters of Nicephorus Blemmydes to Patriarch Manuel II', *Porphyrogenita: essays on the history and literature of Byzantium and the Latin East in honour of Julian Chrysostomides*, ed. C. Dendrinos, J. Harris, E. Harvalia-Crook, and J. Herrin (Aldershot, 2003), 379, where there is a reference to another work of Blemmydes with a complicated prooimion, but mention might also have been made of the other letters of Blemmydes to Theodore II Laskaris.

claims that these can only be understood as an esoteric exhortation to spiritual rebirth.[10]

Byzantine writers who particularly test the ingenuity of readers are a cluster of extraordinary writers active shortly before or after the capture of Constantinople in 1204: Niketas Choniates, Eustathios of Thessalonike and, to a lesser degree, Nikephoros Blemmydes. Both Choniates and Eustathios combine an exceptional richness of vocabulary with an ingenious concatenation of words and sentences. It may be helpful to consider how best to deal with such complicated sentence structures as are to be found in Choniates.

Here is a sample, first presented as a straightforward text without line numbers and later analysed and displayed with line numbers at the end of this paper:

> Συνέβη δέ τι καὶ ἕτερον εἰς τὴν τοσαύτην αὐτὸν ἐκτραχηλίσαν ἀνοσιότητα. Ὁρῶν γὰρ ἀπανταχόθεν στενά οἱ τὰ πράγματα, καὶ τοὺς ἐκ Σικελίας ὅσον οὐδέπω κατὰ κεφαλῆς αὐτῷ ἐπιστησομένους, καὶ ὡς ἑκατογκέφαλον Τυφῶνα καταπιέσοντας, τοὺς δ' ἐντὸς τὸν αὐτοῦ θάνατον διψῶντας ἐπισκοπήν τε ἡγουμένους θεοῦ καὶ λύσιν δοξάζοντας τῶν κακῶν τὴν αὐτοῦ ἀνάλυσιν ἐκ τοῦ σώματος, καὶ τὴν ἀπὸ τοῦ θείου δὲ ὑφορώμενος ἐγκατάλειψιν, οἷς πολυτρόπως τὸ ὑπερέχον ἐδάμασε, καὶ ταῦτα διατεινόμενος ἐκ τῆς αὐλῆς εἶναι Χριστοῦ καὶ τὸ αὐτὸ γένος τοῖς ἐκθλιβομένοις λαχών, πρὸς τὴν διὰ θωπείας εἴτε καὶ θεραπείας τῶν ἐναγῶν δαιμόνων πρόγνωσιν τῶν μελλόντων ὁρμᾷ, καθὰ καὶ ὁ παλαιὸς ἐκεῖνος Σαοὺλ εἰς τὰς ἐγγαστριμύθους ὕστερον ἔβλεψεν, ἃς ἐδίωκε πρότερον τὸ θεῖον ἑαυτῷ ἱλεούμενος.[11]

A text that at first sight may appear quite intractable begins to make sense when it is split up into verse-size lines; it becomes so obvious that this is literature written to be declaimed aloud. Whatever doubts may arise about its historical value, there can be no denying that it is the work of a writer who delights in words.[12] The analysis of this paragraph will serve as an illustration. Choniates begins with an apparently simple sentence, then follows it up with a long complicated period in which

---

[10] A text is available in *PG*, 107, 1129–1149, but for a summary of Dr Vereecken's interpretation, cf. the précis of her communication in the Paris XX ByzIntCong, *Pré-Actes* III *Communications Libres*, 44 (entitled: 'The oracles of Leo the Wise and the philosopher's stone').

[11] The Greek text has been established by J.-L. Van Dieten, *Nicetae Choniatae Historia* (CFHB 11.1, Berlin and New York, 1975) (earlier ed. Bekker, 440–441). For an understanding of the text I have been greatly helped by the Italian translation of Anna Pontani published in *Niceta Coniata Grandezza e Catastrofe di Bisanzio* [Fondazione Lorenzo Valla] (Arnoldo Mondadori, 1999), II, 272–275, Book XI §6.1.

[12] R. Maisano, 'Letteratura e storiografia nell'opera di Niceta Coniata', *Messana: Rassegna di Studi Filologici Linguistici e Storici*, (Sicania, 16, 1993), 41–57: he points out (55) that the work of Choniates survives in many manuscripts (plus an epitome, a paraphrase, and a synopsis); this is very unlike many Byzantine historical works that survived by the skin of their teeth in single or very few manuscripts.

clauses balance one another and the main verb (in line 28) is almost submerged. But even in the first sentence Choniates has inserted a vivid visual image – the bucking horse toppling the rider over its neck. Choniates is a writer who avoids the obvious, whether in words or in construction: e.g. one might have expected a μὲν at line 5 (preparing for the δὲ at line 9). He indulges in wordplay: λύσιν answered by ἀνάλυσιν at line 13, θωπείας at line 26 echoed by θεραπείας in the same line, and ὕστερον ironically followed by a πρότερον in line 32. He draws on both classical myths (Typhon, line 7, confused with the hundred-headed Typhoeus) and Biblical parallels (King Saul, line 30). There is good illustration of the idiomatic use of καὶ in line 19. In fact, the more one looks at these lines the more one discovers of the mastery they display.

There are of course other aspects of Choniates that may be considered less admirable: one finds a morbid lingering over pain and suffering that seems pathological in origin. But for the purposes of this short tribute, one may hope that this passage has served its purpose.

Difficulties with genre

Finally, mention must be made of the hurdles that anyone reading Greek texts has to face with different categories (or genres) of texts. The most obvious case is of course that connected with verse, where sensitivity to metre and stress becomes so important in medieval poems; stress of course can also play an important role in Byzantine prose.[13] But medical or astrological texts present special problems, though fortunately work is progressing on a table of 'abbreviations' that should solve many problems.[14] And, to return to our honorand, the whole genre of monastic *typika*, especially the liturgical, with their recondite terminology can be a daunting prospect. This is a good example of how the work of Robert Jordan can contribute to the advance of Greek studies and to a greater appreciation of the wonders of the Greek language.

---

[13] The work of Wolfram Hörandner is a great help here: *Der Prosarhythmus in der rhetorischen Literatur der Byzantiner* (WByzSt, 16, Vienna, 1981).

[14] A project launched by the indefatigable Julian Chrysostomides with the help of Charalambos Dendrinos, and likely to be published by Porphyrogenitus in the near future.

Analysis of the passage of Niketas Choniates

Συνέβη δέ τι καὶ ἕτερον εἰς τὴν τοσαύτην αὐτὸν ἐκτραχηλίσαν ἀνοσιότητα.
There occurred something else that like a bucking horse flung him into such unholiness.
Ὁρῶν γὰρ ἀπανταχόθεν στενά οἱ τὰ πράγματα,
Seeing that from all sides circumstances were narrowly hemming him in
5 καὶ τοὺς ἐκ Σικελίας ὅσον οὐδέπω κατὰ κεφαλῆς αὐτῷ ἐπιστησομένους,
and that those <Normans> from Sicily were almost about landed on his head
καὶ ὡς ἑκατογκέφαλον Τυφῶνα καταπιέσοντας,
and like the hundred-headed Typhon would be squeezing him to death
τοὺς δ' ἐντὸς τὸν αὐτοῦ θάνατον διψῶντας
10 while those inside <the city> were thirsting for his death,
ἐπισκοπήν τε ἡγουμένους Θεοῦ
both considering it <to be> a visitation from God
καὶ λύσιν δοξάζοντας τῶν κακῶν τὴν αὐτοῦ ἀνάλυσιν ἐκ τοῦ σώματος,
and regarding his extraction from his body as a solution to <their> ills,
15 καὶ τὴν ἀπὸ τοῦ θείου δὲ ὑφορώμενος ἐγκατάλειψιν,
and suspecting that he was abandoned by the divinity
οἷς πολυτρόπως τὸ ὑπερέχον ἐδάμασε,
for the many ways in which he had crushed anything outstanding,
καὶ ταῦτα
20   despite moreover
διατεινόμενος ἐκ τῆς αὐλῆς εἶναι Χριστοῦ
his contending that he belonged to the fold [John 10:16] of Christ
καὶ τὸ αὐτὸ γένος τοῖς ἐκθλιβομένοις λαχών,
and that he shared the same nature as those who were being mistreated
25 πρὸς τὴν
διὰ θωπείας, εἴτε καὶ θεραπείας τῶν ἐναγῶν δαιμόνων,
through flattery or even through service of the accursed demons
πρόγνωσιν τῶν μελλόντων ὁρμᾷ
foreknowledge of what is to happen he rushes after (πρὸς),
30 καθὰ καὶ ὁ παλαιὸς ἐκεῖνος Σαοὺλ εἰς τὰς ἐγγαστριμύθους
just like that famous Saul of old [1 Kings 28], to the ventriloquist women
ὕστερον ἔβλεψεν, ἃς ἐδίωκε πρότερον,
later he looked, whom earlier he had been expelling
τὸ θεῖον ἑαυτῷ ἱλεούμενος.
35 when seeking to placate the divinity on his behalf.

4

The Letter and the Spirit: some problems in transmitting patristic texts to a modern audience

Mary Cunningham

Translation of Greek patristic and Byzantine texts has taken off in the last twenty years or so. Readers wishing to consult the writings of the fathers, hagiography, church histories, as well as more secular texts of the late antique and medieval periods, now have access to a wide range of modern, as well as older, translations.[1] With respect to early Christian and Byzantine spirituality, it is especially worth mentioning the excellent translations of the *Apophthegmata* and *Lives* of the Desert Fathers by Benedicta Ward and Norman Russell,[2] the work of G.E.H. Palmer, Philip Sherrard, and Kallistos Ware on the four volumes of the *Philokalia*,[3] and series such as the Classics of Western Spirituality and Cistercian Studies.[4] For the later Byzantine period we now have the excellent publications of Dumbarton Oaks, many of which are also available online.[5] The Evergetis Project at Queen's University Belfast has contributed to this growing body of translated material: Robert Jordan's meticulous rendering of the Evergetis *Synaxarion* into English represents a

---

[1] Most of the older English translations of post-apostolic and patristic texts were composed in the nineteenth century. These very comprehensive and useful volumes remain accessible in the Ante-Nicene Fathers and Nicene and Post-Nicene Fathers series, republished in the 1990s by Hendrickson Publishers, Inc. Both series may also be consulted on the internet at ccel.org/fathers2/

[2] *The sayings of the Desert Fathers. The alphabetical collection*, tr. B. Ward, SLG (London and Oxford, 1981); N. Russell, *The lives of the Desert Fathers* (Oxford, 1981).

[3] *The Philokalia. The complete text compiled by St Nikodimos of the Holy Mountain and St Makarios of Corinth*, tr. G.E.H. Palmer, P. Sherrard and K. Ware, 4 vols (London, 1979–1995).

[4] Published by Paulist Press, New Jersey, and in Kalamazoo, Michigan, respectively.

[5] For example, the translations of Byzantine saints' *Lives* such as *Holy women of Byzantium. Ten saints' Lives in English translation*, ed. A.-M. Talbot (Washington, DC, 1996); *Byzantine defenders of images. Eight saints' Lives in English translation*, ed. A.-M. Talbot (Washington, DC, 1998); R.P.H. Greenfield, *The Life of Lazaros of Mt Galesion. An eleventh-century pillar saint* (Washington, DC, 2000). The website is at: www.doaks.org/

splendid addition to the corpus of monastic and liturgical texts now available to students of Byzantine spirituality.[6]

With the loss of classics teaching in many private as well as state schools in the British Isles, students wishing to study patristics and Byzantine studies often arrive without the solid grounding in Greek and Latin that they used to have. Undergraduates are no longer required to learn Hebrew or New Testament Greek for theological degrees; ancient and medieval historians can study texts in translation rather than learning to read the original primary sources. It is even possible in some universities for graduate students to gain higher degrees in church history, patristics, or Byzantine studies without learning New Testament, patristic, or medieval Greek. These developments should not really be deplored – instead we should celebrate the wealth of translations that makes such open access possible! These academic fields no longer remain the esoteric and inevitably elitist disciplines that they used to be. Their availability to students who come from a wide range of disciplines, not just classics, history, or theology, means that fresh approaches are being applied and traditional boundaries between subjects are breaking down.

It is necessary to sound a note of caution, however, with respect to the widespread use of translated source material both in teaching and research. How many students, especially undergraduates, are taught to handle translations with critical insight and special care? Certainly, they are all taught the pitfalls of interpreting biased or classicising primary sources, the 'distorting mirror' presented by Byzantine writers, as Cyril Mango memorably described it.[7] However, there is another layer of distortion towards which we may remain less alert: this is the inevitable disjunction which exists between two different languages and rhetorical traditions. It is the aim of this paper to explore some of the problems associated with the apparently straightforward task of translating patristic and medieval Greek texts into English. Various solutions to the problem will be examined, using examples of recent translations.

To begin with some of the issues surrounding the translation of patristic and Byzantine texts, we face first the imperfect textual state of many primary sources. Although many important religious texts have been critically edited, the majority remain in editions prepared largely in the seventeenth century, usually on the basis of one manuscript. While most of these editions, reproduced in J.-P. Migne's *Patrologia Graeca*, are reliable and accurate, they do represent only one strand of what may be in many cases a large and diverse manuscript tradition. Secondly, a more general problem intrinsic to translation is the fact that it is by its nature an *interpretation* of the text. Space forbids going into the history or theory of translation. This is

---

[6] *The Synaxarion of the monastery of the Theotokos Evergetis: September to February*, ed. tr. R.H. Jordan (BBTT, 6.5, Belfast, 2000).
[7] C. Mango, 'Byzantine literature as a distorting mirror', *History and culture of the Byzantine empire and its heritage* (London, 1984), II.

a discipline that has received considerable scholarly attention in recent years and is served by a growing body of methodological studies.[8] For our purposes, it is simply important to reiterate that translation represents, by its very nature, interpretation.[9] Translators do not merely transpose words from one language to another; they embark on a complex process of rendering texts which were composed in distinct cultural circumstances into versions which will be comprehensible to contemporary, English-speaking audiences.

The issue of audience thus applies to both sides of the equation. Firstly, translators need to understand as much as possible the circumstances of their texts' composition and reception by early Christian or Byzantine audiences. Secondly, however, they will be influenced by the needs of the readers for whom the translations are intended. Modern publishers appear to have various audiences in mind when they commission and produce translations of patristic and Byzantine texts. These include members of the scholarly community, both students and more advanced researchers, as well as pious and lay readers. The intended audience will affect the nature of translations and commentaries, although of course there is overlap with many publications serving the needs of more than one of these audiences. Translations thus range from more literal renderings, prepared for scholars who need to know as closely as possible how the original text is worded, to paraphrases enabling easy comprehension in the second language. Translators of highly rhetorical Byzantine texts face the extra problem of transmitting this style faithfully to audiences with very different literary tastes. As George Steiner expresses it, 'Different civilizations, different epochs do not necessarily produce the same "speech mass"; certain cultures speak less than others; some modes of sensibility prize taciturnity and elision, others reward prolixity and semantic ornamentation.'[10] Translators must inevitably compromise between remaining faithful to their textual sources and sensitive to the needs and enjoyment of modern readers.

Let us turn now to some specific examples in order to illustrate some of the problems associated with translation. Two English translations of the fifth-century treatise by Diadochos of Photike, *On spiritual knowledge and discrimination*, adopt somewhat different approaches to this difficult and highly technical text. The more recent version, published by Janet Rutherford in the Belfast Byzantine Texts and

---

[8] Useful introductory bibliography includes *Routledge encyclopedia of translation studies*, ed. M. Baker and K. Malmkjaer (London and New York, 1998); *Western translation theory from Herodotus to Nietzsche*, ed. D. Robinson, 2nd ed. (Manchester, UK and Northampton, MA, 1997, 2002); L. Venuti, *The translator's invisibility. A history of translation* (London and New York, 1995); L. Venuti, *The scandals of translation. Towards an ethics of difference* (London and New York, 1998), and many other recent studies.

[9] See G. Steiner, *After Babel. Aspects of language and translation* (Oxford, 1975).

[10] Steiner, *After Babel*, 18.

Translations series,[11] sets out its method in a short Introduction. Envisaging an audience which is interested in knowing what terms Diadochos himself used, Rutherford defends her choice of a fairly literal translation which is based on a precise understanding of technical vocabulary. Words such as 'soul' (ψυχή), 'heart' (καρδία), 'intellect' (νοῦς), 'sense' (αἴσθησις), and 'reason' (διάνοια) reflect a systematic and highly sophisticated understanding of the human person by Diadochos.[12] Although Rutherford states that defining these terms in isolation may be misleading and decides against providing a glossary, she does aim to translate words such as αἴσθησις consistently when they are used in a technical sense.[13]

We may contrast this method with the looser, but more readable translation of the same text which appears in the English version of the *Philokalia* which is intended as much for a devout lay audience as for a scholarly audience.[14] That it satisfies both types of reader is ensured by its accurate, but also lucid translation, useful introductions and notes, as well as a full glossary at the back. When compared to Rutherford's more literal translation of Diadochos, however, the *Philokalia*'s rendering of *On spiritual knowledge* is more dynamic; that is, it attempts to create a meaningful interpretation of the text even when this involves departing from the exact wording of the original.

The following examples will serve to illustrate these two approaches:

Chapter 14:

Greek text	Rutherford	Philokalia
Ὁ ἐν αἰσθήσει καρδίας ἀγαπῶν τὸν Θεὸν ἐκεῖνος ἔγνωσται ὑπ' αὐτοῦ· ὅσον γάρ τις ἐν αἰσθήσει τῆς ψυχῆς παραδέχεται τὴν ἀγάπην τοῦ Θεοῦ, τοσοῦτον γίνεται ἐν τῇ ἀγάπῃ τοῦ Θεοῦ.[15]	Whoever loves God in the sense of the heart, this man has been perceived by Him; (cf. I Cor 8:3) for one comes to live in love for God to the same extent that one receives the love of God in the sense of the soul.[16]	He who loves God consciously in his heart is known by God (cf. I Cor 8:3), for to the degree that he receives the love of God consciously in his soul, he truly enters into God's love.[17]

---

[11] *One hundred practical texts of perception and spiritual discernment from Diadochos of Photike*, ed. J.E. Rutherford (BBTT, 8, Belfast, 2000).
[12] For a discussion of Diadochos's place in the development of Byzantine monastic theology, and his debt to both Evagrios and Messalianism, see A. Louth, *The origins of the Christian mystical tradition from Plato to Denys* (Oxford, 1981), 125–131.
[13] Rutherford, *One hundred practical texts*, 7.
[14] See n.3 above.
[15] The Greek text is based on that produced by E. des Places, *Oeuvres spirituelles – Diadoque de Photicé* (Paris, 1966), but it has been substantially revised in the light of a newly discovered manuscript, Lavra Γ 42, by Janet Rutherford. See Rutherford, *One hundred practical texts*, 8–9.
[16] Rutherford, *One hundred practical texts*, 25.
[17] *Philokalia*, tr. Palmer, Sherrard and Ware, I, 256.

Chapter 30:

Greek text	Rutherford	Philokalia
Αἴσθησίς ἐστι νοὸς γεῦσις ἀκριβὴς τῶν διακρινομένων.	The Sense of the intellect is the precise taste of things discerned.[18]	The perceptive faculty of the intellect consists in the power to discriminate accurately between the tastes of different realities.[19]

Comparison of these two translations raises issues which have implications for other patristic texts as well. Firstly, Rutherford's decision to translate terms such as 'sense' (αἴσθησις) in a consistent manner alerts the reader to the presence of this word, but sometimes detracts from the fluency of the English. In fact, whereas some technical terms such as 'intellect' (νοῦς) or 'soul' (ψυχή) can usually be translated by one English word, others such as 'passion' (πάθος) and indeed 'sense' (αἴσθησις) can be used in different ways.[20] Rutherford of course acknowledges this problem, but does adhere as much as possible to her scheme of Evagrios's anthropology, preferring consistency to variation. A related problem faced by translators not only of monastic treatises, but of all forms of theological literature, is the fact that there do not appear to be enough words in English to correspond to the plethora of synonyms, or near synonyms, in Greek. 'Thought' may be used for νόημα, νόησις, ἔννοια, or λογισμός, although it is clear that there are subtle differences in the meanings of these words.[21] It is a real problem when translating Byzantine homilies on the Theotokos to find enough English words to express the variations contained in at least a dozen words and their superlatives meaning 'pure' or 'unblemished'.[22]

In fact there is a strong argument for using the increasingly accepted body of English technical terms which have been established especially by the translators of the *Philokalia*.[23] Just as readers of the original texts recognised the meanings of

---

[18] Rutherford, *One hundred practical texts*, 41.

[19] *Philokalia*, tr. Palmer, Sherrard, and Ware, I, 261.

[20] In Greek the word πάθος means literally that which happens to a person or thing: it comes from the aorist root of the verb πάσχω, 'to experience' or 'to suffer'. In the realm of Christian asceticism, the word has a variety of meanings and can be used differently by individual writers. Some Fathers, beginning with Evagrios, regard the passions as inherently evil and describe them as assailing the human being from outside. Others such as Isaac of Nineveh, however, believed that the passions represent impulses which God placed in humankind in order that they might apprehend higher things, but which have become distorted because of the Fall from grace. By means of ascetic training, the passions may be trained and ultimately transfigured so that they will operate once again in a positive way. See *Philokalia*, tr. Palmer, Sherrard, and Ware, I, 363–364.

[21] *Philokalia*, ed. Palmer, Sherrard and Ware, I, 367.

[22] ἁγνός, ἀκηλίδωτος, ἀμόλυντος, ἄχραντος, πανάμωμος, πανάχραντος, ὑπέραγνος, etc.

[23] *Philokalia*, Palmer, Sherrard and Ware, I–IV. This glossary appears at the back of each volume and includes detailed discussions of the meanings of each word.

words which had a long history not only in monastic theology, but before that in pagan philosophy, English readers increasingly recognise the background of such words in the range of translations that are now available to them. Innovation in the translation of technical vocabulary, although not inadmissible, should be undertaken with good justification and, perhaps, should be clearly signalled.[24]

A separate, but related problem lies in the translation of biblical quotations. There is not space in this paper to enter into scholarly and lay debates about all the English translations of the Bible which currently exist.[25] Suffice it to say that in addition to the differences between translations which use the Hebrew or the Greek Septuagint versions of the Old Testament, we are faced with choices between the flowing, but archaic elegance of the authorised version and the more colloquial but comprehensible style of modern translations. It is important to remember that the Byzantines, like their contemporary Orthodox counterparts, used the Septuagint version of the Old Testament, believing the production of this text by seventy-two Greek-speaking Jews in the third century BC to be divinely inspired.[26] Although the Septuagint is generally faithful to the Hebrew text of the Bible,[27] it, like any other translation, represents an interpretation especially in passages which are ambiguous in meaning.[28] Perhaps one of the most famous examples of this is Isaiah 7:14, but many other passages could also be cited.[29] Translators of patristic or Byzantine religious texts are faced with the problem not only of rendering whole scriptural quo-

---

[24] Rutherford has of course done this and provides full explanations, both in her Introduction and in notes. See Rutherford, *One hundred practical texts*, esp. 6–7.

[25] For an excellent overview and criticism of five recent translations, see Archimandrite Ephrem's review of these in *Sourozh. A journal of Orthodox life and thought*, 47 (February 1992), 42–55.

[26] See M. Hengel, *The Septuagint as Christian scripture: its prehistory and the problem of its canon* (Edinburgh, 2002); *On the trail of the Septuagint translators*, ed. A. Aejmelaeus (Kampen, 1994).

[27] Note, however, that various editions of the Septuagint are available, not all of which are critical. The Göttingen edition is the most reliable so far, but it differs from the text which was accepted in the Byzantine church. English translations are also scarce: the nineteenth-century version by Sir Lancelot Brenton is still available in print, but newer versions are in progress, intended for both scholarly and pious audiences.

[28] See S. Sipila, *Between literalness and freedom: translation technique in the Septuagint* (Helsinki, 1999); *The Greek and Hebrew Bible: collected essays on the Septuagint*, ed. E. Tov (Leiden and Boston, 1999). The earliest systematic study of the differences between the Greek Septuagint and the Hebrew Bible, as well as three later translations into Greek was Origen's *Hexapla*, in which he arranged them in six columns. For versions of this text, which survives only in fragments, see *Clavis patrum graecorum*, I: *patres antenicaeni*, ed. M. Geerard (Turnhout, 1983), no. 1500, 174–175.

[29] Archimandrite Ephrem provides some interesting examples in his review article, illustrating the fact that versions are often influenced by translators' theological or political agendas. Thus we see wide variations in the rendering of Genesis 1:2, from the old *Revised Standard Version*, which reads, 'The earth was without form and void, and darkness was upon the face of the deep; and the Spirit of God was moving over the face of the waters' to the *New American Bible*'s 'the earth was formless waste land, and darkness covered the abyss, while a mighty wind swept over the waters'. See *Sourozh*, 47 (1992), 46.

tations, but also of signalling allusions or even inaccurately remembered biblical passages or words.[30] The advantage of using an established English version, especially one used in contemporary church services, is that readers will immediately recognise the biblical reference, even before they have checked the footnote or commentary. On the other hand, many accepted translations in fact represent paraphrases or have moved significantly away from the original Hebrew or Greek.[31] Translators usually choose some form of compromise in response to this problem. Words which echo an established English version may be chosen, but a more literal rendering of grammar or other idiosyncrasies of the original text may simultaneously be adopted.

Oddly enough, it is the more colloquial patristic and Byzantine texts which are the most difficult to translate, rather than the high-style, classicising ones.[32] This is due partly to the lack of critical editions of some texts, such as the alphabetical collection of the *Sayings of the Desert Fathers* and John Moschos's *Spiritual meadow*, which means that the corruption of the published texts causes problems which are occasionally insurmountable. However, colloquial style may also lead to ambiguity in meaning; in such cases translators are entitled to make what sense of the text they can.[33] The meaning of unusual words for objects belonging to daily life may have to be guessed on the basis of their context; more often, however, the laconic use of grammar and syntax leads to ambiguity. An experienced translator begins quickly to gain a 'feel' for the meaning of medieval Greek texts written in a lower style. An

---

[30] Byzantine hymns and homilies, for example, are packed with allusions to scripture, sometimes referring to many different passages in the same verse or line. This represents the direct continuation of a practice which was used by biblical writers themselves, providing not only authority but also a seamless tapestry of allusive meaning which serves to bind together the whole of God's historical dispensation for humankind.

[31] An interesting example, since it has repercussions for Marian typology, is Ps 67 (68): 15, referring to the mountain of God. The authorised version (King James) and NRSV translate a rare Hebrew word by 'high' or 'many-peaked', whereas the Septuagint renders it τετυρωμένον. Brenton translates this as 'swelling' mountain, but in fact the word means 'made into cheese' or 'curdled'. According to Archimandrite Ephrem, 'this is not as odd as it appears since the Hebrew word *gavonon* is certainly cognate with the word for 'curd' or 'cheese', *g'vinah*.' The image in this psalm of 'a fat mountain, a curdled mountain' was understood by Greek Fathers to represent the gestation of Christ in Mary's womb, 'because the growth of the foetus was believed by ancient medicine to be the result of the solidifying of the mother's blood by interaction with the male seed, a sort of "curdling" process.' See Archimandrite Ephrem, 'Mary in eastern Church literature', *Mary in doctrine and devotion*, ed. A. Stacpoole (Dublin, 1990), 70–71.

[32] The classic study of the distinction between 'high', 'middle' and 'low' rhetorical styles remains I. Ševčenko, 'Levels of style in Byzantine prose', *JÖB*, 31/1 (XIV Int.Byz.Cong. Akten, I/1, Vienna, 1981), 289–312.

[33] See J. Wortley, *The spiritual meadow (pratum spirituale) by John Moschos* (CS 139, Kalamazoo, MI, 1992), xii.

understanding of the historical background represents an essential prerequisite for understanding the sayings and activities of desert fathers and mothers.

Higher style texts, such as the homilies of the fifth-century preacher, Proklos of Constantinople, on the other hand, require a translation which will convey something of the florid and poetic character of the Greek. Nicholas Constas's recent translation of five Marian homilies which Proklos delivered in Constantinople between AD 427 and 446 succeed brilliantly in conveying the measured eloquence of these works, which positively shimmer with typological and poetic images.[34] Another recent translator of Proklos, Jan Barkhuizen, has chosen to present the homilies in metrical lines in order to demonstrate their poetic character.[35] This method not only demonstrates Proklos's use of prose rhythm as a rhetorical device, but it also sets out clearly the parallelism and repetitive nature of his asianic style.[36] Translators may thus adopt various solutions in their efforts to convey the rhetorical quality, as well as the meaning, of ancient texts to a modern audience. Readers of high-style patristic and Byzantine texts will inevitably struggle, however, with the differences in rhetorical taste between two cultures.

Many texts, especially the more poetic or philosophical ones, are difficult to translate because their meaning is opaque even in the original Greek. A good example of such an enigma is the anonymous fifth- or sixth-century Akathistos hymn.[37] Various translators have attempted to interpret the metaphorical and typological meaning of the verses called *chairetismoi*, which express greetings to the all-holy and invincible Theotokos, the Virgin Mary. Vassiliki Limberis, in a study which links the Theotokos with pagan goddess cults and sees the imagery in the Akathistos as linked with these, stresses the non-Christian background of symbols such as light, power, water, and fertility.[38] Leena Peltomaa argues on the other hand that all of these images are inspired purely by Christian tradition, stressing especially their links with the sacraments of baptism and the eucharist. Occasionally

---

[34] N. Constas, *Proclus of Constantinople and the cult of the Virgin in antiquity. Homilies 1–5, texts and translations* (Leiden, 2003).

[35] J. Barkhuizen, *Proclus of Constantinople. Homilies on the life of Christ* (Early Christian Studies 1, Brisbane, 2001).

[36] On prose rhythm in Byzantine texts, see W. Hörandner, *Der Prosarhythmus in der rhetorischen Literatur der Byzantiner* (WByzSt, 16, Vienna, 1981). The characteristics of asianic style are described in G.A. Kennedy, *A new history of classical rhetoric* (Princeton, 1994), 95–96.

[37] Editions and translations of this text abound. The most easily accessible and most recent include *The Penguin book of Greek verse*, ed. C.A. Trypanis (Harmondsworth, 1971; repr. 1979), 474–389; C.A. Trypanis, *Fourteen early byzantine cantica* (WByzSt, 5, Vienna, 1968), 17–39; E. Wellesz, *The Akathistos hymn* (Monumenta Musicae Byzantinae Transcripta, 9, Copenhagen, 1957); L.M. Peltomaa, *The image of the Virgin Mary in the Akathistos hymn* (Leiden, 2001), 2–19; *The Lenten Triodion*, tr. Mother Mary and K. Ware (London and Boston, 1978), 422–437.

[38] V. Limberis, *Divine heiress. The Virgin Mary and the creation of Christian Constantinople* (London and New York, 1994), esp. 121–142.

these separate interpretations affect the wording of the translation, as we see in a few lines of Strophe 21:

Greek	Limberis	Peltomaa
Χαῖρε, ὅτι τὸν πολύφωτον ἀνατέλλεις φωτισμόν·	Hail! that you shed the light of great brilliancy.	Hail, since you kindle the many-beamed lantern;
Χαῖρε, ὅτι τὸν πολύρρυτον ἀναβλύζεις ποταμόν·	Hail! that you spring forth the multi-streamed river.	Hail, since you make the many-streamed river gush forth;
Χαῖρε, τῆς κολυμβήθρας ζωγραφοῦσα τὸν τύπον·	Hail! to you, who depicts the sign of the font of Siloam.	Hail, you who prefigure the baptismal font;
Χαῖρε, τῆς ἁμαρτίας ἀναιροῦσα τὸν ῥύπον·	Hail! to you, who did remove the stain of sin…	Hail, you who take away the filth of sin…

Apart from the fact that Peltomaa's translation is more often accurate than that of Limberis, we do not see huge differences in these two versions. However, Peltomaa stresses in her commentary the baptismal resonances of Strophe 21, whereas Limberis writes that the 'multi-streamed river'… 'is an inexplicable image without any context unless one remembers how extremely important the waterways were to Isis and the Egyptians.'[39] The Greek word κολυμβήθρα, in the next line, could refer either to a pool or to a font;[40] whereas Limberis chooses 'font of Siloam', Peltomaa glosses it as 'baptismal font'. Both of these versions represent paraphrases, reflecting the translators' understanding of the metaphor.[41] Whether because it was composed before most other liturgical texts honouring the Virgin, as Peltomaa believes,[42] or because it simply represents a highly original exploration of typological and poetic images for the Theotokos, some lines in the Akathistos hymn may never allow a final interpretation. Translators do need to arrive at a version which expresses their understanding of the text, but it is not necessary for critics to be dogmatic since in some cases various interpretations are possible.[43]

---

[39] Limberis, *Divine heiress*, 133.
[40] G.W.H. Lampe, *A patristic Greek lexicon* (Oxford, 1961, repr. 1976), 766.
[41] Limberis follows P.M. Addison in understanding this line as a reference to the pool of Siloam where Christ healed the man who had been blind since birth (John 9): cf. P.M. Addison, *Akathistos. Byzantine hymn to the Mother of God, translation for chant and choral recitation* (Mater ecclesiae, Centre for Marian Study, Rome, 1983), 33, 51. Most other translators, however, including Trypanis, understand it as a baptismal font, although they may be less explicit than Peltomaa: cf. Trypanis, *The Penguin book of Greek verse*, 387.
[42] Peltomaa, *The image of the Virgin Mary*, 28 and *passim*.
[43] In a thought-provoking section of her study, Peltomaa examines the nature of metaphorical language and concludes that metaphors can only be understood if we know something about the religious or cultural context out of which they come, and further, that 'metaphor is a process of transfer which gives rise to only one meaning.' See Peltomaa, *The image of the Virgin Mary*, 116–

In conclusion, it is perhaps worth emphasising again that translators are engaged in a much more complicated process than simply transposing words from one language to another. The ambiguities inherent in both languages may well render even a 'literal' translation impossible. If we recognise that translators are in fact interpreters of texts, it becomes apparent that various processes must take place. Firstly, it is necessary for translators to understand as fully as possible the meaning of the text in its original context. What is the relation between word and object in that culture, how did it employ rhetoric, what resonances did words or expressions possess in particular contexts – these are only a few of the questions which the translator will need to consider. Secondly, she or he must understand the meaning of the text in its actual context; this involves research into the author's intentions and its reception by a contemporary audience.[44] Finally, the translator seeks to make the text understandable to readers of his or her own period. Choices and compromises will be required in this process too: should the text, in order to be appreciated properly, be rendered in an idiom or rhetorical style which is familiar in the modern world or should it evoke the literary style of a previous era?[45]

Once it is recognised that translators are creative interpreters, we may accept that the decision to adopt any of the methods described above is entirely their own. Consideration of their audiences will influence most translators in making these choices. Whereas pious or lay readers may seek universal meanings in patristic texts, scholars will be keen to understand the idiosyncrasies of the original sources. The fact that such problems which will be solved differently by individual translators, exist, suggests the benefit of multiple translations of important texts. Just as a Bach cello suite may be interpreted entirely differently by individual performers, so

---

125. It is the second of these hypotheses which is perhaps the more debatable: when symbolic language is used as obliquely as it is in the Akathistos hymn, it is possible that more than one type or image may be in the author's mind. See M.B. Cunningham, 'Divine banquet: the Theotokos as a source of spiritual nourishment', *Eat, drink, and be merry, Proceedings of the 37th Spring Symposium of Byzantine Studies*, ed. L. Brubaker, Birmingham, 2002 (SPBS, 13, Aldershot, 2006).

[44] Sometimes there are in fact three audiences to consider, as in the case of anthologies such as Paul of Evergetis's *Synagoge*, in which much earlier texts are collected and arranged for the benefit of an eleventh-century monastic audience. See Paul Evergetinos, Εὐεργετινὸς ἤτοι Συναγωγὴ τῶν θεοφθόγγων ῥημάτων καὶ διδασκαλίων τῶν θεοφόρων καὶ ἁγίων πατέρων, ed. Makarios of Corinth and Nikodemos Hagiorites (Venice, 1783; 7th ed. in 4 vols, Athens, 1983).

[45] We see different choices being made in the translation of Byzantine saints' *Lives* in *Holy women of Byzantium*, ed. Talbot. Compare, for example, the fairly colloquial rendering of the life of St Mary/ Marinos by Nicholas Constas with Jeffrey Featherstone's more archaic version of the Life of St Matrona of Perge. Different English styles may usefully be exploited to convey the difference between high- and low-style Byzantine texts. Wendy Mayer and Pauline Allen's recent translation of homilies by John Chrysostom admirably conveys the colloquial and extempore qualities of these texts. See W. Mayer and P. Allen, *John Chrysostom* (London and New York, 2000).

may a sermon by Gregory of Nazianzos or liturgical hymn be rendered in various versions by translators.[46]

Readers of these texts, however, should always bear in mind the fact that the texts they are reading are interpretations, not original sources. Translators, especially when conveying texts to a scholarly audience, should endeavour to be as transparent as possible in their methods. Footnotes, commentaries, and, when appropriate, a glossary all help students to understand the background and resonances of individual words or expressions. Corruption or ambiguities in the original text should always be signalled, as should allusions or citations of earlier texts. At the same time, it is necessary, as Cicero, Pliny the Younger, Quintilian, and many other translators from antiquity to the present day have reminded us, to produce a version which will be meaningful and eloquent in the language one has chosen to express it.[47] Faithfulness to the author's meaning and sympathy for one's own audience represent the two prerequisites of an effective translation.

---

[46] It could be argued on the other hand that a theological or monastic treatise expresses one authentic message; translators may differ in how they convey that message in another language, but they would be diverging from its underlying meaning if they interpret it too loosely.

[47] Cicero, *De optimo genere oratorum*, V–VI, tr. H.M. Hubbell, Cicero, *De inventione, De optimo genere oratorum, Topica* (Cambridge, MA, 1949), 364–369; Pliny the Younger, *Epistulae*, VII, ix, tr. W. Melmoth, *Pliny Letters*, II (Cambridge, MA, 1957), 20–23; *Quintilian, Institutio oratoria*, X, v, tr. H.E. Butler, *The Institutio oratoria of Quintilian*, IV (Cambridge, MA, 1968), 112–117.

5

Bishops, monks and holy men: military defence and the shedding of blood

Stephen McCotter

This short essay was prompted by a passage in the *Wars* of Procopius which Bob had helped me to translate while I was working on my PhD. It referred to the capture of Amida by the Persians in 503 as a result of some monks, who were guarding the walls, allegedly getting drunk and not spotting the enemy getting in to their assigned tower. While Bob found it quite amusing and paralleled it with other instances of drunken monks, for me it prompted the question of how active a role did religious men, particularly monks, play in defending their monasteries or towns when under attack in late antiquity. The transition from being in the relative calm of the recently Christianised empire at the start of monasticism, to being the target of raids as the frontiers became unstable was bound to challenge the pacifist values of many monks. The passage from Procopius is later mirrored in the diary of Nicolo Barbaro who relates that 'the monks were guarding about a mile of the circuit of the walls on the seaward side,' during the Turkish siege of Constantinople in 1453.[1] In the sixteenth century sultan Selim II permitted the monks of St Sabas to bear arms to protect themselves against local raiders.[2] It appears that monks were sometimes involved in the defence of their cities and towns, but was it passive or active defence, just how often did it happen and, most importantly, is there any evidence from late antiquity of monks or other religious men being willing to do more than rely on the power of prayer and actually shed blood in a conflict? Did they ever step from a world of prayer to a world of blood?

According to George Dennis the Byzantines did not subscribe to the concept of Holy War be it Jihad or a Crusade (strictly speaking the latter was a pilgrimage).[3] Such aggressive activity aside, how was the use of military force in a defensive capacity actually viewed? St Basil's influential Canon 13 admitted that sometimes

---

[1] N. Barbaro, *Diary of the siege of Constantinople 1453*, tr. J. Melville-Jones (New York, 1969). http://www.deremilitari.org/resources/sources/constantinople3.htm
[2] http://stmaryofegypt.org/typika/typ055.html
[3] G.T. Dennis, 'Defenders of the Christian people: holy war in Byzantium', *The crusades from the perspective of Byzantium and the muslim world*, ed. A. Laiou and R.P. Mottahedeh (Washington, DC, 2001), 31–40.

military force was a necessity but even so those who shed blood, albeit in self-defence, were to be excluded from communion for three years.[4] His simple premise was that any killing, however justified, involved sin. However others apparently regarded this as too harsh a measure against those who had defended the empire and its Christian people to spare them from greater harm. Surely such necessary military activity was justified by God and should not incur punishment, argued St Athanasios.[5] The issue was still alive centuries later. In the fourteenth century Matthew Blastares continued to uphold Basil's prohibition, but the twelfth-century writers Zonaras and Theodore Balsamon both argue that such a punishment is best ignored. Evidence that they present regarding a synod's refusal to accept Nikephoros Phokas's attempt to have those who fell in battle regarded as martyrs certainly implies that the thirteenth Canon of Basil was generally not enforced.[6]

So much for the theological attitude to those lay people who took up the sword in defence of the empire, but what about monks and clergy who became involved in warfare? In 1213 Constantine Stilbes vehemently denounced those Latin clergy who took up the sword,[7] hardly surprising given that his home town of Kyzikos had just been overrun by the Latins. While I have found no clear cases of clergy wielding weapons from the late antique period, Balsamon and Blastares both provide a later example of religious men participating in warfare, again from the synodical discussion following Nikephoros Phokas's proposal regarding fallen soldiers. In the discussion several clergy confessed that they had fought and killed some of the enemy. Blastares says they were defrocked on the basis of the thirteenth and fifty-fifth canons. The fifty-fifth canon ordained that those clerics who defended themselves against robbers be removed from their office and that was obviously regarded as being equal to fighting an enemy of the state in this case.

So much for the bishops, but what of monks and holy men? Is there any evidence in antiquity of them ever resorting to violence? The *typikon* of St Sabas set out the punishments for violent actions against other monks in the monastery, a feature not found in other contemporary *typika*, at least not until the twelfth century.[8] A passage dated to 386 certainly seems to suggest that monks were prepared to behave violently against pagans. Writing to the emperor Theodosius to request imperial protection for pagan temples, Libanius says that the monks '…hasten to

---

[4] Cf. N. Oikonomides, 'The concept of "holy war" and two tenth-century Byzantine ivories', *Peace and war in Byzantium. Essays in honour of George T. Dennis S.J.*, ed. T.S. Miller and J. Nesbitt (Washington, DC, 1995), 62–86, esp. 65–68.
[5] P. Viscuso, 'Christian participation in warfare: a Byzantine view', *Peace and war in Byzantium. Essays in honour of George T. Dennis S.J.*, ed. T.S. Miller and J. Nesbitt (Washington, DC, 1995), 33–40.
[6] Viscuso, 'Christian participation in warfare', 38.
[7] J. Darrouzès, 'Le mémoire de Constantine Stilbès contre les Latins', *REB*, 21 (1963), 50–100.
[8] *Typikon* of St Sabas, ed. E. Kurtz, Τύπος καὶ παράδοσις καὶ νόμος τῆς σεβασμίας λαύρας τοῦ ἁγίου Σάββα', *BZ*, 3 (1894), 168–170; tr. G. Fiaccadori, *Byzantine monastic foundation documents*, ed. J. Thomas and A.C. Hero, 5 vols (DOS, 35, Washington, DC, 2000), IV, 1314, 1317.

attack the temples with sticks and stones and bars of iron, and in some cases, disdaining these, with hands and feet. Then utter desolation follows, with the stripping of roofs, demolition of walls, the tearing down of statues and the overthrow of altars, and the priests must either keep quiet or die.'[9] There are certainly many instances of monks engaging in physical violence against other 'heretics'.[10] Mark the Deacon actually praises Porphyry of Gaza for his incomplete *apatheia*. He describes him as σωφρονέστατος for having gained control over all his emotions except his anger, which he directed against enemies of the faith. These and other examples of violence have recently been discussed by Danny Praet of Ghent University in his paper on 'The moral and psychological views on violence in the eastern christian ascetical tradition' delivered to the fifth *Shifting Frontiers* conference.[11] This attitude may be compared with that of the Monophysite archimandrites in the sixth century who, when Ephrem launched his persecution of their monasteries, met to discuss their response and declared, 'It is not laid down that we should fight.'[12] If Orthodox monks and clergy were prepared to use violence against others within the empire who did not share their faith would it be logical to conclude they could actively fight non-Christians from outside the empire?

Given the foregoing paragraph which suggests some monks were engaged in violent activity inside the empire, it is perhaps surprising that there is virtually no record of monks or clergy being engaged in combat with Byzantium's external opponents. In contrast to the quantity of evidence of monastic violence against heretics, there are reported instances of monastic communities and individual holy men showing great pacifism in the face of foreign invasion and internal persecution. The *Apophthegmata Patrum*, a work Bob knows well, provides one of the earliest examples. Abba Moses of Sketis was apparently killed[13] when Mazices raided Egypt in 407-408. When the younger monks asked Abba Moses why he was not trying to escape the raid, he replied, 'For so many years I have been looking forward to this day, that the words of the Master Christ might be fulfilled which he spoke, "All who take the sword shall die by the sword". They say to him, 'Then neither do we flee, but will die with you'. He said, 'It is no business of mine: let each one see how he is settled.' There were seven brethren, and he says to them, 'Look, the barbari-

---

[9] Libanius, *Oratio* 30.8–10, tr. A.F. Norman, *Libanius: selected works* (Harvard, 1969).

[10] See Michael Gaddis's forthcoming paper, 'The anger of God: extremist violence in the late fourth and early fifth centuries', delivered at the fifth *Shifting Frontiers* conference in Santa Barbara in March 2003.

[11] The proceedings have yet to be published.

[12] Pseudo-Dionysius of Tel-Mahre, *Chronicle* Part III, 43, tr. W. Witakowski (TTH, 22, Liverpool, 1996), 40.

[13] There is some debate as to whether Abba Moses did die in the raid, but there is little doubt that Mazices devastated the monastery in 407–408. Palladius does not mention the raid when referring to Moses's passing. Palladius, *Lausiac history*, 19, ed. D.C. Butler, 2 vols (Cambridge, 1898–1904), II, 62.13–15.

ans are drawing near the door.' They came in and slew them. But one of the brethren hid behind the pile of rope: and he saw seven crowns coming down and crowning them."[14] Is this the general monastic view of how great monks should behave in the face of danger? Sketis itself was devastated again c.434 and c.577.

It is worth noting though that in the account by the Sabite monk, Antiochos Strategios, of the Persian siege of Jerusalem in 614, and in many other instances, bishops and monks often attempt to be peacemakers rather than being drawn in to the conflict. Bishops regularly acted as negotiators in sieges but when they took sides there are few cases of them doing anything more active than encouraging the defenders spiritually. At Constantina in 503 the bishop Bar-Hadad sprinkled the walls and the defenders with holy water (despite their massacre of the 'treacherous' Jews in the city).[15] Nonetheless there is also some evidence to suggest that bishops co-ordinated or at least helped to organise the defence of cities in earthly as well as spiritual ways. Possibly the earliest example comes from the siege of Nisibis in 337. Jacob appears to be the key person responsible for saving the city, particularly after the wall's breach, but this may well be later religious bias on the part of his followers to show the spiritual power and favour of a devout man Ephraem as not all the sources mention Jacob's role.[16] The holy men also called upon God to send a plague of gnats and mosquitoes against the Persian army and drive them away to end the city's suffering. In 614 the patriarch Zacharias, after trying to act as peacemaker and being abused for doing so by the 'factions', actively organised the defence of Jerusalem and sent Modestos, superior of the monastery of Thevdos, to bring the troops from Jericho to Jerusalem.[17] Probably the most famous case of a cleric participating in defensive activity is that of the patriarch Sergios, alongside the patrician Bonos, helping to organise the defence of Constantinople against the Avars in 626.

---

[14] Cf. D.J. Chitty, *The desert a city* (Oxford, 1966), 60–61.

[15] Pseudo-Joshua the Stylite, *Chronicle*, 58, *The chronicle of Pseudo-Joshua the Stylite*, ed. tr. F.R. Trombley and J.W. Watt (TTH, 32, Liverpool, 2000), 73–74.

[16] Jerome Chronicle ann.388, ed. R. Helm, 2nd ed. (Gr.Schr., 1956); Theodoret, *Historia Religiosa*, I.11–12, *PG*, 82, 1283–148; Theodoret, *Historia Ecclesiastica*, II.30,1–14, ed. L.Parmentier (Gr.Schr., 84, 1911); Ephraem, *Carmina Nisibena*, XIII.19–21, ed. G. Bickell (Leipzig, 1866); Theophanes, *Chronographia* AM 5829 and AM 5841, ed. C. de Boor (Leipzig, 1883–1885), tr. C. Mango and R. Scott with G. Greatrex (Oxford, 1997); *Chronicon Paschale* 337 and 350, ed. L. Dindorf (CSHB, 1832), ed. tr. M. Whitby and M. Whitby, *Chronicon Paschale 284–628 AD* (TTH, 7, Liverpool, 1989). It should be noted that the various accounts of this siege are confused and many conflate the sieges of 337 and 350. For more detail see C.S. Lightfoot, 'Facts and fiction: the third siege of Nisibis (AD 350)', *Historia*, 37 (1988), 105–125.

[17] Antiochos Strategios, ed. tr. C.F. Conybeare, 'Antiochus Strategius's account of the sack of Jerusalem in AD 614', *EHR*, 25 (1910), 502–517; tr. G. Garitte, *La prise de Jérusalem par les Perses en 614* (CSCO, 203, Scriptores Iberici, 12, Louvain, 1960).

The clearest example of involvement in practical preparation is probably set out in Synesios of Cyrene's letter to Olympios where the bishop details his own actions.

> We do not know, my dearest and best friend, if we shall ever have a chance of conversing together again. The cowardice of our generals has delivered up our country to the enemy without a single battle; there are no survivors except those of us who have seized fortified places. Those who have been captured in the plains have been butchered like victims for sacrifice. We are now afraid of a prolonged siege, lest it should compel most of the fortresses to surrender to thirst. This is the reason why I did not answer your counter-charges on the subject of the presents. I had no leisure, for I was taken up with a machine which I am constructing, that we may hurl long-distance missiles from the turrets, stones of really substantial weight. I shall leave you, however, entirely at liberty to send me gifts, for of course Synesios must yield to Olympios, but they must not be gifts of a luxurious sort. I disapprove of the luxury of the quarters assigned to the company. Send me, then, things that are useful for soldiers, such as bows and arrows, and above all arrows with heads attached to them. As far as the bows are concerned, I can at a pinch buy them elsewhere, or repair those which I have already, but it is not easy to procure arrows, I mean really good ones. The Egyptian arrows that we have bulge at the knots and sink in between the knots, so that they deviate from their right course.[18]

More striking may be an example from 421. When the Persians attacked Theodosiopolis:

> ...and had brought up many *helepoles*, and employed innumerable engines, and built up lofty towers outside the wall, resistance was offered, and the assault of the attacking engines repelled, by the bishop Eunomios alone. Our men had refused to fight against the foe, and were shrinking from bringing aid to the besieged, when the bishop, by opposing himself to them, preserved the city from being taken. When one of the barbarian chieftains ventured on his wonted blasphemy, and with words like those of Rabshakeh and Sennacherib, madly threatened to burn the temple of God, the holy bishop could not endure his furious wrath, but himself commanded a ballista, which went by the name of the Apostle Thomas, to be set up upon the battlements, and a mighty stone to be adjusted to it. Then, in the name of the Lord who had been blasphemed, he gave the word to let go, – down crashed the stone on that impious chief and hit him on his wicked mouth, and crushed in his face, and broke his head in pieces, and sprinkled his brains upon the ground. When the commander of the army who had hoped to take the city saw what was done, he confessed himself beaten and withdrew, and in his alarm made peace.[19]

Quite apart from the giving of a holy name to a weapon of war at this date, this passage is intriguing. Even here the evidence is not that the bishop fired at the barbarians, only that he commanded them to be shot at. Neither does Synesios say

---

[18] Synesios of Cyrene, ep. 133, tr. A. FitzGerald, *The Letters of Synesius of Cyrene* (London, 1926).
[19] Theodoret, *Historia Ecclesiastica*, V.36, ed. L. Parmentier (Gr.Schr., 84, 1911).

he fired the weapon. Is either cleric breaking his vows if he does not actually shed blood and is this the best evidence that we have for holy men being actively involved in the violent defence of cities?

There is actually one cleric who we are told did participate in an act of warfare and while it was hardly a full scale battle, Faustos's actions were certainly violent. All the more surprising is the praise heaped upon him by, again, Synesios of Cyrene.

> May all good things befall the priests of Axomis! While the soldiers were hiding themselves in the gorges of the mountains to take care of their precious lives, these priests called the peasants about them, and led them straight from the very church door against the enemy, and then they called upon God, and erected a trophy in the Myrtle Valley! This is a long ravine, deep and covered with forests. The barbarians, when they found no resistance in their way, rashly entered this dangerous defile, but they had to meet the valiant Faustos, the deacon of the church. This man, unarmed, when marching at the head of his troops, was himself the first to encounter a hoplite. He snatches up a stone, not to hurl it, but, holding it in his hand and leaping upon him as with a clenched fist he strikes the other violently on the temple. He knocks him down, strips him of his armour, and heaps many of the barbarians upon him. If any other man gave proof of courage in that battle, it is to Faustos that credit is due, both on account of his personal bravery, and for the orders which he gave at the critical moment. For my part, I would willingly give a victor's wreath to all those who participated in the engagement, and I would have their names proclaimed by the voice of a herald, for they were the first to do brave deeds, and to show panic-stricken souls that the barbarians are not Corybantes nor the demons who serve Rhea, but men like ourselves, who can be wounded and killed. And if only we are men in such a crisis as this, even the second prize will be honourable. Fate perchance might accord us even the first, if instead of being fifteen irregulars, hiking in a valley to forage, we were able to give battle in the open, in regular warfare, mass against mass.[20]

Letter 125 similarly expresses dissatisfaction with the army's inaction and Synesios's own preparedness to raise troops and lead them into battle.[21] While this seems to be clear evidence of the involvement of holy men in war it must be remembered that Synesios appears to have had a somewhat different outlook on many aspects of Christianity and war and that he cannot be regarded as typical.[22]

However, by the sixth century monks and particularly holy men were seemingly defending themselves more actively, by the power of God, without shedding blood. Anyone who has taken Bob's Byzantine Texts Foundation course with its

---

[20] Synesios of Cyrene, ep. 122, *The Letters of Synesius of Cyrene*, tr. FitzGerald. Also available on http://www.geocities.com/athens/acropolis/5164/sletter122.html
[21] Synesios of Cyrene, ep. 125, *The Letters of Synesius of Cyrene*, tr. FitzGerald. Also available on http://www.geocities.com/athens/acropolis/5164/sletter125.html
[22] J. Bregman, *Synesius of Cyrene: philosopher-bishop* (Berkeley, 1982).

tales of Saracens being swallowed up by the desert in response to the prayers of an early monk will certainly see echoes in these later texts. For example, the Abba Moses incident is paralleled by that of Maro the Stylite near Amida. He had a vision foretelling the arrival of a raiding party of Epthalite 'Huns' serving with the Persians and it scared most of the brethren of his community into flight. Only Maro and three other monks remained behind and were not found by the Huns.[23] Another group of Epthalites around Amida in 502 tried to attack the anchorite Jacob but were paralyzed by him. They stayed in this state until the Persian king Kavades begged the hermit to forgive and release his men, which he did. In gratitude he granted any favour that Jacob named. The anchorite asked for the right to shelter any refugees who came to him during the war and Kavades agreed.[24] Similar western examples of holy men using their powers to repel and thwart barbarian attacks on undefended towns can be found in Eugippius' accounts of St Severinus of Noricum in the fifth century.[25]

It is immediately after the aforementioned incident with the anchorite Jacob in 502 that our point of departure, the tale of the monks at Amida, occurs. Procopius relates the siege of Amida and the reason for its fall he lays squarely with the monks guarding the wall: 'Not many days later one of the Persians saw close by one of the towers the mouth of an old underground passage, which was insecurely concealed with some small stones. In the night he came there alone, and, making trial of the entrance, got inside the circuit-wall; then at daybreak he reported the whole matter to Kavades. The king himself on the following night came to the spot with a few men, bringing ladders which he had made ready. And he was favoured by a piece of good fortune; for the defence of the very tower which happened to be nearest to the passage had fallen by lot to those of the Christians who are most careful in their observances, whom they call monks. These men, as chance would have it, were keeping some annual religious festival to God on that day. When night came on they all felt great weariness on account of the festival, and, having sated themselves with food and drink beyond their wont, they fell into a sweet and gentle sleep, and were consequently quite unaware of what was going on. So the Persians made their way through the passage inside the fortifications, a few at a time, and, mounting the tower, they found the monks still sleeping and slew them to a man. When Kavades learned this he brought his ladders up to the wall close by this tower.'[26] Procopius clearly lays the blame for the fall with the drunken monks who had been assigned to watch this sector of the walls, but it seems clear that monks were expected to play a role in the defence of the city other

---

[23] John of Ephesus, *Lives*, 4, *Patrologia Orientalis*, ed. tr. E. W. Brooks, 17:78–83 (Paris 1923).
[24] Procopius, *Wars* I.7,5–11, ed. tr. H. B. Dewing, 5 vols (Cambridge, MA, 1914–1928), I, 51–53.
[25] Eugippius, *Vita Severini*, ed. P. Knoell (CSEL, 9, Vienna, 1886); *The Life of St Severin*, tr. L. Bieler with the collaboration of L. Krestan (Fathers of the Church, 55, Washington, DC, 1965).
[26] Procopius, *Wars* I.7, 20–25, ed. tr. Dewing, I, 57.

than simply through prayer. Were they expected to repel invaders in the event of an assault? Procopius does not give us any evidence either way.

However there are other detailed accounts of the fall of the Amida in 503 and it would be instructive to examine them all. The next version of the fall of the city comes from Pseudo-Joshua the Stylite:

> The Amidans, however, became overconfident of their victory, and fell into negligence, and did not guard the wall with the care that [they had exercised] before. On 10 January, the guards on the wall drank much wine because of the cold, and when night came, [some] fell asleep and sank into a deep slumber; while others abandoned their posts because it was raining, and went down to take shelter in their houses. Whether by this ill-discipline, as we think, or by a treacherous plot, as some have said, or as a punishment from God, the Persians gained control of the wall of Amid [merely] with ladders, while the gates were not opened nor the wall breached.[27]

The passage is interesting on several accounts but two concern us. First there is no mention of the monastic defenders, though the other elements of drunkenness and deep sleep are mentioned. Secondly, ill-discipline is mentioned as one possible reason for the fall, but Joshua does not expand upon this. For that we must turn to Pseudo-Zachariah of Mitylene.

Zachariah's account is fuller and covers the elements mentioned in Procopius and Joshua:

> And when he [Kavades] was greatly grieved at this, and was preparing to withdraw in disgrace, Christ appeared to him in a vision of the night, as he himself afterwards related it, and said to him, that within three days He would deliver up to him the inhabitants of the city, because they had sinned against Him; and this took place as follows: on the western side of the city by the *Tripyrgion* was a guard of monks who were told off from the monastery of John of Anzetene, and their archimandrite was a Persian. And on the outside, right opposite this watch-tower, a certain Marzban, named Kanarak the Lame, was encamped. And day after day, vigilantly watching by night and by day, he was diligent and clever in devising plans for the subjugation of the city. For there was one whom they called in the city Kutrigo, a turbulent and thievish fellow; this man was very daring in all kinds of attacks upon the Persians, and he used to make raids and snatch away from them cattle and goods; so that they also, being accustomed to hear the men on the wall crying out, used to call him Kutrigo. Kanarak observed this man, and perceived that he went out by the aqueducts adjoining the *Tripyrgion,* and snatched up spoil, and went in again. And for a time the Persians let him accomplish his will, marking and examining his actions, and they ran after him and saw the place from which he came out and where he went in. But it happened on that night on which the city was subdued, that there was darkness, and a dense cloud sending down soft rain; and a certain man gave a friendly entertainment to the monks who guarded the *Tripyrgion,* and he gave them wine to drink late in the night, and consequently sleep overtook them, and they did not watch dili-

---

[27] Pseudo-Joshua the Stylite, *Chronicle*, 53, ed. tr. Trombley and Watt, 60–61.

gently upon their guard, according to their usual custom. And when Kanarak and a few soldiers came up, pursuing Kutrigo, and drew near to the wall, the monks did not cry out nor cast stones; and the man perceived that they were asleep, and he sent for scaling-ladders and for his troops; and his followers went in by the aqueducts, and climbed the tower of the monks, and killed them. And they took the tower and also the battlement; and they set up the scaling-ladders against the wall, and sent to the king. But when those who were in charge of another tower, their neighbours, heard it, they cried out, and tried to come to the monks who were being killed, and were not able; but some of them were wounded by arrows from the Persians, and died.[28]

Amida's fall was a great blow for the Byzantines on the eastern frontier. For many, as was often the case when cities fell to the enemy, the disaster was divine retribution for the city's impiety. The monastery of John Anzetene, more commonly known as that of John Urtaye, was located just outside the walls of Amida so the monks were obviously taking refuge inside the city. Some doubtless wondered how God deserted them, and the drunkenness of the monks could have been regarded as the reason – in other words the monks' lax behaviour was to blame for the slaughter inflicted on them by the Persians once they got inside the walls.[29] Susan Ashbrook-Harvey has certainly regarded it as 'slanderous' to blame the monks.[30] There have been arguments put forward that this passage, and other contemporary incidents, betray a willingness on the part of Monophysites to side with the Persians and play the role of fifth columnists.[31] Pseudo-Zachariah of Mitylene, perhaps pointedly, observes that the archimandrite of the monks was a Persian, leaving an implication of treachery in the mind of the reader. Procopius says the monks were drunk but implies dereliction of duty rather than treachery. Later Theophanes was happy to lay the blame at the door of the Monophysite monks.[32] However Pseudo-Joshua says merely that the guards were drunk without any mention of them being monks. The net result is that the differences in the various accounts and possible prejudices do not allow us to conclude anything beyond the monks being on the walls in a passive capacity. They may simply have been watching for the enemy as opposed to being prepared to repel the Persians forcibly.

One last piece of near-contemporary evidence is perhaps significant. Canon seven of Jacob of Edessa's *typikon* is quite clear that monks who are forced into

---

[28] Zacharias Rhetor, *Historia Ecclesiastica*, VII.4, ed. tr. E.W. Brooks (CSCO, Scr. Syr., III.5–6, 1919, 1921 and 1924).
[29] John of Ephesus, *Lives*, 58. ed. tr. E.W. Brooks, PO, 19:217–9.
[30] S. Ashbrook Harvey, *Asceticism and society in crisis: John of Ephesus and the lives of the eastern saints* (Berkeley, 1990), 60.
[31] W.H.C. Frend, *The rise of the monophysite movement: chapters in the history of the church in the fifth and sixth centuries*, 2nd ed. (Cambridge, 1978).
[32] Theophanes, *Chronographia*, AM 5996, ed. C. de Boor (Leipzig, 1883–1885), tr. C. Mango and R. Scott with G. Greatrex (Oxford, 1997), 223–225.

crewing artillery are not to be punished.[33] In other words monks could be used to man artillery pieces, weapons designed to kill and maim. If coercion is used to force the monks into such action, they are not to be punished. This is the main point that the canon is concerned with, and it implies that it did happen. Possibly crewing, probably simply acting as a loader, was not considered to be too reprehensible for a monk, as opposed to actually aiming and firing the device, the more skilled roles.

In 607 when the Byzantines were at war with the Persians, Mardin was besieged. At one point, presumably well into the thirty-month siege, the garrison abandoned the town after hearing that Hesno d-Kfo had fallen after being besieged for two years. Michael the Syrian goes on to say that at this point, '…the monks flocked to the castle and occupied it, ready for the Persian attack. They were all priests and they sent to ask Basil, the bishop of Kafar Tutho, whether they were permitted to kill the Persians.'[34] Frustratingly we are not given the answer but the city did fall to the Persians. Did the monks actively defend the walls? Ten years later Severos of Ushmanain[35] tells us that many Coptic monks at some sort of church convocation were slain when Nikiou in Egypt was taken by the Persians and that just a short time before, around the great city of Alexandria, some monks engaged in open acts of defiance against the Persians.[36] However these acts of defiance are not defined any further and certainly cannot be conclusive evidence of sword-wielding holy men, but as time moved on it does seem as though attitudes towards active participation softened.

In addition to these texts there is also some archaeological evidence to consider. One of the earliest figures in eastern asceticism, Pachomios, was a former soldier. The community which he founded was surrounded by a wall and resembled in shape a standard Roman camp.[37] Was this due to the influence of his military service and possible need for defence against brigands or was it simply to cut the community off from the outside world more forcefully? Of course the two are not mutually exclusive. Raids were the Arabs' main form of military contact with settled peoples and there are many examples of them terrorising the monks of Pales-

---

[33] A. Vööbus, *Syriac and Arabic documents regarding legislation relative to Syrian asceticism* (Papers of the Estonian Theological Society in Exile, 11, Stockholm, 1960), 96.
[34] Michael the Syrian, AG 915–918, *Michel le Syrien, Chronique*, ed. tr. J.B. Chabot, 3 vols (Paris, 1899–1910).
[35] Severos of Ushmunain, *History of the Patriarchs of the Coptic Church of Alexandria*, ed. tr. B. Evetts, PO, 1 (Paris, 1907), 99–214 and 381–518.
[36] A.J. Butler, *The Arab conquest of Egypt, and the last thirty years of the Roman dominion*, 2nd ed., ed. P.M. Fraser (Oxford, 1978), 75.
[37] *Vita prima* of Pachomios, 42, 81, ed. F. Halkin, *Sancti Pachomii Vitae Graecae* (SubsHag, 19, Brussels, 1932), 26.14; 54.21–25.

tine.[38] Sketis may have received its first towers, admittedly just single structures rather than a walled complex, as early as the mid fifth century.[39] The *phylarchs* even warned the monasteries to guard themselves against the incursions of the barbarians c.506.[40] What form would this guarding take? St Sabas successfully petitioned Justinian for a fort to be built near the monasteries to protect them.[41] Some captured monasteries were even fortified by the Persians because of their strategic location.[42] St Catherine's monastery in Sinai is protected by a very strong set of walls with projecting towers. The monastery of Daphni near Athens also has projecting towers, as does St Sabas. As projecting towers stand proud of the curtain wall to permit the defenders to fire along it (enfilading fire), it would suggest that the walls were built for active not passive defence. But would the monks actually man the walls and fight the enemy? Unfortunately we have no evidence of this actually happening, and indeed Procopius also makes it quite clear that the heavily fortified monastery of St Catherine in Sinai was to be garrisoned by a detachment of soldiers.[43] Similarly Justinian's fortification of Zeno's church on Mt Gazirim in Samaritan territory appears to have barracks included.[44] Given Daphni's location on the road into Athens it too may have been intended as a garrison base, though Krautheimer does not believe so.[45]

In conclusion, apart from Synesios's account of Faustos's actions, none of the available textual evidence from siege accounts or from the archaeological evidence from late antiquity can confirm the active participation of monks or clergy in warfare. There are certainly indicators that it probably happened, particularly the intriguing request from Hesno d-Kfo and the implicit information in Jacob of Edessa's *typikon*. Human nature being what it is, some religious men probably departed from the strictest interpretations of Christ's views on violence. Many, like those who debated Nikephoros Phokas's proposal, felt times had moved on and the teachings of Christ had to be interpreted bearing in mind the realities of the world and the attacks of pagans and heretics. The empire could no longer guaran-

---

[38] B. Isaac, 'Bandits in Judaea and Arabica', *Harvard Studies in Classical Philology*, 88 (1984), 171–203.

[39] Chitty, *The desert a city*, 79, and note 48.

[40] Cyril of Skythopolis, *Life of John the Hesychast*, 13, ed. E. Schwartz, *Kyrill von Skythopolis* (TU, 49, Leipzig, 1939), 211.15–25; *Cyril of Scythopolis: The lives of the monks of Palestine*, tr. R.M. Price (CS, 114, Kalamazoo, 1991), 63.

[41] Cyril of Skythopolis, *Life of Sabas*, 72–73, ed. Schwartz, 174.23–178.17. See also I. Shahid, *Byzantium and the Arabs in the sixth century*, I.1.2 (Washington, DC, 1995), 192.

[42] The Persians fortified the monastery called Sebanos on the border between Lazica and Persia with a wall. It should have been handed back to the Byzantines under the terms of the peace treaty, but was not. Menander Proctector, f.6, 155–162 (Exc.de.leg.Rom.3), *The history of Menander the Guardsman*, ed. tr. R.C. Blockley (Liverpool, 1985), 63.

[43] Procopius, *De aedificiis*, V.8.9, ed. tr. H.B. Dewing (Cambridge, MA, 1940), VII, 357.

[44] R. Krautheimer, *Early Christian and Byzantine architecture* (Middlesex, 1965), 186.

[45] Krautheimer, *Early Christian and Byzantine architecture*, 187.

tee the protection of those inside it and the earthly reflection of God's kingdom was being assailed on all sides. As the situation on the eastern frontier in particular worsened, especially from the reign of Justinian onwards as the Arabs became more independent of the two great powers, many religious men were bound to have felt the increasing anxiety caused by the precarious security situation. Many cities and monasteries were sacked, particularly in the Persian invasion of Palestine in 614 and while some stayed and participated, actively or passively in their defence, many others fled. This period of transition was a challenge. St Augustine was prepared to justify war under certain circumstances. Even St Basil did not utterly condemn the use of violence as those who participated were not to be excommunicated, but merely placed under penance. Others took a more steadfast Christian approach to participation in warfare. Was this down to deep religious belief and a total rejection of violence on their part or is it a matter that hagiographers preferred to omit from their accounts? We can probably never know but the pacifism, or at least the perceived pacifism, seemingly exercised by these religious men at the end of antiquity did not go unnoticed among the Muslim Arab raiders who were now in the ascendant. What started as a brief survey of Byzantine monastic practices when caught up in violent events outside their control is perhaps fittingly ended with the instructions issued by Abu Bakr, one of the most successful opponents of the empire.

> Stop, O people, that I may give you ten rules for your guidance in the battlefield. Do not commit treachery or deviate from the right path. You must not mutilate dead bodies. Neither kill a child, nor a woman, nor an aged man. Bring no harm to the trees, nor burn them with fire, especially those which are fruitful. Slay not any of the enemy's flock, save for your food. You are likely to pass by people who have devoted their lives to monastic services; leave them alone.[46]

---

[46] http://cwis.usc.edu/dept/MSA/fundamentals/hadithsunnah/muslim/019.smt.html

6

Cutting the tusk

Lyn Rodley

I could, I suppose, devise some elaborate route by which a note on early Byzantine ivories would be appropriate to a volume whose theme is 'translation'. Ivory is certainly translated in the now obsolete sense (except when speaking of saintly relics) of movement from one place to another – from African scrubland to the palaces of Rome and Constantinople; and a change of language could be paralleled with a change of function – from foraging or fighting implement to elegant status-symbol. But no! This is the sort of silliness to which much modern scholarship is often reduced in order to meet research assessment targets. I'd rather come clean, and admit that I just don't want to be left out of this tribute to an old friend and colleague whom I admire for several reasons: for his facility in winkling out the meaning of even those passages of Greek that he himself describes as 'fierce'; for the priority he gives to clear communication of his knowledge to others; for his generosity in using his rare skills to help others over linguistic obstacles; and for never engaging in the dreary academic sport of denigrating fellow scholars. So here it is.

Most ivory used to make Byzantine objects would have come from African elephants, the tusks of which could be shipped up the Nile and into the east Mediterranean, for delivery to the workshops of the empire. A small amount of ivory probably came still attached to the elephants which were occasionally imported to astonish the crowds in the arenas of the late Roman and early Byzantine world,[1] where spectators doubtless included those ivory carvers whose highly naturalistic renderings of the elephant suggest first-hand knowledge.[2] The arena was probably also the setting for which some of the most splendid surviving examples of early Byzantine ivory carving – the consular diptychs – were made.

The diptych was the notebook of antiquity: a pair of hinged panels,[3] one side of

---
[1] *ODB*, ed. A.P. Kazhdan and A.-M. Talbot, 3 vols (New York and Oxford, 1991), I, 684–685.
[2] Naturalistic elephants appear on the Apotheosis ivory (British Museum, London; illustrated in D. Buckton, *Byzantium* (London, 1994), 57; also on the Barberini ivory, for which see n.13 below. The ivory carvers may also have used as models the statues of elephants known to have been in Constantinople (*ODB*, I, 684–685).
[3] No diptych survives with hinges intact, nor with any obvious provision for the attachment of hinges (many panels have drilled holes, but not arranged in a manner suitable for the attachment

1. Diptych of Areobindus

each slightly recessed to take a layer of wax which formed a tablet for temporary writing, using a stylus to scratch the wax surface. Everyday diptychs were probably made of wood, and the ivory variety was a luxury object, its outer surfaces embellished with carving. Some were made to commemorate events such as weddings and funerals[4] and (most importantly for the history of art, because they are datable) the accession of a consul to the office he held for a single year.[5] There are over thirty-five surviving consular diptychs (or single panels once part of a pair) and of these some seventeen are decorated with images showing the consul engaged in his most public function – the supervision of the games in the arena or hippodrome.[6] Typically, as in the diptych of Areobindus, consul of Constantinople in 506 (fig. 1) they show the consul seated, wearing the distinctive garments of his office, holding a sceptre and the cloth (*mappa*) he waves to signal the start of events. Beneath him, the events of the arena are variously represented: fighting men and animals, racing chariots, or functionaries emptying sacks of coin to indicate the scale of the consul's largesse.

Since more than one diptych survives for several of the consuls (and the material we have must be only a fraction of the original quantity) it is likely that these diptychs were commissioned by the consul himself, as elegant gifts for those he wished to honour (or whose favours he wished to engage, or keep). Indeed, like the business gift of today, the diptychs appear to have been produced in various qualities, reflecting the status of the recipient: Areobindus had three types: the most elaborate of the kind just described, showing the consul officiating, a second, simpler type, with a bust medallion and some ornament, and a third, simpler still, with ornament alone.[7]

---

of hinges. Probably the hinge was a strip of leather, held in place by glue, or accommodated within a metal rim originally set around the edges of the panels.

[4] The Symmachi and Nicomachi panels in (respectively) the Victoria & Albert Museum, London, and the Musée de Cluny, Paris, form a diptych probably made to celebrate a wedding; illustrated in D. Talbot Rice, *Byzantine art* (Harmondsworth, 1968), 422. The Apotheosis diptych (see n.2) commemorates a funeral. By the fifth century, the diptych had been adopted by the church, for use in noting non-standard elements of liturgy, such as the names of those to be prayed for on a particular occasion.

[5] *ODB*, I, 525–526.

[6] W.F. Volbach, *Elfenbeinarbeiten der Spätantike und des frühen Mittelalters*, 3rd ed. (Mainz, 1976) cat. nos. 1–33; nos. 5, 8–11, 15–21 have scenes below a seated consul. See also R. Delbrück, *Die Consular-Diptychen und verwandte Denkmäler* (Berlin and Leipzig, 1929).

[7] All three types are illustrated in L. Rodley, *Byzantine art and architecture: an introduction* (Cambridge, 1994), 90.

An often noted feature shared by the consular (and some other) diptychs, is their large size – typically in the region of 13 x 35cm, making a rather ungainly form: a long rectangle, the height almost three times the width. This shape is, of course, related to the form of the source of ivory, the elephant tusk, and it prompts me to a consideration of the way in which the tusk was processed by the early Byzantine craftsman. Like the profound Irish observation that the best way to reach a particular destination is 'not to start from here', the elephant tusk is of a form that no sensible artisan would choose as a starting point for the production of regular rectangular panels. The tusk curves, tapers to a point, and is hollowed by a pulp cavity which extends for as much as half the whole length (fig. 2a).[8] Rectangular panels for carving, therefore, may be obtained only by first cutting across the tusk beyond the pulp cavity, and again just before the tapering and curvature become pronounced, producing a solid cylinder, tapering slightly (area 3 on the diagram); this would then be sliced lengthwise into panels (as with wood, the panels are cut with the grain, rather than across it.) To obtain the largest possible panels, the cylinder would be left entire, its length determined by the curvature and tapering of the tusk, but smaller rectangles of more harmonious proportions might be obtained by cutting the cylinder into two or more sections. The diagram shows how the remaining parts of the tusk might be cut to make good use of the rest: area 2, hollowed by the pulp cavity, could be used for cylindrical boxes (pyxides), area 4 for small panels, area 5 possibly for beads or small gaming pieces; area 1, which is rather fibrous, would probably be discarded. Lengthwise cutting of the main cylinder to make panels could adopt one of two schemes, to produce either several pairs of panels of decreasing size (fig. 2b) or a single panel larger than the rest at the centre, flanked by pairs as before (fig. 2c).[9] In either cutting scheme, the pairs of panels obviously get progressively narrower, ending up as narrow strips.

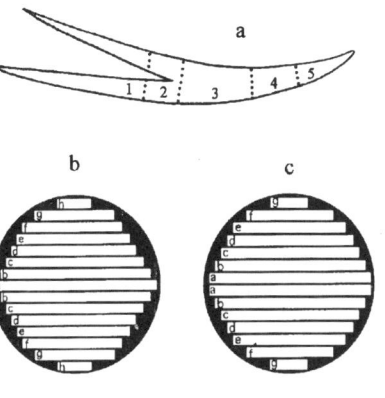

2. Tusk diagram

---

[8] A. Cutler, *The craft of ivory* (Washington, DC, 1985), 1–7.

[9] My diagram supposes a large tusk, with a diameter of 170mm and panels 8mm thick, allowing a loss of 3mm for each cut and a loss of 10mm all round for stripping the outer 'husk' of the tusk. Cutting may cause greater wastage than my diagram supposes, resulting in fewer panels, but the principle is the same. The choice of which scheme to use for a particular tusk may often have been dictated by the location of the fine continuation of the pulp cavity into the otherwise solid area of tusk.

3. Cathedra of Maximian

Such a cutting scheme is consistent with the known forms of early Byzantine ivories: we have over sixty pyxides,[10] over eighty of the large diptychs already described, and a variety of 'composite' pieces made by combining panels of different sizes. The famous cathedra of Maximian, in Ravenna (fig. 3),[11] for example, has five large figure panels on its front, all of the same height, but the central one (John the Baptist) is 12.5cm wide, the outer pair of evangelists 11.5cm, and the inner pair 9cm, an arrangement consistent with cutting pattern (2c).[12] There are also several ivories made of five panels – a wide central one framed by four others, made up of two pairs of slightly different widths. On the Barberini ivory, for instance, which has an equestrian emperor, cut in quite deep relief, in the central panel, the lateral panels are c. 6.4cm wide and the top and bottom ones c. 7.5cm wide (fig. 4).[13] As well as making efficient use of valuable material, such schemes made it possible to combine panels cut from a single tusk, which would ensure uniform colour and texture for the piece as a whole.

Practical efficiency was probably not the only reason for the development of the five-part design, however: the rectangle resulting from the assemblage is of a more pleasing form than that of the long, narrow diptych panels. This is not just the judgement of the modern eye, for at least one Byzantine ivory carver found the diptych shape difficult: a panel in Milan (fig. 5) shows the holy sepulchre on the morning after the Resurrection, in a composition divided into two square fields by a band of decoration matching that of the border of the panel as a whole.[14] The

---

[10] Volbach, *Elfenbeinarbeiten*, cat. nos. 161–205.

[11] *ODB*, II, 1321–1322.

[12] These panels would have taken much of the 'cylinder' (3 in my diagram). For the long strips of foliage ornament that frame the figure panels, a second tusk would have been used (probably the twin of the first, for uniform colour) using a longer 'cylinder' (possible because the strips were narrow (4.5cm) so the curve of the tusk would be less of a problem.

As often noted, the front panels are of much better quality than those on the sides and back of the chair. Conceivably the former were a gift from Justinian to bishop Maximianus, intended to decorate a chest or screen, but the ambitious cleric had more panels made locally in order to cover the more impressive cathedra. We may, therefore, have a new means of measuring respect in the early Byzantine period: Justinian saw Maximian as a bishop worth two tusks, but Maximian rated himself a four-tusker.

[13] Paris, Louvre, illustrated in: J. Durand et al., *Byzance. L'art byzantin dans les collections publiques françaises* (Paris, 1992), cat. no. 20.

[14] Milan, Castello Sforzesco, illustrated in J. Beckwith, *Early Christian and Byzantine art* (Harmondsworth, 1970), pl. 36. The two evangelist symbols at the top of the panel, flanking the

4. Barberini ivory

band is redundant, since a single narrative episode is depicted – indeed, it is awkward, since it cuts the holy sepulchre in two, separating the drum of its dome from the body of the building with its open door below, and making only a half-hearted attempt to rationalise the arrangement by suggesting that the band might be part of the architecture of the building. The real reason for the band is that it gave the artist two squarish fields, permitting two balanced compositions (soldiers on the roof flanking the dome in the upper part; the angel greeting the women below).

Writing-tablet diptych-makers could not, of course, solve the problem of inelegant proportions by using multi-panel schemes.[15] As we have seen, the carvers of consular diptychs coped with the long, narrow field by using a tiered composition, placing the portrait of the consul in the upper part, and the arena activities below (still they often had to add a panel with busts, angels or inscription at the very top to fill the whole long space). They could have avoided the problem altogether, however, by cutting a shorter panel, thereby not only improving the proportions of the diptych, but also making it less unwieldy. Indeed, it has been suggested that the consular diptychs were not actually used as writing tablets, because of their large size, and it is certainly true that they would have made very clumsy toga-pocket notebooks. But the recipients of consular diptychs were of the social order that has servants to carry its bits and pieces, so their size need not preclude a practical function, suggesting rather that it was likely to be a fairly formal one: we may imagine a dignitary attending the games, with an entourage of servants, one of them responsible for the writing diptych upon which the bets were to be recorded.[16] Such a context surely ex-

5. Milan panel

---

dome of the sepulchre, show this to have been one panel of a diptych, since the other two evangelist symbols must have been on a lost second panel.

[15] They would need a wooden backing to hold the panels on one side and the wax on the other, which would result in an object even more cumbersome than the large single-panel diptychs. Five-part panels are often called diptychs because some come in pairs, and were probably made to serve as book covers, a function that some examples still have (see Durand *et al.*, *Byzance*, cat. no. 27).

[16] The 'circus' diptych in the Hermitage (Volbach, *Elfenbeinarbeiten*, cat. no. 60) has both panels decorated entirely with images of men fighting animals, with no inscriptions or reference to consuls, reinforcing the association of elaborate diptychs with the games – it was not only those who had the consul's favour who used them.

plains precisely why the diptychs were *not* made smaller, easier to handle and easier for the artists to decorate pleasingly: the large panels were a declaration of wealth and status. Given the cutting formula described, ivory cannot have been priced by weight, like gold and silver, but by size, like precious stones, and each tusk supplies only one really large pair of panels. As noted at the start of this excursion, the early Byzantine world had first-hand knowledge of the elephant as an awe-inspiring, powerful, exotic beast, qualities transferred (translated, perhaps, in deference to this volume?) to the dignitary whose servant carried for him a diptych representing the best cut of a large tusk.[17] Inconvenience was therefore a secondary matter – the consular diptychs were like the Rolls Royce that the A-list celebrity in our own day uses for a journey that could be more conveniently made on a bicycle.

---

[17] The tusk of a mature African elephant is typically 2–2.5 metres long, with a maximum diameter of c. 16cm, which would be necessary to produce the 13–14cm widths of many consular diptychs. G.F. Kunz, *Ivory and the elephant in art, in archaeology and in science* (New York, 1926).

7

The limits of translation: multiple meanings in a Byzantine religious poem

Dirk Krausmüller

A classicist by training, Robert Jordan has used his linguistic skills to make Byzantine texts like the Phoberou and Pakourianos *typika* and the *Hypotyposis* and *Synaxarion* of the Evergetis monastery available to a wider audience. With the decline of linguistic skills such translations are becoming an ever more important research tool. The fact that a large part of the readership may not be able to check their accuracy puts great responsibility on the translators since a translation, unlike a paraphrase or a summary, is expected to be a faithful rendering of the original. The complexity of Byzantine literature makes it difficult to meet such expectations: more often than not texts are crammed with allusions, double-entendres and wordplay, which may all be crucial for their understanding. Therefore it is not sufficient to restrict oneself to the level of meaning immediately accessible to modern readers; one must also identify less obvious features and attempt to reproduce them in the translation.

In the following I shall address one of the problems faced by modern translators: the presence of multiple meanings in Byzantine texts. The discussion will be based on a liturgical poem or *kanon* in honour of the fourth-century Constantinopolitan abbot Dios, which in the manuscripts is attributed to patriarch Germanos of Constantinople (715–730).[1] In accordance with the conventions for the composition of *kanones* that had developed in the seventh century, this poem consists of nine 'odes'. The first stanza of the third ode reads as follows:

ὄρει προσιὼν
ἐνθέου πολιτείας
ἔλυσας σαυτὸν

---

[1] *AHG*, XI: *Canones Iulii*, ed. I. Schirò (Rome, 1966–1983), 347–358: text, 604–605: commentary.

τῶν βάσεων τοῦ βίου
τὰ ὑποδείγματα πάντα τῆς ἀλογίας
τῶν παθημάτων τὴν οἰκείωσιν. [2]

The syntactical structure of this passage cannot be established with absolute certainty. However, it seems most likely that the finite verb λύειν is construed with the genitive τῶν βάσεων and with two parallel accusative objects, σαυτόν and τὰ ὑποδείγματα, followed by the apposition τὴν οἰκείωσιν. Therefore I propose the following translation:

> Having approached the mountain of godly life, you have loosened from the feet yourself as regards all signs of the life of irrationality, which creates an affinity with the passions.

As is typical of Byzantine church poetry, the odes of the *kanon* of Dios do not give a linear biographical overview but are variations of the theme of Christian perfection. The stanza that I have translated speaks about the saint's progress from a 'life-style of irrationality', βίος τῆς ἀλογίας, to a 'godly life-style', ἔνθεος πολιτεία, and presents this process as the consequence of a liberation from 'the affinity with the passions', τῶν παθημάτων ἡ οἰκείωσις. This understanding of spiritual development and the terms with which it is expressed derive from the teachings of late antique writers who had adapted the Platonic concept of the tripartite soul for a Christian context. The author of the *kanon* combines this abstract terminology with metaphorical language. In the first half of the sentence 'godly life-style' is equated with a mountain and the saint's progress to this state is compared with the climbing of this mountain. This imagery has its origin in the Bible: the phrase ὄρει προσιὼν ἐνθέου πολιτείας is evidently derived from the sentence 'you have come to Mt Sion and the city of the living God, the heavenly Jerusalem', προσεληλύθατε Σιὼν ὄρει καὶ πόλει θεοῦ ζῶντος Ἰερουσαλὴμ ἐπουρανίῳ/, in Hebrews 12:18.

The context of the complementary formula 'life-style of irrationality' is much less straightforward. It is combined with τὰ ὑποδείγματα, 'types' or 'signs'. In itself this combination is commonplace in late antique and Byzantine Christian texts.[3] However, its appearance in this particular context is rather surprising: in-

---

[2] Ode 3, 350.46–51: ὄρει προσιὼν ἐνθέου πολιτείας ἔλυσας σαυτὸν (Sn: αὐτοῦ, ΟΑ: αὐτὸν) τῶν βάσεων (Co: θλίψεων) τοῦ βίου τὰ ὑποδείγματα (Co: ὑποδήματα) πάντα τῆς ἀλογίας τῶν παθημάτων τὴν οἰκείωσιν.

[3] Cf. Gregory of Nyssa, *In Canticum Canticorum*, ed. H. Langerbeck (Gregorii Nysseni Opera, VI, Leiden, 1960), 7.4: εἴπερ ἐπὶ ψιλῶν σταίημεν τῶν πραγμάτων οὐκ ἀγαθοῦ βίου παρεχομένης ἡμῖν τὰ ὑποδείγματα, cf. also *In Canticum Canticorum*, ed. Langerbeck, 126.10: διὰ τῆς ἐν σαρκὶ φανερώσεως πάντων τῶν ἀγαθῶν πολιτευμάτων ἐν ἑαυτῷ δείξας τὰ ὑποδείγματα.

stead of an abstract term one would have expected a concrete noun comparable to 'mountain' at the beginning of the stanza. The choice of ὑποδείγματα is even more startling when we consider how this term is integrated into the sentence: the saint loosens the types 'from the feet', τῶν βάσεων.[4] The result is an awkward mixture of the concrete and the abstract.

These problems could be easily overcome if one replaced ὑποδείγματα with ὑποδήματα, 'sandals', which can be considered as its homonym because in Byzantine Greek both eta and epsilon-iota were pronounced as 'i' and the gamma before the consonant would have been barely audible. This alternative reading has a Biblical fundament in the well-known episode from Exodus where God speaks to Moses through the burning bush: 'Do not approach here: loosen the shoe from your feet, for the place on which you stand is holy ground', καὶ εἶπεν· μὴ ἐγγίσῃς ὧδε· λῦσαι τὸ ὑπόδημα τῶν ποδῶν σου· ὁ γὰρ τόπος ἐν ᾧ σὺ ἕστηκας γῆ ἁγία ἐστίν. The affinity between the Biblical λῦσαι τὸ ὑπόδημα τῶν ποδῶν and the words ἔλυσας... τῶν βάσεων... τὰ ὑποδήματα is immediately obvious: differences are limited to the replacement of the synonyms.[5] Thus we can conclude that the author expected his audience to recognise the meaning 'sandals' in the text.

When we look at the manuscript tradition for the *kanon* we find that one codex has indeed the reading ὑποδήματα.[6] I have already pointed out that to a contemporary listener the two words would have sounded virtually identical. Can we conclude that the alternative ὑποδείγματα is the result of a spelling mistake? For a number of reasons such an explanation must be ruled out. The reading ὑποδείγματα is not only found in four of the five manuscripts that served as basis for the edition; its spelling is also more complex than that of its alternative and is therefore unlikely to be the result of a *lapsus calami*. Moreover, not all words in the context support the decoding as ὑποδήματα: it is evident that the attribute 'all', πάντα, makes much better sense in the combination 'all types' than it does in 'all sandals'. Most importantly, however, the use of ὑποδείγματα also has a recognisable biblical model. We have seen before that the first part of the sentence is adapted from Hebrews 12:18. There the Christians' ascent to the heavenly Sion is juxtaposed with Moses' encounter with God on Mt Sinai: 'for you have not come to a mountain that may be touched... but you have come to Mt Sion and the city of the living God, the heavenly Jerusalem.' Such juxtaposition between the 'material' Old Testament and the 'spiritual' New Testament is one of the central themes of the Letter to the Hebrews. In this framework the author of Hebrews uses the noun ὑπόδειγμα to define Old Testament religious practice as a mere foreshadowing of what finds its realisation in the New Testament through the ultimate self-

---

[4] Cf. Acts 3:7: παραχρῆμα δὲ ἐστερεώθησαν αἱ βάσεις αὐτοῦ.
[5] Cf. below note 9.
[6] Cf. Codex Cryptoferratensis D.a. XI.

sacrifice of the high priest Jesus Christ. In Hebrews 9:23 where Christ's ascension to heaven is compared with the entering of the high priest into the tabernacle this hierarchy is expressed through the juxtaposition of 'the heavenly things', αὐτὰ τὰ ἐπουράνια, with 'the types of that which is in heaven', τὰ ὑποδείγματα τῶν ἐν τοῖς οὐρανοῖς.[7] The juxtaposition between Sinai and Sion in Hebrew 12:18 must be understood in the same way. This is evident from Hebrews 8:5 where the 'type and shadow of the heavenly things', ὑπόδειγμα καὶ σκιά... τῶν ἐπουρανίων, is identified with the 'type' of the tabernacle that was shown to Moses when he had climbed up the visible mountain.[8]

Thus there can be no doubt that the author of the *kanon* deliberately created this ambivalence and that he expected his audience to recognise the presence of both spellings and their respective meanings in his text. This raises the question: what were his reasons for creating this double meaning? I suggest that the answer lies in the Christian tradition of allegorical interpretation of Exodus 3:5. This tradition identified the leather shoes of Moses with the garments of skin which according to Genesis 3:21 God made for Adam and Eve. These garments were in turn interpreted as the coarse body, which was given to man after the fall.[9] Whereas before the fall man only had disembodied reason for the contemplation of the spiritual realm, this material body contained the faculties of sense perception and imagination. These faculties allowed him to exist in the material world, which had only diminished reality and thus can be called ὑπόδειγμα, 'type' or 'shadow', of the spiritual realm. In order to achieve dispassion, the link with the parts of the soul that connect man with the sensible world must be severed and this severing is symbolised by the taking-off of Moses' shoes.[10] The use of homophones allows the author of the *kanon* to express in one word both the concrete image and the abstract concept it stands for. Thus, the superimposition of 'sandals' and 'types' becomes a reflection of the principle that underlies allegorical exegesis: namely that the Biblical text contains two layers, the 'obvious' narrative and its 'hidden' significance.

Analysis of a stanza from the *kanon* of Dios has thus given an insight into the creation of multiple meanings. The author chose the sound pattern 'ipódhi(g)ma', which can be decoded both as ὑπόδειγμα and as ὑπόδημα, and put it into a context that contains clues for both readings. At the same time he took care that audiences did not content themselves with one of these meanings by inserting elements

---

[7] Hebrews 9:23: ἀνάγκη οὖν τὰ μὲν ὑποδείγματα τῶν ἐν τοῖς οὐρανοῖς τούτοις καθαρίζεσθαι αὐτὰ δὲ τὰ ἐπουράνια κρείττοσιν θυσίαις παρὰ ταύταις.
[8] Hebrews 8:5: οἵτινες ὑποδείγματι καὶ σκιᾷ λατρεύουσιν τῶν ἐπουρανίων καθὼς κεχρημάτισται Μωυσῆς μέλλων ἐπιτελεῖν τὴν σκηνήν· ὅρα γάρ φησιν ποιήσεις πάντα κατὰ τὸν τύπον τὸν δειχθέντα σοι ἐν τῷ ὄρει.
[9] Cf. e.g. Maximus, *Ambigua*, PG, 91, 1148D.
[10] Gregory of Nyssa, *Vita Moysis*, PG, 45, 333A: εἰ μὴ περιλυθείη τῶν τῆς ψυχῆς βάσεων ἡ νεκρὰ... τῶν δερμάτων περιβολή.

into the text that question the appropriateness of either term: the genitive τῶν βάσεων sits ill with ὑποδείγματα and πάντα cannot be reconciled with ὑποδήματα. This raises the question: do these tensions remain unresolved? There is no reason to believe that equivocation in this passage is limited to only one term. At least one further case is found at the beginning of the sentence. We saw that the author of the *kanon* adapted both the verb προσεληλύθατε and the noun ὄρει from Hebrews whereas the name Sion does not appear in the adaptation. However, it is nevertheless present in the text: with the participle προσιών the author has chosen a form in which two different statements in his model, the movement of approaching and the destination Σιών, are superimposed. Thus it is perfectly possible that other parts of the sentence are open to alternative interpretations, which would have allowed contemporary audiences to discover meaningful combinations behind apparent absurdities.[11] If this hypothesis were correct an adequate understanding of the text would require the extension of the search for multiple meanings to all words appearing in this passage. Only systematic study of this phenomenon in Byzantine texts can provide us with a definite answer.

It is evident that the technique of superimposition poses considerable problems for translators. Since both versions are clearly part of the text any decision to reproduce only one alternative must be arbitrary. However, usually instances of superimposition cannot be reproduced in other languages because the equivalent terms do not resemble each other. In these cases one can only present the two alternatives in a linear fashion. Such a rendering at least reproduces the whole range of intended meanings even if it does not recreate the experience of ambiguity that is offered in the original.

---

[11] One such case may be τῶν βάσεων. A search of late antique Christian texts reveals that ὑπόδειγμα has a synonym in the noun ἔμφασις, 'image' or 'reflection'. Cf. Gregory of Nyssa, *In canticum canticorum*, ed. Langerbeck, 25.4: μή τις ἐμπαθὴς καὶ σαρκώδης ἔτι τῆς νεκρᾶς τοῦ παλαιοῦ ἀνθρώπου ἀπόζων πρὸς τὰς κτηνώδεις ἀλογίας κατασυρέτω τὰς τῶν θεοπνεύστων νοημάτων τε καὶ ῥημάτων ἐμφάσεις. Therefore one can argue that the author of the *kanon* expected his readers to decode the genitive object τῶν βάσεων as τῶν φάσεων, which would fit the context much better.

8

Constantine's Constantinople

Liz James

A translation of Constantine Rhodios's verse account of the wonders of Constantinople and the church of the Holy Apostles was begun many years ago.[1] Now, finally, with Bob Jordan's guidance, it has reached its conclusion and I offer him this brief note in celebration of that and in thanks!

Constantine Rhodios's poem (I will refer to the author as Rhodios rather than Constantine for reasons that will become clear) is 981 lines long. It is an unfinished or an incomplete text – it breaks off abruptly in the middle of a lament made by the Virgin at the foot of the cross – that deals with the seven wonders of Constantinople and the church of the Holy Apostles. The poem is a tenth-century piece, written at some point in the reign of Constantine VII, and what I will discuss here is something of what it says about Constantine's Constantinople.[2]

Like Byzantine accounts of works of art generally, the poem was not written with the purpose of providing what we might understand as a full and accurate description of the buildings and monuments of Constantinople.[3] It was written for a purpose and to make points. Like the tenth-century *Patria*, it reads very much as an insider's view of the city, with few guides or pointers for those who might be unfamiliar with Constantinople, and, also like the *Patria*, it offers a 'Constantinople imaginaire' to its readers.[4]

Rhodios's dealings with the past are quite specific and focused. In the historic figures he mentions, he reveals tenth-century memories of a very specific past, the

---

[1] *Constantine the Rhodian, the wonders of Constantinople and the church of the Holy Apostles*. A new Greek edition, ed. I. Vassis. English tr. V. Dimitropoulou, L. James and R. Jordan (BBTT, Belfast, forthcoming). My thanks to Ioannis Vassis for allowing us to use his new edition of the text.

[2] For the date, see P. Speck, 'Konstantinos von Rhodes. Zweck und Datum der Ekphrasis der sieben Wunder von Konstantinopel und der Apostelkirchen', Varia III, *Poikila Byzantina*, 11 (Bonn, 1991). Ioannis Vassis will discuss this further in *Constantine the Rhodian*.

[3] Ruth Webb in particular has discussed the ways in which the technique of ekphrasis, the rhetorical technique of vivid description, was employed in Byzantium not to recreate monuments and works of art accurately but to bring an image of them vividly to the mind's eye of the listener. See, for example, R. Webb, 'The aesthetics of sacred space: narrative, metaphor and motion in *ekphraseis* of church buildings', *DOP*, 53 (1999), 59–74.

[4] G. Dagron, *Constantinople imaginaire. Etudes sur le receuil des* 'Patria' (Paris, 1984), esp. 54–60.

glories of the fourth, fifth and sixth centuries.[5] Six dead emperors appear in the poem. Five date to this period: Constantine the Great, Theodosios I, his son, Arkadios, Leo I and Justinian. The most important of these for Rhodios is Justinian.[6] The first wonder of the city, 'holding first rank among the wonders', is the mounted statue of Justinian outside Hagia Sophia.[7] Justinian himself is mentioned four times in the poem: twice with his statue; once in relation to rebuilding the church of the Holy Apostles; and finally in a panegyric in relation to Hagia Sophia and other unnamed building works throughout the city. He is always described as 'the great' and 'victorious', 'mighty and noble', and his piety is emphasised.

However, Constantine the Great is almost as significant as Justinian in the poem. What Rhodios describes memorably as 'the especially wondrous porphyry column' of Constantine the Great is the second-ranked marvel within the city.[8] Constantine the Great appears twice more, as the importer of sculptures from Ephesos and as founder of the church of the Holy Apostles. He is described as 'most powerful' and 'triumphant' and 'wise', and his actions make it clear that he is also 'pious'. Rhodios also talks at line 18, of Constantinople as 'the city of Constantine'.

Both Constantine and Justinian recur regularly in tenth-century texts as major figures in the history of the empire; indeed, they seem to be perceived as semi-divine heroic figures.[9] This is an image also made visible in the ninth- or tenth-century mosaic from the south-west vestibule of Hagia Sophia, depicting Constantine offering his city and Justinian his church to the Virgin and Christ. Magdalino has suggested that this representation offers a synchronic snapshot of imperial Christian history, a visual demonstration of the way in which the medieval Byzantines constructed the idea that they were living in the Roman Empire of Constantine and Justinian.[10]

Of the remaining five early Byzantine emperors, Theodosios I appears three times, as builder of the Anemodoulion and as the subject of his son's work in setting up both the column of Theodosios and the mounted statue of Theodosios.

---

[5] For these themes, see P. Magdalino, 'The distance of the past in early medieval Byzantium', *Ideologie e pratiche del reimpiego nell'alto medioeve* (Settimane di Studio del Centro Italiano di Studi sull'alto medioevo, Spoleto, 1999), 115–146. I am very grateful to Paul Magdalino for this reference. On the theme of relation of present, past and future, see P. Magdalino, 'The history of the future and its uses: prophecy, policy and propaganda', *The making of Byzantine history*, ed. R. Beaton and C. Roueché (Aldershot, 1993), 1–34.

[6] As Magdalino, 'Distance of the past', pointed out, suggesting that Rhodios saw himself as presenting the Holy Apostles as an implicit companion piece to Paul the Silentiary's account of Hagia Sophia. If, as Alan Cameron has suggested, Constantine was the compiler of the *Palatine Anthology*, he would certainly have been familiar with Paul's work.

[7] Lines 39–51.

[8] Line 52.

[9] Magdalino, 'Distance of the past', 124–125.

[10] Magdalino, 'Distance of the past', 124–125 and on the mosaic, 116.

Theodosios too is 'pious', 'godly', 'all-wise', ' a marvellous man' and, above all, victorious in war. Arkadios is mentioned twice as builder of monuments commemorating his father, Theodosios I. Arkadios's own column is rather dismissed at line 244: 'it is like in all ways to the column of Taurus' and Arkadios himself is only described as 'famed' – and famed for honouring his father at that. Finally, Leo I makes a brief appearance as Rhodios describes how the Senate burnt down in the major fire in the city in his reign.

Rhodios's choice of these five emperors was not random. All were buried in the church of the Holy Apostles. In addition, all are emperors who appear in other texts, most notably in the *Patria*, as emperors who built monuments and churches throughout the city.[11] Rhodios, in portraying these emperors as the men responsible for many of the original glories of the city, including several of his seven wonders and both Hagia Sophia and the Holy Apostles, maintained tenth-century traditions of who the great emperors of Byzantine history were.[12]

However, the real hero of the piece was a living emperor, Constantine Rhodios's own 'compassionate lord', who had commanded him to write the poem, Constantine VII. When, immediately after his opening lines of dedication, Rhodios referred to 'the city of Constantine', that Constantine was both Constantine the Great and Constantine VII. Markopoulos has suggested that Constantine VII deliberately sought to associate himself with his namesake, seen, for example, in Constantine's writing of the *Vita Basilii*.[13] In Rhodios's poem, this association is again apparent for the reiteration of the name 'Constantine' throughout the poem in reference to Constantine I continually evokes his tenth-century heir.

In this context, Rhodios's emphasis on past glories was not a nostalgic yearning for the good old days. Rather, his references to the imperial past of the city served to illuminate its imperial present. The final dead emperor he mentioned is Constantine VII's own father, Leo VI. Rhodios describes Constantine as 'scion of the purple', 'seed of my celebrated king', 'son of the most famous Leo'.[14] These emphasise the legitimacy of Constantine VII as true heir of Leo, rebutting the slurs on his birth. It is a theme also apparent in the *Book of Ceremonies*, which associates Constantine with the heroic past, in contrast to the newness of the usurping Romanos Lekapenos. The *Book of Ceremonies* invoked a familiar trinity: whilst Romanos ignored the traditions of 'those great and renowned emperors', Constantine,

---

[11] On this theme and for more figures, see L. James, 'Building and rebuilding: imperial women and religious foundations in Constantinople in the fourth to the eighth centuries', *Basilissa*, 1 (forthcoming).

[12] Only the column with the cross on it is the exception though, as Rhodios emphasises, this guards the city. Mango has suggested that this monument had special links with Constantine the Great.

[13] A. Markopoulos, 'Constantine the Great in Macedonian historiography: models and approaches', *New Constantines*, ed. P. Magdalino (Ashgate, 1994), 159–170.

[14] Lines 1 and 26; 26–27, 277.

Leo I and Justinian, Constantine VII restored order. Both Leo VI and Basil I, Constantine's grandfather, positioned themselves within this same tradition. Leo portrayed himself as the successor to Justinian, in, for example, his reworking of Justinian's legal code, where he claimed to take over the roles of that emperor and even to surpass him. Basil, for his part, claimed descent from Constantine the Great on his mother's side and was renowned for rebuilding churches founded by his imperial predecessors, above all Constantine and Justinian. Thus Rhodios's invocation of imperial predecessors matches the official line of the Macedonian dynasty and its construction of the past, underlining part of his poem's role as imperial propaganda.[15] This theme of praising the present through association with the past is apparent throughout the poem. In using a vocabulary of piety, wisdom, triumph, nobility and greatness to describe both the late antique emperors and Constantine VII, Rhodios establishes Constantine both as a righteous emperor, and as the latest in a series of Good and Great Emperors whose glories he shares.

Rhodios's city is the city of three Constantines. The first is the poet himself whose creation this city is. The second is the divine founder, Constantine the Great. The third is Constantine's heir, 'the most famous Constantine/scion of the purple', Constantine VII, for whom Rhodios was writing. Although it was the great figures from the past who were responsible for the glories of the city of Constantine and who dominate Rhodios's picture of the city, Constantine VII is irrevocably linked with his great imperial building predecessors and their works, even if he personally had little to do with building. Thus the city is made out to be his city. Its monuments, directly and indirectly, reflect him; its previous rulers, above all Constantine and Justinian, whose images Constantine VII may have placed in Hagia Sophia, are models of his own imperial virtues.[16] Constantine's presence within the poem is maintained by Rhodios addressing him directly on at least six occasions. This may have been flattery, it may have been an assertion of Constantine's role as legitimate emperor, but it was also a way of maintaining the emperor as a perpetual audience for the poem. Through his eternal presence, Constantine VII remained present whenever and wherever the poem was read.

---

[15] S.F. Tougher, *The reign of Leo VI (886–912)* (The Medieval Mediterranean, 15, Leiden, 1997).
[16] Magdalino, 'Distance of the past', 116, proposes that this mosaic made a statement that the reigning emperor, whoever that was, had been prefigured by Constantine and Justinian, and that they were present in him.

9

Stephanites kai Ichnelates
and the tale of the swindler, the simpleton
and the buried treasure

Alison Noble

The text known in Greek as *Stephanites kai Ichnelates*[1] is a translation of a translation of a translation[2] of the Sanskrit work of uncertain date known as the *Pancatantra*, the 'Five Chapters', the story of which is as follows: a king, in desperation over the stupidity of his three sons and their inability to learn the art of government, calls a council. There he is informed that it normally takes decades to teach all that a king needs to know, even more if the pupil is stupid. There is only one man who can help, a Brahmin, and he is summoned. He promises to teach the sons all they need to know in only one year, with the help of fables. These fables, most of which have animal protagonists, form the substance of the work in this and all subsequent versions. The sixth-century Middle Persian version of the *Pancatantra* is now lost, but it is clear from the two translations made directly from it, into Arabic and old Syriac, that a considerable amount of new material was added at this stage. This new material consists of two introductory chapters, and five more chapters within the body of the work. Three of these were taken from the *Mahabharata*, one from a Buddhist legend, and the remaining story is possibly of Persian origin.

The Arabic version/translation dates from the eighth century, and, like the Middle Persian one it was taken from, contains material additional to its predecessors. Its author, Ibn al-Muqaffa', was employed at the Umayyad and Abbasid courts,

---

[1] The principal editions of *Stephanites kai Ichnelates* are: *Stephanites kai Ichnelates. Quattro recensioni della versione greca del Kitab Kalila wa-Dimna*, ed. V. Puntoni (Florence, 1889) and *Stephanites und Ichnelates. Überleiferungsgeschicht und Text*, ed. L.O. Sjöberg (Uppsala, 1962). From 1997 until 2003 Dr Jordan very kindly spent time helping me to make sense of this text, from deciphering manuscripts to producing a finished translation, both for my MA dissertation and my PhD thesis. It is no exaggeration to say that without his assistance and encouragement it is most unlikely that either would have been completed!

[2] It is perhaps misleading to call these texts 'translations': versions would be a more accurate term.

where he wrote and translated works belonging to the Arabic literary genre of *'adab*: the presentation of essential knowledge in an aesthetically pleasing literary style. He added an introduction of his own to the work, as well as (probably) five more chapters: two of Indian origin, two from unknown sources, and one of his own invention, in which justice is done and the wicked man, or rather jackal, is punished for his wrongdoings.

From Arabic the work was translated into (in chronological order) Syriac, Greek, Hebrew and medieval Spanish. Only the Greek versions will be discussed here. The earliest of these is thought to date from between 980 and 1050 and to come from southern Italy, but the only extant manuscript contains just three episodes from the end of the work.[3] A second Greek version is attributable to Symeon Seth,[4] a doctor, astronomer and mathematician, as well as translator, who dedicated his version to the emperor Alexios I Komnenos, thus giving it a date of post 1081. It exists in so many manuscripts, however, with such variation between them, that the question of the history of the text has still not been resolved. It is likely that this version was a much abbreviated one, compared to the Arabic, containing just eight chapters, the last of which was probably left unfinished at Seth's death. He omitted all the prologues and also cut the content within the chapters. A third Greek version, based on Seth's, is believed to date from twelfth-century Constantinople. It contains the rest of the chapter left unfinished by Seth and two more, taken from the Arabic. This version is the basis for the thirteenth- or fourteenth-century Church Slavonic one, which in turn was used for the sixteenth-century Italian translation, known as *Del Governo de' Regni*.

A fourth version, also dating from the twelfth century, and which also includes Seth's version more or less unchanged, is known as the Eugenian Recension because of its mention by name of the known historical figure admiral Eugenios of Palermo. This version contains a considerable amount of additional material translated from the Arabic compared with Seth's: all three prologues and six more chapters, as well as the material Seth left out from within the chapters that he did translate. In addition, there are three new prefaces, whose principal theme is to advise the reader to appreciate the value of the book and not to regard it as just a story. It is within one of these prefaces that Eugenios's name is mentioned, although it is unclear from the text whether or not he carried out the translation himself.

---

[3] For this version see E. Husselman, *A fragment of Kalilah and Dimnah from Ms.397 in the Pierpont Morgan Library* (London, 1938).
[4] For Seth and his version see *Stephanites*, ed. Sjöberg.

With so many versions and manuscripts to take into account[5] any large-scale comparison between them would be extremely difficult. The various 'translators' and authors did not feel obliged to remain faithful to their source text when dealing with a work of this nature, in which the original didactic purpose has over the centuries given way to an emphasis on the stories themselves, as stories, for entertainment. Deliberate changes to the text were also made in order to make the content more acceptable to the target audience. Examples of these are Ibn al-Muqaffa's addition of the chapter in which justice is done, and Ichnelates is punished, and the insertion into the Greek version of many biblical and classical quotations and references. The work's popularity meant that old copies quickly became worn out and were replaced, adding to the difficulties of going back to any sort of 'original'.

Bearing this in mind, a short sample passage has been selected in order to make a comparison between the Greek (one printed edition and one manuscript) and the Arabic (three printed editions and two manuscripts), and to bring to light the extent and the nature of the variations between the versions and, indeed, the manuscripts. The passage selected comes from the story of 'The swindler, the simpleton and the buried treasure', which is found towards the end of the first chapter when the wicked jackal Ichnelates has achieved his purpose of tricking the lion into killing the bull. Ichnelates's friend, Stephanites, is lamenting the fact that Ichnelates ignored his advice not to embark on such a course of action, and is now warning him by means of this story what happens to villains and traitors like him. A translation of the whole story, as found in Sjöberg's edition, follows the comparison exercise.

Textual comparison

The different versions which are compared below are taken from the following printed editions: Sjöberg's edition of the Greek *Stephanites kai Ichnelates*, and Cheikho, 'Azzam and de Sacy's editions of the Arabic *Kalila wa-Dimna*.[6] The Greek manuscript used is the fifteenth-century Leiden codex Bonaventurae Vulcanii 93 (L), the oldest representative of the Eugenian recension. The two Arabic manuscripts are London.Or.4044 (L5) (thought to be fifteenth century) and

---

[5] M. Sprengling, 'Kalila studies I', *The American Journal of Semitic Languages and Literatures*, 40 (1924), 82, mentions 'eighty-odd manuscripts, versions, and lists of chapters'; *Stephanites*, ed. Sjöberg, 24–46, gives details of over forty Greek manuscripts.

[6] 'Abdullah ibn al-Muqaffa', *Kalila wa-Dimna*, ed. L. Cheikho, *La version arabe de Kalilah et Dimnah ou les fables de Bidpaï, traduit du persan par Abdallah Ibn al-Muqaffa'. Texte arabe, publié d'après le plus ancien manuscrit daté, avec une preface, des additions et des notes critiques et linguistiques* (Beirut, 1905, repr. Amsterdam, 1981); ed. 'Abd al-Wahhab 'Azzam, *Kalila wa-Dimna of 'Abdallah ibn al-Muqaffa'* (Cairo, 1941, repr. Beirut, 1973); ed. S. de Sacy, *Calila et Dimna, ou fables de Bidpaï, en arabe* (Paris, 1816).

Paris.Ar.3469 (P15) (attributed variously to the fourteenth and sixteenth centuries). It is worth noting that each of the printed Arabic editions is based on only one manuscript.

Firstly, a comparison was made between Sjöberg's text and Greek manuscript L, which revealed only the few minor variants detailed below.

Sjöberg	L
ἐξελθόντες οὖν	ἀπελθόντες
(καὶ) τύπτειν τὸ στῆθος	(καὶ) τύπτων τὸ στῆθος αὐτοῦ
(ὡς οὐδὲν) τοιοῦτον (ἔδρασε)	(ὡς οὐδὲν) τοιούτων (ἔδρασε)

Then translations were made of the text as found in the Arabic manuscripts L5 and P15, and compared with the translated text from the three Arabic editions and with that from Sjöberg's edition of the Greek.

L5 (52r, 1–3)
They set off together, and when they dug in the place they found nothing. The swindler began to pull his hair out, and to beat his chest, and cried out and said, 'One cannot trust one's brother, and should not be blind about one's friends. You have betrayed me for the dinars, and you have taken them.' And the simpleton began to get angry and to curse...

P15 (133, 14–17)
The swindler set off, and the simpleton with him, and they went to the place, and when they got there they did not find anything. The swindler began to pull his hair out, and to strike his face, and to beat his chest, and to say, 'One should not trust anyone.' Then he said to the simpleton, 'You are the one who took the dinars,' and the simpleton began to swear...

Cheikho (96, 1–5)
They went together to the tree and dug in the place where the dinars were, and found nothing. The swindler began to tear his hair out and to beat his chest and to shout, saying, 'No one can trust anyone, and one should not be blind about one's brother or friend. You have betrayed me for the dinars and have taken them.' And the simpleton began to deny this, and to swear...

'Azzam (92, 6–9)
So they set off to the place, and dug there, and did not find them. The swindler began to tear his hair out and to bear his chest, saying, 'No one can trust anyone, you came back and took them. The simpleton began to swear...

de Sacy (130, 5–8)
They went to the place, and dug, and did not find anything, and the swindler began to strike his face, and to say, 'No one can trust anyone, and a friend should not be blind about a friend. You have betrayed me for the dinars and have taken them.' And the simpleton began to swear and curse...

Sjöberg (187, 12–15)
Therefore they set off, and having dug up the ground and found nothing, the swindler started to tear his hair and beat his breast and cry out against the simpleton that he had stolen the treasure. The simpleton assured him with countless oaths that he had not done any such thing.

As can be seen, none of these Arabic versions is an exact match for the Greek; neither is any Arabic version exactly the same as any other. Amongst the Arabic printed editions, Cheikho's is the longest, and is also the closest to L5: both mention pulling the hair and striking the chest, trusting and being blind, the brother and the friend, betrayal and taking the dinars. Cheikho alone of all the versions mentions the tree. 'Azzam's version is much abbreviated compared with the others; there is no mention in de Sacy of pulling the hair or beating the chest, but de Sacy, alone of the printed editions and in common with P15, includes the striking of the face. The variations found in this short passage give some indication of the difficulties involved in attempting to reconstruct the version of Ibn al-Muqaffa', or the source text for the Greek translation.

The whole story
(Stephanites is speaking to Ichnelates)
Exactly thus, so you also, possessed by wickedness and selfishness, do not listen to advice, and you will suffer the same fate as that of the swindler who was the companion of the simpleton. For it is said that a swindler and a simpleton established a relationship, and once while walking around they found one thousand gold talents. The simpleton said to the swindler, 'Divide the windfall equally between us.' But the swindler said, 'No, but let us take with us as much of it as we want now, and let us bury the rest underground. When we want something we will come and take out sufficient, a little at a time. For in this way our relationship will also last a long time, and, through companionship, affection.' The simpleton was persuaded by his advice and they buried the gold beneath a large shady tree. But some days later the swindler secretly went out and appropriated the whole of the stored gold. Some days after this the simpleton said to him, 'Let us go, if you like, and take some of the buried gold.' Therefore they set off, and having dug up the ground and found nothing, the swindler started to tear his hair and beat his breast and cry out against the simpleton that he had stolen the treasure. The simpleton assured him with

countless oaths that he had not done any such thing. And after a while the swindler also dragged him before one of the judges, who said, 'The burden of proof is on the plaintiff, and he must show this.' The swindler said, 'The tree itself, even though it is dumb, will testify to the truth in my favour.' And going off to his own father he reported his situation to him and requested him to get into that tree secretly and, in reply to the person who asked, to answer that the simpleton had stolen the treasure. 'I will do this,' said the father, 'but look, don't get caught in your own trap.'

He went off and secretly got into the tree. When the judge arrived there, and asked the tree who had taken the treasure, a voice answered that the simpleton had stolen it. Having heard which, the judge discovered the trick and gave orders for the tree to be burned to the ground. The fire was lit, and when the smoke blazed up towards him the father cried out immediately. Having fallen out of the tree, he confessed to the trick and was severely punished by the judge, together with his son. All the gold was taken from them and given to the simpleton alone. Such, therefore, is what results to a villainous and treacherous man.

10

Byzantine marriages and classical transmission in the *Cliges* of Chrétien de Troyes

Evelyn Mullally

Bob Jordan's network of interests covers such a wide field, from Byzantium to the west of Ireland, that I trust it will be appropriate to pay tribute to his contribution to literature and history by evoking a moment in the second half of the twelfth century when a western vernacular romance was coloured by both the classical tradition and the Byzantine empire. There has been massive interest in the works of Chrétien de Troyes over the past half-century.[1] Chrétien's five narratives undoubtedly make a significant contribution to the twelfth-century renaissance. His originality is uncontested: four of the five romances are firsts in their fields: *Erec et Enide* is the first known Arthurian romance, and many would say the first European novel, insofar as it deals with an individual psychological problem, the conflict between the personal and the professional in the life of the hero; *Le Chevalier de la Charrette* is the invention of the adulterous love between Lancelot and Guinevere; *Le Chevalier au Lion* is the first romance to incorporate a degree of social realism and *Le Conte du Graal* gives us the first known account of Perceval and the quest for the Grail. Chrétien's second romance, *Cliges*, is however markedly different from all the others and, while it has not lacked commentators, one aspect of the romance is relatively neglected and that is the context in which it was written. The fullest account of the historical background was given by Anthime Fourrier, who used it in an attempt to show that the romance was written in the 1170s.[2] Fourrier's dating has not won general acceptance: more recent scholars have preferred to place it in the 1180s on the basis of literary influence. As Douglas Kelly has stated: 'There have been no widely accepted advances in the chronology of Chrétien's ro-

---

[1] The explosion of academic interest in recent decades in the romances of Chrétien de Troyes is evidenced by the sheer size of the scholarly bibliographies compiled by Douglas Kelly: the first volume, which appeared in 1976, ran to a mere 153 pages, while his first supplement, published two years ago, is four times that length. See D. Kelly, *Chrétien de Troyes, an analytic bibliography* (London, 1976); D. Kelly, *Chrétien de Troyes, an analytic bibliography*. Supplement 1 (London, 2002).
[2] A. Fourrier, *Le Courant réaliste dans le roman courtois en France au moyen-âge* (Paris, 1960), 160–178.

mances.³ However, it is not at all necessary to agree with Fourrier's conclusions about dating to accept the interest of the historical background he opened up to Chrétien's work.⁴

It is generally accepted that Chrétien was writing some time between 1170 and 1190, but, despite the popularity and the enormous influence of his romances, we know practically nothing about the man himself. Only two facts are certain: the names of his two patrons, which he includes in the prologues to his third and fifth romances. Both these figures were powerful aristocrats with connections to all the ruling families of east and west. The first patron mentioned is Marie de Champagne (1145–1198), the first child born to Louis VII and Eleanor of Aquitaine. Marie was only a very small child when her parents set off on the Second Crusade and they divorced when she was still very young. It is not however unreasonable to assume that she received some echo of that momentous if ill-starred event. Her father was certainly dazzled by the sights shown him by the emperor Manuel I Komnenos during his passage through Constantinople, according to his chaplain, Odo of Deuil.⁵ Her mother's activities in Antioch provided disapproving material for the chroniclers and no doubt for court intrigue.⁶

A much more positive reference to Marie's mother occurs some years later in a purely literary context. It is noteworthy that there is a marked change of tone and genre in vernacular French literature after the Second Crusade. The first half of the twelfth century had been dominated by *chansons de geste* which celebrated national legends in a heroic mode. But a new genre emerges alongside them from the midcentury, that of the proto-romance, the *romans d'antiquité*. These early romances are all set in Greece or Rome and they are in fact French adaptations of classical epics. As regards the content, one element of these early romances may perhaps have been inspired by reports from Constantinople: there are numerous elaborate rhetorical descriptions of luxurious objects such as robes, harnesses, silk materials and pavilions. So we have the *Roman de Thèbes,* based on Statius, the *Roman d'Eneas*, adapted from Virgil and the vast *Roman de Troie*, composed c.1165–1170 by Benoît de Sainte-Maure, who used not Homer but Dares Phrygius and Dictys Cretensis.

---

³ Kelly, *Supplement 1*, 485.
⁴ Following Fourrier, Henry and Renée Kahane sought to derive the name Cligès from the enemy of Manuel I Komnenos, Kilidj Arslan II, sultan of Iconium (1156–1192): 'L'énigme du nom de Cligès', *Romania*, 82 (1961), 113–121. The attempt to forge a definite historical link between the romance and the Byzantine world did not meet general acceptance: see D.L. Maddox, 'Critical trends and recent work on the *Cligès* of Chrétien de Troyes', *Neuphilologische Mitteilungen*, 74 (1973), 730–745. There has however, been a revival of interest by M. Wis, 'Hartmanns Connelant und Chrétiens *Cligès*: Der Dichter und der Stauferhof', *Neuphilologische Mittteilungen*, 92 (1991), 269–280.
⁵ *Odo of Deuil: De profectione Ludovici VII in orientem*, ed. V.G. Berry (New York, 1948), 62–69.
⁶ P. McCracken, 'Scandalizing desire: Eleanor of Aquitaine and the chroniclers', *Eleanor of Aquitaine: lord and lady*, ed. B. Wheeler and J. Carmi Parsons (New York, 2002), 247–264.

In the course of his romance Benoît, after indulging in a routine tirade against women, pulls himself up abruptly to make an elaborately flattering exception of a certain *riche dame de riche rei*, who can only be Eleanor, now queen of England.[7]

Meanwhile, her daughter Marie by her first marriage had become part of the triple marriage alliance made by King Louis with the siblings of the powerful house of Blois-Champagne, great-grand-children of William the Conqueror through William's daughter Adèle of Normandy (and so second cousins of Eleanor's second husband, Henry II Plantagenet). After the divorce from Eleanor and the death of his second wife Constance of Castile, Louis VII married again in 1160. He himself married Adèle (or Alix) of Blois-Champagne and four years later his two daughters by Eleanor married Adèle's brothers: Marie's younger sister Alix married Thibaut V of Blois and she herself married Henry I of Champagne.

Besides his connections with William the Conqueror, Henry had Germanic connections through his mother, the princess Matilda, daughter of the duke of Carinthia. Furthermore, the house of Blois-Champagne had Byzantine contacts going back to the late eleventh century. In 1097 Henry's grandmother Adèle of Normandy received letters from her husband Stephen of Blois, absent on the First Crusade, in which he told her of the gracious reception he had received from the Byzantine emperor, Alexios I Komnenos.[8] Alexios had even offered to take one of Stephen's sons to his court, perhaps Thibaut, the future Thibaut IV of Champagne, Henry's father. Fifty years later, contact was renewed. On the occasion of the Second Crusade, St Bernard addressed a ceremonial letter of recommendation to the grandson of Alexios, the emperor Manuel I Komnenos, on behalf of the bearer, son of the illustrious Thibaut IV, requesting the honour of having the young man knighted by the Byzantine emperor himself.[9] They must always have remained on cordial terms for, in 1180, near the end of both their lives, Manuel ransomed Henry, who had fallen into the hands of the Turks on his return from Jerusalem.[10]

By birth and marriage therefore, the court of Champagne at Troyes had connections with all the most powerful families of Europe. On her marriage to Henry the princess Marie acquired considerable personal power. She was ruler of Champagne during her husband's absence in the east, regent after his death during the minority of their son and in charge again during his absence on the Third Crusade. Like her mother, she took an interest in literature, and was therefore a highly desirable patroness. For a native of Troyes like Chrétien she was the natural person to turn to

---

[7] T.F. O'Callaghan, 'Tempering scandal: Eleanor of Aquitaine and Benoît de Sainte-Maure's *Roman de Troie*', *Eleanor of Aquitaine*, ed. Wheeler and Carmi Parsons, 301–318.

[8] H. Hagenmeyer, *Epistulae et chartae ad historiam primi belli sacri spectantes : Die Kreuzzugsbriefe aus den Jahren 1088–1100* (Innsbruck, 1901; repr. Hildesheim, New York, 1973), 138–152.

[9] *PL*, 182, 672–673.

[10] *Monumenta Germaniae historica, Scriptores (in folio)* vol. 26: *Ex rerum Francogallicarum scriptoribus*, ed. G. Waitz (Hanover, 1882), 244.

for patronage.[11] It is true that Chrétien's first romance, *Erec et Enide*, contains no reference to a patron, but the confident, indeed arrogant tone of the prologue may indicate that he already has a position at the countess's court as he feels able to be contemptuous of those mere professional storytellers who have already told the story so badly 'before counts and kings'.[12]

Chrétien mentions Marie specifically in the opening lines of the prologue to his third romance:[13]

> Puis que ma dame de Chanpaigne
> vialt que romans a feire anpraigne,
> je l'anprendrai molt volentiers
> 4 come cil qui est suens antiers
> de quan qu'il puet el monde feire
> sanz rien de losange avant treire.

(Since my lady of Champagne wants me to undertake a romance, I shall do so most willingly as one who is entirely at her disposal to do whatever he can, without prefacing it with any flattery).

Flattery is then laid on with a trowel, but Chrétien concludes his prologue on a point that must have some fact behind it:

> 24 Del Chevalier de la charrete
> comance Crestïens son livre;
> matiere et san li done et livre
> la contesse, et il s'antrement
> 28 de panser, que gueres n'i met
> fors sa painne et s'antancïon.

(Chrétien begins his book on the Knight of the Cart [*Lancelot*]; the countess gives him the matter and sense of it and he undertakes to think it through, for he puts nothing into it except his trouble and his understanding).

It is impossible to establish the exact level of Marie de Champagne's input into *Lancelot*, but there was certainly some degree of personal interest. She was not merely a nominal patroness, but had at least discussed the subject of the romance with Chrétien. It is also reasonable to suppose that she was conversant with his earlier romances, or she would hardly have commissioned him to write a new one. So, if Chrétien was thus relatively intimate with the house of Blois-Champagne, it

---

[11] J.F. Benton, 'The Court of Champagne as a literary center', *Speculum*, 36 (1961), 551–591.
[12] 'Devant rois et devant contes': *Erec et Enide*, l.1, ed. M. Roques (Classiques français du moyen âge, 80, Paris, 1952), 1.
[13] *Le chevalier de la charrete*, ed. M. Roques (Classiques français du moyen âge, 86, Paris, 1958).

is not unlikely that he had had some echoes of high-level marriage negotiations at the time he was writing *Cliges*.

Erec had clearly been a success, and the prologue of his second romance, Cliges, reads almost like a job application for future patronage as Chrétien outlines his work to date in the opening lines:[14]

>   Cil qui fist *D'Erec et d'Enide*
>   Et *Les comandemanz d'Ovide*
>   Et *L'art d'amors an romans mist*
> 4   Et *Le mors de l'espaule* fist,
>   *Del roi Marc et d'Ysalt la blonde*
>   Et *De la hupe et de l'aronde*
>   Et *Del rossignol la muance,*
> 8   Un novel conte recomance
>   D'un vaslet qui an Grece fu
>   Del linage le roi Artu.

(He who wrote of Erec and Enide, and the commandments of Ovid, and put the art of love into the vernacular, and wrote of the shoulder bite, of King Mark and Iseut the Fair, of the hoopoe and the swallow and the metamorphosis of the nightingale, is starting a new tale about a young man who lived in Greece, of the lineage of King Arthur).

It thus appears that his works to date have been transformations of Arthurian material and translations of Ovid. In the Arthurian domain he has composed two works: *Erec and Enide* and *King Mark and Iseut the Fair*. *Erec and Enide* has survived as the earliest known Arthurian romance; his Mark and Iseut story has been lost. We shall never know why there is no mention here of Iseut's lover Tristan, but the influence of that famous triangle is felt in all of Chrétien's surviving works, most notably the one we are about to discuss. But besides the Celtic tradition of Arthur, Chrétien puts himself on record as having translated into French at least three works of Ovid: the *Ars amatoria* and two stories from the *Metamorphoses*: the shoulder wound of Pelops and the transformations of Philomela, Procne and Tereus. Chrétien's second romance is introduced into this combination of the Celtic and the classical: he is now starting a new tale about a young man of King Arthur's lineage, but one who lived in Greece. But first he will embark on the parental romance:

---

[14] *Chrétien de Troyes: Cliges*, ed. S. Gregory and C. Luttrell (Cambridge, 1993). The name Cliges has no accents in the original manuscript. It has been variously edited as Cligès or Cligés but I have omitted either accent in all my references.

>   Mes ainz que de lui rien vos die,
> 12 Orroiz de son pere la vie,
>   Dom il fu et de quel linage,
>   Tant fu preuz et de fier corage
>   Que por pris et por los conquerre
> 16 Ala de Grece an Engleterre,
>   Qui lors estoit Bretaigne dite.

(But before I tell you anything about him, hear the life of his father and where he came from and from what lineage. He was so brave and courageous that, in order to win honour and praise, he went from Greece to England, which was called Britain at that time).

The story will move from Byzantium to Britain. There follows immediately the alleged source of this wide-ranging tale:

>   Ceste estoire trovons escrite,
>   Que conter vos vuel et retraire,
> 20 En un des livres de l'aumaire
>   Mon seignor saint Pere a Biauvez.
>   De la fut li contes estrez
>   Don cest romans fist Crestïens.
> 24 Li livres est molt ancïens
>   Qui tesmoingne l'estoire a voire;
>   Por ce fet ele mialz a croire.

(We find this story that I want to relate to you written in one of the books in the library of St Peter in Beauvais. The story that Chrétien has made a romance from was taken from there. The book is very ancient which testifies to the truth of the story and makes it all the more worthy of belief).

The alleged ancient source may be nothing more than a conventional medieval fiction,[15] but the appeal to venerable antiquity sends Chrétien off on an oft-quoted evocation of the *translatio imperii* and the *translatio studii*, the translation or rather the transfer of political power and cultural knowledge from the ancient world to the modern:[16]

---

[15] The main part of the story appears to be Chrétien's own original reworking of the Tristan plot. The final part of the romance, which deals with the case of the woman who feigns death, is closely related to an exemplum which has not been traced back further than the thirteenth century; see *Marques de Rome*, ed. J. Alton (Tubingen, 1889), 135.

[16] On the *translatio imperii* and the *translatio studii* in this type of context, see E.R. Curtius, *European literature and the Latin Middle Ages*, tr. from German by W.R. Trask (London and Henley, 1952), 28–29; for the rhetoric of this prologue, see M.A. Freeman, *The poetics of* Translatio Studii *and* Conjointure: *Chrétien de Troyes's* Cliges (Lexington, KY, 1979).

>   Par les livres que nos avons
> 28 Le fez des ancïens savons
>   Et del siegle qui fu jadis.
>   Ce nos ont nostre livre apris
>   Qu'an Grece ot de chevalerie
> 32 Le premier los et de clergie.
>   Puis vint la chevalerie a Rome
>   Et de la clergie la some,
>   Qui or est an France venue.

(Through the books which we have we know the deeds of the ancients and the world of long ago. Our books have taught us this: that the first glory of chivalry and learning was in Greece. Then chivalry and the summa of learning came to Rome, which has now come to France).

Certainly France in the twelfth century had a fair claim to being the heir of Rome and Greece. Almost all the creations of the twelfth-century renaissance had their birth there. But this is more than simple chauvinism. Chrétien is aware that these gifts are indeed only loans: they were taken back from Greece and Rome in the past and could be taken back too from France:

> 36 Dex doint qu'ele i soit retenue,
>   Et que li leus li abelisse
>   Tant que ja mes de France n'isse
>   L'enors qui s'i est arestee.
> 40 Dex l'avoit as altres prestee,
>   Car des Grezois ne des Romains
>   Ne dit an mes ne plus ne mains:
>   D'ax est la parole remese
> 44 Et estainte la vive brese.

(God grant that it be retained here and that the country may be pleasing to it so that the honour that has come to France may never leave it. God had lent it others: for nothing more is heard of the Greeks and Romans: nothing is said of them any more and their living embers have burnt out).

God has not actually given this honour to France: He had only lent it to the Greeks and the Romans and France too is presumably only the recipient of a loan. National disaster is frequently seen as punishment for sin, so God may well take back this honour if France proves herself unworthy. But for the moment France is undoubtedly where glory and culture reign. We might well expect that the romance to follow would therefore be set in contemporary France. But on the contrary, the ancient world is not dead after all for we are instantly plunged into a fictional Byzantium of long ago:

> Crestïens comance son conte.
> Si con li livres nos reconte
> Qui treite d'un empereor
> 48 Puissant de richesce et d'enor,
> Qui tint Grece et Costantinoble....

(Chretien begins his story: As the book tells us, which is about an emperor, powerful in riches and honour who held Greece and Constantinople...)

This fictional emperor, Alexander, has a son also called Alexander who insists on pursuing chivalry at the court of King Arthur in far away Britain. After various adventures, he returns to Constantinople, having crowned his successes abroad by marrying an English princess, King Arthur's niece. His story turns out to be a prologue in itself to the real romance, that of their son, Cliges. The model for a parental romance of this kind is the Tristan story, where the tragedy of the hero's parents foreshadows events in the life of their son. Chrétien's romance will also involve the adulterous triangle of a ruler, his wife and his nephew but with more moral and social complications. His hero, the young Byzantine prince Cliges, falls in love with the daughter of the emperor of Germany, who has been treacherously sought by his uncle and treacherously promised to him by her father.

In real life, Chrétien was in a position to receive some echoes of the complicated politics of royal marriage negotiations, as both his patrons moved in the highest circles. After Marie, Chrétien's patron was her former suitor, her cousin's husband, Philippe d'Alsace, count of Flanders. (Philippe had married Isabelle, daughter of Raoul de Vermandois and Petronille, younger sister of Eleanor of Aquitaine. Marie de Champagne and Isabelle de Vermandois were thus first cousins). For Philippe, Chrétien undertook to write Perceval, the story of the Grail, but Philippe died on the Third Crusade and Chrétien himself died before he could finish the romance.

In the lives of powerful families, both premature death and changing circumstances resulted in marriage negotiations being continually undertaken and broken off as political interests dictated, so it is not improbable that Chrétien's fictional account of Byzantine marriage negotiations should contain echoes of historical fact. The whole tone of *Cliges* is realistic, at least with regard to externals. His treatment of geography contrasts sharply with his first romance. *Erec* had taken place in a fantastic Arthurian world, where it seemed possible to move from Britain to Brittany without crossing the channel. *Cliges* is precisely realistic in its evocation of the cities of the south of England and Chrétien also shows himself to be aware of the place of Köln and Regensburg in the relations between the German empire and Byzantium.

There are certainly some resemblances between the plot of Cliges and the accession of Manuel I Komnenos.[17] In the romance Alexander, the emperor's son, returns on the death of his father to find that his younger brother Alis has usurped the imperial Byzantine crown. The ensuing conflict is resolved when it is agreed that Alis shall have the title, but Alexander shall have the power. The real Byzantine succession had experienced something similar: when John Komnenos was dying in 1143, he designated his younger son Manuel as successor over his elder son Isaac. Manuel had Isaac confined to the monastery of the Pantokrator until his succession was assured, but was then reconciled with him and an arrangement was reached whereby Isaac kept the title of sebastokrator but Manuel kept the power.

The sharing of power and prestige between two rival imperial brothers, where the stronger keeps the power and the weaker is consoled with a title does certainly recall the case in Cliges, though it has to be said that the romance presents a simpler moral situation. Here the older brother and natural heir is also the stronger physically and morally and the younger brother is both vain and weak and thus content with empty appearances. He subsequently breaks his word to allow Alexander's son Cliges to succeed and instead seeks a marriage alliance for himself with the daughter of the German emperor.

In real life, the Emperor Manuel, unlike his father and grandfather, 'not only gave increased priority to foreign marriages, but sought these almost exclusively in the Latin world.'[18] Manuel himself married Bertha, sister of Gertrude of Sulzbach, the wife of the German emperor Conrad III. As Byzantine empress Bertha took the name of Eirene and sought to further relations between Constantinople and Germany. In the 1150s a marriage was negotiated between Conrad's nephew and successor, Frederick Barbarossa (c.1112–1190), and a Byzantine princess, but negotiations fell through when Barbarossa married Beatrice of Burgundy instead and bad feeling resulted between the two empires, intensified by Manuel's Italian policy which conflicted with Barbarossa's interests.

The fictional Byzantine emperor Alis is doubly treacherous in his negotiations with the German emperor. On the one hand he hopes to produce his own heir who will oust the legitimate heir, his nephew Cliges. On the other hand, he induces the German emperor to break his word to the Duke of Saxony to whom his daughter was already promised and the Duke is understandably furious.

In real life, there was a very high-profile duke of Saxony in the twelfth century, also in conflict with the real-life German emperor. This real duke was none other than Henry the Lion (1129–1195), son of the princess Gertrude, daughter of the

---

[17] F. Chalandon, *Les Comnène. Jean II Comnène et Manuel Comnène* (New York, 1912 ; repr. 1971), II, 192–193, 195–200, 215. P. Magdalino, *The Empire of Manuel Komnenos 1143–80* (Cambridge, 1993), 195.

[18] Magdalino, *Manuel Komnenos*, 209. For the following negotiations, see Fourrier, *Le Courant réaliste dans le roman courtois*.

previous German emperor Lothair II. When Conrad III of Hohenstaufen succeeded as emperor he deprived Duke Henry of his territories of Saxony and Bavaria. As in the romance, there is produced a serious sense of grievance between the Duke of Saxony and the German emperor. The real-life Duke of Saxony fared rather better than his fictional counterpart, at least in the short term. Henry recovered Saxony in 1142 and had Bavaria restored to him in 1156 at the diet of Regensburg by Conrad's successor, Frederick Barbarossa. (Henry the Lion, as well as being the grandson of the previous emperor through his mother Gertrude, was also the first cousin of the new emperor through his father, Henry the Proud, who was the brother of Judith of Bavaria, Barbarossa's mother). However, when Henry the Lion became too powerful and refused to support Barbarossa's Italian ambitions, he was once again deprived of his lands, both Saxony and Bavaria, in 1181. Meanwhile, however, in 1168, Henry (having divorced his first wife Clementia some years earlier) had married Matilda, daughter of Henry Plantagenet and Eleanor of Aquitaine; Eleanor, from her marriage with Louis VII, was already the mother of Marie de Champagne, so Henry the Lion's wife was the half-sister of Chrétien's patroness.

With this close family connection, we might expect the fictional duke of Saxony to play a heroic role in the romance, but this is not the case. He is indeed a champion, but one that the real hero Cliges will be called upon to defeat. Henry the Lion was closely linked to the house of Blois-Champagne, so the household was very probably fully aware of all his doings, but in fact Marie's husband, Henry the Liberal, was a life-long supporter of the duke of Saxony's first cousin, the emperor Barbarossa himself, so fictional balance is maintained by having the fictional duke defeated, but not disgraced or killed.

Marriage negotiations between the Byzantine and German emperors were long drawn out and complicated. In 1171 Barbarossa met in Köln messengers from Manuel, who had come to negotiate with him the proposed marriage of Manuel's daughter, the princess Maria, with one of Barbarossa's sons. Manuel had already pledged her to William II of Sicily but finally decided that a son of the German emperor was the most advantageous match for his daughter and broke the agreement with William of Sicily. Early in 1172 the bishop of Worms made his way to Constantinople on Barbarossa's behalf to further the marriage project, in the company of Henry the Lion, who was on pilgrimage to the Holy Land with 500 knights. Bishop and duke were magnificently received in Constantinople on Easter Sunday 1172. On his way back from Palestine, Henry once again stopped in Byzantium and was given magnificent presents.

In 1174 Barbarossa held a diet in Regensburg, an assembly of all princes including Henry the Lion and ambassadors from Manuel, anxious to conclude the marriage deal. But Barbarossa, though he kept up negotiations with Manuel, in the hope of winning over to his side an ally of his enemy the pope, was already thinking of backing out of a marriage between his son and Manuel's daughter. He was also planning a new expedition to Italy and was annoyed that his cousin Henry the Lion was refusing to support him, leaning more towards the pope and the Byzantine connection. Henry had long ago been designated by Barbarossa as his heir, but Barbarossa had subsequently had several sons who would certainly inherit. Barbarossa was able to blame his cousin Henry, duke of Saxony for his defeat in northern Italy in 1176.

As we have seen, Marie's husband Henry the Liberal of Champagne, was a life-long supporter of Barbarossa, to whom he was connected through Barbarossa's wife, Beatrice of Burgundy. (His great uncle, Hugh I of Champagne, had married Beatrice's aunt Elizabeth). Henry had even received the honorific title of prince of the Empire (as did Chrétien's second patron, Philip of Flanders). Up to his death in 1181, he was on Barbarossa's side against Henry the Lion. Meanwhile, Henry had supported a proposed marriage between his niece, the princess Agnes (daughter of Louis VII's marriage to Henry's sister Alix de Blois) with a son of Barbarossa's, in order to consolidate an alliance with the German empire. However, Pope Alexander III, determined to prevent an alliance that would strengthen his enemy Barbarossa, proposed instead to Louis that she should be married to Alexios, the son and heir of Manuel, an alliance that duly came about in 1179–1180.

We can only speculate on Chrétien's awareness of all these manoeuvres, but it was in his interest to be informed of his patrons' interests and he certainly knew enough to be able to transform real imperial marriage negotiations into fiction. At the same time Chrétien saw France as the heir of Greece and Rome both as regards culture and political power. His classical background made the eastern Mediterranean an obvious starting point for a literary work, and the great power there in his period was the Byzantine empire. His two patrons were great aristocrats connected to all the ruling families of both east and west and he spent all his working life connected with the courts of the great with their constantly changing alliances. So, when he undertook to compose a radically new version of a plot based on the Tristan triangle, he chose to place it in a new setting as far as possible from the Celtic world of the original. He moves his story from west to east and, using echoes of the complex marriage negotiations available at the court of Champagne, imagines an intrigue involving the German empire, and makes his hero heir to the throne of Constantinople.

11

Urbs parva, sed loco munita: translation, culture and the institution

David Johnston

What happens when the contours of a language and culture no longer match the landscape of fact?

The words are – almost literally – those of George Steiner, but the question is posed most powerfully by the hedge-school teacher, Hugh O'Donnell, in Brian Friel's *Translations*.[1] In its recognition of the need to look outwards from the cultural matrix, the question provides a positive counterbalance to Jimmy Jack's dire warning to Maire, who is in love with the English soldier Yolland, about the difficulty of escaping from the heartland of a culture, of crossing boundaries.[2] So that when, accordingly, O'Donnell declares his willingness to teach Maire English, he is affirming a moment of what Marxist historical materialism would describe as dialectic shift, or contemporary cultural theory as paradigm change. It is the recognition of a time of transition, of the need to create a place for otherness within those outmoded contours.

Translations, of course, primarily presents the act of translation, through its capacity for appropriation, as a dramatic device for exploring the mapping of one culture's military power over another. But in the way that translation can also seek to 'interpret between privacies', as O'Donnell finally recognises, translation – as method and practice – becomes a mode that shatters frontiers, breaking out of those provinces bordering only on silence in which many of us still dwell. In that way, and in the specific context of Field Day, who challenged Irish audiences to 'imagine alternatives' at a time when the Irish historical imagination seemed to have grown stunted and myopic, translation stands here as a paradigm for a mod-

---

[1] See G. Steiner, *After Babel* (London, Oxford and New York, 1975). B. Friel, '*Translations*', *Friel: selected plays*, ed. S. Deane (London, 1984). Friel has, of course, openly acknowledged the relationship between his play and Steiner's thought. See A. Roche, *Contemporary Irish drama* (Dublin, 1994), esp. 245.

[2] The idea of 'crossing boundaries' is much in vogue at the moment. This brief essay is an attempt to tease out what some of the implications of such cross-overs may be, outside the remit of translation theory.

ernity that refuses to be constrained within self-absorbed – and self-serving – definitions of cultural nationalism.[3]

This is all about a willingness to move into uncharted territory, to move beyond the terrible dyadic unity of Tiocfaidh ár lá agus/and No surrender, abbreviated form both, in the final analysis, for a ring-fenced future. Just as the play ends on a signal moment of uncertainty – 'But will that help you to interpret between privacies? I have no idea. But it's all we have. I have no idea at all' – so all translational activity is inevitably contingent. When translators refer to their *trouvailles*, or talk – as they will do – about the creative misreadings that have yielded up unexpected but startlingly fresh meanings, it is this same sense of contingency they are describing, and which, indeed, many feel to be a defining feature of the process of translating literary texts.[4] Not surprisingly, perhaps, all of this arouses a marked philological/new critical hostility that is still much in evidence within the institution today.

'We have here indeed what may very probably be the most complex type of event yet produced in the evolution of the cosmos.'[5] I.A. Richards' hyperbolic description of literary translation derives, of course, from his view of works of literature as 'vastly complex systems'. Such complexity, in Richards' scheme, however, is open to a 'perfect understanding' that, in turn, maps itself from the original onto a translated text that is duty-bound to reformulate exactly that understanding. Underlying this is a clear distrust of contingency, a functioning of the 'error terror' that characterises, and arguably has impoverished, much humanities thinking.[6] But there is also an authoritarianism here, as there is indeed in any close-reading model that pre-supposes that only one interpretive line is valid, that there is a single 'correct' response to what a text is about and how it inscribes itself within a culture.

There is a curious parallel between Jimmy Jack's threatening depiction of the dangers of exogamy and Richards' belief that translation is solely concerned with mapping the 'interanimation of words' in the source text onto the verbal surface of the target text. By ignoring the translation process as the site of dialogic interaction

---

[3] Symbolically, Field Day launched itself as a company with the Derry premiere of *Translations* in 1980. The company staged a large number of translated plays in their fifteen years or so of existence.

[4] Contingency arising from what Edwin Gentzler has called 'laws that are unique to the mode of translation itself', in *Contemporary translation theories* (Clevedon, 2001), 15.

[5] I.A. Richards, 'Toward a theory of translating', *Studies in Chinese thought*, ed. A. Wright (Chicago, 1953), 247–262. Richards' theory has proved remarkably resistant. It is still alive in a number of class-room practices, including the so-called translation workshop, which tests participants' ability to approximate to a notionally 'correct' version, and, most notoriously, the undying foreign-language prose class, in which, all too often, translation is reduced to a mechanical exercise of interlingual photocopying.

[6] Stephen Kelly has very recently drawn my attention to Seth Lerer's fascinating *Error and the academic self. The scholarly imagination, medieval to modern* (New York, 2002).

between cultures, Richards – and the school of thinking that followed him – is no less guilty of a cultural fundamentalism that still pervades much critical thinking today, in the institution no less than in the media.[7] Jimmy Jack's reaction to the encroachment of the sappers (and with them their language) is to declare a culture of ourselves alone, while Richards urges no surrender to the new developments in cultural and literary theory that were increasingly challenging the whole notion of the textual master key, and that in doing so threatened the power base of philology in the institution.[8]

Such power was vested in the control of language itself, a control that in the specific context of translation maintained itself through an intertextual (and therefore intercultural) paradigm of clear subservience. But empirical evidence shows that translations constantly open up new heterogeneous perspectives that breach the barriers of our linguistic and cultural homogeneity. If we think less of translation as a product, as the sort of linguistic big bang so admired by Richards, and regard it instead in terms of process – the process of understanding and writing the other – then its central relationship with alterity asserts translation as one of the key methods of our times, a compelling paradigm of our modernity.

The hedge-school in *Translations* provides a powerful image of what the institution can and should be. Under Hugh O'Donnell's stewardship it is a group of people in search of disinterested learning across a variety of disciplines, most particularly through a network of linguistic encounter; disinterested but not unconnected, necessarily alive to the shifting patterns of the cultural landscape that is being re-mapped and re-named around them. *Translations* ends with the image of looking outwards. In a recent essay, the French translator Jean-Charles Vegliante refers to translation as 'mon Eurydice'.[9] No matter how comforting the backward glance, no matter how compelling, the textual and cultural journeying of the translator is only viable when he or she keeps their gaze resolutely on the crossings still to be negotiated. Yet in many of our universities we continue to dwell behind the philological divides that are the shadow of the nineteenth-century construction of the nation state. Philological scholarship, with its principal method of exegesis, frequently makes claims for its own particular parcel of culture that are not substantiated when set against the bigger picture framed by the intercultural spaces set in and

---

[7] Consider, for example, this excerpt from a recent review of a play (taken from the British Theatre Guide, online) by Lope de Vega in English translation: 'This is undeniably not Shakespeare. The language is easy to understand and sounds modern. It doesn't have the richness or depth of the Bard's work, but it has a more universal appeal.' Leaving aside the simplicities of the botched linguistic mapping, the writer ignores the fact that the translation occupies a 'new space' that is neither Spanish nor English.

[8] See also Gentzler, *Contemporary translation theories*, esp. ch. 1.

[9] J.-C. Vegliante, 'Traduction et traductologie', *Les écrivains italiens et leurs traducteurs français* (Caen, 1996), 55–70. Quoted by P. Broome, 'Translating the untranslatable', *Reading across the lines*, ed. C. Shorley and M. McCusker (Dublin, 2000), 70.

around that particular parcel. The organisation of any humanities curriculum captures the vision of a culture. It bears a paradigmatic relationship to the culture it seeks to explicate. All too often, however, our philological curricula fail to acknowledge the processes and connections of cultural kinetics. And they do so at their peril, because it is precisely the idea of process and connection, rather than knowledge drawn from systematic overview, that chimes with the intellectual climate of postmodernism and excites the best of our students today.

None of this is to suggest that internal explanations of the factors of cultural change should be ignored; but the process of intercultural dynamics must be accounted for and integrated into any method or model of cultural study that pretends to be anything other than partial, or indeed self-serving. An awareness of such process is in itself central to translation history, a discipline that goes beyond philology in its attempt to say why textual translations occurred, when they did, where they did, and, crucially, how they related to change. Answers to these questions bring a sharper awareness of power relations across society, and between languages and cultures, an awareness that in turn deepens our understanding of whole periods or networks. By way of example: the sudden surge of Shakespeare productions in Japan after the Second World War may be identified as marking the recognition of a qualitative change within Japanese culture stemming from military defeat. That is undoubtedly so, but it is stating only a partial case. Unless we look at how those translations were written, how that intercultural space between Japanese and English cultures was actually defined by the receiving culture, and how that writing subsequently changed – as it did, radically – thereby changing that unique third space, we will remain largely unaware of how Japanese society and culture have been profiling their own deep-rooted changes through this contact. Indeed, we will also have only the sketchiest idea of how that contact has in itself acted as an agent of change within Japanese culture.

At the heart of this methodology is, of course, the translator as social actor and cultural enabler. In other words, the methodology of translation history does not ignore the properly human dimension of the act of translation, but at the same time it is subsequently concerned to insert that dimension into an explanation of how change occurs in and across a culture. In other words, the individual act of translation, rather than a philological exercise, creates an interstice between two cultures, unique in its own way, but also part of a discontinuous but ongoing borderline.

The School of Translators, which flourished in Toledo in the twelfth and thirteenth centuries, provides a very good example of such a borderline. Situated about 70km to the south of Madrid, perched high above a dramatic curve in the River Tagus, Toledo is first mentioned by Livy as an 'urbs parva, sed loco munita'. It is a city of rich cultural palimpsest, Roman, Visigothic, Christian, Sephardic and Islamic. It was the Moors who first practised translation in any consistent way in the

Peninsula, mainly of Greek and Latin works into Arabic from the eighth to the twelfth centuries. There were important links with the House of Wisdom, created in Baghdad under the caliphate of Al-Mamun in the ninth century, and it was from there that a number of texts translated into Arabic, by authors such as Hippocrates, Galen, Archimedes, and Ptolemy, began to arrive in the Peninsula. The scientific knowledge that these texts brought with them inspired the first period of the school's functioning when Bishop Raimundus (who was originally French) organised teams of Christian, Arabic and Jewish translators. The second period of translation began around 1250, under the influence and inspiration of King Alfonso X the Wise, when the first Arabic literature was translated into Romance. There are distinct differences between both periods of the School, in terms of translation theories and protocols, but both are extraordinary in terms of the international network of influence they established, as well as the rich variety in the origins of patrons and translators alike.

Livy's description of this 'small city, but fortified by its position' possesses a neat symbolism. There are numerous examples of philological scholarship annexing the endeavour of the School, re-constructing it squarely within monolithic models of a self-enclosed, fortified culture. Such re-constructions, of course, serve their own political purpose, both within and outside the institution. There has been much research, for example, conducted in the interests of Spanish national glory, that has tended to ignore the intercultural and deracinated nature of the translation teams and the individual translators who journeyed from afar to work there. Typical is this view of José Sangrador Gil, articulated in 1997:

> The historical moment in which the School of Translators flourished was of capital importance for western civilization. Without this contribution from Spain, Europe would have continued locked into cultural isolation, or at the very least, cultural scientific development in the West would have been considerably impeded.[10]

Spain and Europe are presented as clearly defined cultural entities, schematised so as to extend the appeal and power base of a systematic discipline, as well as to corroborate the validity of Spain's claims to international recognition as an appropriate venue for the first round of peace talks – the so-called Madrid talks – that were talking place between Arafat and Begin at about the same time. But Sangrador Gil's cultural nationalism is as absurd and misplaced today as would be a view from the twenty-fifth century claiming the work of the European Parliament in Brussels

---

[10] 'Por otra parte, el momento histórico en que esta escuela de traductores floreció fue de capital importancia dentro de la civilización occidental. Sin esta aportación desde Espana, Europa habría continuado en el ostracismo cultural o al menos el desarrollo científico cultural en el Occidente se habría retrasado considerablemente'. My translation. J. Sangrador Gil, 'La Escuela de Traductores de Toledo durante la edad media', *Pensamiento y circulación de ideas en el Mediterráneo*, ed. M. Hernando de Larramendi and G. Fernández Parrilla (Cuenca, 1997), 25–52.

as a significant Belgian contribution to European unity. There is clearly an issue of mapping here.

The history of the Toledo School of Translators is one of exchange and movement. This was, of course, enabled in the first instance by the complex network of exchanges between Islamic, Sephardic and Christian peoples and cultures that was operative in and around Toledo. Those changeovers encouraged translators to flood to the city, in much the same way as artists flooded to the Paris of the interwar years. An early arrival was Daniel de Morlei, an Englishman of Norman descent.[11] He provides us with one of the first accounts of work in the School, justifying his desire to remain 'since it is at Toledo that Arabic teachings, almost all in the quadrivium, are widely celebrated, I hurried there to listen to the world's wisest philosophers'.[12] This movement of people was paralleled by an extraordinary influx and exodus of texts that created a network of influence and contact across the continent in its entirety.[13] Translators have been continuing that work ever since, operating as uprooted intermediaries in an intercultural space whose borders remain constantly open.

And yet we talk so easily about incipient Spanish literature, or French literature, at this time. However, even this extremely brief sketch of the borderlands that created and, in turn, were created by the School of Translators indicates the difficulties in conceptualising the areas occupied by languages, literatures and cultures. As Hugh O'Donnell recognises, and as the history of the School demonstrates, these areas are in constant flux, developing through processes of exchange, fragmentation, displacement and renewal. How should a curriculum map these areas? Is it enough to replace 'Spanish literature' with 'the literature written in Spain' when we know that national borders, in cultural terms at least, are the fictions of political mapping?

The problem is, of course, that we somehow envisage cultures as firmly located, unmoving. Sangrador Gil's observation implies that it is the rootedness of Spanish culture that is to be admired. Similarly, the organisation of modern-language philologically-based curricula promotes the idea that both culture and identity belong to a certain place, inherited from the land, rather than realities that are constantly in the process of becoming, as people, ideas and texts migrate through time and space, acquiring and accumulating new meanings, new beliefs, new values and new practices as they do so. Culture, as Jimmy Jack sees it, and philology represents it, requires permanence, a clinging to what is inherited from birth, an inheritance that must be organised and fortified through the sharing of secrets that keep others out.

---

[11] See A. Pym for a fuller account of de Morlei, *Method in translation history* (Manchester, 1998), esp. ch.1.

[12] Pym, *Translation history*, 12.

[13] See, for example, the book cited in n.10 above, or J. Francisco Ruiz Casanova *Aproximación a una historia de la traducción en España* (Madrid, 2000), esp. ch.2.

The contours of the land rapidly become the contours of the intellectual equivalent of a fortress mentality.

And this makes us guilty of privileging the history of those who refuse to let go, of those who erect mental and virtual barriers, of the cultural protectionists. And in the process we increasingly allow culture to be reduced to the desire for permanent belonging. Most worryingly, the institution both replicates and interprets that desire. And meanwhile we undervalue the contribution of those who journey, who act as intermediaries between cultures and whose nomadic activities create the genuinely intercultural spaces in which so much real discovery and innovation takes place. Such spaces are only created through the act of translation, just as languages and cultures only interact through specific moments of exchange. There are no pre-ordained coordinates, no consistently marked interfaces, any more than we can meaningfully determine the pre-existing frontiers around cultures.[14] Contingency becomes the medium in which we must operate.

There is no room in an essay of this brief extension to rehearse the very good reasons, inside and outside the institution, why we should not only recognise interculturality and transcultural movement, but also assert them both as significant shaping forces of our cultural heritage and as defining features of the knowledge-based society of the twenty-first century. The history of that small city, fortified by position but open to the world, speaks of the way understanding, information and knowledge flow with the movement of peoples and texts. The translators of Toledo were aware that translation opens up discursive bridges between cultures, not just encouraging intellectual travel, but also establishing new categories of thought that bridge, transcend, fragment, even shatter, the contours of the known.

This is where Steiner emphasises the importance of the hermeneutic motion. The translators of Toledo were, of course, early examples of hermeneuts. In 1199 the great Sephardic philosopher Maimonides wrote a letter to Ben Tibbon, one of the most prolific translators of the first period of the school:

> The translator must above all clarify the development of thought in the original, then write it, comment upon it, and explain it so that the same process of thought is clear and comprehensible in the new language. That is how Hunain ben Ishaq translated Galen and his son Ishaq translated Aristotle.[15]

---

[14] For example, we know that the twelfth-century scholars Hermannus Dalmata (also known as Herman of Carinthia) and Robertus Ketenensis (Robert of Chester, or Kent) left France and England respectively and moved to then Hispania in search of Arabic science. They met each other, became translators, and between 1141 and 1143 they wrote the first translation of the Koran into a European language – Latin.

[15] The full letter in quoted in *Textos clásicos de teoría de la traducción*, ed. M. Angel Vega (Madrid, 1994). My translation.

In Maimonides's words we hear the early spirit of the Renaissance, an acknowledgement of the lessons that may be learned from varied experience, a recognition that, from that point on, identity would be increasingly forged through diaspora and difference. The act of translation is both a function of and a working model for the new possibilities of relationships between peoples and cultures, holding out the hope of transcending our over-specificities. We study the past presumably because we are aware that greater knowledge of the past gives us wider frames for assessing the future. The history of the School of Translators of Toledo allows us to affirm the validity of intercultural specificity, 'a kind of specificity that is not wholly compatible with histories and theories of what might be called sedentary cultures, the cultures that stay in place, the ones that have states and money to subsidise their products'.[16] These histories and theories work together with philology and exegesis to suggest that cultures, texts – and, by extension, identity – are enclosed, self-referential, knowable entities. And in that collusion they coalesce, with great authority, to keep power – the power to read, the power to know, the power to appropriate and own – lodged well within the institution.

In its day, the School of Translators of Toledo was at the forefront of advanced education.[17] We have already noted Daniel de Morlei's professed reason for journeying to the *urbs parva*. The School of Translators of Toledo, with its quadrivial teaching system and work deriving from both theory and practice, was already insisting on interdisciplinary teaching and research, on the ability to reason analogically, to recognise patterns in common among seemingly unrelated areas of knowledge and experience. It is the same recognition that prompts O'Donnell to teach English to the love-struck Maire. This is the pedagogy of the human borderlands, of a time of historical transition and cultural shift. Today, however, the specialisation of knowledge has reached extreme proportions, locking scholars and students into critical and philosophical monads. The philosophical and scientific convergences, the moments of qualitative change, that emerged when somebody mapped the third space between cultures or a discipline, have been well documented throughout history.[18]

But today? What happens when the contours of a curriculum no longer match the landscape of need?

---

[16] Pym, *Translation history*, 17.

[17] The fourfold intellectual model of the quadrivium was based on mathematics, geometry, music and astronomy. Each of the quadrivial sciences was – either by open acknowledgement or careful allusion – accompanied by its complementary metaphysical art (and its underpinning, the trivium of grammar, rhetoric and logic).

[18] Think, for example, of Kepler, who was led to his discovery of the mathematical laws of planetary motion by his investigation of the music of the spheres.

12

Translating cultures: suggestions from the Middle English Prose *Brut*

Stephen Kelly

I

While *translatio studii* – the translation of classical learning into new situations of pertinence – has been at the heart of Robert Jordan's career,[1] this essay is concerned with the associated, and arguably more controversial, rhetorical and historical trope, *translatio imperii*: the transmission and continuity of imperial, and imperialising, cultural forms and political structures. The beginnings of a larger study of the poetics of translation in what I'll refer to as the '*Brut* tradition', this essay seeks to foreground some of the contradictions inherent in the performance of *translatio imperii* in the culmination of the tradition, the Middle English Prose *Brut* chronicle. Nowhere, to my sorrow, does the essay engage in a sustained interrogation of the *Brut* – there simply isn't space to do justice to this amorphous text. Rather, the essay is concerned, in common with the themes of this volume, to outline some of the implications of translation, in theory and practice, for the *Brut* and its sponsoring historiographical tradition. The most popular secular English text of the Middle Ages, the Prose *Brut* represents a vernacular rendition of a tradition, from Geoffrey of Monmouth through Wace, Layamon and the Anglo-Norman and Latin *Bruts*, grounded in the mythic foundation of Britain by the Trojan Prince Brutus.[2] At the heart of this multilingual historiographical tradition is the project of articulating the

---

[1] While I have never worked directly with Bob, his reputation reached me through students we had in common, James George and Edward Moss. They spoke in reverential tones of his erudition, generosity and good humour – values which University Square, where I regularly bump into Bob, will sorely miss.

[2] Edited by F.W. Brie, *The* Brut, *or the chronicles of England* (repr. Woodbridge, 2000). For a survey of the Prose *Brut* in textual and manuscript form, see L. Matheson, *The Prose* Brut: *the development of a Middle English chronicle* (Medieval and Renaissance Texts and Studies, Tempe, AZ, 1998).

ethnic and political pre-eminence of the English in later medieval Britain.[3] The gestures and predispositions of *translatio imperii* are central to this enterprise, but, as this essay hopes to begin to suggest, the cultural dynamics implicit in the processes of translation reveal a series of paradoxes disruptive of the *Brut* tradition's colonial project.

II

Originating with Geoffrey of Monmouth's *Historia Regum Britanniae* (c.1136), which Geoffrey claims, with all the irony of a postmodern novelist, is based on a lost and 'very ancient book in the Welsh tongue', the history of Britain rooted in the conquest of the island by the Trojan Prince Brutus quickly became the principal historical account of British origins in the Middle Ages, surviving well into the early modern period. The appeal of the tradition lies in its totalising imagination: it glosses over ethnic upheaval and dynastic rupture by the sheer force of its mythographic vision of the ethnic integrity of Britain's rulers. Dismissed by its contemporaries, such as William of Malmesbury, and too often by modern historians, as a work of deceit and invention, the extraordinary achievement of Geoffrey's *Historia* is to have provided a culturally flexible template for an Anglo-Norman and, subsequently, English colonial polity. The work of an Anglo-Welsh cleric with an eye to pleasing his Norman masters, Geoffrey's *Historia* functioned to describe the inevitability, and therefore legitimacy, of the Norman invasion. Quickly translated and adapted – in Gaimar's *L'Estoire des Engleis*; in, most significantly, Wace's *Roman de Brut*; in Piers Langtoft's chronicle, which in turn adapts Wace – Geoffrey's version of the Brutus narrative first reaches English in the form of Layamon's *Brut*, but permeates the textual cultures of thirteenth- and fourteenth-century Britain in myriad forms. Anglo-Norman and Latin antecedents of what we now recognise as the English Prose *Brut* appear from the reign of Edward I onwards, with the Latin versions, interestingly, succeeding the Anglo-Norman texts. What Lister Matheson suggests of the Middle English Prose *Brut* – that it 'develops by a process of accretion'[4] – is arguably true of the entire tradition. Indeed, that process of accretion occurs both textually – the Middle English *Brut* draws various other historiographical texts, such as *The short English metrical chronicle*, into its vortex – and linguistically; Brutus narratives exist in Welsh, English, Scots English, Latin and Anglo-Norman,

---

[3] After the Wycliffite Bible, the *Brut* is the single most copied extant text in Middle English. While adjudging popularity in manuscript cultures is a notorious and treacherous business, it is fair to say that, with one hundred and eighty three manuscript versions – a figure far outnumbering the manuscript remains of Chaucer, Gower, Langland or Lydgate – the *Brut* was enormously popular in late medieval England and further afield.
[4] Matheson, *The Prose Brut*, 6.

and the Middle English *Brut* frequently draws on these multiple versions.⁵ The consummation of the Galfridian tradition, the Prose *Brut* survives in forty-nine Anglo-Norman manuscripts; 183 Middle English manuscripts and around twenty Latin manuscripts; as Matheson states:

> The amount of time and labour that went into the production of such a number of manuscripts... must have made the *Brut* omnipresent for those engaged and interested in the book trade in the fifteenth century, whether as scribes, illuminators, binders, and booksellers or as librarians, readers, hearers, and owners.⁶

It has as much to do with its status as the continuation and extension of an historiographical tradition as to any claims it makes to the historical record that the *Brut* remains the definitive history of Britain in the late medieval and early modern periods. And I will argue that translation as an operation must play a crucial role in maintaining the text's cultural momentum. The Prose *Brut* is therefore a multilingual text *par excellence*, drawing on texts in a range of insular languages in its attempts to delineate the inevitability of English dominance of Britain. But already, there is a contradiction in this: the Prose *Brut* both necessitates and denies the multiple ethnicities of the British Isles in its assertions of English dominance.

Thanks to their investment in Anglophone cultures contemporary medievalists often assume that the process of 'vernacularisation' begins in Britain in the fourteenth century, but it would probably be more accurate to say that the twelfth century sees the first expansive use of a vernacular language, Norman French. Users of French appear, according to Ian Short, 'as alternative voices to that of the ecclesiastical establishment.' French is the language of 'a powerful lay majority'; while it by no means subsumes Latin, it contributes to a multilingualism with powerful cultural connotations: 'not so much a *vox populi*... as a plurality of *voces communes*'.⁷

Together with Latin and French, myriad other languages, including of course English, persist so that we have, according to Short, a situation of genuine 'ethnic plurality':

> [W]hen we... consider the inventiveness and the precociousness of the literature of England it will be difficult to believe that this was not due in large measure to the

---

⁵ Work carried out by William Marx and by Jason O'Rourke demonstrates that for the compiler of one Prose *Brut* manuscript, National Library of Wales MS 21608, the comparison of the English text with the distinct counter-tradition of Welsh *Brut* narratives was a procedural necessity. See W. Marx, 'Aberystwyth, National Library of Wales, MS 21608 and the Middle English Prose *Brut*', *Journal of the Early Book Society*, 1 (1997), 1–16, and S. Kelly and J. O'Rourke, 'Culturally mapping the Middle English Prose *Brut*: a report from the Imagining History project', *Journal of the Early Book Society*, 6 (2003), 41–60.

⁶ Kelly and O'Rourke: 'Culturally mapping the Middle English Prose *Brut*', 9.

⁷ I. Short, 'Language and literature', *A companion to the Anglo-Norman world*, ed. C. Harper-Bill and E. van Houts (Woodbridge, 2003), 192.

> multi-culturalism and multi-lingualism of the wider community of which it was formed... In addition to the five major dialects of English, the languages that were in use in twelfth century Britain included Welsh, Cornish, Irish, Gaelic (not to mention Manx and a presumably moribund Cumbric), alongside the Anglo-Norman dialect of French... and of course... the Church's *lingua franca* of Latin.

As I shall argue later, it is not enough, as scholars of multilingualism often do, to argue that medieval England has a marketplace of languages from which speakers or writers might consciously or unconsciously choose, in the form of 'loaning' or 'code-switching'.[8] Linguistic anthropology alerts us to the cultural embeddedness of language: its rootedness in historical, social, political and ideological archives and 'life-worlds'. By the time the *Brut* is being translated into English in the fourteenth and fifteenth centuries, the situation of English and Anglo-Norman may have changed, with Anglo-Norman displaced by a Continental form of French in the court of Richard II,[9] but the ethnic plurality recognised by Short has not dissipated. While the myriad language communities of the twelfth century may have undergone greater homogeneity, the languages of Britain remain freighted with the experience of intercultural negotiation and exchange. The Middle English Prose *Brut*, then, in its account of a Britain dominated by the English, is therefore inevitably and paradoxically intercultural. Indeed, the operations of translation guarantee the transmission of an intercultural account of English ethnicity, even while subsuming ethnic plurality within a programme of *translatio imperii*.

If the *Brut* has suffered almost universal neglect in twentieth-century literary studies, its contribution to our understanding of forms of national self-consciousness and ethnicity in later medieval Britain is arguably invaluable. However, in critical surveys of 'nascent' nationalism in medieval Britain, the *Brut* hardly features. In Thorlac Turville-Petre's influential *England the nation*, the *Brut* is completely absent; in Kathy Lavezzo's more recent collection of essays, *Imagining a medieval English nation*, the *Brut* registers barely four fleeting references.[10] And in his controversial contribution to the new Oxford English Literary History series, *Reform and cultural revolution* James Simpson dismisses the *Brut* as 'an uncritical reproduction and continuation' of earlier Anglo-Norman and Latin versions of the Brutus story.[11] The *Brut* is ignored by literary critics because it is insufficiently artful

---

[8] See for example an otherwise extremely useful collection edited by D.A. Trotter: *Multilingualism in later medieval Britain* (Woodbridge, 2000).

[9] N. Watson, 'The politics of Middle English writing', *The idea of the vernacular: an anthology of Middle English literary theory, 1280–1520*, ed. J. Wogan-Browne, N. Watson, A. Taylor and R. Evans (Exeter, 1999), 332–333.

[10] T. Turville-Petre, *England the nation: language, literature and national identity, 1290–1340* (Oxford, 1996); *Imagining a Medieval English nation*, ed. K. Lavezzo (Minneapolis, 2004).

[11] J. Simpson, *Reform and cultural revolution: the Oxford English literary history, 1350–1547* (Oxford, 2002), 76.

and it is distrusted by historians because it is altogether too fanciful.[12] It occupies a discursive realm for which modern literary or cultural history has no name.[13] And yet, we might come to a better sense of that 'discursive realm' if we attend to the *Brut*'s status as a *translation* and to the considerable cultural potency and utility translation granted it for its fifteenth- and sixteenth-century readers.

III

Translation is inevitably intercultural. After all, translation represents the 'replication' in one language and grammar of an act of discourse in an alien, or 'other' (with all the connotations postmodernism has granted that term) language and grammar. The process of translation produces, according to Wolfgang Iser, a liminal space in which two cultures intermingle, before what might be termed a 'third space', the space of the translation as text, is elaborated.[14] 'Translation,' says Willis Barnstone, 'as with all transcription and reading of texts, creates a difference.'[15] For Lawrence Venuti, 'a translated text should be a site at which a different culture emerges, where a reader gets a glimpse of a cultural order and resistency.'[16] Venuti's notion of translation as a process in which a 'target' language is 'foreignised' by its 'source' language arguably underpins much of contemporary translation theory. Concerned to elaborate a liberal ethics of difference, with as much pragmatic political utility as theoretical sophistication, translation theory as practised by Venuti, Barnstone, Iser and others resists what might be termed 'canonising' translation, by which the cultural significance of the text to be translated is reaffirmed. For Venuti, this form of translation is to be avoided precisely because it supersedes the original text: 'a translation canonises the foreign text, validating its fame by enabling its survival. Yet the afterlife made possible by translation simultaneously cancels the originality of the foreign text.'[17]

---

[12] The AHRB-funded Imagining History project at Queen's, under the direction of Professor John Thompson, will for the first time provide the scholarly community with access to accounts of the manuscripts of the *Brut*. Alongside other work undertaken by the project team, we hope that this will lead to an increased interest in the text and its traditions. For further information, see: http://www.qub.ac.uk/imagining-history/

[13] While the *Brut* is nominally a chronicle, attention to the text reveals it to be vertiginously intertextual, incorporating a wide variety of late medieval discourses and genres, including insular and continental romance, monastic cartularies, hagiography, annalistic historiography, folklore, Arthuriana and so on.

[14] W. Iser, *The range of interpretation* (New York, 2000), 5–12 *passim*, and W. Iser, 'The emergence of a cross-cultural discourse: Thomas Carlyle's *Sartor Resartus*', *The translatability of cultures: figurations of the space between*, ed. S. Budick and W. Iser (Stanford, 1996), 264.

[15] W. Barnstone, *The poetics of translation: history, theory, practice* (New Haven, 1993), 18.

[16] L. Venuti, *The translator's invisibility: a history of translation* (London, 1995), 305.

[17] *Rethinking translation: Discourse, subjectivity, ideology*, ed. L. Venuti (London, 1992), 7.

It will be clear from this brief survey that contemporary translation theory is extremely anxious about translation as an act of cultural negotiation: 'in its broadest sense, translation means cross-cultural understanding.'[18] I think Rubel and Rosman's anthropological optimism here had better be tempered by suggesting that for most of its theorists, translation represents the *hope* of cross-cultural understanding. As Michael Cronin points out, 'translation relationships between minority and majority languages are rarely divorced from issues of power and identity, that in turn destabilise universalist theoretical prescriptions on the translation process.'[19] For Richard Jacquemond,

> Translation is not only the intellectual, creative process by which a text written in a given language is transferred into another. Rather, like any human activity, it takes place in a specific social and historical context that informs and structures it... In the case of translation, the operation becomes doubly complicated since, by definition, two languages and thus two cultures and societies are involved.[20]

I shall not repeat I.A. Richard's famous description of translation, reported in David Johnston's essay in this volume; suffice to say that the complexity of translation as a cultural process demands that we approach any translated text with theoretical sensitivity and historical care. In the case of the Middle English Prose *Brut*, the cultural and literary contexts, and philosophical complexity, of translation cut across any account of the text as an 'uncritical reproduction or continuation' (in James Simpson's thoughtless terms) of an earlier *Brut* tradition. Translation, as we shall see, is the key to the *Brut* tradition's cultural success but also to the ultimate failure of its imperialising literary project.

IV

However, nowhere does the Middle English Prose *Brut* signal its status as translation. The work of translation occurs silently, invisibly, inevitably. English ethnicity is assumed, unproblematically (but, of course, extremely problematically) to be multilingual. While the fact that the manuscript remains of the Prose *Brut* regularly present us with multilingual, and particularly Latin, annotations of the English text is not extraordinary, it does record the passage of the English text through communities which continue to be actively multilingual. In the case of one manuscript, Columbia University MS. Plimpton 261, we have translation and compilation taking place from a Latin version of the *Brut*, probably Oxford Bodleian Library MS.

---

[18] A. Rosman and P. Rubel, *Translating cultures: perspectives on translation and anthropology* (Oxford, 2003), 1.
[19] M. Cronin, *Translating Ireland: translation, languages and cultures* (Cork, 1996), 4.
[20] R. Jacquemond, 'Translation and cultural hegemony: the case of French-Arabic translation', ed. Venuti, *Rethinking translation*, 139.

Rawlinson C.398, either by or ascribed to 'Richardus Rede.' Throughout the fifteenth century, when English is beginning to assert its linguistic pre-eminence in the circles traditionally dominated by Latin, Anglo-Norman and French, we continue to have Anglo-Norman *Bruts* copied and disseminated. The Latin versions of the *Brut* derive from Anglo-Norman sources and sire translations into English which bear no or little relation to the other strands of English translation.[21]

The *Brut*'s multilingual status therefore articulates a series of cultural paradoxes. How could the *Brut*'s model of English ethnicity – which is predicated on the distinctiveness of the English in comparison to their insular neighbours – tolerate such a multilingual situation? I would suggest that the model of British identity presumed by the text attempts to transcend linguistic specificity by subsuming all languages in which the *Brut* appears to a notional English identity. Furthermore, ethnicity is modelled *spatially* and *territorially* rather than in an explicitly linguistic way. This is a strategy of considerable audacity by the *Brut*'s translators and copyists; the *Brut* elides difference in its concern to discern an English hegemony. Interestingly, this tendency goes against the grain of many concurrent translations into Middle English. Robert Mannyng's *Chronicle*, written in the mid fourteenth century, is an adaptation of Wace's *Roman de Brut* and Piers Langtoft's chronicle, both Anglo-Norman texts. However, according to Helen Philips:

> Despite his use of two texts written in French, one of Mannyng's themes is the oppression under which the 'true' English are still said to labour almost three centuries after the Norman Conquest. Written... in what Mannyng presents as the 'native' language of the country, the *Chronicle* thus offers itself as an attempt to repatriate a historical narrative that has too long been the property of readers of French – that is, the aristocracy.[22]

As Mannyng puts it, his translation is 'not for the lerid [learned] bot for the lewed,/ For tho that in this land won [dwell].'[23] Mannyng's association of the English vernacular with the 'communes' and the land – that is, his equation of people, language and space – naturalises English, arguing for its inevitable superiority to 'foreign' languages. Indeed, its superiority, in a gesture whose dynamics are familiar from postcolonial translations, is demonstrated paradoxically by its cultural *inferiority* and subservience to other languages:

> Mannyng's *Chronicle* and similar texts create a sense of English linguistic community by at once implying that the degraded status of the language is a token of forced servitude and that it is as flexible a medium as its rivals... But any attempt to accept

---

[21] Matheson, *The Prose Brut*, 4–7.
[22] H. Philips, 'Robert Mannyng, *Chronicle*: prologue', *The idea of the vernacular*, ed. Wogan-Browne et al., 19.
[23] *The idea of the vernacular*, ed. Wogan-Browne et al., 20.

Mannyng's view literally by portraying Middle English as an underdog, fighting a war of resistance against a powerful enemy, badly oversimplifies the issues.[24]

Indeed; and yet even when the status of English is becoming settled, a text like the *Speculum Vitae*, written within twenty of so years of Mannyng's *Chronicle*, and in a cultural moment when the use of English is being promoted by the clergy in the York diocese, feels compelled to distinguish itself linguistically:

> In Inglysche toung I shall you telle
> And ye sa lang with me wyll dwell
> Nat Latyn I wylle speke na waster
> Bot Inglysche that men uses maste. [*mostly use*]
> For that es our knyde langage [*natural language*]
> That we have here maste of usage,
> That canne ilk a man understand
> That es borne in Inglande.[25]

English is being explicitly promoted as a 'natural' language in the *Speculum Vitae*, with all the connotations of national integrity, ethnic distinctiveness and universalism which that entails. Albeit while the Middle English Prose *Brut* is disseminated a few decades later, it is surely significant that nowhere does it feel compelled to distinguish its version of the *Brut* from those in other languages. Figuratively speaking, the *Brut* nowhere lays claim to the land; it merely occupies it and dominates it. Its reach is national rather than local, and its implied audience is of masters rather than the 'communes.' In this it enacts the tactics of power symptomatic of *translatio imperii* and draws on the capacities of translation to transform both meanings and places.

V

While *translatio studii et imperii* pervades late medieval thinking about translation, the clichéd view that it underpinned medieval notions of authority and therefore of how cultural forms from earlier societies were inherited needs to be reviewed.[26] As Rita Copeland has shown, in the later Middle Ages *translatio* was also synonymous with invention; with the creation of new rhetorical forms, by Dante, Gower, Chaucer and others, rooted in a broad range of discursive and interlingual traditions.[27]

---

[24] Watson, 'The politics of Middle English writing', 335.
[25] Watson, 'The politics of Middle English writing', 336.
[26] On the development and range of meanings of *translatio studii et imperii*, see E.R. Curtius, *European literature and the Latin Middle Ages* (London, 1953), 29, 128, 384, and R. Copeland, *Rhetoric, hermeneutics and translation in the Middle Ages* (Cambridge, 1991). The classic account is E.H. Kantorowicz, *The king's two bodies: a study in medieval political theory* (Princeton, NJ, 1957).
[27] Copeland, *Rhetoric*, 179–220, *passim*.

The Prose *Brut*, however, has little truck with the innovations of insular or continental poets. It does not need to engage with these developments; rather, in its status as a translation of an established literary and textual tradition, it re-emphasises the historical need to 'translate' empire – its version of empire. In its vernacular versions, the *Brut* tradition reaffirms the inevitability of its model of an insular English empire precisely because it is the 'latest' in a concatenation of multilingual accounts of the Brutus story.

That 'inevitability' is arguably sustained by the dynamics of translation, and the functions that translation serves in the hermeneutical imagination of medieval readers. It should be remembered that in the Middle Ages, *translatio* doesn't just mean translation:

> In medieval Latin, the word *translatio* was often taken to be synonymous with *expositio* (interpretation). If this equation is taken seriously it provides a justification for understanding vernacular translations not simply as attempts to transfer meaning unchanged from one language to another but as readings of source texts, part of whose purpose may indeed lie in their difference from those texts.[28]

The act of translation-as-interpretation revivifies the earlier text, relocating it within a new register, with the result that the language into which a text is translated reactivates the semantic charge and hermeneutic surplus of the 'original' text. 'We have to remind ourselves,' says Wolfgang Iser, 'what interpretation has always been: an act of translation.' Furthermore, and in a crucial idea for my sense of the Prose *Brut*'s conception of *translatio imperii*, Iser adds: 'Each interpretation transposes something into something else. We should therefore shift our focus away from underlying presuppositions [regarding interpretation] *to the space that is opened when something is translated* into a different register [my italics].'[29]

The idea that the act of translation is also an act of transposition – literally, of taking something into a different space – has radical connotations for the colonial project of the *Brut* tradition and of the Prose *Brut* particularly. At the heart of the tradition is the project of asserting the dominance of the English over the main ethnic groups of Britain and Ireland. A concomitant concern of this project is the elaboration of a symbolic and narrative justification for the occupation of space within the archipelagic context of the British Isles. From Geoffrey of Monmouth to the Prose *Brut*, the Brutus legend serves to delineate the ownership of space in late medieval Britain.[30] I have already argued that Geoffrey's text is produced to in-

---

[28] R. Evans, A. Taylor, N. Watson and J. Wogan-Browne, 'The notion of vernacular theory', *The idea of the vernacular*, ed. Wogan-Browne et al., 317.
[29] Iser, *The range of interpretation*, 5.
[30] For the spatial politics and cultural utility of the Troy legend in the Middle Ages, see F. Ingledew, 'The book of Troy and the genealogical construction of history: the case of Geoffrey of Monmouth's *Historia Regum Britanniae*', *Speculum*, 69 (1994), 665–704.

gratiate himself with the Norman colonists of England, and to provide them with a narrative identity and colonial claim capable of counter-acting indigenous accounts.[31] By the time the Prose *Brut* is being disseminated, the English claim to ethnic superiority has all but been materially settled; but it has not yet achieved the status of cultural hegemony (indeed, does it ever?). Thus the necessity of translation: as the English language comes to acquire greater cultural cachet in the fourteenth and fifteenth centuries, the *Brut*'s model of the English cultural hegemony must be reasserted in a new situation of semantic pertinence; or, following the view of translation as *trans*-position, it must be relocated to satisfy the particularities of English language communities.

VI

And yet we return to the paradoxes of this extraordinary cultural project. If translation allows for the *Brut*'s emplotment of an English 'narrative identity' to be reinterpreted in a new linguistic context, the text must remain, given the nature of translation, marked by the *difference*, the *otherness*, of the cultures it translates and relocates in its *grand récit* of English ethnic and political mastery. We will remember that translation creates difference and ignites hermeneutical reflection. In its commitment to the cultural integrity of the source language, contemporary translation theory advocates 'foreignising' the target language. According to Rosman and Rubel, 'foreignising a text means that one must disrupt the cultural codes of the target language in the course of translation.'[32] This recalls Venuti's assessment of translation as the site at which a different culture emerges, or Iser's conception of the liminal space born of translation. But need the translator be consciously concerned with importing cultural difference in the act of translation for that difference to survive in the translated text?

I would suggest that difference is an inevitable feature of the multivalence of all discourses; indeed, it may be more primordial than that. Rosman and Rubel remind us of the Sapir-Whorf hypothesis, which 'asserts that human beings speaking different languages do not live in the same "real" world with different labels attached; they live in different worlds – language itself acts as a filter on reality, moulding our perceptions of the world around us.'[33] One need not subscribe to the controversial Sapir-Whorf position. Instead, take the Greek view of man as a language animal, or Heidegger's sense of language as the plane of Being; or Wittgenstein's assertion in the *Tractatus* that the limits of language are the limits of the world; or Paul Ri-

---

[31] See J. Gillingham, *The English in the twelfth century: imperialism, national identity and political values* (Woodbridge, 2000).
[32] Rosman and Rubel, *Translating cultures*, 7.
[33] Rosman and Rubel, *Translating cultures*, 12.

coeur's argument that the capacities of 'semantic innovation' inherent in language provide actions with templates of possibility. Languages are more profoundly part of our being than historical linguistics allows; the memories latent in contemporary language forms provide an etymological counter-history of our present self-conceptions. What happens to us when our languages mix? Is it any different in the case of the *Brut* and the cultures it translates?

Difference, then, and *histories* of difference, haunt any attempt to render one language into another. While the fifteenth- and sixteenth-century readers of the Anglo-Norman and Middle English *Bruts* read the same texts, the cultures which the texts embody, while nominally 'English', are radically different. The English text is perhaps marked by myths of indigenousness; the Anglo-Norman remembers better its colonial claim and asserts belonging to a now lost notion of Englishness, neither English or French. And one interpenetrates the other in the act of translation and interpretation, destabilising and undercutting the text's hope of ideological certainty. As Paul de Man remains us, 'the translation canonises, freezes, an original and shows in the original a mobility, an instability which at first one did not notice.'[34] Derrida goes further: 'The translation will truly be a moment in the growth of the original, which will complete itself in enlarging itself... And if the original calls for a complement, it is because at the origin it was not there without fault, full, complete, identical to itself.'[35]

VII

Derrida's suggestion chimes with my concluding thoughts on translation in the Middle English Prose *Brut*. Let us recall the situation of Geoffrey of Monmouth's *Historia Regum Britanniae*. 'No single figure,' says Ian Short, 'better illustrates the productive mix of England's pluralistic and trilingual society than the Anglo-Welshman Geoffrey of Monmouth.'[36] From its very origin, the colonial narrative begun by Geoffrey represents a negotiation of cultural difference; the Galfridian achievement is not to banish that difference but to distil it into a cultural resource of extraordinary utility and malleability. But what Geoffrey also illustrates, which is in turn amplified by the translation of the Brutus narrative back and forth between the languages of Britain, is the fundamental instability of the *Brut* tradition's colonial project and the inevitability of its failure. The *Brut*'s facility for translation, its deployment in multiple linguistic and cultural contexts, deconstructs its power as an ethnic myth of origin and reveals the paradoxes of insular colonialism as a po-

---

[34] P. de Man, '"Conclusions": Walter Benjamin's "the task of the translator"', *The resistance to theory* (Minneapolis, 1986), 82.
[35] Quoted in *Rethinking translation*, ed. Venuti, 7. Derrida's notion of *différance* has an obvious utility here.
[36] Short, 'Language and literature', 193.

litical and ideological enterprise. Indeed, the *Brut* begins in otherness, 'in the noble lande of Surrye [Syria]', and the exile, first of Diocletian's daughters, and then of Brutus himself, marks the subsequent colonisation of Britain in terms of loss rather than gain. Moreover, in the *Brut* the island of Britain is originally alien even to itself: 'and þe v day afterward they aryued in an hauene of Totnesse, & commen into þe Ile of Albion; & þer þey founde neiþer man ne woman, as þe story telleþ but Geantz.'[37] Giants, not the English (or French, or Saxons and Angles before them), are indigenous to Britain; when Brutus slays them, asserting a colonising polity as the guarantee of the legitimacy of English ethnicity, he merely subsumes, rather than overturns, the difference at the heart of English, and subsequently British, identity. Even as they deny their intercultural origins, the texts of the *Brut* tradition finally betray, like the processes and negotiations of translation, the inevitability of pluralism.

---

[37] Brie, *The Brut*, 1 and 10.

13

A Virgin 'lost in translation'?: another fine mess for Geoffrey Chaucer, John Lydgate and English literary history

John Thompson

The topic of this essay is the bibliographical misadventures of a short Middle English Marian poem generally known as 'An ABC to the Virgin'.[1] This is a work that was translated from continental French by Geoffrey Chaucer, and, apparently, greatly admired by Chaucer's near-contemporaries, but it only finally appeared in print as late as 1602, at a time when Chaucer was chiefly admired as a proto-protestant English poet. Such a decadent and late topic may well seem like small potatoes to someone such as Bob Jordan, who has worked for so much of his career on an enormous documentary archive from the eleventh-century monastery of Theotokos Evergetis, itself an institution dedicated to the Virgin and a productive religious house near Constantinople that has provided 'probably the largest and most detailed guide to medieval monastic liturgical practice to have come down to us'. My only excuse for offering Bob the following account of an abecedarian poem that was 'lost in translation' in the gutters of English printing history for over a century following Caxton's *Chaucer* (1478) is that my case study raises issues of fundamental importance for twenty-first-century humanities generally, and English literary history in particular. We have here a poem by a major English author, one that almost no undergraduate or postgraduate student is ever likely to want to read or enjoy as part of their experience of the English literary canon. But how is literary history formed? Who secures the writings that make up the canon or archive? What is their objective in so doing? What happens to texts and documents that do not fit the temper of the times? How do we counter the blind prejudice, educational ignorance, and intellectual arrogance that influences such decisions? Can ancient and unfashionable texts even have an afterlife that is worth retrieving? Can later readers complete (or erase) the work of much more ancient authors? How do we recover the evidence that bears witness to

---

[1] The standard modern edition is *The Riverside Chaucer*, ed. L.D. Benson, 3rd ed. (Oxford, 1988), 637–640 (text), 1076–1077 (explanatory notes), 1185 (ms and textual notes).

the various processes and textual 'events' outlined above and how do we make them tell their story in a twenty-first-century context?

I feel sure that these are all issues and questions that Bob himself will have already encountered, perhaps in slightly different forms, as a gifted teacher, translator and researcher of Greek and Latin texts. In writing this celebratory essay, I trust too that the general issues raised above will remain important and relevant for other likely readers of this volume, if only because of the current institutionalised and often narrow view of the Middle Ages, where both medievalists and postmodernist critics alike have sometimes been guilty of encouraging the presupposition that the so-called 'medieval' era is much more difficult to understand, more alien, more specialised and more cut off from early modern, modern and postmodern critical sensibilities, methodologies and interests than almost any other historical period that one can imagine.[2] From the academic vantage point provided by our various quite narrow disciplinary enclaves and dark corners, however, one is often now forced to witness the inevitable corollary of this unthinking endorsement of the supposed 'alterity' of the Middle Ages: that is the trend, so prevalent in certain influential and bullish contemporary political settings, including the media, where humanities disciplines, as represented by medieval studies, are considered largely irrelevant in the higher educational scheme of things. None of this bodes well for Chaucer's 'An ABC', of course. On the other hand, Bob is an obvious and fortunate exception to the recent fashionable critical trends described above. The values he has exemplified throughout his career are, indeed, worthy of continuing celebration in a festschrift volume of this kind.

For those of us interested in the literary implications of book history (arguably one of the most vibrant cross-disciplinary areas of study in today's highly-specialised RAE-driven research work in the humanities), the issues discussed in this essay can obviously contribute to our contemporary understanding of Chaucer's place as a translator in the English literary canon. I am thinking, in particular, of the largely synthetic and transcendent role Chaucer's poetical reputation was granted in the decades immediately following his death in 1400.[3] It was during those years that Chaucer was hailed for the first time, by Deschamps, as the 'grant translateur', and by Thomas Hoccleve, John Lydgate and many other near-contemporary writers, as the 'Father' of English poetry, an achievement that Lydgate, in particular, was careful to define according to classical literary models

---

[2] A view depressingly endorsed most recently by the intellectual presuppositions underlying a new Oxford series; see J. Simpson, *Reform and cultural revolution, 1350–1547* (The Oxford English Literary History, Oxford, 2002), II, esp. 1–6.

[3] I elaborate on the general points made here in J.J. Thompson, 'Reception: fifteenth to seventeenth centuries', *Chaucer: an Oxford guide*, ed. S. Ellis (Oxford, 2004), 497–511. The truly monumental documentary archive relating to this general topic remains C.F.E. Spurgeon, *Five hundred years of Chaucer criticism and allusion, 1357–1900*, 3 vols (Cambridge, 1925).

and precedents. It seems no coincidence that it was during the politically uncertain period immediately following the Lancastrian usurpation of 'England's empty throne' that Chaucer's posthumous reputation as a pious and completely conformist English translator-poet was secured among his metropolitan and courtly readers, again largely through the efforts of poet-followers such as Thomas Hoccleve and John Lydgate. Both poets were obviously active within the orbit of Lancastrian courtly patronage and both would appear to have been determinedly anxious to establish a 'Chaucer' literary aesthetic that would work to their professional advantage. The relevance of this to the puzzling bibliographical afterlife of Chaucer's only extant self-contained Marian poem in the years immediately following his death will become apparent shortly. On the other hand, Chaucer's reputation in the sixteenth century was largely as a proto-protestant satirical writer. According to John Foxe, in his *Actes and monumentes*, Chaucer was 'a right Wiclevian' – a largely reductive view of the poet as Wycliffite satirist that is often expressed in more sophisticated fashion but is still basically clung to in one myopic or ideologically-driven form or another by certain second and third-level English students, teachers and examination setters across Ireland, the UK, North America, Australia, and in the surprising number of other places in the world where Chaucer is simply and uncritically revered as the 'father' of Anglophone literature.[4] In this respect, Chaucer's reputation reached its apogee during the period of the English Reformations, at which time (so the story goes) Chaucer was fully 'protestantised' in print for a nation of reformed and chauvinistic English readers. Precisely how and why this happened still remains largely a mystery, but its effects are clear. Paradoxically, it was at exactly the same time, and in one of the same supposedly 'protestantised' printed texts (Thomas Speght's 1602 second edition of Chaucer's works), that Chaucer's most undeniably papist work, his short Marian translation, now the focus of this essay, finally emerged from a lengthy period of hibernation to appear in print for the first time.[5]

My opening paragraphs have obviously already consigned considerable socio-literary significance to Chaucer's inoffensive short Marian lyric. Indeed, the evidence of its earliest textual transmission in manuscript form suggests that 'An ABC' quickly became an English poetical translation that was expected to bear considerable weight, particularly the baggage of other translated versions of its ultimate source which directly influenced John Lydgate's 'Lancastrian' translation of that source, and Lydgate's own version of Chaucer's posthumous reputation, as I shall demonstrate slightly later in this discussion.[6] The Chaucer poem itself is an

---

[4] For an infuriating but also stimulating polemical account of our investment in claiming a transhistorical familiarity with Chaucer, while always attempting to shape him in our own likeness, see S. Trigg, *Congenial souls: readings in Chaucer from medieval to postmodern* (Minneapolis, 2002).

[5] J.J. Thompson, 'Chaucer's "an ABC" in and out of context', *Poetica*, 37 (1993), 38–48.

[6] See also D. Pearsall, *John Lydgate (1371–1449): a bio-bibliography* (Victoria, BC, 1997).

imaginative translated version of a similarly-structured French prayer that had been originally etched into Guillaume de Deguileville's *Pèlerinage de la vie humaine*. The English poem is more than simply a line-for-line translation, however, since Chaucer has clearly ransacked other parts of de Deguileville's lengthy allegorical work for inspiration throughout his ambitious experimentation with the abecedarian translation process. The resultant translation now survives as a fully independent Middle English poem in nine extant fifteenth-century English manuscript miscellanies, often in literary anthologies that preserve other short works by Chaucer alongside it, also numerous short religious, amatory or moral items written in a similarly 'metropolitan' and 'courtly' vernacular English style.[7] Sometimes the other items in these collections were written by Hoccleve or Lydgate, but more often they are by unnamed English poets who were obviously capitalising on the developing fifteenth-century English taste for French-style polite reading, without feeling any particular need to identify themselves or assemble their own poetical canon within the manuscript culture in which they operated.

Modern editors have agreed that the seven other surviving fifteenth-century manuscripts of 'An ABC' form a single distinctive textual grouping.[8] In six of these, Chaucer's poem is no longer self-contained but has instead been reinserted in an anonymous early fifteenth-century Middle English prose translation of the de Deguileville work.[9] It is added at the equivalent point in the *Pèlerinage de la vie humaine* narrative from which Chaucer had first derived it, at the point where the allegorical character Grace Dieu presents a miraculously-produced abecedarian scriptural prayer for the Pilgrim sinner. The miracle text is now Chaucer's, of course, but, perhaps surprisingly, this skilful relocation and reintegration of his translated text is achieved without the anonymous later English translator-compiler showing readers the slightest sign that 'An ABC' in the English prose version was in fact originally translated/written by the Father of English poetry. In these codicological contexts, Chaucer's authorship of the poem simply does not appear to have been relevant or an issue worth recording. Similarly, in the only other extant manuscript belonging to this distinctive textual grouping, 'An ABC' is presented anonymously. It was apparently derived directly from the de Deguileville English prose version to make good a perceived flaw in the truncated text of the Middle English *Cursor Mundi*, an encyclopaedic and surprisingly entertaining and informative Christian version of world history structured largely along Augustinian

---

[7] J. Boffey and J.J. Thompson, 'Anthologies and miscellanies: production and choice of text', *Book production and publishing in Britain, 1375–1475* (Cambridge, 1989), 279–315.
[8] Benson, *Riverside Chaucer*, 1185.
[9] *The pilgrimage of the lyfe of the manhode*, ed. A. Henry, 2 vols (EETS, o.s. 288, 292, Oxford, 1985, 1988).

lines that immediately precedes the Marian poem in this particular anthology setting.[10]

John Lydgate was much more effusive in his praise of Chaucer's achievement as a translator in 1426 when he took on a commission to produce another de Deguileville English verse translation, on this occasion for a prominent Lancastrian, Thomas Montagu, Earl of Salisbury. Salisbury was the husband of Chaucer's granddaughter, Alice, so it is hardly unexpected that Lydgate should attempt to capitalize on the translation work of his illustrious predecessor. As such, Lydgate inserts a lengthy encomium, just before the point in his own translation at which one might reasonably have expected him to insert Chaucer's 'An ABC'.[11] His lines invoke the image of the dead master poet of Britain who dutifully approached the task as if he was undertaking a vernacular biblical translation – as such, he writes of the translator's art in terms that maintain the conventional distinction often made by medieval authors between 'substance'/matiere/matter and 'sentence'/sens/meaning.[12] He credits Chaucer, ahistorically, for what might pass as a 'Lancastrian-sponsored' attitude of unimpeachable religious orthodoxy and translatorly accuracy and thoroughness:

> Affter the French he dyde yt ryme,
> Word by word, as in substaunce,
> Ryght as yt ys ymad in fraunce,
> Fful devoutly, in sentence… (19756–19759).

Lydgate is not renowned for the innovatory nature of his own translation activities and he seems a writer who would have valued precisely those characteristics here attributed to Chaucer. His words seem a very odd way to characterise Chaucer's achievement as translator in 'An ABC', especially his judicious selection and pruning of the French source and his evident delight in playing with current vernacular legal jargon, manipulating certain technical terms to provide potent metaphors for contemporary religious practices. Lydgate's words also fail to appreciate the other adventurous forms of linguistic and metrical experimentation that enabled Chaucer to develop a fresh approach to the standard religious treatment of Marian themes he found in de Deguileville's French text. Instead, Lydgate invokes an image of Chaucer as the totally orthodox and religious poet, an image that closely follows up and elaborates on Thomas Hoccleve's earlier

---

[10] J.J. Thompson, *The cursor mundi: poem, texts and contexts* (Oxford, 1998), 88–96.

[11] All references are to the text and line numbering in *The pilgrimage of the life of man, Englisht by John Lydgate*, ed. F.J. Furnivall and K.B. Locock, (EETS, e.s. 77, 83, 92 (1899, 1901, 1904), repr. 1 vol., 1973).

[12] A.J. Minnis, *Medieval theory of authorship: scholastic literary attitudes in the later Middle Ages* (London, 1984).

claim in the *Regiment of princes* (written over a decade previously) that Chaucer had written 'ful many a lyne' in praise of the Virgin. This is probably an exaggeration. Apart from 'An ABC', Chaucer did indeed write a few lines in praise of the Virgin, some of which (the *Invocacio ad Mariam*) ended up in the *Second nun's prologue*, while other lines on a similar Marian theme form part of the *Prioress's prologue*, with both sets of material now submerged within the linking passages in the narrative frame structure of the *Canterbury tales*. Intriguingly, Lydgate's reconstructed version of Chaucer's orthodox and unadventurous piety as a writer/translator also reflects the apparently lifelike image variously pressed into service in the earliest visual representations of Chaucer as an English poet, in the Ellesmere manuscript of the *Canterbury tales* (San Marino, Huntington Library, MS Ellesmere 26.C.9), possibly completed during Chaucer's lifetime, and in an early copy of Hoccleve's *Regiment of princes* (London, British Library MS Harley 4866), produced about fifteen years after Chaucer's death.[13] Both were projects in which Thomas Hoccleve probably had a hand, as a London scribe, a poet-translator and Chaucer aficionado who probably knew Chaucer from his Westminster dealings and was also involved in the early fifteenth-century London book trade.[14] Lancastrian propaganda purposes, it seems, were served well by the iconic value of the seemingly 'authentic' and 'lifelike' conventionally pious Chaucer image so created, although the image itself was ultimately compromised (in reformed Tudor eyes, at least) by the eventual emergence, just over a century later, of an ideologically sounder proto-protestant and quintessentially 'English' Chaucer.

While Lydgate obviously acknowledged Chaucer as the 'grant translateur' of English literary history, the encomium in his de Deguileville translation also allows the later poet to take upon himself the role of compiler-translator. In order for him to 'enlwmyne' his 'lytyl book' (19782–19783), Lydgate says he will graft ('ympen', 19779) Chaucer's poem onto his text:

> And as he made thys Orysoun
> Off ful devout entencioun,
> And by maner off a prayere
> Ryht so I wyl yt settyn here,
> That men may knowe and pleynly se
> Off Our Lady the .A. b. c. (19785–19790).

---

[13] Discussion and reproduction of the images in D. Pearsall, *The life of Geoffrey Chaucer* (Oxford, 1992), 285–305.

[14] J.J. Thompson, 'A poet's contacts with the great and the good: further consideration of Thomas Hoccleve's texts and manuscripts', *Prestige, authority and power: studies in later medieval manuscripts*, ed. F. Riddy (York, 2000), 77–101.

The emphasis is on 'illuminating' the book and 'seeing' the grafted text, thus suggesting that the visual experience of Lydgate's readers and their participatory function in the production of his text was an important consideration for him at this juncture. 'An ABC' here seems set fair to take on some of the same iconic value as the 'lifelike' Chaucer portraits that were pressed into service in some, but not all, manuscripts of Hoccleve's *Regiment of princes*.[15] The use of the future tense here also seems relevant; Lydgate says he *will* set the Chaucer text in place, yet in all four extant manuscripts preserving his de Deguileville translation, there is absolutely no evidence that the planned insertion of 'An ABC' took place. Instead, an appropriate space has been reserved for the short Chaucer text at the relevant point in each of the copies, without the text itself ever having been added. Chaucer's 'An ABC' was evidently 'lost in translation' in the transition from translator/compiler to scribe/book producer and reader at this intriguingly well-documented moment in its eventful textual history.

A later sixteenth-century owner and second copyist of one of these Lydgate manuscripts (London, British Library, MS Stowe 952) was the famous Londoner and Chaucer editor, John Stow.[16] Stow is renowned for his ability to patch and repair the damaged and incomplete texts he found in fifteenth-century manuscripts that passed through his hands. At some stage, probably after his 1561 Chaucer edition, he examined and annotated no fewer than four of the surviving manuscript collections containing short works by Chaucer, Hoccleve, Lydgate and others, referred to briefly above, all of which also preserve texts of Chaucer's 'An ABC'. Any one of these codices could have provided him with copy to make good the apparent and heavily-advertised textual lacuna in MS Stowe 952. Quite uncharacteristically, Stow seems to have been content to ignore that fact, with the result that Chaucer's Marian poem remained lost from sight until 1602 and its first printing in Thomas Speght's second Chaucer edition.[17] But Stow probably also played a slightly more illustrious role in the final chapter in this story of the wilful editorial neglect of an authentic Chaucer text. In publishing his two Chaucer editions, Speght relied heavily on Stow's continuing scholarly detective work among an extraordinarily broad range of Chaucer manuscripts. The recognisably modern process of best text editing on the basis of careful textual collation was clearly an option for Stow that he never fully explored. Yet, when 'An ABC' was finally printed by Speght, its text was taken from one of the manuscripts Stow is known to have consulted (Cambridge, University Library, MS Gg. 4. 27), with its

---

[15] On the implications of this see J.J. Thompson, 'After Chaucer: resituating middle English poetry in the late medieval and early modern period', *New directions in later medieval manuscript studies*, ed. D. Pearsall (York, 2000), 183–199.

[16] A. Hudson, 'John Stow', *Editing Chaucer, the great tradition*, ed. P.G. Ruggiers (Norman, OK, 1984), 53–70.

[17] D. Pearsall, 'Thomas Speght', *Editing Chaucer*, ed. Ruggiers, 71–92.

title probably derived from a heading now extant only in Cambridge, Magdalene College, MS Pepys 2006, another copy that is known to have passed through Stow's hands.[18]

Stow's continuing interest in and involvement with the textual history of 'An ABC' was probably crucial since its inclusion in Speght's 1602 Chaucer edition serves to temper the strident reformed voice of Jack Upland's *Complaint against friars,* a text that had also forced its way into the Chaucer canon at this point, in a text Speght derived from John Foxe's *Actes and monumentes*. Speght's rubric for the authentic Chaucer item, by contrast, emphasises its early date, claiming that it was 'made, as some say, at the request of Blanch, Duchesse of Lancaster, as a praier for her priuat vse, being a woman in her religion very deuout'. In other words, in addition to its impeccable textual pedigree, the text is here presented as a genteel curiosity from the old religion, reflecting the private devotional habits of the first wife of John of Gaunt, Chaucer's earliest known literary patron. It was for the Lancaster household that Chaucer's earliest dateable poem, the *Book of the duchess,* had been written in commemoration of Blanch's death. As such, the terms in which 'An ABC' enters the Chaucer canon are particularly noteworthy since the 1602 'Speght' rubric reminds one strikingly of the nostalgic tone of Stow's reminiscences in his *Survey of London*. It is in the Survey that Stow recalls the vestiges of the old religion that still survive in the scarred remains of the city churches he had patiently walked around and inventorised. Through such processes of reminiscence and myth making, London's pre-Reformation history was located by Stow who, unlike Speght, was not a gentleman, and whose Elizabethan religious beliefs had long remained suspect, in an old-fashioned world that was far too rapidly becoming, for Stow, almost completely lost from sight. By the same token, it was probably through Stow's good graces that Chaucer's short Marian poem was at last allowed to come in from the cold to take its newly-prepared place in Speght as an antiquated but interesting part of Chaucer's life record and the stridently-protestantised English literary canon to which the father of English poetry obviously belonged as the English Virgil.

---

[18] Thompson, 'After Chaucer', 195–197.

14

'The adorning of my native tongue': linguistic metamorphosis in Milton

Estelle Haan

> It were as wise to cast a violet into a crucible that you might discover the formal principle of its colour and odour, as seek to transfuse from one language into another the creations of a poet.
>
> (Shelley, *A defence of poetry*)[1]

Thus proclaimed Shelley in a famous caveat about the perils of translation. A whole host of literary examples spanning several centuries and as many languages could be cited as a means of determining the truth or otherwise of this statement. But something of its rather blinkered nature emerges once it is acknowledged that translation in itself may possess an ability to recreate. It is an ability, it will be argued, that manifests itself on several levels, whereby the very nature and process of 'transfusing' an original creation from one language into another can in fact function as a liberating process – liberating from at least two different perspectives. Firstly, it enhances the dissemination and consequently the reception of a text by rendering it accessible to a wider readership; secondly, it can simultaneously result in the enrichment of the language into which that text has been transfused. Contrary to Shelley's viewpoint, then, surely there is much to be 'gained in translation' in linguistic as well as in methodological terms? Or, as Walter Benjamin puts it:

> Translation is so far removed from being the sterile equation of two dead languages that of all literary forms it is the one charged with the special mission of watching over the maturing process of the original language and the birth pangs of its own.[2]

This discussion will concern itself both with an 'original' language (Latin), and with the 'maturing process' of two further languages: one, a pseudo-original, as it were

---

[1] Text is that of *Percy Bysshe Shelley: selected poetry and prose*, ed. A.D.F. Macrae (London and New York, 1991), 209.
[2] W. Benjamin, 'The task of the translator,' *Illuminations*, tr. H. Zohn, ed. H. Arendt (London, 1970), 69–82, at 73. For further discussion see C. Martindale, *Redeeming the text: Latin poetry and the hermeneutics of reception* (Cambridge, 1993), 75–77.

(neo-Latin); the other, a seventeenth-century English vernacular. It will do so by focusing on one case in point: that of John Milton, for whom, it will be argued, 'translation' in a variety of guises helped to engender differing forms of linguistic metamorphosis: the 'birth pangs' of innovative neo-Latin and vernacular tongues. It will interpret 'translation' in its broadest of senses, not merely as a rendering from one language into another, but also and essentially as appropriation, invention, and linguistic experimentation: from neo-Latin (Mantuan) into neo-Latin (Milton); from classical Latin (Horace) into the vernacular (Milton); from neo-Latin (Milton) into the vernacular (Milton), as a Renaissance poet eventually 'translates' himself in a variety of ways. It will emerge, moreover, that 'translation', as exemplified by Milton, is inextricably linked to Renaissance debate on the relative merits of Latin and the vernacular (the *Questione della lingua*), to pedagogical theory and practice (as manifested in such exercises as the 'double translation system', the 'turning of verses', and the 'metaphrase'), and especially to that peculiarly distinctive form of bilingualism so integral to Milton's poetic practice.

And it is with that bilingualism, and what would appear to be its associated paradoxes, that this discussion commences. While Milton has been regarded (and quite justifiably so) as a polyglot,[3] his poetic corpus proclaims what is for the most part an irrefutable bilingualism.[4] At first glance his comparative use of Latin and the vernacular is not without several tensions. I enumerate here what could be termed (in a reinvention of Empson's famous phrase) 'seven types of ambiguity,'[5] or, more accurately, seven types of linguistic ambiguity[6] attending Milton's respective usages of Latin and the vernacular.

1) A prolific author of Latin verse during his Cambridge years,[7] Milton is nonetheless conspicuous by his absence from bilingual anthologies endlessly produced by Cambridge University on the occasions of royal births, marriages or deaths. 2)

---

[3] See, for example, J.K. Hale, *Milton's languages: the impact of multilingualism on style* (Cambridge, 1997), *passim*. Hale, 1, describes Milton as 'a humanist who wrote poems in four languages (Latin, Greek and Italian as well as his mother-tongue)… a lifelong polyglot whose writings evince knowledge of three Semitic languages and further modern languages.'

[4] As noted below, the 1645 volume: *Poems of Mr John Milton: both English and Latin* is presented as a bilingual volume. Furthermore almost half of Milton's prose writings are in Latin.

[5] Cf. W. Empson, *Seven types of ambiguity* (New York, 1947; revised ed. 1966).

[6] On 'ambiguity', cf. Empson, *Seven types of ambiguity*, 1: 'I propose to use the word in an extended sense, and shall think relevant to my subject any verbal nuance, however slight, which gives room for alternative reactions to the same piece of language.' The present discussion 'extends' this even further to embrace the level of reader response, or 'alternative reactions' to Milton's languages themselves, and to his apparently fluctuating choice between various linguistic media.

[7] Datable to Milton's Cambridge period are seven Latin elegies, several occasional pieces on university academics, a miniature Latin epic poem on the Gunpowder Plot (and five associated Latin epigrams), and two quasi-philosophical pieces on the decay of nature and the Aristotle/Plato controversy respectively.

When he does make his sole contribution to such (famously in his pastoral poem *Lycidas*, mourning the death of Edward King, a Latin poet),[8] he writes it not in Latin, but in English, producing a piece that functions as the resounding climax of the vernacular section of a bipartite Cambridge volume, the *Iusta Edovardo King* (1638).[9] 3) While Milton through the publication of *Comus* (1637) and *Lycidas* (1638) had achieved no small acclaim as an English poet, later that very year in the course of his Italian journey it was as a neo-Latin poet that he promoted himself among foreign litterati. Here the benefits of Latin as a universal language are self-evident. Hence it is for his recitation of Latin verse that he is acclaimed in the minutes of a Florentine academy.[10] Likewise it was Latin poetry that he composed during that sojourn and presented to Italian academicians.[11] 4) Hand in hand with such self-promotion, however, is Milton's associated announcement that it was at this time that he began to contemplate writing a great English epic, stating that his so-called decision in favour of the vernacular over Latin[12] was governed very much by

---

[8] On King as a Latin poet, see the excellent edition and discussion by Nigel Postlethwaite and Gordon Campbell: 'Edward King, Milton's *Lycidas*: poems and documents', *Milton Quarterly*, 28.4 (1994), 77–111.

[9] Part I of the *Iusta* consists of twenty Latin and three Greek poems; part II: of thirteen English poems. Milton's *Lycidas* is the last and the longest. See *Iusta Edovardo King: a facsimile edition of the memorial volume in which Milton's Lycidas first appeared*, ed. E. Le Comte (Norwood, 1978). Hale, *Milton's languages*, 21, interestingly suggests that Milton may have derived from the *Iusta* the idea for his own bilingual 1645 volume.

[10] That Milton recited his Latin poetry before the Florentine Accademia degli Svogliati is attested by its minutes of 6/16 September 1638, which single him out for his reading of 'a very erudite Latin hexameter poem': 'furono lett' alcune compositioni et particolarmente il Giovanni Miltone Inglese lesse una poesia Latina di versi esametri multo erudita' (Biblioteca Nazionale Centrale, Florence, MSS Magliabecchiana, MSS. Cl. IX, cod. 60, f. 48). The minutes of 7/17 March 1639 include Milton among those who read 'some noble Latin verses': 'nell' Accademia si trovarono li signori... Miltonio... Furon ... letti alcuni nobili versi latini' (Biblioteca Nazionale Centrale, Florence, MSS Magliabecchiana, MSS. Cl. IX, cod. 60, f. 52). For a full discussion, see E. Haan, *From academia to amicitia: Milton's Latin writings and the Italian academies* (Transactions of the American Philosophical Society, 88.6: Philadelphia, 1998), 10–28. Milton's skill as a Latinist is highlighted in the written encomia he received in his honour from academicians in Florence, Rome and Naples. See Haan, *From academia to amicitia*, 38–52, 82–85, 130–136.

[11] See, for example, *Ad Salsillum, Mansus*, and the three Latin epigrams in honour of Leonora Baroni. For fuller discussion, see Haan, *From academia to amicitia, passim*.

[12] However, Milton's 'decision' in favour of his native language is anticipated in such an early work as *At a vacation exercise*, significantly entitled *Part Latin, part English*. After a Latin section consisting of an *Oratio* and a *Prolusio*, Milton somewhat self-consciously asserts: 'The Latin Speeches ended, the English thus began.' He proceeds (lines 1–10) to salute the English language, assuming an apologetic tone as he invokes its assistance and begs pardon for his neglect. He recalls the mispronunciations he uttered as a child, and humbly speaks of his inability to do full justice to his native tongue. The implication is that it is English rather than Latin which is

the precedent of such Italian poets as Ariosto.[13] 5) In what is by now a characteristic paradox Milton announces that decision almost in the same breath as his boast about the 'written encomiums'[14] which he received (and those for his Latin poems) from Italian academicians. And the ambiguities do not end here. 6) Upon his return to England in 1639, he composed a pastoral poem, the *Epitaphium Damonis*, lamenting the premature death of his close boyhood friend Charles Diodati. But here he does what he did not do in the case of *Lycidas*: composes it in Latin. And once again there is an implicit irony. 7) It is in this Latin pastoral (lines 168–178) that he announces what would appear to be his decision to abandon Latin verse altogether, and to assume the vernacular henceforth.[15] While it is certainly true that after 1639 Milton composed only one further Latin poem (a piece sent to the Bodleian Librarian to accompany a replacement of a lost copy of his 1645 volume of poetry),[16] the precise nature of that decision is something to which this discussion will have reason to return.

---

inbred in him. All quotations from Milton's Latin and minor English poems are from *Milton: complete shorter poems*, ed. J. Carey, 2nd ed. (London, 1997).

[13] 'For which cause, and not only for that I knew it would be hard to arrive at the second rank among the Latines, I apply'd my selfe to that resolution which Ariosto follow'd against the perswasions of Bembo, to fix all the industry and art I could unite to the adorning of my native tongue; not to make verbal curiosities the end, that were a toylsom vanity, but to be an interpreter and relater of the best and sagest things among mine own Citizens throughout this Iland in the mother dialect. That what the greatest and choycest wits of Athens, Rome, or modern Italy, and those Hebrews of old did for their country, I in my proportion with this over and above of being a Christian, might doe for mine: not caring to be once nam'd abroad, though perhaps I could attaine to that, but content with these British Ilands as my world.' (*Reason of church government*). All quotations from Milton's prose works are from *The works of John Milton*, ed. F.A. Patterson, et al (New York, 1931–1940), hereinafter abbreviated to *CM*. The present extract occurs at *CM* 3, 236–237. It is likely too that Milton was influenced in no small degree by his witnessing or participating in debates in the Italian academies on the relative merits of Latin and the vernacular. On Milton's interest in the Italian vernacular as expressed during his Florentine periods, cf. his Latin letter to Benedetto Buonmattei (31 August/10 September 1638), in which he asks him to include in his forthcoming work on the Tuscan dialect a guide to pronunciation for foreigners (*CM*, 12, 34). See Haan, *From academia to amicitia*, 17–18.

[14] 'But much latelier in the privat Academies of Italy... some trifles which I had in memory, compos'd at under twenty or thereabout (for the manner is, that every one must give some proof of his wit and reading there), met with acceptance above what was lookt for, and other things which I had shifted in scarsity of books and conveniences to patch up amongst them, were receiv'd with written Encomiums, which the Italian is not forward to bestow on men of this side the Alps... ' (*Reason of church government*: *CM*, 3, 235–236).

[15] Cf. Hale, *Milton's languages*, 57–61.

[16] The *Ad Ioannem Rousium*. See S.P. Revard, '*Ad Ioannem Rousium*: Elegiac wit and pindaric mode', *Milton Studies*, 19 (1984), 205–226, reworked in her *Milton and the tangles of Neaera's hair* (Missouri, 1997), 237–263; E. Haan, 'Milton's *Ad Ioannem Rousium* and the 1645 volume,' *Notes and Queries*, 51.4 (December 2004), 356–360.

Do these apparent paradoxes, these seven types of linguistic ambiguity, as I have termed them, necessarily imply a tension between Latin and the vernacular in terms of Milton's methodology and poetic career? Did all roads lead to that decision enunciated in a somewhat grandiloquently self-conscious pronouncement? Or might not the obvious felicity with which he shifts between the two languages suggest something rather different? Perhaps Latin and the vernacular were not always 'conscious' alternatives or mutually exclusive media, but rather, to appropriate a famous Miltonic image, parts of a linguistic 'two-handed engine',[17] so to speak. This possibility is actually corroborated by the fact that the published Milton, the author of the 1645 volume, presented himself as a bilingual poet. This is evident in the title-page: *Poems of Mr John Milton, both English and Latin*, and in the clear-cut division of the volume into two distinct sections (with separate pagination) of English and Latin poetry respectively.[18] As Hale remarks, 'we see that the book is actually two books.'[19] Significantly, like the languages themselves, they are bound together.

One approach to the linguistic versatility exhibited by Milton's bilingualism, this felicitous ability to shift or to choose between Latin and the vernacular, might be to regard it as a consequence, at least in part, of Renaissance pedagogical theory and practice. According to John Aubrey, Milton was already a poet when he had his portrait painted at the age of ten.[20] While the precise truth of such a viewpoint is open to question, it is clear that his linguistic experimentation would have had its inception while he was a student at St Paul's School, London. And in many ways such experimentation was inevitable. 'Translations' into and out of a variety of languages formed a central part of the educational system of the day. In Renaissance England, as Moss has shown, translation functioned as 'the "natural" medium through which pupils learn[ed] to manipulate the phraseology of "rhetorically" contrived Latin.'[21] That Latin be taught through the medium of translation was one of the precepts of the Renaissance educator John Brinsley. According to this system the tutor would recite a Latin poem to his pupils, who would translate it into

---

[17] Cf. *Lycidas*, 130.

[18] Among useful surveys of the volume are L.L. Martz, *Poet of exile: a study of Milton's poetry* (New Haven, 1980), 31–59, C.W.R.D. Moseley, *The poetic birth: Milton's poems of 1645* (Aldershot, 1991), 79–85, J.K. Hale, 'Milton's self-presentation in poems… 1645', *Milton Quarterly*, 25.2 (1991), 37–48.

[19] Hale, 'Milton's self-presentation', 37. Hale, 38, proceeds to point out that while bilingual volumes by diverse hands abounded, 'volumes of verse by one author, assembled for a book by the poet, were still rare in the England of 1645.'

[20] J. Aubrey, 'Minutes of the life of Mr John Milton', *The early lives of Milton*, ed. H. Darbishire (London, 1932), 2.

[21] A. Moss, *Printed commonplace-books and the structuring of Renaissance thought* (Oxford, 1996), 216.

English as it was being dictated in Latin.[22] It was a system which, as Moss observes, was 'aimed quite explicitly at bringing the English language within the scope of the verbal competence inculcated by classroom method.'[23] There was no shortage of types of translation. Such indeed were seen as a means of enhancing the very language(s) into which the pupil was 'translating', whether that language be neo-Latin, Greek, Hebrew or English, to name but a few. And classical precedent was not lacking: Cicero had recommended translation from Greek into Latin as a way of enhancing the pupil's command of his own language, as well as a means of enriching the Latin language itself,[24] while Quintilian announced that in the very act of translating Greek into Latin 'we may use the very best words since all that we use are our own.'[25] As Donald Clark succinctly puts it: 'Milton had to become a little Roman boy of sorts before he could make Latin translations from the Greek classics as he did from the beginning of the Fifth Form.'[26] In seventeenth-century London, even more so than in ancient Rome, translation might function as a means of enriching other languages. How then might this have worked in practice?

One exercise expected of the grammar school pupil was that of the 'double translation system'. According to this practice, recommended by such Renaissance educators as Roger Ascham, the pupil would translate a Latin piece into English; then, without looking at the original, translate his own English into Latin, finally comparing what was now his own neo-Latin version with the original.[27] Clark

---

[22] J. Brinsley, *Ludus literarius or the grammar school*, ed. E.T. Campagnac (Liverpool and London, 1917), 193: 'Take *Flores Poetarum*, and in every Common place make choise of Ovid's verses, or if you find any other which be pleasant and easie... Cause also as many as you would have to learne together to set downe the English as you dictate [the Latin verses].'

[23] Moss, *Printed commonplace-books*, 216. For further discussion of links between bilingualism and Renaissance pedagogy, see E. Haan, *Andrew Marvell's Latin poetry: from text to context* (Collection Latomus, 275, Brussels, 2003), 66–72.

[24] Cicero, *De Oratore* 1.155: *postea mihi placuit, eoque sum usus adulescens, ut summorum oratorum Graecas orationes explicarem, quibus lectis hoc adsequebar, ut, cum ea, quae legeram Graece, Latine redderem, non solum optimis verbis uterer et tamen usitatis, sed etiam exprimerem quaedam verba imitando, quae nova nostris essent, dum modo essent idonea.* Text is that of *Cicero: De Oratore*, ed. A.S. Wilkins (Oxford, 1879), I, 130.

[25] Quintilian, *De Institutione Oratoria*, 10.5.2: *vertere Graeca in Latinum veteres nostri oratores optimum iudicabant... nam et rerum copia Graeci auctores abundant et plurimum artis in eloquentiam intulerunt et hos transferentibus verbis uti optimis licet: omnibus enim utimur nostris.* Text is that of *Institutionis Oratoriae Libri Duodecim*, ed. M. Winterbottom (Oxford, 1970), 607.

[26] D.L. Clark, *John Milton at St Paul's School* (New York, 1948; repr. Hamden, 1964), 172.

[27] Thus R. Ascham, *The scholemaster*, ed. E. Arber (London, 1870), 26, advises as to how Cicero should be double translated: 'The childe must take a paper booke, and sitting in some place, where no man shall prompt him, by him self, let him translate into Englishe his former lesson. Then shewing it to his master, let the master take from him his Latin booke, and pausing an houre, at the least, then let the childe translate his own Englishe into Latin againe, in an other paper booke. When the childe bringeth it, turned into Latin, the master must compare it with *Tullies* book, and lay them both together.' Cf. Clark, *John Milton at St Paul's school*, 172–173.

speculates that 'Milton must have done a great deal of translating as well as keeping up of paper books at school – translation from Latin into English, from English into Latin, from Greek into English and into Latin, from Hebrew into English and into Latin.'[28] If he did (as undoubtedly he must have) these do not survive.

Nonetheless evidence of the precise methodology of the 'double translation system' does survive, and is most eloquently exemplified by Milton's friend and contemporary, Andrew Marvell, albeit from the other side of the desk, so to speak. For Marvell, as for Milton, bilingualism and pedagogy were inextricably intertwined. It was probably while acting as tutor to Mary Fairfax at Nun Appleton House that Marvell produced his parallel neo-Latin and vernacular poems: *Ros*/'On a Drop of Dew'; *Hortus*/'The Garden'.[29] In so doing he may well have been composing his own 'originals', so to speak, his pseudo-classical models, which he then seems to have reworked into English verse, perhaps as a means of illustrating the system to his young pupil.[30] The literary repercussions of this methodology should not be underestimated. Marvell, through 'translating' his own neo-Latin into an experimental vernacular, simultaneously enhanced that vernacular by quasi-Baroque wordplay manifested in a whole series of puns, macaronic and otherwise, appropriated from one language and poem into its vernacular equivalent.[31] The very language, rhetoric, form and subject matter of Marvell's celebrated English poems would be altogether very different were it not for the fact that he had composed these works in Latin first. Gordon Campbell compares this practice to that of Samuel Beckett, who 'disciplined his dramatic prose by writing his plays in French and then translating them into English.'[32] For Marvell then the double translation system was surely much more than 'translating'. Regarded in the light of Shelley's dictum, the appropriation of one's own neo-Latin into an experimental vernacular could serve perhaps as a means of both discovering that original 'violet' and actually enhancing the poem and indeed the language into which it was 'translated'.

Can the same be said to be true of translation from neo-Latin into neo-Latin? Or to approach this from the perspective of Clark: did not Milton have to become a little neo-Latin boy as well as a little Roman one? The answer is a resounding affirmative. In his *Apology for Smectymnuus* (1642) Milton describes the ease and pleasure that attended his schoolboy 'imitations' of Latin elegiac poetry, a likely allusion

---

[28] Clark, *John Milton at St Paul's school*, 177.
[29] See Haan, *Andrew Marvell's Latin poetry*, 57–94.
[30] See Haan, *Andrew Marvell's Latin poetry*, 64–72.
[31] See Haan, *Andrew Marvell's Latin poetry*, 77–87.
[32] *Andrew Marvell*, ed. G. Campbell (London, 1997), xii.

to his very act of composing neo-Latin verse at St Paul's School.[33] Indeed a key aim of the Renaissance educational system was to equip its subjects with the necessary tools for Latin verse-composition. One way in which it did so was through a practice known as the 'turning of verses'. This exercise, recommended and illustrated by Brinsley, required the pupil to rework a Latin poem into a Latin equivalent, substituting alternative words or phrases while preserving the metre and form of the original or applying the subject matter to another, frequently contemporary, topic.[34] This practice is exemplified by both Marvell and Milton. Marvell's university *Parodia* on Horace, *Odes* 1.2, published in a Cambridge anthology (1637) celebrating the birth of princess Anne, reworks Horace's grim prediction of divine retribution for civil war into a depiction of the bitter consequences of plague in seventeenth-century Cambridge.[35]

A more succinct example is provided by Milton's *Apologus de Rustico et Hero*, which in all probability dates to his St Paul's period. Here, as I have illustrated elsewhere,[36] he reworks a neo-Latin fable by Mantuan (on a farmer's loss of an apple-tree as a consequence of his rash transplantation of the same). As Milton describes that 'transposition' (*transtulit* [4]) of an apple-tree from its native soil, he does so by 'transposing' the very language of Mantuan's poem, making the Latin his own. By substituting words and phrases, while preserving the metre and sense of the fable, he excels in two ways: firstly, by fulfilling the prerequisites of the set exercise; secondly, by moving beyond his 'original' through careful choice of nouns or adjectives, and linguistic and syntactical innovation. Thus hissing sibilants convey the enticing juices of the apple; cleverly juxtaposed phrases reach a climax in the decay of the tree; there is a pun on *malus-i* (f.) 'apple' and *malum-i* (n.) 'evil', while the tragic sense of loss experienced by the master is heightened and personal-

---

[33] He alludes to 'the smooth Elegiack Poets, whereof the Schooles are not scarce. Whom both for the pleasing sound of their numerous writing, which in imitation I found most easie; and most agreeable to nature's part in me, and for their matter which what it is, there be few who know not, I was so allur'd to read, that no recreation came to me better welcome.' (*CM*, 3, 302).

[34] Brinsley, *Ludus literarius*, 194, states: 'Cause them to turne the verses of their Lecture into other verses, either to the same purpose, which is easiest for young beginners, or turne to some other purpose, to express some other matter; yet ever to keep the very phrase of the poet, there or in other places, only transposing the words or phrase, or changing some word or phrase, or the numbers or persons or applying them to matters which are familiar.' Clark, *John Milton at St Paul's school*, 181, notes that 'the exercise depends in part on the relative indifference of Latin elegiac verse to word order so long as the metre is kept regular.'

[35] See Haan, *Andrew Marvell's Latin poetry*, 19–56.

[36] See E. Haan, 'Mantuan, Milton and "the fruit of that forbidden tree" ', *Medievalia et Humanistica*, 35 (1998), 75–92, which argues that Milton's poem is an exercise in the 'turning of verses' (contrary to Fletcher's reading of the same as exemplifying the 'double translation' system. Cf. H.F. Fletcher, 'Milton's *apologus* and its Mantuan model,' *Journal of English and Germanic Philology*, 55 (1956), 230–233).

ised.[37] Indeed in this, as in other instances, Milton's methodology anticipates that implemented in his mature vernacular epic: in the laments uttered by Adam and Eve, having eaten of the forbidden fruit, and in their consequential 'transplantation', as it were, from the Garden of Eden, their 'native soil'.[38]

What then of classical Latin into the vernacular? Certainly Milton's most obvious example of such is his 'translation' of Horace, *Odes* 1. 5, to which we now turn:

Horace, *Odes* 1.5   John Milton

*Rendered almost word for word without
Rhyme according to the Latin Measure, as
near as the Language will permit*

Quis multa gracilis te puer in rosa	What slender Youth bedew'd with liquid odours
perfusus liquidis urget odoribus	Courts thee on Roses in some pleasant Cave,
grato, Pyrrha, sub antro?	Pyrrha for whom bindst thou
cui flavam religas comam	In wreaths thy golden Hair,
simplex munditiis? Heu quotiens fidem	Plain in thy neatness; O how oft shall he 5
mutatosque deos flebit et aspera	On Faith and changed Gods complain: and Seas
nigris aequora ventis	Rough with black winds and storms
emirabitur insolens,	Unwonted shall admire:
qui nunc te fruitur credulus aurea,	Who now enjoys thee credulous, all Gold,
qui semper vacuam, semper amabilem	Who alwayes vacant alwayes amiable 10
sperat, nescius aurae	Hopes thee; of flattering gales
fallacis; miseri, quibus	Unmindfull. Hapless they
intemptata nites; me tabula sacer	To whom thou untry'd seem'st fair. Me in my vow'd
votiva paries indicat uvida	Picture the sacred wall declares t'have hung
suspendisse potenti	My dank and dropping weeds 15
vestimenta maris deo.[39]	To the stern God of Sea.

The date of the poem is unknown, with suggestions ranging from 1624 to as late as 1655. Fletcher,[40] Hughes[41] and Carey[42] regard it as either a school or university exercise, while Clark leaves the question open.[43] By contrast Shawcross and others

---

[37] See Haan, 'Mantuan', *passim*.

[38] Cf. Michael to Adam at *Paradise Lost* 11. 259–262: 'But longer in this Paradise to dwell/Permits not; to remove thee I am come,/And send thee from the garden forth to till/The ground whence thou wast taken, fitter soil,' or Eve's lament at 11.269–270: 'Must I thus leave thee, Paradise? Thus leave/Thee, native soil!' All quotations from *Paradise Lost* are from *Paradise Lost*, ed. A. Fowler, 2nd ed. (London, 1998).

[39] Text of both Latin and English is that printed in *Poems &c upon several occasions by Mr John Milton: both English and Latin &c composed at several times* (London, 1673). I have modernised punctuation.

[40] H.F. Fletcher, *The intellectual development of John Milton* (Illinois, 1956), I, 238.

[41] M.Y. Hughes, *Milton: the minor poems* (New York, 1947), li.

[42] Carey, *Complete shorter poems*, 99, suggests late 1629.

[43] Clark, *John Milton at St Paul's school*, 178.

have argued at length for a later date,[44] while Gordon Campbell has cautiously described the piece as 'wholly undatable'.[45] True as this may be, there are, however, several indications that might support the argument that this is a school or university exercise. Like the *Apologus de Rustico et Hero*, it was published only in 1673 (with the Latin text subjoined), at a time when the elderly Milton seems to have been gathering together his life's work (including his school-exercises) for publication. But more striking is the fact that the methodology exemplified by the piece closely approximates that of the 'metaphrase,' one of the key exercises practised in Renaissance schools.

In his Preface to Ovid's *Epistles*, published in 1680, John Dryden discusses three different types of 'translation': 'metaphrase', 'paraphrase', and 'imitation'. He defines 'metaphrase' as 'turning an author word by word, and line by line, from one language into another.'[46] In terms of Renaissance pedagogy metaphrase was a rigorously effective means of instilling into a pupil sensitivity to metre and form, to the inflected syntax of the Latin language, and not least to ways in which such could be replicated via creative experimentation in a vernacular translation. For Ascham 'Metaphrasis is to take some notable place out of a good poet and turn the same sense into meter or into other words in prose.'[47] In some respects then it was seen as the vernacular equivalent of the 'turning of verses', and demanded of its subject a mental alertness,[48] the ability to substitute words for words, phrases for phrases, while still retaining the structure of the original. But there was, of course, one important distinction: the result was an English version of a Latin original, but

---

[44] J.T. Shawcross, 'Of chronology and the dates of Milton's translation from Horace and the new forcers of conscience,' *Studies in English Literature*, 3 (1963), 77–84, argues for a late date, noting (80) that the Latin text supplied in the 1673 volume of Milton's poetry seems not to have been published before 1636. Cf. D.P. Harding, *The club of Hercules: Studies in the classical background of Paradise Lost* (Illinois, 1962), 128–134, who detects the development of Milton's mature style, while R. Flannagan, *Riverside Milton* (Boston, 1998), 260, dates it 1646–1648. There is, however, no reason to assume (as Shawcross and others do) that the Latin text published by Milton in 1673 is necessarily the text he used at the time of composing his English version. For a convincing rejection of Shawcross's reasons, see *A variorum commentary on the poems of John Milton*, ed. M.Y. Hughes (New York, 1972), II, 502–505. Cf. 504: 'If the style does not resemble that of the early Milton, it does not much resemble that of the later poet either; in fact it is unique.'

[45] G. Campbell, *A Milton chronology* (London and New York, 1997), 214.

[46] John Dryden, *Preface to Ovid's Epistles* (London, 1680). Text is that of *The works of John Dryden*, ed. E. Niles Hooker and H.T. Swedenberg Jr (London, 1956), I, 114.

[47] Ascham, *The scholemaster*, 93.

[48] Cf. Ascham, *The scholemaster*, 109–110: 'This exercise may bring much profit to ripe heads and staid judgements because in traveling in it the mind must needs be very attentive and busily occupied in turning and tossing itself many ways and conferrying with great pleasure the variety of worthy wits and judgements together.'

one which might seek to recreate that original through the use of Latinate vocabulary, word-order and syntax.

In terms of its reception through the centuries, it might be remarked that Horace's *Odes* 1.5, with its interconnected themes of love, credulity, betrayal, and retirement from love,[49] is one of the most, if not *the* most, translated of Latin lyrics.[50] Such may also have been the case in the Renaissance classroom. One way into Milton's 'translation' is via the headnote he provided, in which, as Clark remarks, he seems to show 'a very schoolboy pride.'[51] It is a pride, it could be argued, that is closely linked to pedagogical practice, and to Milton's experience and perceptions of the same, both as schoolboy and (by the time he was publishing the version in 1673) as erstwhile schoolmaster.[52] In the following discussion pedagogical methodology (and Milton's consciousness of the same) will be used to support and augment Charles Martindale's reading of the poem as metaphrase.[53]

At the outset it is important to remember that Milton's provision of headnotes to many of his poems frequently acted as a means of self-advertisement, and for the most part as a way of boasting about his youthfulness at the time of composition. For example, in the 1645 volume he takes pains to indicate the date or his precise age at the time of his early compositions, and he does so in both English[54] and Latin. Indeed very frequently his age in Latin becomes part of the heading of a poem.[55] As such Milton's headnotes may in themselves act as a means of guiding

---

[49] For studies of the Ode, see among others, E.A. Fredricksmeyer, 'Horace's Ode to Pyrrha (*Carm*. 1.5)', *Classical Philology*, 60 (1965), 180–185; V. Pöschl, 'Die Pyrrhaode des Horaz (c. 1.5)', *Hommages à J. Bayet*, ed. M. Renard and R. Schilling (*Collection Latomus*, 70, Brussels, 1964), 579–586; M.C.J. Putnam, 'Horace, *Carm*. 1.5: Love and death', *Classical Philology*, 65 (1970), 251–254; K. Quinn, 'Horace as a love poet: a reading of *Odes* 1.5', *Arion*, 2 (1963), 59–77; J.C. Brown, 'The verbal art of Horace's *Ode to Pyrrha*', *Transactions of the American Philological Association*, 111 (1981), 17–22; D. Coffta, 'Programme and persona in Horace, *Odes* 1.5', *Eranos*, 96 (1998), 26–31; D.W. Thomson Vessey, 'Pyrrha's grotto and the farewell to love: a study of Horace, *Odes* 1.5', *Why Horace? A collection of interpretive essays*, ed. W.S. Anderson (Bolchazy-Cardicci, 1999), 20–30.

[50] See R. Storrs, *Ad Pyrrham: a polyglot collection of translations of Horace's Ode to Pyrrha (Book 1, Ode 5)* (London, 1959).

[51] Clark, *John Milton at St Paul's school*, 178.

[52] See in general A.F. Leach, *Milton as schoolboy and schoolmaster* (Proceedings of the British Academy, 3, London, 1908, repr. 1976).

[53] See C. Martindale, 'Unlocking the word-hoard: in praise of metaphrase', *Comparative Criticism*, 6 (1984), 47–72, reworked in his *Redeeming the text*, 75–100 (= Chapter 4: 'Translation as rereading: symphony in three movements').

[54] *On the morning of Christ's nativity, compos'd 1629*; *A paraphrase on psalm 114, this and the following psalm were done by the author at fifteen yeers old*; *On Shakespeare, 1630*; *Comus*, 1634, *Lycidas... 1637*.

[55] *Elegia Secunda, Anno aetatis 17*; *Elegia Tertia, Anno aetatis 17*; *Elegia Quarta, Anno aetatis 18*; *Elegia Quinta, Anno aetatis 20*; *Elegia Septima, Anno aetatis undevigesimo*; *Anno aetatis 16: In Obitum Procancellarii Medici*; *In Quintum Novembris, Anno aetatis 17*; *Anno aetatis 17: In Obitum Praesulis Eliensis*. The

reader response or at the very least as a form of careful sign-posting for his audience.

What aspects of his 'translation' then does Milton highlight? Firstly, he points out that his version is verbally close to the original: it is 'rendered almost word for word.' As remarked above, this was perhaps the chief characteristic of the Renaissance metaphrase. Hence Milton is, by implication, revealing himself as master of that art, so to speak, as excelling in this methodology. Secondly, he announces that his version does not rhyme. Rhyming translations were criticised by Roger Ascham, especially if the inclusion of such was likely to hamper the rendering.[56] In fact rhyme and the metaphrase were virtually incompatible. Thirdly, he draws attention to the fact that his poem seeks (on a visual level perhaps)[57] to mirror 'the Latin measure' of the original – 'measure' here encompassing metre, but also perhaps the stanzaic structure of the whole.[58] The ability of English verse to reproduce the metre of a classical original is discussed by Ascham, who contrasts the respective clumsiness and felicity of English poetry in rendering hexameter and iambic verse.[59] Indeed Milton's poem proper may (in the number and shape of its stanzas: two iambic pentameters followed by two iambic trimeters) attempt to mirror Horace's metre (third Asclepiad) and line-length.[60] Fourthly, he conveys the fact that his poem approximates a Latin original in the English language – or at least 'as near as the Language will permit.' The headnote as a whole, and the latter phrase in particular, is strikingly similar to Brinsley's precepts concerning translation:

> In all such translating either English or Latine this is carefully to be observed; ever to consider well the scope and drift of the Author and the circumstances of the place;

---

title-page of the second (Latin) section of the 1645 volume has the following heading: *Ioannis Miltoni Londiniensis Poemata Quorum Pleraque Intra Annum Aetatis Vigesimum Conscripsit.*

[56] Ascham, *The scholemaster*, 145–146, in criticising rhyming, musters the support of Quintilian: 'Quintilian in his learned Chapter *de Compositione*... doth justly inveigh against all rhyming; if there be any, who be angry with me, for misliking of rhyming may be angry... with Quintilian also for the same thing.' Cf. his criticism of 'that barbarous and rude rhyming' (145). Contrast his praise of the Earl of Surrey and of Gonsalvo Periz, who 'avoided the fault of rhyming' in their translations of Virgil, *Georgics* 4, and Homer's *Odyssey* respectively (147).

[57] For a possible parallel in terms of an English poem's attempt to replicate (on a visual level) Horatian stanzaic structure, cf. Marvell's *An Horatian ode upon Cromwell's return from Ireland*. See Haan, *Andrew Marvell's Latin poetry*, 53–55.

[58] Contrast Hale, *Milton's languages*, 71: 'even if "measure" refers only to the metre...'

[59] Ascham, *The scholemaster*, 146: 'Athough *Carmen Exametrum* doth rather trot and hobble than run smoothly in our English tongue yet I am sure our English tongue will receive *Carmen Iambicum* as naturally as either Greek or Latin.'

[60] Cf. Martindale, 'In praise of metaphrase', 54.

and to labour to express lively, not only the matter, but also the force of each phrase, *so near as the propriety of the tongue will permit.*[61]

If Milton's headnote alerts us to ways in which his poem fulfils the necessary prerequisites of the metaphrase, it also, at least by implication, emphasises the essentially Latinate English of the poem proper. This works on both a verbal and a syntactical level: verbally, in terms of his choice of nouns and adjectives,[62] and the preference for English words with Latin roots as a means of rendering their Horatian equivalent: thus 'liquid odours'(1)/*liquidis... odoribus* (2); 'admire' (8)/*emirabitur* (8); 'credulous' (9)/*credulus* (9); 'vacant' (10)/*vacuam* (10); 'amiable' (10)/*amabilem* (10). Through such Latinisms Milton's metaphrase transposes the 'turning of verses' to the dimension of a Latinate vernacular, its linguistic alterity mirroring 'the alterity of Horace's lyric manner'.[63] But if it looks back to Horace, it also looks ahead to the mature vernacular Milton, the poet of *Paradise Lost*, an epic permeated by precisely such Latinisms, by English words used in a Latinate sense.[64]

The poem's Latinity operates on a syntactical level also as Milton replicates the inflected word-order of the ancient language by postponing verbs until the end of clauses ('complain' [6], 'admire' [8], 'hopes thee' [11]).[65] He uses enjambment as a means of enabling his vernacular version (like its Horatian equivalent) to cut across stanzaic division.[66] As in Horace, he holds back the *simplex munditiis* phrase to enable it to open the second stanza,[67] and he replicates the repetition of *qui... qui* (9–10) in 'who... who' (9–10) and of *semper... semper* (10) in 'always... always' (10). His emphatically positioned 'me' at the beginning of the final clause (13) balances its precise Latin equivalent *me* (13), thereby achieving complete verbal assimilation, and he reproduces the archaism of the accusative and infinitive construction: *me.../... indicat.../suspendisse* (13–15) in 'me.../... declares t'have hung' (13–14).

---

[61] Brinsley, *Ludus literarius*, 156–157. Italics are mine.
[62] A. Burnett, 'The Fifth Ode of Horace, *Lib.* I, and Milton's style', *Milton Quarterly*, 16 (1982), 68–72, remarks on the high frequency of adjectives in Milton's version.
[63] Martindale, *Redeeming the text*, 79.
[64] A few examples will suffice: 'abject' (from *abicio-ere* [to cast down]): 'so thick bestrewn/Abject and lost lay these, covering the flood' (*PL* 1. 311–312); 'reluctant' (from *reluctor-ari* [to struggle]): 'till supplanted down he fell/A monstrous serpent on his belly prone/Reluctant but in vain' (*PL* 10. 513–515); 'involved' (from *involvo-ere* [to roll/wrap around]): 'Satan involved in rising mist' (*PL* 9. 75).
[65] On the 'hopes thee...' construction, Hale, *Milton's languages*, 71, remarks: '[Milton's] English, forced into the Latin word-order, cannot make clear who is "credulous" and who is "amiable" nor what "vacant" means. What inflection can clarify readily, English fails to: the syntax crumples into nonsense.'
[66] Cf. Martindale, 'In praise of metaphrase', 54; Martindale, *Redeeming the text*, 79.
[67] Cf. Martindale, 'In Praise of metaphrase', 54; Martindale, *Redeeming the text*, 79.

One question remains to be answered: is anything 'lost in translation' in terms of Milton's metaphrastic version? Martindale, while regarding the poem as 'astonishingly innovatory, both linguistically and rhythmically,'[68] concedes that 'Milton does not really capture the elegance that rather unexpectedly goes with the dense and difficult textures of the original.'[69] This is a judgement that is certainly open to question. Scholars have criticised the poem for its overly puritanical tone. For example, the difficult phrase *simplex munditiis*,[70] is rendered by the unsatisfactory 'plain in thy neatness'.[71] But perhaps in such an instance a wholly adequate rendering is impossible. Is this 'as near as the language will permit?'[72] Is this as near as any language will permit? Likewise it might be observed that in Milton's version the sexual undertones of the Horatian *te… /…urget* (1–2) are not only suppressed but actually countered in the politely refined 'courts thee' (2). But perhaps criticism of the poem's supposedly 'puritanical' nature may be answered by noting that Renaissance pedagogy had an explicitly moral purpose. I would suggest that Roy Flannagan's viewpoint is nearer to the truth:

> For anyone who has struggled to translate the sophisticated and intricate poetry of Horace into English, Milton's translation is a marvel: it is concise, precise, definitive; it is faithful to the original; and it creates its own integrity as an English poem. The English is not in Milton's poetic style, because its style deeply honors Horace's in Latin; it is an exercise on how to write poetry in either language.[73]

Read in this light this 'exercise on how to write poetry' seems to transcend the level of mere pedagogy. As such it is symptomatic of Milton's poetic method.

In *Epitaphium Damonis* (168–178) Milton announces what would seem at first glance to be his contemplated abandonment of Latin in favour of English. This is depicted through the symbol of the *fistula*, or shepherd's pipe, which will either be hung up for good and forgotten, or else, having undergone a metamorphosis of sorts, it will utter a British theme in the vernacular:

---

[68] Martindale, *Redeeming the text*, 79.
[69] Martindale, 'In praise of metaphrase,' 56.
[70] R.G.M. Nisbet and M. Hubbard, *A commentary on Horace Odes Book I* (Oxford, 1970), 75, state '*munditiis* does not make an oxymoron with *simplex* but points in the same direction.'
[71] For Martindale, 'In praise of metaphrase', 56, this rendition 'seems too puritanical.' He speculates, however, that 'perhaps there was a seventeenth-century (sub-Puritan) usage of the word neat that meant something like "chic." '
[72] Nisbet and Hubbard, *A commentary on Horace Odes Book I*, 76, remark of the phrase: 'in the present context an adequate English translation seems impossible.'
[73] Flannagan, ed. *Riverside Milton*, 260.

> ...O mihi tum si vita supersit,
> tu procul annosa pendebis fistula pinu
> multum oblita mihi, aut patriis mutata camoenis[74]
> Brittonicum strides. (*Ep. Dam.*, 168–171)

Do these lines really bid farewell to the Latin language? Admittedly, Milton, in aiming to be a national poet, must move outside the Latin world of the poem and assume the vernacular (just as the poem itself has to break through the confines of a pagan, pastoral genre in order to describe the apotheosis of Diodati in a Christian Heaven). But what sort of vernacular? Is it not the case that his vernacular is in fact a Latin that has undergone a linguistic metamorphosis (*patriis mutata camoenis*), or rather (as though mirroring the rebirth of Diodati in Heaven) a linguistic apotheosis? If so, Milton's English is thus a Latinate English in a very unique way. It is, in those words of the 1645 volume, 'Both English and Latin.'

It has been argued of Joachim Du Bellay that he translated his own Latin lines into the vernacular.[75] While the present discussion makes no such claim for Milton, it concludes by reverting to 'translation' as the manifold intersections between languages, and by positing some instances of the frequently complex interplay between Milton's neo-Latin and English poetry.[76] Perhaps Milton's poetic practice as a whole can (in a quasi-revisionist version of Marvell's 'double translation' methodology?) exemplify different ways of 'translating' his own neo-Latin into an experimental vernacular. Several examples will suffice:

(i) The nightingale of *Elegia Quinta* (*iam Philomela tuos foliis adoperta novellis/instituis modulos, dum silet omne nemus* [25–26]) finds a parallel in the opening lines of the first English Sonnet: 'O nightingale, that on yon bloomy spray/warblest at eve, when all the woods are still.' (1–2). The *pendulus orbis* (*El.*1.76) or *pendulum telluris orbem* (*In Obitum Procancellarii Medici* (3) become 'this pendent world' of *Paradise Lost* 2. 1052.[77]

---

[74] Lines 170–171 have received various interpretations. W. MacKellar, *The Latin poems of John Milton* (New Haven, 1930), 169, translates *patriis mutata camoenis* as 'forsaking your [the pipe's] native songs,' and explains in a note (347) 'its paternal Muses, i.e. Latin.' I would disagree with this interpretation. It is much more likely that the phrase means *Milton's* native Muses, i.e. the English language. The lines are well translated by Mary Campbell in *John Milton: the complete poems*, ed. G. Campbell (London and New York, 1980), 543: '... unless, changed, you will utter a British theme in native songs.' D. Bush, *A variorum commentary on the poems of John Milton*, I, *The Latin and Greek poems* (New York, 1970), 316–317, notes that Ovid (*Epistulae Ex Ponto* 4.13.33) uses *patria... Camena* for his native language in contrast with Getic.

[75] See G. Demerson, 'Joachim Du Bellay: traducteur de lui-même,' *Neo-Latin and the vernacular in renaissance France*, ed. G. Castor and T. Cave (Oxford, 1984), 113–128.

[76] It is complex in the sense that this interplay would seem to move beyond that verbal and psychological patterning illustrated by such scholars as Le Comte. See in general E.S. Le Comte, *Yet once more: verbal and psychological pattern in Milton* (New York, 1953).

[77] Cf. *PL.* 4.1000: 'The pendulous round Earth.'

(ii) In *Naturam Non Pati Senium* the collapse of the universe is envisaged in a simile of Vulcan's fall (*qualis in Aegaeam proles Iunonia Lemnon/deturbata sacro cecidit de limine caeli* (23–24).[78] This receives a much fuller treatment in *Paradise Lost*, in the depiction of Mulciber ('and how he fell/From Heav'n... On Lemnos th'Aegaean Isle' [*PL* 1.740–746]).

(iii) Aspects of *In Quintum Novembris* recur in a transmuted form in *Paradise Lost*:[79] Satan as the *fraudumque magister* (17)/'artificer of fraud' (*PL* 4.121); as the exile from heaven (*aethereo vagus exul Olympo* [8])/[evicted] 'from the ethereal sky' (*PL* 1.45); as the sower of hatred (*unanimes odium struit inter amicos* (13)/ 'these acts of hateful strife' [*PL* 6. 264]); as the disturber of peace (*regnaque olivifera vertit florentia pace* (15)/'how hast thou disturb'd/Heav'ns blessed peace' [*PL* 6. 266–267]); as the flying demon, whose pitchy wings oppress the air (*et piceis liquido natat aere pennis* [45]/'Then with expanded wings he steers his flight/Aloft, incumbent on the dusky air/That felt unusual weight' [*PL* 1.225–227]). Satan's address to a sleeping pope (*dormis nate? Etiamne tuos sopor opprimit artus/immemor O fidei, pecorumque oblite tuorum* [92–93]) is closely mirrored in his attempts to waken Beelzebub: 'Sleepst thou Companion dear? What sleep can close/Thy eye-lids? and remembrest what Decree...' (*PL* 5. 673–674). And King James, described as *sedebat/in solio, occultique doli securus et hostis* (5–6), becomes God the Father 'till then as one secure/Sat on his throne' (*PL* 1. 638–639). But God is a supreme power who laughs from Heaven at the vain attempts of conspirators (*vanaque perversae ridet conamina turbae* [168]/'He from heaven's height/All these our motions vain, sees and derides' [*PL* 2. 190–191]/ 'Mighty Father, thou thy foes/Justly hast in derision, and secure/Laughst at their vain designs and tumults vain' [*PL* 5.735–737]).

This discussion commenced with a Shellean violet. It concludes with Miltonic (or perhaps Horatian?) roses: with the 'translation' of *Odes* 1.5 into a prelapsarian Eden. It is an Eden which possesses its own *multa in rosa* (1) ('flowers of all hue, and without thorn the rose' [*PL* 4. 256]/ 'And on their naked limbs the flowery roof/Showered roses, which the morn repaired' (4.772–773]);[80] its *liquidis... odoribus* (2) ('odorous sweets' [4. 166]; 'odorous gums' [4. 248]; 'each odorous bushy shrub' [4. 696]); its *grato... antro* (3) ('umbrageous grots and caves/of cool recess' [4. 257–258]);[81] its golden-haired female (*flavam religas comam* [4]), her tresses now unbound, as Eve 'her unadorned golden tresses wore/Dishevelled, but in wanton ringlets

---

[78] Cf. *El*.7.81–82: *sic dolet amissum proles Iunonia caelum,/inter Lemniacos praecipitata focos*.
[79] See M. Cheek, 'Milton's *In Quintum Novembris*: an epic foreshadowing,' *Studies in Philology*, 54 (1957), 172–184.
[80] Cf. 'A sylvan scene' (140), 'herself a fairer flower' (270), 'the soft downy bank damasked with flowers' (334), 'underfoot the violet,/crocus, and hyacinth with rich inlay/broidered the ground' (700–702).
[81] Cf. 'under a tuft of shade' (325), 'blissful bower' (690), 'inmost bower' (738).

waved' (4. 305–306), while 'half her swelling breast/Naked met his under the flowing gold/Of her loose tresses hid' (4. 495–497). And if the Horatian *simplex munditiis* (5) has been transmuted into 'simplicity and spotless innocence' (4. 318), it is a state that will not endure:

> Ah gentle pair, ye little think how nigh
> Your change approaches, when all these delights
> Will vanish and deliver ye to woe,
> More woe, the more your taste is now of joy (*PL* 4. 366–369)[82]

A young lover's credulity (*credulus* [9]), his lack of knowledge (*nescius* [11]) of future betrayal, have become for two lovers an essentially transient present in which prelapsarian ignorance is bliss:

> Sleep on
> Blest pair; and O yet happiest if ye seek
> No happier state, and know to know no more. (*PL* 4. 773–775)[83]

---

[82] Cf. 'close the serpent sly/Insinuating.../... of his fatal guile/Gave proof unheeded.' (347–350).

[83] Cf. 'Can it be sin to know,/Can it be death? And do they only stand/By ignorance, is that their happy state' (517–519).

15

Richard Mant's translations from the Roman breviary

George Woodman

The late 1830s saw the publication of several books of translations of Latin hymnody. In 1837 there appeared *Ancient hymns from the Roman Breviary, for domestick use… to which are added, original hymns…*[1] It was the work of Richard Mant, an Englishman and bishop of Down and Connor, a diocese of what was then the United Church of England and Ireland. He belonged to the High Church school of Anglicans that long predated the Tractarians. It shared many of their ideas before parting company with them and subsequently being superseded by them, although it lived on longer in Ireland than elsewhere. In his lifetime an important figure in his church and in north-east Ulster, Richard Mant is today best remembered for two of his hymns, *Bright the vision that delighted* and *For all thy saints, O Lord*. It is the purpose of this article to introduce his translations and set them in their context.

Richard Mant was born in 1776 in Southampton, the son of the master at the grammar school.[2] After initial teaching from his father, he was educated at Winchester College and Trinity College, Oxford. He was elected a Fellow of Oriel in 1798 and in 1812 was Bampton Lecturer. From 1802 he ministered in country parishes in the south of England before moving to London in 1815 as rector of St Botulph's, Bishopsgate. In 1820 he went to Ireland as bishop of Killaloe, whence he was translated to Down and Connor in 1823. (Dromore was added to these two dioceses in 1842.) He lived at Knocknagoney, outside Belfast. He remained as bishop of the three dioceses until his death in 1848. He devoted much effort to building churches for the expanding population of Belfast and its surrounding area. He was frequently embroiled in controversies with Roman Catholics, Protestant Nonconformists and other Anglicans (including those of his own flock) who did not share his views. In his later years he was a strong critic of the Tractarians. He

---

[1] R. Mant, *Ancient hymns from the Roman Breviary for domestick use, every morning and evening of the week, and on the holy-days of the church: to which are added, original hymns, principally of commemoration and thanksgiving for Christ's holy ordinances* (London, 1837).
[2] F.R. Bolton, 'Richard Mant (1776–1848), Bishop of Down, Connor and Dromore', *Theology*, lii, 341 (1948), 403–411.

was a prolific writer. Much of this writing arose out of the controversies, but he also wrote commentaries on the Book of Common Prayer and poetry. Before looking at his translations it is necessary to consider the background against which they were written.[3]

The Evangelical Revival in the eighteenth century had brought about a great age of hymn writing. By the 1830s hymn singing had become a major feature of non-conformist worship, particularly among Methodists and Independents, and demand was growing in the established church, where hymns were displacing the metrical Psalters which had been a staple of worship since the late sixteenth century. Old High Churchmen like bishop Mant and the early Tractarians were united in resisting this trend. They disliked the idea of adding unauthorised material to the appointed services of the church and also found the subjectivity of Evangelical hymns theologically unacceptable. In a charge delivered to his clergy in Killaloe in 1821 Bishop Mant admonished them not to use '... all that variety of modern compositions under the name of hymns...' which could be considered '...as tricking out the chaste and matronly simplicity of the church with the meretricious trappings of the conventicle.' He expressed similar views in 1830 and 1836.[4] At the same time hymns and poems were seen as a valuable aid to personal devotion and this was the intention of Mant and Tractarians such as John Keble and Isaac Williams in the poetry they wrote.

From the seventeenth century onwards there was a tradition of translating devotional works of Roman Catholic writers, many of them major figures of the Counter-Reformation, and adapting them for Protestant use.[5] As a translator, Mant was very much working within this tradition. At the same time the growing interest of hymnody in the established church led to a greater awareness among its clergy of Latin hymns. They had been written for liturgical worship and those that did not contain specifically Roman Catholic teaching were seen as containing sound doctrine to counter the subjectivity of Evangelical hymns. Bishop Reginald Heber in his pioneering hymnbook, published posthumously in 1827, included three Latin translations from the seventeenth-century poet William Drummond of Hawthornden. In 1837, the same year as Mant's collection, John Chandler's *The Hymns of the Primitive Church now first Collected, Translated and Arranged* appeared. Isaac Williams published his *Hymns translated from the Paris Breviary* in 1839.[6] Both Williams and Chandler belonged to the Tractarians, among whom at this period there were proposals to translate the whole of the Roman Breviary, although in the end these did not materialise. Their interest arose out of a wish to reconnect Anglicanism

---

[3] This is well discussed in O. Chadwick, *The Victorian Church: part 1* (London, 1966).
[4] F.R. Bolton, *The Caroline tradition of the Church of Ireland* (London, 1958), 149.
[5] Described in detail in J.Wickham Legg, *English church life from the restoration to the Tractarian movement* (London, 1914).
[6] For a description of developments in Anglican hymnody at this period see *Historical companion to hymns ancient and modern*, ed. M. Frost (London, 1962).

with the wider heritage of the western church and to provide more varied sources of liturgical worship. Here they parted company from Mant. He was a firm Protestant who saw it as his duty to counteract Romish errors and, as will be seen, was anxious not to translate anything he regarded as theologically suspect. He was scathing about the Tractarian view of the Breviary as devotionally richer than the Book of Common Prayer, something which makes his achievement in his collection of translations all the more remarkable.

The book consists of 120 hymns. It is divided into two parts. The first section comprises sixty-four 'translations from the Roman Breviary' and the second 'original hymns'. In fact the first section includes four original hymns and the second one translation. Mant uses the 1632 edition of the Breviary, in which certain medieval hymns were revised in rather more classical Latin. One hymn is selected from the Paris Breviary. He translates some of the greatest Latin hymns, including *Veni, Creator Spiritus, Jesu dulcis memoria* and *Stabat mater dolorosa*.

Mant was a medievalist who had edited the poems of Thomas Warton, the eighteenth-century precursor of the Gothic Revival. He had a strong sense of the past and had been responsible for the discovery of an ancient doorway in Killaloe Cathedral. These considerations are worth remembering in addition to the reasons for compiling the collection that he sets out in its preface. Here he explains that he is in the tradition of the English Reformers who derived much of the Book of Common Prayer from 'the Breviary or Daily Service book of the Romish Church, purified from corruption and reduced to the standard of Holy Scripture'. He cites the example of the *Veni, Creator*, the Breviary hymn included in the Book of Common Prayer services for the ordination of priests and the consecration of bishops. Interestingly, he goes on to acknowledge the influence of singing the morning office hymn *Jam lucis orto sidere* as one of William of Wykeham's scholars. This had been part of Winchester since the fourteenth century so that Mant's translations were not merely a revival. For all his Protestantism Mant was very aware of being part of an unbroken pattern of reciting the daily office extending back to pre-Reformation times. He saw his fellow Winchester scholar Thomas Ken as part of this tradition. Ken's morning and evening hymns were important to churchmen of Mant's school and Ken probably influenced his arrangement and selection of Breviary hymns.

There are two sets of morning and evening hymns for each of the seven days of the week. These are followed by a set of twenty-five hymns for the feasts of the Christian year (most feasts have two hymns and Easter has three) and there is a final set of eleven hymns for saints' days. These consist of two for All Saints and others cover the categories of angels, prophets, apostles, evangelists and martyrs. The one translation in the second section *Alto ex Olympi* is included as a 'hymn of thanksgiving for God's presence in his church'.

Mant has made a selection which 'rendered into English verse... would be an acceptable and useful manual to many individuals and families in our reformed Church, who are pleased with a metrical form, as an eligible vehicle of their devotions'. Some of his translations are rather free. In some cases he has combined short hymns or verses from different hymns. In others he has added verses to extend the thought. Sentiments in some hymns make him uneasy as a Protestant with the result that he alters them or adds verses to 'correct' the theology! Nevertheless he is capable of effective translation in his rather eighteenth-century and Latinate style. He is punctilious in providing an index of first lines so that any reader who wishes to check his work against the original can do so.

Mant naturally chose *Veni, Creator Spiritus* for Whitsunday. This would have been familiar to Mant and his readers through Bishop John Cosin's compressed version, which could have influenced Mant towards a certain freedom in translating texts. His own version makes a good starting point for an examination of his actual translations. The first verse is rendered thus:

Veni, Creator Spiritus,
mentes tuorum visita
imple superna gratia
quae tu creasti pectoral.[7]

Come, Holy Ghost, Creator blest
Come, visit Thou each willing breast
And with thy grace celestial aid
Those whom thy genial influence made.

'Genial influence' reads a little oddly today but these lines provide a solemn and effective version of the hymn. There is no English translation that does not in some way amplify this opening verse – with the exception of John Cosin, who contracts it. For Advent Mant chooses

En clara vox redarguit,
Obscura quaeque personans.
Procul fugentur somnia;
Ab alto Jesus promicat

He translates it as:

---

[7] Sources of the Latin texts in this paper are: *The Penguin book of Latin verse*, ed. F. Brittain (Harmondsworth, 1962); *Breviarum Romanum: ex decreto sacrosancti Concilii Tridentini restitutum...jussu editum Clementis VIII et Urbani VIII* (Ratisbon, 1862–1863); *Historical companion to hymns*, ed. Frost.

> Hark! A voice of warning, hark!
> Sounds it through the nations dark.
> Hence, ye baseless visions, fly!
> Jesus lightens from on high.

This is a vivid, thoroughly anglicised and yet accurate version of the original, the office hymn during Advent at Lauds. Mant conveys the feeling of a hymn for a service sung at dawn. 'A voice of warning' is an excellent rendering of the rather unusual Ciceronian word 'redarguit' (not used in the original hymn but inserted in the 1632 revision).

Mant's version of one of the best-known Latin hymns, the Compline office hymn *Te lucis ante terminum* provides a good example of his freer translations:

> *Te lucis ante terminum*
> *Rerum creator, poscimus*
> *Ut solita clementia*
> *Sis praesul ad custodiam.*

> Ere the waning light decay,
> God of all, to Thee we pray,
> Thee thy healthful grace to send,
> Thee to guard us and defend.

What is offered here is more something suggested by the original rather than the original itself. No attempt is made to translate the phrase *solita clementia* (the most familiar English translation renders it as 'wonted favour'), and there is no Latin equivalent of the word 'healthful'. The second verse also shows some interesting variations:

> *Procul recedant somnia*
> *Et noctium phantasmata;*
> *Hostemque nostrum comprime,*
> *Ne polluantur corpora.*

> Guard from dreams that may affright;
> Guard from terrors of the night;
> Guard from foes, without, within;
> Outward danger, inward sin.

Perhaps no nineteenth-century translator could be expected fully to rise to the challenge of the last line! However, the familiar translation comes close in

> Tread underfoot our ghostly foe,
> That no pollution we may know.

More unexpectedly, by rendering 'hostem' in the plural he moves away from the idea of Satan, the 'great enemy' and he does not attempt to match the physicality of 'comprime'. The third and final Latin verse is, as is customary, a doxology. Mant renders this fairly freely and adds a verse expanding the thought of the original:

> Mindful of our only stay,
> Duly thus to Thee we pray;
> Duly thus to Thee we raise
> Trophies of our grateful praise.
>
> Hear the prayer, Almighty King!
> Hear Thy praises while we sing,
> Hymning with Thy heavenly Host,
> Father, Son and Holy Ghost.

This is a homage rather than a translation. It is a solemn, dignified and thoughtful evening hymn, very suitable for the purposes of personal devotion for which it was intended. If it is not an exact translation of the original, it certainly derives from it.

The results can be rather strange when Mant encounters theology he finds unacceptable as a Protestant. As might be expected hymns in honour of the Blessed Virgin Mary and the Saints cause him problems. For his first hymn to the Annunciation Mant chose a great hymn attributed to Venantius Fortunatus:

> *Quem terra, pontus, sidera,*
> *Colunt, adorant, praedicant,*
> *Trinam regentem machinam,*
> *Claustrum Mariae bajulat.*

This appears as:

> Him whom the skies, the earth, the sea,
> Confess, adore, declare
> Lord of that threefold regency,
> Behold a Virgin bear!

Mant makes no attempt to convey the physicality of the last line or the specific reference to Mary rather than a Virgin. The name Mary nowhere appears in his translation. He thus renders the verse:

Beata caeli nuntio,
Fecunda Sancto Spiritu
Desideratus gentibus
Cujus per alvum fusus est.

Blest, whom the Angel hail'd, on whom
The Holy Ghost came down;
Whose Son, desired their health to come,
Their health the nations own!

Once more, Mant does not attempt to render the physicality of this very physical hymn and moves the focus from the Mother of God to Christ himself. He adds an extra verse:

But blest, more blest than she, are they
By whom His will is done,
Who hear His precepts, and obey,
The Father in the Son.

This entirely biblical sentiment has the effect of completely altering the intentions of the hymn writer. It is significant that for his second Annunciation hymn Mant supplies an original rather than attempts another translation. The Latin original of the All Saints' hymn *Salutis aeternae dator* is specifically addressed to the various categories of Saints, praising them and offering thanksgiving:

Vos Angelorum Millia
Patrumque coetus, agmina
Canora Vatum, vos reis
Precamini indulgentiam

Mant turns this into:

All glory for Thy angel train,
Who heaven's high temple throng;
All glory for those ancient men,
Bards of prophetick song.

Any idea of a direct address is unthinkable. For a doxology he adds this somewhat reproving final verse:

But not to them or hymn or prayer
Present we, due alone

> To Thee, and those with Thee who share,
> The everlasting throne.

The effect is of a schoolmaster pointing out the errors of a good-hearted but wayward pupil.

However it would be wrong to present Mant as totally negative about the Saints and the Blessed Virgin Mary. In other places his strong sense of the Kingdom of Heaven asserts itself triumphantly. His praise of the archangel Michael from his version of 'Te splendor et virtus patris' provide a fine example:

> He, the ancient dragon fell
> Smote and drove to nether hell;
> He both chief, and rebel crew,
> Victor from heaven's rampart threw.

It might be expected that the spirituality of *Stabat Mater*, the great meditation on the sufferings of Christ's mother at the foot of the Cross, might be remote from the sensibilities of an English churchman of Mant's generation. However he chooses the first five verses of this long poem as one of his hymns for Good Friday and his fine version deserves to be quoted in full:

> By the cross, sad vigil keeping,
> Stood the Mother, doleful, weeping,
> Where her Son extended hung;
> For her soul, of joy bereaved,
> Smit with anguish, deeply grieved,
> Lo! the piercing sword had wrung.
>
> O how sad and sore distressed
> Now was she, that Mother blessed
> Of the sole begotten One!
> Woe-begone, with heart's prostration,
> Mother meek, the bitter passion
> Saw she of her glorious Son.
>
> Who on Christ's fond Mother looking,
> Such extreme affliction brooking,
> Born of woman, would not weep?
> Who on Christ's fond Mother thinking,
> With her Son in sorrow sinking,
> Would not share her sorrow deep?

> For His people's sins rejected,
> She her Jesus, unprotected,
> Saw with thorns, with scourges rent:
> Saw her Son from judgment taken,
> Her beloved in death forsaken,
> Till His spirit forth He sent.
>
> With Thy Mother's deep devotion,
> Make me feel her strong emotion,
> Fount of love, Redeemer kind!
> That my heart, fresh ardour proving,
> Thee my God and Saviour Loving,
> May with Thee acceptance find!

Mant's version of the eastern hymn *Aurora coelum purpurat* is in the great tradition of both Easter and western writing on the Harrowing of Hell. Its first three verses make an appropriate conclusion to this survey:

> Morning spreads her crimson rays,
> Heaven resounds with hymns of praise,
> Through the earth loud anthems swell
> Heard with rage in vanquish'd hell.
>
> From the dark sepulchral gloom
> See the King of Glory come:
> See Him now from bondage freed
> All His saints to daylight lead.
>
> Vain the tomb securely barr'd,
> Sealed stone, armed guard:
> Death is crush'd, and finds his bier
> In the Conqueror's sepulchre.

The years following 1837 saw the emergence of a group of distinguished translators of hymns. As has been said, Mant, Williams and Chandler wrote for a literary audience. However, such was the demand for hymns that their versions were seized on for congregational use. Chandler bowed to the trend and produced a second volume in 1841 for public use. This set the trend for the translators that followed, writers like Edward Caswall and John Mason Neale.[8] Neale, who came from a slightly younger generation, was perhaps the greatest of them all. These, es-

---

[8] See L. Litvack, *John Mason Neale and the quest for sobornost* (Oxford, 1994); M. Chandler, *The life and work of John Mason Neale 1818–1866* (Leominster, 1995).

pecially Neale, were all more poetically accomplished than Mant and more concerned with fidelity to the original text, to which they applied greater scholarship. Neale stated that the hostility of the early Tractarians to hymns had been a mistake. He wrote very much with congregations in mind. He, and others, paved the way for the more literary hymn versions of Robert Bridges towards the end of the nineteenth century. As a result of all this, while a couple of his own hymns have entered the standard repertoire, Mant's translations were soon superseded and are now largely forgotten. Indeed Isaac Williams is described by his modern biographer as having made 'the first attempt to restore the hymns of Latin Christendom to the English church'.[9] His collection appeared in 1839, two years after Mant's.

Yet it is right to remember Mant's translations. They demonstrate the value of translated hymns in the religious life of the English-speaking world. Through them insights from other Christian traditions were absorbed into the bloodstream of English worship. These insights were domesticated through the medium of hymnody and any strain of the exotic removed. Thus medieval, and indeed post-Reformation, Latin hymns became part of Anglican and, at a slightly later stage, Nonconformist services. Neale and others translated Greek hymns and so insights from the eastern church were absorbed in the same way. The part played by Mant in this process should be acknowledged.

In his lifetime Richard Mant was in constant battle with other Christians, especially Roman Catholics. While this conflict was theological there is no evidence that Mant made any personal friendships with those on the other side. His biography by his son is in many ways painful reading.[10] The 1840s were a time of bitter religious conflict, in Belfast and elsewhere. Yet at a devotional level his strong faith could encounter constructively and draw from the faith of those with whom he disagreed. This devotional meeting among Christians has been relatively little acknowledged, although the work of A.M. Allchin is an outstanding exception.[11] I would argue that it has laid the groundwork for closer personal contacts between Christians. Richard Mant's engagement with Latin hymnody still has lessons for us today.

It is particularly appropriate that it should be remembered as we honour a classical scholar and a musician, a son of both the Church of Ireland and the Church of England, who, like Mant, has made his home in Belfast and has contributed so richly to its culture and educational life.

---

[9] O.W. Jones, *Isaac Williams and his circle* (London, 1971), 161.

[10] W.H. Mant, *Memoirs of the Right Reverend Richard Mant, D.D., M.R.I.A., Lord Bishop of Down and Connor, and of Dromore* (Dublin, 1857).

[11] See especially his *The dynamic of tradition* (London, 1981).

TRANSLATIONS

16

Verse translation of Horace, *Odes* 1.5

Estelle Haan

As I show above,[1] 'translation', whether in the form of 'the double translation system', 'the turning of verses' or the 'metaphrase' was a central part of the Renaissance educational system. Certainly Horace's *Odes* I.5 has been translated through the centuries (and in a multitude of ways) by schoolboys, schoolmasters, undergraduates, and scholars alike.[2] We have already seen how Milton's express delight in imitating classical Latin poets is exemplified by his skillful metaphrastic version. Not all schoolboys, however, were so talented. In the early eighteenth century Richard Steele relays an affectionately humorous anecdote of a proud mother who asked a classics master to test her son's (extremely dubious) knowledge of the Latin Ode in question. He examined him thus:

> In the first Place I asked him, Who this same Pyrrha was? He answered very readily: 'She was the Wife of Pyrrhus, one of Alexander's Captains'. I lifted up my Hands. The Mother courtesies 'Nay', says she, 'I knew you would stand in Admiration. I assure you', continued she, 'for he looks so tall, he is but very young. Pray ask him some more, never spare him'. With that I took the Liberty to ask him, What was the Character of this Gentlewoman? He read the Three first Verses.
>
> > Quis multa gracilis te Puer in rosa
> > Perfusus liquidis urget Odoribus
> > Grato, Pyrrha, sub Antro?
>
> And very gravely told me: 'She lived at the Sign of the Rose in a Cellar'. I took Care to be very much astonished at the Lad's Improvements; but withal advised her, as soon as possible, to take him from School, for he could learn no more there.[3]

---

[1] E. Haan, 'The adorning of my native tongue: linguistic metamorphosis in Milton', 119.
[2] See R. Storrs, *Ad Pyrrham: A polyglot collection of translations of Horace's Ode to Pyrrha (Book 1, Ode 5)* (London, 1959).
[3] *The Tatler*, no. 173 (18 May, 1710) in *The Tatler*, ed. Donald F. Bond (Oxford, 1987), II, 447–451, at 448–449. I have modernised punctuation.

The master's obvious sensitivity to the boy's feelings, reflected in his feigned admiration of the child's futile attempts to understand or interpret the poem, anticipates the gentleness, patience, good humour, and expertise of another teacher, translator and scholar almost three centuries later – except that Dr Bob Jordan would not have sent the schoolboy (or girl) away.

In my verse rendering of *Odes* 1.5 below I have aimed to fuse aspects of the Renaissance metaphrase with the linguistic experimentalism afforded by eighteenth-century translational methodology and practice. Like Milton's version,[4] it replicates the stanzaic structure, linguistic alterity, and at times the Latinate word-order of the original, but it moves beyond metaphrase in its liberal use of rhyme and rhythm as a means of enhancing the accessibility of the text to a modern readership. Composed in iambic pentameters and employing the heroic couplet – a form which would achieve its fullest manifestation in the verse translations of Dryden and Pope – it is in many respects a pseudo-eighteenth-century experiment:

> With liquid scents bedew'd what slender boy
> 'Mid roses 'neath sweet cave with thee doth toy?
>   For whom, o Pyrrha, unadorn'd, refin'd,
>   Dost thou thy tresses gold in fast'nings bind?
>
> How oft, alas, shall he have cause to weep
> O'er changèd gods and faith thou didst not keep,
>   And, unaccustom'd, shall with wonder mark
>   The seas that will be rough with storm winds dark,
>
> Who, trusting, now enjoyeth golden thee,
> Who thee e'er loving hopeth, thee e'er free,
>   While he the breeze beguiling doth not know;
>   O wretches for whom thou untri'd dost glow;
>
> On my account the hallow'd wall doth state
> (with tablet vow'd it thus doth indicate):
>   That I have hung up dripping vestments mine
>   In honour of the powerful God of brine.

---

[4] E. Haan, 'The adorning of my native tongue: linguistic metamorphosis in Milton', 111–127.

17

Romanos's *kontakion* On Elijah

James Peden

I first encountered Romanos's *kontakia* in a reading class of Dr Jordan's. Like all his students I can recall with great pleasure the experience of these classes animated by the good humour and sustained by the expertise and boundless patience of our teacher. It is with a great sense of honour that I dedicate this translation of Romanos's *On Elijah* to him.

On Elijah is a good starting point to undertake a study of the work of this great Byzantine writer for it is highly representative of his narrative, dramatic and poetic techniques. In it he employs a full range of figures of speech which form his rhetorical panoply,[1] and it is doing justice to this that provides any translator with such a challenge.

There is the question of tense. I have tended to render Romanos's historic presents as pasts in my English version but am well aware that in doing so I am missing something of the immediacy and timelessness of the original. The present tenses of some of the prooimia illustrate what I mean.

Romanos's prooimia usually fulfil what Barkhuizen calls an 'indicative function' that is, they define the thematic context of the hymn.[2] He also argues that the prooimion serves a 'liturgical function.' For example, in *On the Resurrection I* this takes on what he terms 'a doxological perspective' with words such as ἑορτάζοντες and ἀγαλλιῶντες βοῶμεν. In the first *kontakion On the Nativity*[3] it acts a sort of *dramatis personae* and is very visual.[4] As it brings on stage one by one the various protagonists we can almost see the characters take their place in the mosaic or fresco: the Virgin in the cave, the angels with shepherds, the magi following the star. That is its indicative function. However, the visual aspect which we

---

[1] See K. Mitsakis, 'Figures of speech', *The language of Romanos the Melodist* (Munich, 1967) where the author discusses word order, repetition and redundancy, figures of vivacity, the contribution of sound, and of metaphor and comparison.
[2] J.H. Barkhuizen, 'Romanos Melodos: essay on the poetics of his *kontakion* "Resurrection of Christ"', *Maas-Trypanis*, 24', *BZ*, 79 (1986), 268–281.
[3] P. Maas and C.A. Trypanis, *Sancti Romani Melodi cantica: cantica genuina* (Oxford, 1961), 1.
[4] E.C. Topping, 'St Romanos the Melodos and the first nativity *kontakion*', *Three Byzantine sacred poets*, ed. N.M. Vaporis (Brookline, MA, 1979).

have already noticed takes on a liturgical perspective once we remember that the *kontakion* was performed in churches where the congregation was literally in the presence of the Theotokos and the angels as they gazed down from gilded domes and painted walls. The present tenses likewise introduce us into 'eternal' or 'liturgical time' as does the poet's σήμερον (v.1). Bishop Kallistos of Diokleia puts it this way:

> During the Divine Liturgy… the earthly and heavenly realms are joined in unity. Whether few or many, the members of the earthly congregation invariably form part of a larger, all-embracing drama; they are taken up into an action far greater than themselves… Those on earth are made concelebrants at the heavenly Liturgy with Christ himself, with the Mother of God, the angels and the saints.[5]

In the same way, the prooimion of *On Elijah* demands our present participation with its

> Intercede for us with
> Man's only Friend

And the present tenses throughout the narrative set the events of the *kontakion* firmly within our sphere of reality. It is in this eternal drama that the prooemion urges the congregation to participate as actors deeply involved in the redemptive process of which Elijah himself is the principal object. The *kontakion* as developed by Romanos is a form of instruction and story-telling, but it is much more than that. First and foremost it has a liturgical function. Andrew Louth compares the *kontakion* in general to an icon, for like the icon its setting is not an event of Scripture but a liturgical feast (in this case the feast of Elijah the Prophet, 20 July) and it invites and enables the worshipper to participate in the mystery which is being celebrated.[6] In this sense the *kontakion*, like the liturgy, is timeless, permitting us to bridge the span of centuries separating us from the events being commemorated and to become involved in them.[7] This aspect of invitation and participation is a common motif in much of Romanos's work. In stanza 4 of the Elijah *kontakion* we are invited

---

[5] Bishop Kallistos of Diokleia, 'The meaning of the Divine Liturgy for the Byzantine worshipper', *Church and people in Byzantium*, ed. R. Morris (Manchester, 1986).
[6] A. Louth, 'An invitation to the Christian mystery', Kontakia *on the Life of Christ: Saint Romanos the Melodist*, tr. E. Lash (San Francisco, CA, 1995).
[7] Indeed in a number of kontakia such as *On Mary at the Cross* and *On the Victory of the Cross* we travel not only in sacred time but in sacred space also as the scene shifts from earth to Hades and back again.

ἀλλ' εἰ βούλεσθε,   πρὸς τὴν βίβλον ἀναδράμωμεν
καὶ γνῶμεν τὰ ῥήματα.

The prooimion and the refrain are intimately linked since it is the final clause of the prooimion that provides the refrain. It is important for the translator to so work with the text that this relationship is upheld clearly and consistently. The refrain like the prooimion fulfils various functions. Often it keeps before us the central point or doctrine which the poet is investigating and making explicit. We observe this in the Elijah *kontakion* where it continually reminds us of God's compassion as he is 'Man's only Friend' – but on the lips of the various characters with what different tones and connotations it is endowed! Sometimes it is God revealing himself in a longing plea, sometimes it is Elijah resentfully throwing the epithet in God's face, and it is even found on the widow's lips with scathing, disbelieving irony. These subtle shifts in tone invite us to muse on the real meaning and depth of the words. *On the Presentation in the Temple*[8] uses the same refrain as *On Elijah*. There it is interesting to see how the poet similarly moves through a series of divine titles, such as those by which Elijah addresses God here – Κύριος, δεσπότης, βασιλεύς, κτίστης – as he represents Simeon's spiritual odyssey towards an appreciation of God's *philanthropia*.[9] In this way the refrain keeps before the congregation the goal to which our understanding of God is to progress. This interconnecting web of terms used in prooimia, refrains, and from *kontakion* to *kontakion* provides the translator with a considerable challenge. He must seek to preserve and make identifiable this subtle system of resonances which vibrates not only throughout the various sections of an individual *kontakion* but through the poet's entire *oeuvre*. To do so requires great vigilance in order to be consistent and systematic, yet sensitivity in order not to lose the poetic quality of the work.

It has been impossible to fully respect the divisions of Romanos's *kola* or to represent his mastery of word order in any meaningful way. He likes to place cognates in a chain such as in Strophe 16 where we have the series ξένος... πρόξενος... ξενοδόχῳ which it is extremely difficult to render. I have tried, as far as I understand them, to convey the emphases of the original text whether these be individual words, phrases or concepts.

I have based my translation on the Oxford text of P. Maas and C. Trypanis but have occasionally allowed myself the liberty of preferring a reading from the French edition by J. Grosdidier de Matons.[10] I had a French teacher who used to

---

[8] *Maas-Trypanis*, 4.
[9] E.C. Topping, 'A Byzantine song for Simeon: the fourth *kontakion* of Saint Romanos', *Traditio*, 24 (1968), 409–421.
[10] J. Grosdidier de Matons, *Romanos le Mélode: hymnes* (SC, 99, 110, 114, 128, 283, Paris, 1964–1981).

say of translations: *si elle est belle elle ne peut être fidèle*. I have done my best to walk the tightrope between elegance and literalism and for what it is worth I offer this translation to this collection and take the opportunity of wishing Bob a happy and productive retirement.

Translation *On Elijah*

Prologue
Prophet and seer of the magnificent works of our God,
Magnificent Elijah, who, by your utterance, stayed the watery clouds,
Intercede for us with
Man's only Friend.

Strophe 1
Observing men's great lawlessness and God's great compassion for those men
The prophet Elijah was convulsed with rage
And cast unpitying words at the All-Pitying One
Crying 'Rage against those who have now despised you, most righteous Judge.'[11]
Yet he could by no means move the bowels of him who is good
To wreak vengeance on those who had despised him;
For he always awaits repentance[12] – he who is
Man's only Friend.

Strophe 2
When the prophet saw the whole earth sold to lawlessness,[13]
Nor the Most High raging against them in the least, but rather bearing with them,
He was moved to frenzy and called upon the All-Pitying One to witness:
'I will take over and I will punish the ungodliness of those who anger you;
For these have all scorned you great forbearance, and failed to recognise
You the All-Pitying Father;
But, lover of your children, you pity them as
Man's only Friend.

Strophe 3
Now I will judge on the Creator's behalf, I will cut off the ungodly from the earth,[14]

---

[11] Psalm 7:11 presents the idea of God as a righteous Judge who can be angry with righteous anger.
[12] Wisdom 12:19.
[13] Compare Genesis 6:5.

And I will vote for vengeance; but I fear divine goodness,
For Man's Friend is importuned by just a few tears.[15]
What shall I think up against such great goodness? I have it,[16] I will stay his mercy
Bolstering my stance with an oath so that, even when he is importuned by it,
Being righteous he will not loose
So great a sentence, but as lord will uphold my judgement – he who is
Man's only Friend.'

Strophe 4
The oath preceded the judgement and was a prologue to the decrees.
But if you wish, let us hasten to the Scripture and learn its words,[17]
For the raging prophet says, as is written:
'As the Lord lives, neither dew nor rain shall fall except by my word.'
But immediately the King answered Elijah:
'Yet if I see repentance and welling tears,
I cannot withhold my compassions from men – I, who am
Man's only Friend.

Strophe 5
The prophet immediately argued and alleged the legality of the oath.
'By you,' he said, 'the God of all, have I sworn, most holy Master,
That no more rain would be given – except by my word.
Therefore when I see the people repenting, I will supplicate you.
It is no longer in your power, Most Righteous, to loose the punishment
Of the oath which I have sworn.
Keep it and seal it retracting your bowels of compassion,[18]
Man's only Friend!

Strophe 6
The famine was besieging the land and its inhabitants were wasting away,
Wailing and stretching out their hands to the All-Merciful.

---

[14] 3(1) Kings 21:21. The verb ἐξολοθρεύω is used throughout the Old Testament to mean 'to destroy utterly'. Compare Genesis 17:14, 1 Matthew 3:8, etc.
[15] Compare Basil of Seleucia: *PG,* 85, 149A: Φοβοῦμαι δ'ὅμως τὸ φιλάνθρωπον τοῦ Θεοῦ· οἶδα γὰρ δάκρυσι ταχέως αὐτὸν πειθόμενον· οἶδα ταῖς ἱκεσίαις καμπτόμενον.
[16] Literally: 'Yes!'
[17] 3(1) Kings 17.
[18] In *PG,* 85, 149A Basil uses the verb συστέλλω of God reducing the punishment for men: οἶδα μικρᾷ μετανοίᾳ τὰς τιμωρίας συστέλλοντα; here Romanos uses it in the sense of God contracting his compassion.

The Master was trapped between two causes:[19]
On one hand opening up his bowels of mercy to his suppliants and eager to be merciful;
On the other respecting his prophet and the oath which he had sworn[20]
He did not give the rain but prepared a loop-hole
Which trapped and afflicted the prophet's soul – as
Man's only Friend.

Strophe 7
The Master seeing the Tishbite fuming with rage against his fellows
Decided to afflict that righteous man with hunger along with the others
So that, oppressed by want, he might resolve on compassion in regard to the oath which he had sworn
And bring the punishment to an end.[21]
For truly the inexorable craving of the stomach is a dreadful thing,
But he nourishes each living thing, rational and irrational,
And preserves them through the wisdom of his godhead and with food – he who is
Man's only Friend.

Strophe 8
The stomach began to plead on nature's behalf
And taking up nature's laws[22] set upon the old man wilily
To make him change his resolve.
But he, like unfeeling stone, resisted
Supplied with his zeal instead of any feast[23] – and with this well satisfied!
The Judge, after observing him, relieved his hungering friend's need
Considering it unjust for the just to hunger along with the unjust and lawless[24]
– he
Man's only Friend.

---

[19] Basil of Seleucia writes: *PG*, 85, 149C: Ὑφ'ἑκατέρων δὲ συνεχόμενος ὁ τῶν ὅλων Δεσπότης.

[20] In 'Das Kontakion', 302, Maas indicates a parallel passage in Basil of Seleucia: *PG*, 85, 149C.

[21] The parallel passage in Psuedo-Chrysostom: *PG*, 56, 584 reads: ἵνα τοῦ λιμοῦ καὶ αὐτὸς συνεχόμενος τιμωρίᾳ βουλεύσηται τι περὶ τῆς ἀποφάσεως τῆς ἐνόρκου φιλάνθρωπον.

[22] Here I follow the French edition λαβοῦσα.

[23] Basil of Seleucia also speaks of Elijah revelling luxuriously in revenge: *PG*, 85, 151A: ὡς εἶδεν τρυφῶντα ἀσεβῶν τιμωρίᾳ but Romanos likens it specifically to a hungry man in regaling himself in a feast.

[24] Basil of Seleucia writes: *PG*, 85, 151A: ἵνα μὴ τοῖς ἀσεβέσιν ὁ εὐσεβὴς λιμῷ διαφθείρηται.

Strophe 9
So the All-Merciful, in great wisdom, prepared food for him;
For he commanded compassionless the ravens to provide him food.
Now the race of ravens knows no compassion
As they never bring food to their nestlings as [one ought] to children –
But they are nourished from above.[25]
Now since he was adopting the manners and thinking of a child-hater,
He, in all wisdom, used child-haters – ravens – against this man-hater – he who is
Man's only Friend.

Strophe 10
'This great friendship of yours,' reasoned God with Elijah,
'Let it not bring over you a disposition of hatred towards man; but look upon the crows,
For they, who are always haters of their children, are suddenly,
As you see, zealous towards you and are now transformed.
They have been revealed as ministers of my pity
By providing you with food. But, as I see it,
I am unable to assail[26] your nature in regard to men – I
Man's only Friend.

Strophe 11
Now, prophet, you should feel some shame[27] and imitate the tractability of the brute beasts:
How these merciless creatures – which nonetheless respect[28] me the All-Pitying One – were suddenly transformed.[29]
I value your friendship and do not loose your sentence
But I cannot bear the universal wailing and tribulation of the men whom I created.
The cry of infants and their tears
And the unintelligible bellowing of beasts – how am I to bear it?

---

[25] Job 38:41, Psalm 146(147):9, Luke 12:24.

[26] Basil uses this verb of Elijah assailing God's nature: *PG*, 85, 149B: αὐτὴν τοῦ Θεοῦ φιλανθρωπίαν βιάσομαι.

[27] αἰδεῖσθαι ranges in meaning from 'to fear', 'to reverence', 'to feel shame', and even 'to pardon' – all these nuances are present here in God's address to Elijah.

[28] The verb αἰδεῖσθαι appears in verse 1 where I have translated it 'feel some shame' and here where I have rendered it 'respect.' It has, as I have stated, a wide range of nuances – basically that one's reverence for another binds one by a sense of honour or duty to behave respectfully towards them. I feel that the dual translation is necessary to indicate the somewhat different reactions of the two concerned to God's command.

[29] Basil of Seleucia writes: *PG*, 85, 151A: Ἐνίκησαν οὗτοι τὴν φύσιν τῇ περί σε λειτουργίᾳ.

For as their modeller I will sympathise with them all – I, who am
Man's only Friend.

Strophe 12
In spite of this the prophet grew savage, and then he answered the Master:
'Do not urge the ravens, your ministers, to feed me, Master;
I will choose to perish with hunger, Most Holy One,
And if only I can wreak vengeance on the ungodly, that will be refreshment for me.
Therefore, do not pity me, and in my hunger
Do not spare me, but only
Cut off[30] the ungodly from the earth – You,
Man's only Friend.

Strophe 13
When the Creator heard these words he removed the prophet from that place
And commanded the birds not to provide him with food as before.
And he sent him to Sarepta to a starving widow
Saying: 'I will command a woman to nourish you.' Wise counsel!
For the woman to whom he was sent was a widow and a gentile and cumbered about with children;[31]
That the righteous man hearing her gentile status might cry:
'Give the rain,
Man's only Friend.'

Strophe 14
It was forbidden for Jews ever to eat with other races,
That is why he guided Elijah to a woman of different nationality
That, disgusted by her fare,
He might immediately importune Man's Friend.
But he thought nothing of his flight to the nations,
But, in all haste, ran to the woman demanding of her food:
'He has instructed me, woman,' he said, 'to exact [sustenance] from you – he, who is
Man's only Friend.'

Strophe 15
Now when she heard this the widow replied in all earnestness:

---

[30] See note 4.
[31] The Septuagint speaks of children whereas the Hebrew and Syriac mention only one child.

'I have no loaves baked in the ashes, only a handful of flour
Which I wish to make so that I may eat with my children.
Nothing more than this handful is left to me – except death.[32]
At the widow's voice he was shaken and began to sympathise
As he reasoned thus: 'This widow is pining away and is more afflicted than I,
Unless he intervenes first – who is
Man's only Friend.'

Strophe 16
'Now,' he said, 'the woman's lot troubles me. For if I am famished,
I am alone, but the widow to whom I have come is starving with her children.
Heaven forbid that I the guest should become for her death's host,[33]
I will not be reckoned a child-slayer by my hostess.
But now let me consider mercy. I was at enmity with all, now I will change towards her.
I shall accustom my nature to delight in pity
For he abides pitiful – the author of the universe –
Man's only Friend.'

Strophe 17
The prophet answered the widow, 'You have one handful of flour, as you say:
Your vessel will not run dry, and your jar will overflow with oil.'
And not only did Elijah by his words grant the blessing,
But the Creator immediately, as the zealous and merciful one, brought the act to pass.
The All-Wise fulfilling, [Scripture] says, the prophet's aim,
Or, more exactly, seizing the best pretext,
Granted the widow abundance – he, who is
Man's only Friend.

Strophe 18
God acquiesced with the prophet's words and provided food for him and the widow;
Yet Elijah was totally unmoved by pity and remained inflexible.
Now the All-Pitying One, when he saw the people perishing,

---

[32] Basil of Seleucia puts it neatly: *PG*, 85.153B: Τὸ πέρας ἡμῖν τῆς τροφῆς, ἀρχὴ τελευτῆς.

[33] Here the Greek has a play on words with ξένος and πρόξενος. I have tried to convey the relationship between these two words in English by using 'guest' and 'host' but this is not an exact translation of πρόξενος by any means. Rather, as Carpenter indicates, the noun is linked to the verb προξενέω, which means to be a patron or a means of bringing something to pass.

And the prophet acting in disobedience
Turned, in his righteousness, to another ruse; for he put to death the widow's son[34]
So that, observing the widow's tears and other distress
He might cry: 'Give the rain,
Man's only Friend.'

Strophe 19
When, therefore, the widow saw that her son was dead
She revolted against the prophet, saying: 'O that I had died of starvation first before I saw you.[35]
For it would have been better for me to have starved to death and not see my son stretched out dead in your presence.
Are these the rewards of excellent hospitality?
For I was happy in my children before you came, O man,
But now that you have come you have bereaved me of my children,
As you called upon
Man's only Friend.'

Strophe 20
He who had seized control of the clouds and rain now found himself seized tightly by the widow;
And he who constrained all by his word, was constrained himself by one woman.
And a poor woman, devoid of all power,
By her word and power, held, as a criminal, him who thought he held the rain.[36]
And seizing him in a frenzy she dragged him as a murderer to court, crying:
'Give me my child whom you killed; I have no use for your flour,
Do not nourish me, thinking that you have become
Man's friend.

Strophe 21
You sowed bread in my stomach but have ripped out by the root
The stomach's fruit and branch, and you sell me [and at what a price!] gifts of food,
Craftily exacting a life for some flour and oil.
But I beseech you to overthrow the contract and return what you have taken.
Or were you not satisfied with the deaths of the people

---

[34] Literally: 'he showed the widow's son dead.'
[35] The parallel passage in Basil of Seleucia: *PG*, 85, 153 reads: εἴθε, φησί, τῷ λιμῷ παραπολοίμην.
[36] On both occasions 'held' is κρατέω as in verse 1.

But have hastened to lay your hand on my house?
Loose my son's life and carry off my life instead, and become
Man's friend.'

Strophe 22
Pricked by these words as by goads and shamed by the wailing of the widow,
Who suspected that he had wrested her son's life by force,
Though he tried to persuade her with words – he could not.
Seeing that he was not believed by her – though he made his defence –
He lamented unceasingly. But looking up to heaven, he cried:
'Alas, Lord, irreproachable Witness[37] of this woman who took me as her guest,
You have moved her to demand of me her child – You, who are
Man's only Friend.

Strophe 23
'I do not believe, Saviour,' the prophet cried out to the All-Powerful God,
'That death has come upon the child naturally, as it does upon all.
Rather, this is due to the cunning of your wisdom, Sinless One,
And you have schemed up against me a constraint of pity
So that when I ask you: "Raise up the widow's son who has died,"
You may immediately reply: "Have mercy on my son Israel
In his affliction and on all my people" – You, who are
Man's only Friend.'[38]

Strophe 24
Wishing to save the earth, the All-Pitying One immediately answered Elijah:
'Now pay more attention to my words and listen to me while I speak.
I am suffering the pangs of childbirth and longing for the cancellation of the punishment.
I am eager to give food to all the hungry – for I am the All-Pitying One.
Seeing the floods of tears I am moved as a father,
I am full of pity for those who are wasting away through famine and tribulation.
For I want to save sinners through repentance – I, who am
Man's only Friend.

---

[37] Basil of Seleucia: *PG*, 85, 155A reads: Οἴμοι, Κύριε, ὁ μάρτυς τῆς χήρας...

[38] Basil of Seleucia: *PG*, 85, 155A reads: Ἔγνων σου τὴν κατ'ἐμοῦ μηναχὴν· ᾐσθόμην οἷς παρὰ σοῦ περιβέβλημαι· ἀντιδόσιν ἀπατεῖς με φιλανθρωπίας, ἵν' ὅταν ἐγὼ περὶ τοῦ παιδίου τῆς χήρας ἱκτεύσω, Λῦσον, ὦ Κτίστα, τοῦ παιδίου τὸν θάνατον, ἀντεπαγάγῃς μοι καὶ αὐτὸς Λῦσον οὖν καὶ σὺ τὴν τοῦ παιδός μου τοῦ Ἰσραὴλ τῆς ἀβροχίας ἀπόφασιν.

Strophe 25
Therefore, prophet, listen to me with confidence; for I am very eager that you
    should know
That all men hold me by a treaty of pity[39]
In which I have stated that I do not desire to see the death of trespassers,
But rather their life.[40]
Do not present me before them as a liar but accept my request:
I offer you my mediation,
For in regard to all, I am
Man's Friend.'

Strophe 26
Elijah submitted his mind and thoughts – and his ears to the words of the Most
    High:
He both humbled his soul and beautified it by his words:
He said: 'Master, therefore let your will be done.[41]
Grant both rain – and life to the dead.
God, you who are Life and Resurrection and Redemption,
Grant your grace to man and beast,
For you are the one who can save all creatures – You, who are
Man's only Friend.'

Strophe 27
As soon as the prophet said this the All-Pitying One answered him:
'I accept your decision and praise it, and now I hasten to honour you.
I have received from you grace for them,
Now be my mediator and furnish my grace, for I cannot allow them
To be reconciled without you. But go and declare
The granting of the rain so that all may raise the shout
"He who lately was pitiless has suddenly become all
Men's friend."

Strophe 28
So go quickly, prophet, and when you have shown yourself to Ahab, tell him the
    good news,

---

[39] Basil of Seleucia: *PG*, 85, 157A reads: ἐμοὶ δὲ ὄντι Δεσπότῃ νόμος φιλανθρωπίας ἀνάγραπτος. Ὀφειλέτην αὐτὸς ἐμαυτὸν ἀγαθότητος ἐγγράφως κατέστησα... *Οὐ βούλομαι τὸν θάνατον τοῦ ἁμαρτωλοῦ, ὡς τὸ ἐπιστρέψαι αὐτὸν πρός με, καὶ ζῆν.*
[40] Ezekiel 18:23,32.
[41] Luke 1:38, Matthew 6:10, Luke 11:2.

And I will command the clouds and they will water the earth with their moisture.
You, my friend, reveal the provision of these things,
And I, honouring your generosity, will subscribe to these so mighty decisions.'
When he heard this he instantly prostrated himself before the Most High,
Crying to the All-Pitying One: 'I know that you are rich in mercy,
I realise that you are long-suffering, my God,
Man's only Friend.'

Strophe 29
The prophet, respecting the commandment, ran to Ahab
And announced the glad tidings to him as the All-Pitying One had said.
And immediately, by the Maker's order, the clouds
Pregnant with water glided over the air pouring down showers of rain.
The earth exulted[42] and began to glorify the Lord.
The woman received her child raised [from the dead] and Elijah[43]
Rejoiced and lauded him who is
Man's only Friend.[44]

Strophe 30
When a considerable time had elapsed Elijah saw the wickedness of men
And thought upon making the punishment heavier still.
But, observing this, the All-Pitying One answered the prophet:
'I understand the zeal you have for righteousness, and I know your resolve,
But I feel compassion towards sinners whenever they are punished beyond measure.
You are filled with wrath and cannot bear [them], but I cannot bear
That anyone should perish – I, who am
Man's only Friend.'

Strophe 31
After this, the Master seeing how harsh [he was] towards men,
Gave consideration to their race and removed Elijah from their land,
Saying: 'Friend, withdraw from the dwelling of men,
And, as the All-Pitying One, I will come down to men, having become Man.

---

[42] Psalm 95(96):11, 96(97):1, Isaiah 49:13.

[43] Here I follow the text of the French edition. See commentary.

[44] Basil of Seleucia reads: *PG*, 85, 156D ...ὁ μὲν οὖν τῆς χήρας υἱὸς ταῖς τῆς ἀγκάλαις ἐδίδοτο· Ἠλίας δὲ ταῖς τοῦ Θεοῦ μηχαναῖς πρὸς φιλανθρωπίαν καμφθεὶς τὸν ὑετὸν ἀνθρώποις ἐδίδου· καὶ πάλιν οὐρανὸς νεφέλας ἐνδύεται, γῆ δὲ τὴν τῆς ἀκαρπίας χρείαν ἀπετίθετο· καὶ πάλιν ἡ κτίσις διὰ τῶν ὄμβρων ἐνεάζε...

Ascend up from the earth as one unable to bear men's failures,
But I, the Heavenly One, will mix with sinners
And snatch them from their failures – I, who am
Man's only Friend."[45]

Strophe 32
If, as I have said, prophet, you are unable to live with men who trespass,
Come here and inhabit the sinless regions of my friends.[46]
But I am going down able to bear on my shoulders the sheep that has gone astray[47]
And to cry to those who stumble:
"Sinners, come running to me and find rest;[48]
For I have come
Not to punish those I formed[49], but to pluck sinners from ungodliness – I, who am
Man's only Friend." '

Strophe 33
Behold, Elijah dispatched on high, appeared as a figure of things to come:[50]
For the Tishbite was taken up in a chariot of fire, as is written;[51]
But Christ was taken up among clouds and powers.[52]
The former sent Elisha his mantle from on high;[53]
But Christ sent down upon his apostles the Paraclete, the Holy One,[54]
Whom all we who are baptised have received,[55]
By whom we are sanctified[56] as he teaches us all – He who is
Man's only Friend.

---

[45] Maas compares Basil of Seleucia: *PG*, 85, 156D and strophes 29–31.
[46] Basil of Seleucia: *PG*, 85, 157B reads: Σὺ μὲν οὖν δέχου καταγώγιον ἁμαρτίας ἐλεύθερον, συμπολιτεύου μετὰ σαρκὸς τοῖς ἀγγέλοις· ἐγὼ δὲ πρὸς ἀνθρώπους διὰ τῆς οἰκονομίας ἐλεύσομαι, ἐγὼ πρὸς τὴν τούτων σωτηρίαν δραμήσομαι.
[47] Luke 15:3–7, Isaiah 49:11, Isaiah 53:6.
[48] Matthew 11:28.
[49] John 3:17.
[50] Hebrews 10:1.
[51] 4(2) Kings 2:11.
[52] Acts 1:8,9.
[53] 4(2) Kings 2:13.
[54] John 15:26, Acts 1:5.
[55] 1 Corinthians 12:13.
[56] Romans 15:16.

18

Alexander the monk, *Discovery of the True Cross*

Roger Scott

Alexander the monk's treatise on the *Discovery of the True Cross* not only describes the event of its title but also offers a symbolic explanation of the Cross (since God made 'everything worthy in all creation... in the form of a cross') as well as accounts of early Christian history, the appearance of the Cross over Jerusalem in 351 and finally an encomium of the Cross in the form of a long list of salutations. A translation of the treatise is, I hope, a suitable way of honouring Bob Jordan. For Bob is not only a fine translator but also a teacher of Byzantine Greek who has sought out interesting texts which, with a little help, could be read in the original by those in the early stages of learning the language. The language of much of *Discovery of the True Cross* is straightforward, though in places it also presents challenges which I have not necessarily solved, while its narrative presents a lively account of how Byzantines viewed some intriguing aspects of the history of early Christianity. My hope is that my translation will not only allow Bob to add this text to the repertoire of introductory texts but that he will also now help in improving this preliminary version.

Discovery of the True Cross has not been previously translated into a modern language. The translation will eventually accompany a much-needed new edition of the text which is being prepared by John Nesbitt. The only edition of the Greek text is that of either 1598 or 1620 by Jacob Gretser (1560–1625), of which the 1734 reprint was taken over (probably with misprints) for the edition in *Patrologiae cursus completus, Series graeca*, ed. J.-P. Migne, 161 vols (Paris, 1857–1866). Gretser's edition is not only old but was based on just two witnesses whereas in fact more than thirty manuscripts exist, testimony to the work being widely read. My translation is thus a preliminary version which may possibly assist in solving textual problems but which certainly will need to be revised later when those textual problems have been resolved.

Nothing is known of Alexander. Similarities to criticisms of Origen made in 543 and before 553 provide a *terminus post quem* while a Georgian manuscript of the ninth century provides the *terminus ante quem*.[1] But a traditional date of the late sixth century remains probable, though not certain. Alexander claims that the work was commissioned by holy men, presumably at a monastery. It is unlikely that such a work would have been sought during the period that the Persians held the Cross after their capture of Jerusalem in 614. This, taken together with the absence of any reference to Heraclius' restoration of the Cross, almost certainly in 630, to which Alexander would surely have drawn attention if he had written after that event, suggests a date before 614.

I have noted those citations from the Bible which have so far been spotted and also correspondences with the text of Theophanes's chronicle. It did not seem appropriate to clutter this version with references to correspondences with several other texts, most notably various late *Lives* of Constantine. I have also suggested a few corrections to the corrupt text in *PG*. But although more work is needed, I hope this translation will help make this intriguing work available to a wider audience, as Bob Jordan's translations have also done for significant Byzantine texts.

Notes on the translation
Titles of books from the Bible are given without italics as in the King James version except that specific references to the Septuagint follow LSJ. References are by chapter and verse, not by page. Other works follow the abbreviations given in LSJ or Lampe, including references to editions listed by these works.
The text used is that in *PG*, 87, 4016–4076 (Alexander Salaminus, *de inventione crucis*), so variant readings are corrections to that text. PG column numbers are included in square brackets.
Words that have been added to the English translation for the sake of clarity have been placed in square brackets […].
† is used to indicate an unsolved corrupt reading.

---

[1] M. van Esbroeck, 'L'opuscule "Sur la Croix" d'Alexandre de Chypre et la version géorgienne', *Bedi Kartlisi*, 37 (1979), 107ff. Cf. A.K. Kazhdan, 'Constantinople imaginaire', *B*, 57 (1987), 199–200. Van Esbroeck argued for a date between 543 and 553, while Kazhdan argued for a ninth-century date.

A translation of Alexander Salaminus, *de inventione crucis*
(*PG*, 87, 4016–4076)

[4016A] The command of your paternal holinesses made me exceedingly dizzy. For you had commanded my nothingness to produce an historical narrative of the discovery of the life-bringing Wood, the all-sacred and venerable Cross on which our Lord Jesus Christ was stretched out of his own free will and so both dissolved the power of the devil and the tyranny of death and also bestowed security beyond understanding on those who believed in Him. Accepting your injunction, which went far beyond my own powers, I grew afraid of the undertaking. The work is suited to others rather than to us. For in our initiation we had none of the encyclical education, and we got our education from spiritual training, but we are really ignorant not only of letters but even of knowledge because of the long-lasting power of our sufferings.

[4016B] Although I was unequal [to the task] I feared that disobedience would be dangerous, and through my urge to obey, I shall in the end attempt to carry out the command, thrusting it all on to God and your prayers. And we shall not utter any private view (for we are novices in our scholarship and we lack knowledge), but what things we had strength to discover from the old histories (for many others have toiled at this) and what things we have taken from earlier tradition, these I have attempted to reveal to you with the help of God, after pondering the truth from everywhere. [4017A] But 'you should set in order the things that are wanting'[2] and pray for us, O most holy men.

We shall make the beginning of our account the one who is the beginning of every beginning. O only-begotten Son of God, the one being in the bosom[3] of the Father, the life-making Word being in the beginning from the living Father, with God who is forever; the one 'being the brightness of His glory and the express image of His person'[4] of the eternal Father from the beginning that has no beginning, the unfailing[5] beginning, the life without end from the everlasting life, the source of immortality from the source that makes life, the perfected and unchanging image of the invisible God, the mould of the Father the begetter, the ineffable light of the incomprehensible light, the life-giving stream of the life-producing source, the one of the same substance, same throne, same authority and same goodness as the engendering Father, the one possessing everything [4017B] the Father possesses except for ingenerateness, the one with the Father and the Holy Ghost (always proceeding from the Father) having introduced all things through Himself

---

[2] Titus, 1:5.
[3] 'Bosoms' in Greek! (cf. *A Patristic Greek Lexicon*, ed. G.W.H. Lampe (Oxford, 1961), 765–766 sv κόλπος for parallels).
[4] To the Hebrews, 1:3.
[5] Reading ἀνέκλειπτος for ἀνέκληπτος.

and from non-existence into existence. For there was nothing except for the consubstantial Holy Trinity, always existing in its own properties or rather substances or at any rate persons, the uncreated nature, the unfailing divinity, the lordly majesty[6] the continuous exultation, the simple and uncompounded and unbounded reality, which being always exactly thus did not have a beginning nor will it have an end.

[4017C] So this living, active and omnipotent Word of God, through the will of the Father and in co-operation with the Holy Ghost, introduced every creation both visible and invisible in the needful world into existence out of non-existence, knowing however, through divine foreknowledge, when, where, how and how large it was necessary for things to be. For the everlasting ages passed, so to speak, [4020A] in which there was nothing apart from God alone being glorified in the Trinity. For the three, in which the Divinity is, are one. Nor out of any private need did He introduce the things [created] (for the Divinity is without want) but out of unmeasured goodness, so that more would have a share of His grace. So having introduced and arranged all things in a suitable order, He created man later than everything [else] by fashioning the body out of the earth which had already been created, [adding] from Himself a rational mind to him and the capacity for intelligence which did not exist previously and was not a part of God as the deranged and crazy Origen blasphemed who, in a pagan or rather in an impious way,[7] introduced some pre-existing essence for souls and a monstrous restoration following from this. For the relevant point in the holy and divine Scripture [4020B] is that 'God breathed into his nostrils the breath of life and man became a living soul'[8] which gives no indication of any pre-existence of the soul, not even if it were to have been said 'And man received a living soul.' But that puffing was not the soul of man as is shown by the enigma that the all-holy Ghost does not exist outside of the creative power, according to the Prophet saying 'By the word of the Lord were the heavens made; and all the host of them by the breath of His mouth'[9] and furthermore 'The Spirit of God hath made me and the Almighty hath given me life'.[10]

[4020C] So the Word of God, having created everything magnificently, revealed it all by the tiniest amount of power. I say 'by the tiniest amount of power' since He made and makes everything just by His nod [4021A], always keeping His power appropriate according to the Prophet, saying 'the Lord hath done whatsoever He hath pleased.'[11] But the insane Origen dared to say that the power of God

---

[6] cf. Mac.Aeg. *hom.* 4.23 (*PG*, 34, 489D).
[7] cf. Cyr. S. *v. Euthym.* 26 (Schwartz 39.30), Bars. *resp.* (*PG*, 86, 892B).
[8] Genesis, 2:7.
[9] Psalms, 32 (33):6.
[10] Job, 33:4.
[11] Psalms, 113 (114):3.

was limited, and foaming up[12] with ten thousand other blasphemies and having filled up excessive amounts of evil report in his writings, he filled the world with an infinite amount of nonsense. He was condemned appropriately for his effrontery by synod.

But let me return to the question.

So God after creating man in His own image and likeness put him in paradise just as Scripture relates 'to labour not for the meat which perisheth but for that meat which endureth unto everlasting life,'[13] again manifestly by keeping the life-bringing instruction given to him by the Creator.

[4021B] No one should be critical of an introduction that is as long as this since it is neither without purpose nor without reason. But since our object is to commemorate the Cross, I wanted to reveal the glory of the life-making Cross at the outset, a glory which shines out in every creation from the very beginning. And consider whether it is not just so. For it is possible to see with complete accuracy that God made every created thing both visible and invisible; for having made width, length, height and depth, He clearly described the type of the Cross in a mysterious way as these make up its entirety. [4021C] And it is this, I believe, that is said by the very wise Paul. For he says 'For this cause I bow my knees unto the Father'[14] and so on 'that ye may be able to comprehend with all saints what is the breadth and length and depth and height.[15]

But everything worthy in all creation has been made with a greater wisdom by the Demiurge in the form of a cross. At any rate the fourfold form of living things signals unambiguously the type of the Cross by their shape. For the holy prophet says 'I saw the Lord sitting upon a throne, high and lifted up' and then 'and Seraphim stood in a circle about him and their legs were straight,[16] six wings on one and six wings on the other. And they covered their faces[17] with two wings and their feet with two and they flew with two.' Mystically through the highest powers the glory of the life-bringing Cross was revealed. [4021D] But even the stars flash their light in the shape of the Cross and mankind was fashioned in the shape of the Cross. For all people standing and stretching their hands incontrovertibly typify the Cross in their shape. And paradise has the symbol of the Cross, i.e. the Wood of Life, on which the serpent, the beginner of mischief, [4024A] through its excess of envy, allowed man to eat, quickly hurling him out of paradise because of his

---

[12] Assuming ἀπαφρίζω here equals ἀφρίζω as in Modern Greek. ἀπαφρίζω itself is very rare and its dictionary meaning 'skim' does not seem appropriate.

[13] John, 6:27.

[14] Ephesians, 3:14.

[15] Ephesians, 3:18. Greek word-order differs from King James.

[16] 'and their legs were straight' is Alexander's addition to the Septuagint version (Isaiah, 6:2).

[17] Alexander has the plural as against the singular of the Septuagint, which reads 'above it stood the seraphims; each one had six wings; with twain he covered his face; and with twain he covered his feet and with twain he did fly.'

disobedience [which arose] from the deception, and, because of his most wicked disobedience, delivering him up to sin, and, because of his sin, casting him down into the most bitter death. The sin of the most evil beginning has gone forward from generation to generation until it reached the bottommost pit of evils.

The holy Word was thus not turned aside from its own shape nor did it desert [mankind] whom He had made in His image. Nor did it push aside [mankind] oppressed by the evil skill of the devil [4024B] but it did not leave a gap in its visits upon each generation and recall errant mankind through the life-making Cross by the symbol as in a sign. For [God], since He is good, did not want [mankind], who had been created to be without corruption and was an image of His own character, to go to total perdition through the evil-doing of the devil. And when the whole world perished through unnatural intercourse and was condemned to destruction, then through the tiniest [piece of] Wood He preserved the just Noah with all his household from the universal shipwreck for the regeneration of the cosmos.[18] Likewise Abraham the great patriarch received through the Wood the proclamations of God on oath, when he was sent to a lofty place to sacrifice[19] his beloved son. Accepting the manner of his obedience, God revealed to him a ram, caught by its horns [4024C] in a thicket plant[20] which is interpreted as 'remission' clearly revealing in advance through prefiguration the remission that would come for the sins of the whole world through the nailing of the Lamb of Understanding on the Wood. Just as the tradition has it, the lofty place, which is holy, is [that of] Golgotha.

What does Jacob's adoration for the tip of his staff mean[21] except that the patriarch revealed prophetically that it is necessary that the life-giving Cross be adored by all who trust in Christ? Such signs and marvels as Moses made in Egypt through God's edict and through the forty years in the desert, [4025A] he made with the staff, with the Lawgiver signifying thereby through a symbol that all things are possible to him who trusts in the crucified Christ. Do I need to speak about all the prophets who proclaimed openly the glorious Cross and the salvation for the world that would come to be through it? For what could be clearer than the saying '[with] the fir tree, the pine tree and the box together to beautify the place of my sanctuary.'[22] For since the holy and consubstantial Trinity has brought about the salvation of mankind through the Cross in one of the substances of itself, naturally also the weapon of salvation was fitted together from three Woods. For the holy place is the holy catholic church in which all the faithful, carrying

---

[18] Cf. Genesis, 7 and 8.
[19] Note that this also means 'minister the gospel'.
[20] Cf.Genesis, 22:13. Thicket is 'sabek'.
[21] Genesis, 47:51; To the Hebrews, 11:21.
[22] Isaiah, 60:13

around the life-giving Cross, glorify [4025B] the Trinity, undefiled and worthy of all praise in joy and exultation.

Thus for all those being saved from Adam to Christ, justice was always administered symbolically through the esteemed Cross. And when the fulfilment of time of the glorious coming of the divine Word in the flesh arrived, then indeed He revealed the whole wealth of His natural love for us, not because of our deeds but because of a fitting goodness in the benefactor Himself. For, because of the mercy of His pity that comes from that same love of mankind, He did not want man to be oppressed by the devil's evil until the end [of time] but, by the will of the Father and the consent of the Holy Ghost, which is always present and in no way circumscribed, [4025C] He leant upon the heavens and came down for us and for our salvation, not being separated from the heavens but having settled in the womb of the holy, glorious and ever-virgin Mary, herself previously purified in her soul together with her limbs by the Holy Ghost.[23] 'The Word was made flesh and dwelt among us'[24] not changing His divinity into humanity, for the Word of God is immutable and unchangeable, but uniting with itself in substance the flesh from the womb of the Theotokos, having a rational and intellectual soul, unconfusedly, unchangeably, indivisibly and inseparably. 'In substance' is said because the Word of God is united not in man as fashioned, but the Word itself being perfect in its own substance [4025D] has taken on its own perfection in becoming man, being always one Christ and Son and Lord and King of all.

So He is born from an unwedded maiden [4028A] being from the seed of David and Abraham, in truth and not as a delusion, being the true God after the assumption. And thus the holy virgin is godbearer correctly and in truth, who thus brought Him forth even as she conceived Him. For she conceived [Him] without losing [her] virginity, and begot Him as befits God, for God was made flesh from her and in no way did He use doors to the way in or the way out. But the one born from her [is] in truth Emmanuel, being perfect in His humanity, being one and the same in each nature, always preserving in Him the difference or separate characteristic after the natures came together in one person and one substance.

[4028B] Our Lord Jesus Christ was born in the flesh in Bethlehem of Judaea in the days of king Herod. For the rulers of Juda had already come to an end in accordance with the prophecy, having lasted until Aristoboulos, a chief priest who placed the royal diadem on himself. But after the Roman general Pompey had besieged him and sent him in chains with his children to Rome and then imposed part of the tribute on the Judaeans, [Pompey] appointed Aristoboulos's brother Hyrkanos as chief priest. This Hyrkanos established a friendship with one Antipater of Askalon, a slave of idolatry, the father of Herod whom he established as overseer of the country. His son Herod was a man competent in affairs who dis-

---

[23] Cf. Greg Naz. Or.38.13 (PG, 36, 325B).
[24] John, 1:14.

patched many brigand-leaders by his bravery. After Hyrkanos had been taken prisoner by the Parthians and Antipater had been killed [4028C] and since there was no one left in authority, Herod grabbed the rule after giving the Romans a large amount of money and becoming their client.

After Augustus Caesar had crossed into Egypt with as large an army as was possible for the war against Cleopatra, to whom control of the Egyptian empire had fallen, since she was a Ptolemy by race, Herod met him and provided useful service both to the army and through money. God placed Cleopatra into the hands of Caesar and thus that dynasty in Egypt ended in the twelfth year of Augustus Caesar's rule. On returning [4029A] to Rome, [Augustus] appointed Herod as king of Judaea by decree of the senate because of his goodwill, placing the diadem on him. On his return to Jerusalem and with the Jews being unwilling to accept him on the grounds that he was a foreigner, Herod put many of them to death, plundering the city and the sacred precinct, so abusing his authority, and burned in a fire all the records of the tribes and their families which had been kept since [the time of] Esdra. Thus there would no longer be any knowledge among the Jews of what country they were from or from what tribe or who were autochthonous and who were proselytes, as they are called[25], and he put the holy stole under his own seal, and furthermore, being under no restraint, he sold the high priesthood to obscure people for money.

[4029B] In the forty-second year of Caesar Augustus, an edict from him was sent out for a census of the whole world.[26] This census was the first, as the sacred history of the Gospels states. Caesar entrusted this census (or levying of tribute at any rate) to the kindest and most important member of the senate, Cyrenius, whom he had placed in charge of Syria (i.e. Judaea) in the thirteenth consulate of Augustus and of Sylvanus.[27] It was during this consulate that our Lord Jesus Christ was born in Bethlehem of Judaea in accordance with the prophecy in the thirty-third year of king Herod, the son of Antipater, on the eighth day before the Kalends of January.[28] Epiphanios, the great and holy bishop of the Cyprians, is however firm in maintaining that the true birth of our Lord Jesus Christ from the holy Theotokos and ever-virgin Mary took place on the eighth day [4029C] before the Ides of January.[29] All the other divinely-wise teachers of the holy catholic and apostolic Church, as if with one voice, give the birth day of Christ as the eighth day before the Kalends of January.

But I consider it superfluous to put forward everybody's interpretations at the present time. For our current work is not concerned with this. By introducing one

---

[25] γειῶραι cf. LXX, *Is.* 14.1.
[26] See Luke, 2:1.
[27] 2 BC.
[28] 25 December.
[29] 6 January.

distinguished teacher, whom the holy Epiphanios introduced as a supporter of his own view, I shall leave it to the audience to select the better [interpretation]. Thus Ephraim the Syrian, no ordinary person and himself [4031A] a teacher of piety, states the following in his work on the victory of light: 'In the shining [month of] Xanthikos was the conception of the shining fruit and of light. And the darkness, running quickly, lacked the strength to obscure the shining conception.' And later 'In the cave occurred the birth of light which scattered our darkness. And in the month in which darkness departed, intelligible and movable light began shining on us. He interpreted for you the prefigurement of His conception which Moses revealed in his writings: and the month of His birth has likewise made clear the mystery for us.'

Our Lord Jesus Christ was born in Bethlehem of Judaea in the forty-second year of the rule of Augustus Caesar in the [4031B] afore-mentioned consulship, in the thirty-third year of Herod [the son of] Antipater in the thirtieth year of the subjection of Egypt, on the eighth day before the Kalends of January according to the Fathers, when the Magi were present in Jerusalem seeking the [new-]born king, where the star from the East guided them right to Judaea. Having reached the royal city but lost their guide, they sadly began asking the local inhabitants, revealing to them their heavenly guide. When Herod heard about this, being a clever man, he recognised that the sign was not human. For, he said, although many kings had been born in Jerusalem, a star had appeared in the East for none of them. After questioning the scribes carefully, he learned from the prophecy that it was necessary that Christ be born in Bethlehem. [4031C] So having summoned the Magi to a secret meeting, he interrogated them about the timing of the rising[30] of the star, and then sent them off in a cunning way, having arranged, as was proper, very large gifts for them, so that when they had found the child they would report back to him. As the [star] which had previously been guiding them appeared to them again, they followed it with great joy to Bethlehem and after discovering the King they had been seeking and venerating him with gifts, they were warned by an angel and returned to their own land by another route.

It was then that Joseph, under a command from God, fled to Egypt with the child and his mother and stayed there until Herod's death. [4031D] The sum of time from the arrival of the Magi and Herod's deception and the return to their own country amounts to two years. Then in anger Herod brought about the slaughter of the innocents in the thirty-fifth year of his reign. Immediately divine wrath came down on him, and tortured by severe illnesses he ended his life, having ruled his realm for thirty-eight years. He left four sons as successors to his kingdom and his evil. Then at the Lord's command [4033A] Joseph returned from Egypt with the child and His mother, the child being four years old, and settled in Nazareth while Archelaos was tetrarch of Judaea. The sons of Herod, namely this

---

[30] Reading ἐπιτολή for ἐπιστολή.

Archelaos, plus Herod, Philip and Lysanias, are called tetrarchs since each of them had a quarter of the kingdom. In the eighth year of Archelaos' reign, the Lord began to teach in the temple, going into the midst of the teachers, being twelve years old in His bodily age. Not long after His return to Nazareth with those who were His parents through grace, Joseph reached the end of his life, being thought by all to be the Lord's father.

Archelaos survived for one more year and ended his life without leaving an heir. After completing fifty and a half years Augustus Caesar [4033B] died, handing over the empire to his son Tiberius. The Lord was then fifteen years old. Tiberius Caesar had a genuine love for Pilate and sent him out to be in charge of Judaea, and there he stayed until Caesar's death. In the fifteenth year of Tiberius Caesar's rule, according to the word of the Gospel, John went around all Judaea heralding the baptism of repentance through the revelation from God, and the Lord, being thirty years old, was baptised by him, and began his ministry according to the Gospel.[31]

About that time Herod divorced his wife who was the daughter of Aretas the king of Arabia, whom Paul mentions in his letter to the Corinthians,[32] [4033C] and took up Herodias, the wife of his own brother Philip, even though the latter was still alive. That herald of truth, John the Baptist, did not put up with this impropriety and attacked Herod with severe reproofs. This made Herod absolutely furious, and gratifying the wish of his adulterer, he beheaded the prophet. But he paid the penalty for his shameless behaviour not long afterwards. For after his wife had been driven away in disgrace she went to her father Aretas and complained about her mistreatment. He, since his daughter had been insulted, gathered his whole army and descended upon Herod in war, cut his entire army to pieces and fired and subjugated the land. But not even then did Herod cease from his wickedness.

[4033D] In the eighteenth year of Tiberius Caesar and the twentieth of Herod while Pontius Pilate was presiding over Judaea, the saving passion occurred on the thirteenth day before the Kalends of April.[33] Our Lord Jesus Christ suffered willingly on our behalf, being truly God and man with the two natures in Him [4036A] not admitting either separation or division in any way. For both on the Cross and in the grave the economy of the two natures remained undivided, through which the one and only Lord of us is known, Jesus Christ, only begotten Son and Word of the living God. And since the Cross is glorious in everything and everything is made in the form of the Cross, just as we made clear earlier in this account, naturally the Lord underwent His death on the Cross so that He might sanctify everything through His own blood, redeem us from the curse of the law,[34] free us from

---

[31] Luke, 3:1 ff.
[32] II Corinthians, 11:32.
[33] 20 March.
[34] Galatians, 3:13.

the power of the devil, and deliver us from tyranny and corruption. So on our behalf the Lord died truly and not in imagination. After being crucified during the governorship of Pontius Pilate, He was buried [4036B] and He did rise again on the third day according to the Scriptures, truly, on the eleventh day before the Kalends of April[35] at the spring equinox, without His divinity descending into suffering and death. (Certainly not! Such a thought should stay far away from every Christian, for the divinity is without suffering and is immortal.) But rather [the divinity] is present in a unity with itself according to its substance, consubstantial with us and suffering like us in the flesh, and experiencing the sufferings of the flesh providentially and granting to us a remission of our sins and everlasting life, because of the mystical food of the true body and blood of the rational Lamb, Christ our God.

[4036C] After carrying out the mystery of the Cross and the resurrection, the Lord-slaying Jews fabricated among themselves how to hide the miracle. First they bribed Pilate with a large sum of money to have the tomb sealed and placed under the guard and custody of the army. God allowed them to do all this so that He might affirm the truth all the more through their very own acts of evil. For if they had not guarded it, they would have been able to claim (though the claim would have been false) that it had been robbed by His disciples. But the fact that they did guard the tomb so securely has made the resurrection unambiguous, with the troops [4037A] proclaiming the miracle far and wide even though they had accepted a considerable sum of money from the chief priests.

After the Lord's ascension and the performance of very many miracles in His name by the holy apostles, the chief priests again became divided, saying: 'What shall we do? For since signs and great marvels are being carried out in the name of Jesus by His disciples, it is clear to everyone and we are not able to deny it, but to prevent it being spread further to future generations, let us come and hide the site of his tomb. For if the people see the empty tomb, everyone will believe in Him.' Then they ordered the tomb and the site of Calvary, [4037B] where the most holy Cross stood, to be covered over, striving to bring the signs of salvation to oblivion. This was the worst plan of the law-breaking Jews. God allowed them to do all this, planning future events clearly. For since the city was going to be made desolate and handed over to fire, God allowed the Life-giving Wood and the glorious resurrection to be hidden for a little while, so that these sites would not be subjected to fire during the revolt of the Jews and gentiles. For He knew that at the appropriate time they would be revealed with great glory.

Pilate had reported all that had happened about the Cross to Caesar, namely that the crucified Jesus, called Christ, had risen on the third day [4037C] and that great miracles were being carried out by His disciples in His name. Tiberius, when he heard about this and marvelled at it, believed in the Lord and wanted immediately

---

[35] 22 March.

to proclaim Him as God through an imperial decree. This was rejected by his own senate, who thought that the story of the Cross was stupid. Caesar kept the story of it in his heart and threatened death to those who slandered the Christians. When he learned that Herod had consented to the death of Christ, and that, because of his nefarious adultery with Herodias, he had committed many evil acts in that country and that he had put to death John the Baptist, who was a just man, for convicting him of immorality, [Tiberius] became very angry. He ordered that [Herod] be brought to Rome in chains along with his paramour, and [4037D] after stripping him of his rule and fining him he sent him off along with Herodias to exile in Spain, and there he ended his life painfully. The earth consumed the girl who danced badly while she was still alive, having been begotten by a viper.

Tiberius died after reigning for twenty-two years. In his stead Gaius ruled for four years. He was [4040A] savage and extremely arrogant. When Pilate had been denounced to him and had been brought to Rome to stand trial[36] he fell into such a plight and crisis that he committed suicide. The Jews were driven into greater violence so that many of them were killed by the Romans. The Caesar appointed another Herod, called Agrippa, the son of Antipater, as king of Judaea, entrusting him with all four tetrarchies. Being a dreadful person he began to persecute the disciples of Christ. He killed James the Lord's brother with a sword according to the holy word of the *Acts*, having also attempted to kill Peter and [he would have done so] if [the latter] had not been unexpectedly delivered from his hands by a holy angel. The afore-mentioned Herod did not cease from his arrogance until he experienced divine justice [4040B] and being eaten by worms he gave up the ghost.

Around this time James the just, also known as the Lord's brother, was the first person appointed by God's command as bishop of the holy church of Jerusalem. The Jews were becoming increasingly unruly towards the Lord's disciples and attempted even further acts of violence. Anyway a great many of them were then killed by the Romans. According to St Paul another Agrippa had taken over the kingdom of Judaea.[37] Gaius died and Claudius ruled in his stead for fourteen years. Under him there was a great famine throughout the inhabited world according to the prophecy of Agabos.[38] [4040C] Then the Jews turning to madness slaughtered each other by guile around the agora. Disturbed by this the Caesar sent instructions to the leaders of the gentiles to treat the Jews without mercy and a large crowd of them was put to death and their houses and children were taken as plunder and they were expelled from Italy and Rome with many afflictions and penalties. These things happened to them because of their behaviour towards Christ.

Claudius died and Nero ruled in his stead for fourteen years. He was an awful man and lecherous apart from anything else. He was the first to persecute the

---

[36] Cf. Ioannis Malalas, *Chronographia*, 10.36, ed. I Thurn (Berlin, 2000), 193.
[37] Acts, 25–26.
[38] Acts, 11:1 ff.

Christians. He executed Peter and Paul, the most important of Christ's apostles, and he killed many of their †relatives and many others among the leaders of the senate. [4040D] The governor Festus, who still held office in Judaea, perished at that time. The Jews, grasping the opportunity provided by the lack of a governor, increased even further their attacks. They killed the Lord's brother James and whipped and chased the remaining disciples out of the city. The disciples retreated to the region around the Jordan in accordance with God's revelation and stayed there because of the evils which would befall the city according to the Lord's prediction.

[4041A] Then the whole race [of Jews] began a revolt against the Romans. Agrippa fled to Rome. So Nero wrote in anger and fury to the general of the East (it was Vespasian at the time) ordering him to gather the entire army under his command and to go to the Judaean land and destroy it utterly. When those with power among the Jews heard this, they went down to Jerusalem since it was the strongest and safest place with its walls and huge towers. After overrunning the land and capturing all the cities of Judaea, the general destroyed them by fire. But after reaching Jerusalem and besieging it for a full year and preparing many war machines he was not strong enough to take it because of the city's defensive strength. But those from the city [4041B] made sudden excursions and killed many of the Romans. So going down to Caesarea Vespasian allowed his army to rest.

Meanwhile Nero was killed at Rome and Galba reigned for seven months. He too was killed and Otho reigned for three [months] and after him Vitellius reigned for three months. Amidst much danger and a state of confusion over how affairs stood, and with some of the barbarians pressing on Romania, the army of the East crowned Vespasian as emperor against his wishes with the support of all the rulers in the East. Setting off for Rome at the beginning of winter and appointing his sons Titus and Domitian as Caesars, [4041C] he left Titus to besiege Jerusalem and sent Domitian on an expedition against the barbarians. When he was already close to Rome, the army that was there together with the senate, after killing the rebel[39] joined in welcoming him with a very great deal of feasting and cheering. Established on the throne he put to death all the rioters and quickly the affairs of the Romans were repaired with Domitian too having thoroughly destroyed the invading barbarians.

After Jerusalem had been besieged for two years everyone there was wasting away from hunger, even eating their children because of the siege. After capturing it [4041D] the Caesar, having cut down the inhabitants and plundered everything along with the temple,[40] put it to the flames. Then was fulfilled the saying of the Lord 'There shall not be left here one stone upon another.'[41] Some relate that

---

[39] Reading ἀντάρτην for ἄνταρτον.
[40] Reading ναοῦ for λαοῦ.
[41] Matthew, 24:2.

those killed were three million.[42] After the capture of the city and their return to holy Sion the faithful appointed a second bishop of Jerusalem, Symeon, the son of Cleophas, the one mentioned in the Gospels who had himself seen and heard the Lord and was his cousin. Cleophas was the brother of the Lord's father by grace. [4044A] The period of time from the the saving passion to the capture of Jerusalem was forty years.

The mighty Vespasian reigned for ten years and died, and his son Titus reigned in his stead for three years and died, and his brother Domitian reigned in his stead and again incited a great persecution of the Jews, seeking out those of royal descent. Matters about Christ were reported to him because He came from [the line] of David and had a great family, some of whom were supporters of Christianity, even proclaiming Jesus Christ as the everlasting king who would put an end to all the powers under heaven and who would reign alone. Angered at this the emperor ordered that Christians should not live. After sending orders [4044B] to Jerusalem he led the relatives of the Lord's brother Juda back to Rome and questioned them about Christ and His kingdom. They replied that His kingdom was not on earth but heavenly and that He was intending to come at the fulfilment of time with glory to judge the living and the dead to repay each according to his works. On hearing this the emperor became fearful[43] and released them and stopped the persecution of Christians.

Domitian died after reigning for fifteen years and Nerva reigned in his stead for one year. Nerva died and Trajan reigned in his stead for twenty years. This man incited a persecution [4044C] of Christians to a great degree and slaughtered very many martyrs to the extent that the rulers of the gentiles grew disgusted[44] at the mass of martyrs and referred the matter to the emperor. They gave evidence of the freedom of Christians, [saying] that the Christians did everything in accordance with the appropriate laws and acknowledged Christ as the only God. On hearing this the emperor put an end to the persecution. Under him Ignatius the bishop of Antioch became a martyr in Rome as also did Symeon the son of Cleophas, the bishop of Jerusalem who was crucified at the age of 120 by Atticus, a man of consular status. Around that time the Jews in their very own madness dared to set up their own king. Angered by this the emperor dispatched tough officials to them [4044D] who after subduing the proposed usurper and pursuing the Jews throughout the inhabited world slaughtered a countless number of them.

Trajan died and in his stead Aelius Hadrian reigned for twenty-one years. Since he was maimed he travelled around the empire seeking a cure for his illness. After reaching the holy city and seeing it devastated with only the church of the Christians standing, he gave orders for the entire city to be built except for the temple.

---

[42] Literally 'three hundred ten thousands'.

[43] A new meaning for ἔμφοβος, which normally means 'terrible', 'inspiring fear'.

[44] ἀποκακίζω, *hapaxlegomenon*, cf. ἀποκακέω in *Greek Lexicon*, ed. Lampe, 194.

At this news the Jews flocked together from all over the place and in a short time it was very quickly built. But once more [4045A] the evil demon, which drove them to Bacchic frenzy, prevented them from staying peaceful but after revolting from Roman subjection, they established a revolutionary for themselves called Barchochiba.[45] On hearing this the Caesar dispatched a great many troops against them who laid siege to the city for a long period until the population in it perished from hunger and thirst.

This was the final desolation of Judaea. For having exterminated all the Jews and reduced the city to total desolation, he ordered Greeks[46] to take control of it, proclaiming a law which ordered as a matter of principle that in future the Jews were not to look upon the ground of their ancestral land with their eyes. The inhabitants of Jerusalem, coming from various other peoples, set [4045B] up a column to the emperor in the temple itself by the splendid gate, and also changing the name of the city they called it 'Aelia' from the name of the emperor. Before those times the holy church in Jerusalem, since it was established among the Hebrews, did not accept a bishop who was not circumcised. Your holinesses will allow me in my difficulty not to mark out the times of those people in detail for no one would ever discover this easily. But here is the list of their names. First was the Lord's brother James, then Symeon the son of Cleophas, Justus, Zachaios, Tobias, Benjamin, John, Matthias, Philip, Seneca, Justus, Levi, Ephres, Joseph and Juda. All these were circumcised, fifteen in number. And the period from the capture of Jerusalem until the last siege [4045C] and the final expulsion of the Jews was fifty-eight years.

The holy church at Aelia, when it was made up of foreigners[47] made Mark the first bishop from among the foreigners, a man most holy amongst all. Learning from tradition about the site of Golgotha, which was still covered up and hidden, the faithful used to visit it daily and venerate it reverently. Seeing this the idol-worshippers built a temple there at the devil's prompting with a statue of the impure demon Aphrodite. Since the mass of Christians was prevented from approaching the site, the holy places eventually became unknown to most of them.

[4045D] Hadrian died and Antoninus Pius reigned in his stead for twenty-two years. After him was Marcus Aurelius Verus, whom his son Antoninus succeeded for fourteen years together with his brother Lucius. With a persecution instigated, many were the martyrs who died eagerly for Christ. Many miracles occurred, so that when the Caesar Marcus himself together with his whole army was in danger of perishing from a shortage of water, they were saved [4048A] by the prayers of the Christians with God sending rain for them in the arid regions. On Verus's death, Commodus succeeded to the leadership for twelve years. After him Pertinax

---

[45] Bar Cochba.
[46] I.e. pagans.
[47] I.e. uncircumcised.

reigned for six months, and after him Severus reigned for eighteen years. Under him a great persecution was instigated and many were martyred in all areas.

On his death Antoninus Caracalla reigned for seven years, succeeded by Macrinus for one year, and after him another Antoninus for fourteen years. After him Alexander reigned for thirteen years. The bishops at Aelia from the reign of Hadrian were as follows: [4048B] Marcus, Cassian, Puplius, Maximus, Julian, Gaius, another Julian, Capito, Valens, Dolichianus and Narcissus. Narcissus shone with the apostolic graces, and as a lover of quietude left the bishopric and ran off to unknown places. After he had been looked for thoroughly but not found by the populace and by the bishops of the province, Dios was appointed as bishop in his place and Germanion after him. Gordias succeeded him. In his time, as if from sanctuaries, Narcissus reappeared once more. Advanced much in old age he was with the appointed bishop as the thirtieth since the Saviour's passion. After the bishop with him died and since Narcissus had grown exceedingly old (for he was 116 years old), they appointed in his place through God's revelation someone called [4048C] Alexander as bishop of Jerusalem after much exhortation. (He had come from elsewhere to venerate the holy places). He later would die in martyrdom. In those times there was much peace in the Churches of God. For the emperor's mother, Macrina, was very pious.

After Alexander had ended his rule, Maximinus succeeded to the leadership for three years. He mistreated the house of Alexander and roused a persecution of the Christians, ordering the execution of the church's leaders, holding them responsible [4048D] for blasphemies against the gods. On his death Pupienus and Balbinus took control of the Roman empire for three months. Gordianos succeeded them for six years. After him the emperor Philip reigned for seven years, He truly believed in Christ. But the servant of Satan Decius killed him and took control of the empire for two years. Under him when a severe persecution had been instigated, a number difficult to count became martyrs across the empire. After he had been killed along with his children, Gallus succeeded to the empire along with Volusianus for three years. Valerian [4049A] followed them along with Galienus for fifteen years. He introduced a great persecution against the Christians. After he had been taken prisoner by the barbarians, his son put an end to the persecution.

In Aelia Alexander became a martyr and left Marzabanes as his successor in the ministry, whom Hymenaios succeeded. After Galienus, Claudius reigned for two years. His successor was Aurelian for six years. After him Tacitus and Florianus reigned for nine months. His (*sic*) successor was Probus for six years. On his death Carus received the empire with his sons Carinus and Numerian for two years. After them Diocletian and Maximian followed as emperors for twenty-one years. [4049B] Under them the longest and most violent persecution of the Christians occurred during which a number known to the Lord alone of countless tens of thousands were martyred. In Aelia after Hymenaios ended his ministry he left Zaudas as his successor, and on his death Hermon gained the throne of Jerusalem.

After those around Diocletian and Maximian, surnamed Herculius, had killed many thousands of holy people, as though they had had a surfeit of evils after being driven by the excess of their madness, as masters of impiety under the pretext of religiousness, they set aside their rule following an agreement and returned to private life.[48] Maximian known as Galerius and Maxentius the son of Herculius, [4049C] took control of the Roman leadership for nine years. Maximian resided in the regions of the East while Maxentius made his rule in great Rome itself, they both being wild beasts with a share of every form of evil, especially in their raging madness[49] against the Christians. In Britain Kostas the great, the father of Constantine the great, joined in ruling with them, a man most peaceful and gentle in everything, who embraced piety, detested idols and welcomed Christians strongly.

While Constantine was still a child he was brought up at [the court of] the tyrant of the East and was educated in pagan wisdom. Since he was actually in Palestine, he was able to see all that the servants of Christ were suffering, [4049D] and this stabbed at his soul. For from childhood he was a hater of evil. Then an anger driven by God descended on Diocletian who was residing in Dalmatia, and with his body swollen he was broken into many pieces with his blaspheming tongue turning putrid in his windpipe and gushing out a mass of worms. So it severed his breathing. Herculius ended his life in Cilicia at Tarsus. Galerius Maximian, as though free from fear, usurped power in a way that was godless and inhuman. For since he was a mad womaniser, his officials competed [4052A] for where they might hide their wives and daughters from the sight of the tyrant.[50] To such an extent was he absorbed in the deception of the demons that tricked him that he refused to taste anything without divination. He ordered the complete annihilation of the Christians, not only because of his impiety but also to seize their property.

Seeing Constantine developing into a strong young man, who was endowed too with sagacity, and suspecting or rather having divined that he would be likely to put an end to his tyranny, [Galerius] planned to kill him treacherously. [4052B] But the young man, having learned of the plot through divine providence, like David found safety in flight. With the tyrant [now] venturing into an immense degree of wickedness and attacking the Christians violently, divine justice checked him, sending out a scourge against him. For a nasty festering wound grew out of the hidden member of his licentiousness and became larger than any human could devise. With the spreading of the putrefaction and the most awful stinking smell spreading and the multitude of worms being distributed across his body (the coward was

---

[48] Cf. Theophanes, *Chronographia* volumen 1 textum Graecum continens, ed. C. de Boor (Leipzig, 1883), AM 5796, 10.
[49] ἐπιμαίνομαι meaning different from LSJ and not listed in *Greek Lexicon*, ed. Lampe.
[50] Cf. Theophanes, *Chronographia*, AM 5797, ed. de Boor, 12–13.

grossly fat) he finally came to such despair that he was a pitiable sight to all those around him.[51]

[4052C] Then some recognition crept up on him that this had happened to him through divine justice because of his unjust slaughter of the Christians. So immediately he dispatched edicts to every city setting the Christians free and allowing them to act freely in accordance with their own customs and for everyone to honour the Christians and to call upon them to pray on behalf of the emperor himself. These things happened and immediately God's love of mankind was revealed. And he, who was at his last breath, regained again his health and strength, and through the prayers of the Christians his most awful wound was unexpectedly restored to health. But lest his wound be completely and totally healed, the tyrant, driven to an even greater madness through pressure from the devil, issued godless edicts and laws filled with cruelty [4052D] by which he ordered that Christians were neither to live nor hold office, nor even to dwell in any part of the inhabited world nor even in the desert. For otherwise, he said, 'we cannot live or prosper unless the race of Christians is obliterated.' So for the future the affairs of the Christians were brought to despair among mankind. But God was not forgetful of His own creatures. For He could see the Christians everywhere being driven in herds to death together with their women and children. But divine justice scattered the designs of the lawless. For immediately everywhere [there were] wars and uprisings among the barbarians; and widespread famine, frequent plagues and unseasonable deaths suddenly descended on them, so that the living were not sufficient to bury the dead,[52] and thunder and terror were sent so that each person had a care for himself alone, and [4053A] thus all the decrees of the tyrant were rendered ineffectual.[53]

Constantine, excellent in all respects, got safely away to his father's domain. [The father] after receiving him in good health gave bounteous thanks to God, and shortly after entrusting his rule to [Constantine] exchanged his life. Constantine the great was acclaimed emperor in the first year of the two hundred and seventy first Olympiad, on the 25 July. Maxentius the most wicked of all those before him was harming the inhabitants of Rome and the Christians in particular. Having put to death many of the leaders and exiled many others, [4053B] he used to snatch hold of their property. Following the same licentiousness as Galerius he defiled many of the free women, carrying out tens of thousands of other acts of wickedness and unmentionable vice and became intolerable to everyone through his use of a bewitching evil magic. After the great Constantine had taken control of the northern and western parts as far as the Ocean, there was much peace, happiness and stability throughout his territory.

---

[51] Cf. Theophanes, Ioannis Malalas, *Chronographia*, AM 5797, ed. de Boor, 13.

[52] The same phrase in *Chronographia*, 18.92, ed. Thurn, 407 for the plague of 542.

[53] Cf. Theophanes, *Chronographia*, AM 5797, ed. de Boor, 13.

The inhabitants at Rome sent a request to him, calling on him not to overlook the mother of the emperors, which was being destroyed by the harsh tyrant or rather by a flesh-eating wild beast. When he had heard this and sympathised with them the great Constantine [4053C] put his mind to freeing them from slavery, but he was frightened about this because of that man's witchcraft and evil magic. For by this time [Maxentius] had cut up many children on the pretext of his lawless divination. Troubled much by cares and doubt [Constantine] was actually on campaign with his soldiers when around noon there appeared the Cross made of light in the shape of a column on which was written 'In this conquer'. Filled with fear the emperor asked those with him if they too had seen anything. They agreed that they had seen the same vision, whereupon the emperor was made resolute in mind and was filled with courage and zeal. On the next night the Lord appeared to him and said, 'Use the sign that has appeared [4053D] and you will conquer all your enemies.' Having made a cross without delay on that day, which to this very day is kept in the imperial palace, he commanded that it be carried in front into battle whereas the impious tyrant, placing his trust in his demons, after building a bridge made of many ships across the river which flowed by, went out into battle.[54]

[4056A] When the battle took place, the enemy was crushed by the power of the Cross. Most were massacred, while the rest along with the tyrant, as they fled into the city, were drowned in the river when the bridge collapsed from the greater weight,[55] just like Pharaoh with his whole army. And it was possible to see the whole river full of horses along with their riders. The citizens of Rome after garlanding him received with great joy and hymns of praise the victory-making Cross and the victory-bringing emperor, naming him as their saviour.[56] Then the emperor ordered that the relics of the holy martyrs be gathered and handed over for a holy burial, and that property be returned to those who had been wronged. [4056B] They spent seven days celebrating the victory festival, honouring Christ's Cross. This was the seventh year of Constantine's reign.[57]

After Galerius Maximianus heard of these events, he set out. For he himself awaited the same destiny and had departed a little from his threats against the Christians.[58] The very great Constantine, taking confidence from his unconquerable weapon of the Cross, set out against him. But as his ally against the tyrants he had Licinius, who was pretending to rejoice in the teachings of the Christians.[59] The tyrant, relying upon his deceitful magic, went out to draw up his line against the pious emperor, pictured with a countless mass of troops. When the clash took

---

[54] Cf. Theophanes, *Chronographia*, AM 5802, ed. de Boor, 14.
[55] Or 'the greater power'.
[56] Cf. Theophanes, *Chronographia*, AM 5802, ed. de Boor, 14.
[57] Cf. Theophanes, *Chronographia*, AM 5803, ed. de Boor, 14.
[58] Cf. Theophanes, *Chronographia*, AM 5805, ed. de Boor, 15.
[59] Cf. Theophanes, *Chronographia*, AM 5808, ed. de Boor, 15.

place and the honoured Cross appeared, the tyrant's shield-bearers were unable to resist the attack [4056C] and were turned to flight. As they fled hastily they were pursued strongly, with many thousands of the enemy falling. The rest deserted the tyrant and came over to the emperor.

The impious man threw away [the robes of] his sovereign authority of which he was unworthy, so that he would not be recognised as he fled, and he got away in effect naked, as he travelled from village to village, scarcely kept hidden among a few of his most avid supporters. Having assembled the priests of their supposed gods along with the prophets, seers and those renowned for prophecy, whom previously he had loved and honoured, he put them to death as imposters and deceivers who had plotted against his own security.[60] [4056D] Since he was likely to fall alive into the hands of the emperor (for the war against him still went on) divine anger intervened and came upon him in such a way that he lay prostrate on the ground begging for help but not getting any. For a flame, kindled in the depth of his innards and his marrow, brought unbearable pains on him as he gasped for breath and writhed there so that both his eyes popped out on to the ground and left him blind. With the flame inside him burning to infinity, his flesh became putrid and became separated from his bones, so that he begged for death for himself. So, having rotted away in entirety, he vomited up his soul.[61]

[4057A] With the tyrants put out of the way and with the great Constantine having become the sole emperor, the inhabited world lay in deep peace[62] and the affairs of the Christians daily increased in stature and the Cross of Christ was glorified among all peoples. To Licinius, who had been his ally in the dissolution of the tyrannies, Constantine gave his sister as wife. And after designating an adequate part of Roman territory for him, he proclaimed him as emperor, insisting on pledges from him that he would do nothing contrary to Christian teaching.[63] But Licinius, now that he had gained office, was not content with his good fortune but just as he was forgetful of what had happened to the tyrants before him [so] he became shipwrecked on [the reef of] idolatry.[64] He now modelled his life on those at whose bitter overturning he had been a spectator, becoming infatuated about women, [4057B] and wronging and murdering Christians. When the servant of God, the revered Constantine, learned about this, he was struck with grief and wrote to him urging him to keep away from this madness against the Churches of Christ. But [Licinius] contemptuously and even more madly undertook the persecution. Next he secretly conceived plots against his benefactor and later he hammered out a civil war against him who was sole emperor guarded by divine power.

---

[60] Cf. Theophanes, *Chronographia*, AM 5806, ed. de Boor, 15.
[61] Cf. Theophanes, *Chronographia*, AM 5807, ed. de Boor, 15.
[62] Cf. Theophanes, *Chronographia*, AM 5810, ed. de Boor, 16.
[63] Cf. Theophanes, *Chronographia*, AM 5808, ed. de Boor, 15.
[64] Cf. Theophanes, *Chronographia*, AM 5811, ed. de Boor, 16.

When the clash took place in the regions of Bithynia and with the glorious Cross going ahead, the coward came into the power of the emperor after being captured alive. Acting humanely to his enemy, the emperor, most gentle in everything, ordered him to stay peacefully in Thessalonica. [4057C] [Licinius] kept the peace for a short time but was detected hiring barbarians for the purpose of again renewing the fight. On learning of this Constantine ordered that he undergo capital punishment. Then at last events enjoyed peace and quiet through the power of the invincible Cross with the evil of the tyrants having been removed.[65]

At that time the bishop of Aelia bearing the name Makarios succeeded Hermonas. The great Constantine having become sole emperor gave his mind entirely to holy matters, building churches and enriching them lavishly from public funds with money and expenses and all kinds of treasures and he introduced a first law [4057D] that the offerings made to idols be given to the Church of the Christians and that those who continued to practise idolatry undergo capital punishment. He introduced a second law that Christians alone were to serve in the army and to command foreign races and armies. He introduced a third law that public business was to cease for the week of the Saviour's passion and for Easter week. Thereupon there was deep peace and joy prevailed [4060A] throughout the inhabited world with all peoples rushing daily to holy baptism and smashing their ancestral gods to pieces with their own hands.[66]

But these activities were intolerable to the avenging demon, who once again devised with himself how he might stamp out such great delight among the Christians and bring it about that men should consider creation the invention of gods, but he still could not do this, for his deception was spotted. He attempted to persuade the unstable to equate the creator with the created. And there was no little confusion in the Churches of God with an Alexandrian called Arius causing trouble all over the place and disturbing the inhabited world.[67] Just a few bishops joined him, of whom the first was Eusebius of Nikomedeia [4060B] and also Eusebius Pamphili and others with them. Seeing the quarrel was enormous the mighty Constantine was vexed in his soul and first of all attempted to end the strife between the factions by encouraging words and letters. But when he saw that the trouble was incurable, he gave instructions for an ecumenical synod to take place in the city of the Nicaeans. Three hundred and eighteen bishops gathered of whom the majority were confessors bearing the stigmata of Jesus on their bodies. [4061A] With them was the wholly-blessed and great Constantine and when the matter had been discussed they published a written exposition of the faith which is still now recited as orthodox throughout the whole Church. They publicly renounced those supporters of Arius who persisted in their wrong view and exiled

---

[65] Cf. Theophanes, *Chronographia*, AM 5815, ed. de Boor, 20.
[66] Cf. Theophanes, *Chronographia*, AM 5810, ed. de Boor, 16.
[67] Cf. Theophanes, *Chronographia*, AM 5812, ed. de Boor, 17.

them and others were elected in their place. After honouring and embracing the bishops, the emperor dismissed them in peace to their own lands, rejoicing in the unanimity of the Churches.[68]

Makarios, the bishop of Aelia who was present at the synod and who was a vigorous fighter for the apostolic teachings, was exhorted by the emperor to seek out the life-giving Cross [4061B] and the tomb chosen by God and all the holy sites. The emperor likewise instructed the other bishops each to check if anything [was needed] for the completion of his own church. It was the nineteenth year of his reign when the synod at Nicaea took place. After this the emperor sent his own mother Helen, who was worthy of praise and beloved of God, to Makarios in Jerusalem with a letter and a liberal supply of money both for searching for the life-giving Wood and for the construction of the holy places. The empress herself had asked to do this as she stated that she had seen a divine vision ordering her to go to Jerusalem and to bring to light the holy places that had been buried by those lawless men and removed from sight so long ago. [4061C] When the bishop learned that the empress had arrived he went to meet her with the bishops of his province. [She] immediately instructed the bishops to make a search for the longed-for Wood. But as no one had any idea of the whereabouts of the site and as various people were making different suggestions by guesswork, the city's bishop called on everyone to keep quiet and to offer a very earnest prayer to God about it.

As soon as this was done the site was revealed to the bishop by God in that place where the temple and statue of the impure female demon stood. Then the empress using her imperial authority gathered together a large crowd of craftsmen and workers and ordered that the temple of the female demon be torn down to its foundations, [4061D] and when this was done the divine tomb was revealed and also the site of Golgotha and not far away were three buried crosses. After searching carefully they found the nails. But then the empress felt crushed with helplessness and despair as she sought out which Cross was the Lord's. But the bishop solved the problem through faith. After bringing each of the crosses to a noblewoman who was known to all but who was ill and breathing her last, he discovered which was the only one sought. [4064A] For as the shadow of the saving [Cross] got close to the dead woman, she, though not able to breathe or move, through God's power suddenly leapt up and glorified God in a loud voice. The empress with great joy and fear took up the life-giving Cross and sent part of it along with the nails to her son. After making a silver casket, she handed over the rest to the city's bishop as a memorial for all generations. After commanding that a church be built on the life-giving tomb and also at holy Golgotha and also at Bethlehem where the Lord was born according to the flesh, and on the Mount of Ol-

---

[68] Cf. Theophanes, *Chronographia*, AM 5816, ed. de Boor, 21.

ives, where the Lord after blessing the disciples was taken up, and after performing many other fine deeds, she returned to her son.

After receiving her with joy and placing [4064B] the piece of the honoured Cross in a golden chest he handed it over to the bishop for safe-keeping, commanding that the discovery of the Cross be celebrated at commemorations annually. Of the nails he forged some on to his helmet, and inserted others in his horse's bridle, so that the word of the Lord speaking through the prophet might be fulfilled, saying, 'on that day there will be on the bridle of the horse holiness unto the Lord Almighty.'[69] The emperor wrote to bishop Makarios to hurry with the building and sent out an officer of works with an abundance of money with orders to build the holy places munificently so that there would be nothing so beautiful on all earth. He also wrote to the governors of the province to undertake the work [4064C] totally from the public account in terms of resources both for money and materials. Then the emperor celebrated the festival of his twenty years [of rule] and gave thanks to God for all the good things that he had done in the period of his reign.[70] The period from the coming of Christ until the discovery of the Cross was 352[71] years and from Adam to the coming of Christ was 5475 years.

In Aelia bishop Makarios was succeeded by Maximonas. He was a gentle man and distinguished, and during the persecution he had often been tortured and had lost his right eye which had been cut out. At this time too the blessed Helen died at the age of eighty [4064D] after achieving much for her son out of her reverence for Christ.[72] When the emperor learned that the building of the new Jerusalem had been completed, he ordered the bishop to go there and to assemble a synod of many bishops and to consecrate the holy sites. This was Eusebius of Nikomedeia who adhered to the Arian teachings. This man [4065A] had been anathematised at Nicaea together with his fellow bishops and been exiled. After a period of time they, accepting the emperor's generosity for their travel allowance, had brought an imperial letter to the emperor swearing that they subscribed to the exposition of the faith and that they were guided by the holy Fathers in everything. Persuaded by this the emperor recalled them from exile and treated them with the greatest honour. Since the throne of Constantinople was then vacant, Eusebius relying on his own tricks usurped the throne of the imperial [city]. Grabbing hold of even greater power he placed those of his persuasion in the ministries of the Church, expelling those who justly held these posts.

---

[69] Zachariah, 14:20.
[70] Cf. Theophanes, *Chronographia*, AM 5817, ed. de Boor, 25–27.
[71] So the text as it currently stands, but Alexander has made clear that the calculation should be about 325 years.
[72] Cf. Theophanes, *Chronographia*, AM 5817, ed. de Boor, 27.

[4065B] When this had happened they next devoted [their efforts] against Athanasios in Alexandria, plotting much mischief[73] against him. The emperor thought it right to invite Athanasios to the consecration of the holy places. So first he ordered the synod to gather in Tyre and the case against Athanasios to be examined so that all could set out to the festival away from all division. He sent his nephew Dalmatius to keep watch over the synod. When the bishops had gathered in Tyre, Maximonas the bishop of Aelia was present with them, totally unaware of what was being heaped up against Athanasios. When Athanasios came into the assembly, his accusers stood around him, laying numerous serious charges against him which had been suggested to them by the judges present, namely Eusebius of Nikomedeia [4065C] and his supporters. But they were not able to make their case with Athanasios defending himself and like a spider tearing asunder what was being put forward by them. The accusers, turning to madness with their lies exposed, began obliterating the whole assembly, shouting 'Get rid of the magician! For by using magic he has muzzled everyone.' And Athanasios would have been killed if the emperor's nephew had not got him out of their clutches with the help of the soldiers.

The story goes that Athanasios, having fled from there, went to the holy city, and after praying and after anointing the prayer houses with holy myrrh and consecrating them before the arrival of the other bishops, he went to the emperor and made known to him all the relevant material concerning himself. [4065D] When the emperor had heard and been amazed by the evil of his adversaries and deemed him worthy of the highest honour he sent him off to Alexandria with imperial letters.[74] When the [other] bishops reached Jerusalem, they celebrated the festival of the dedication very splendidly since the emperor had sent treasures and all kinds of gold and silver decorated with precious stones and very expensive decorated curtains and a large sum of money for [4068A] giving to the poor and for honouring all who had gathered for the celebration. When the Christ-loving emperor heard an account of the consecration of the holy places, he gave much thanks to God and associated himself even more with Christianity.

This was the thirtieth year of his reign. He immediately wrote a law with an imperial rescript that no Jew should be seen within a radius of six miles of Jerusalem. He rejoiced in God's grace, looking at the barbarian peoples rushing to the word of truth and gladly subjecting themselves to the emperor. After surviving for another year and a few months he collapsed with some illness and so was baptised and died in Nikomedeia. He had postponed [baptism] [4068B] till this moment as he wanted to be deemed worthy of this in the river Jordan.

Being upright, he disposed [of his property] piously, leaving his three sons as heirs to his kingdom and his piety, proclaiming the elder, who had the same name,

---

[73] Reading σκαιωρίας for σκαιορίας.
[74] Cf. Theophanes, *Chronographia*, AM 5827, ed. de Boor, 30–32.

Constantine, as emperor of the Western regions. He appointed the second, who had the same name as his grandfather Constantius, as emperor of the East and the younger [as emperor] of Europe. None of them was present at his death. The wholly blessed Constantine died as emperor [at the age of] sixty-five; he reigned piously and pleasingly to God for thirty-two years and after departing from his earthly kingdom he received the heavenly one. Soldiers after placing his honoured corpse in a golden coffin, [4068C] lamented loudly as they mourned over him, since they had been deprived of a beloved father rather than an emperor wielding extreme power. When the emperor of the East Constantius arrived and had buried his father regally, he placed him on high in the Church of the Apostles in Constantinople where his mother Helen was placed. For this purpose the blessed Constantine had built that church for burying the emperors and priests there, so that they would not be far from the relics of the apostles. The day of his death was the twenty-first of May on the eleventh day before the Kalends of June[75] in the consulship of Felicianus and Tatianus.[76]

When Constantius had just taken control of the empire, the leaders of the Arian disease approached him, urging him to remove the designation 'consubstantial' from the creed of the faith. [4069A] For they said that this had been the cause of the division among the Churches and when this had been removed there would no longer be any dispute about teachings. Because of the emptiness of his mind he accepted their arguments without question and agreed to do this. Again there was considerable trouble throughout the inhabited world.

Around this time a marvel occurred in Jerusalem surpassing any description. For when during the quarrel over the teachings a fall occurred in the number of those coming over to the faith, being scandalised by the dissension among those consecrated [to God], the God of wonders revealed from heaven that the Word of faith in Him was not the cause of the scandals, but rather it was the stupidity of discredited priests and the lack of discernment[77] in their utterly evil thinking. So in the middle of the day there suddenly appeared above holy Golgotha [4069B] the most enormous Cross made of light which hid the brightness of our sun with its excess of light, in the presence of all the inhabitants of the city, both large and small, both believers and unbelievers. Cyril was at that time bishop of Jerusalem, having succeeded the confessor Maximonas. Eighteen catacheses of his are preserved, gloriously written. In these in his interpretation of the holy creed he made no mention of the word 'consubstantial', as he suspected that the powerful were at that time plotting [against him]. Nevertheless he remained on the side of the holy Fathers, defending the Church [but] not in writing. He did write to the emperor Constan-

---

[75] 22 May. Alexander appears to have made a mistake in cross-referencing the dating systems.
[76] AD 337.
[77] Reading ἀδιακρισία for ἀδιακρασία.

tius about what had happened regarding the sign that had appeared.[78] The very words of the bishop will teach best about this. [4069C] They are as follows:-

'Under your blessed and outstanding father the saving Wood of the life-giving Cross was discovered. Under you, most pious emperor, acknowledging your ancestral piety, [there have been] miracles, naturally not out of the earth but from heaven. For on these holy days of Pentecost, on the Nones of May[79] at the third hour the most enormous Cross made of light appeared in heaven above holy Golgotha and extending as far as the holy Mount of Olives, visible not to one or two alone but revealed most clearly to the whole mass of the city, nor might anyone consider passing over it quickly or assigning it to imagination, [4069D] but it was gazed at for many hours, visible to the eye above the earth, and overpowering the rays of the sun with its flashing gleaming. For assuredly it would have been overwhelmed by these and stayed hidden if it had not provided sources of light for those watching more powerful than the sun, so that as a result of it the whole mass of the holy church has run together, constrained by fear of the vision of God, which had taken place, sent from heaven by God.' These were the words of the bishop.[80]

As a result of this miracle many thousands were brought over to the faith. Up to this point let this be the account of the discovery of the life-giving Cross, [4072A] and let no one deceive himself and by talking idly introduce to the argument absurdities and fables made with foreign names. For there was no other bishop except those previously mentioned, nor another Roman emperor, nor was the honoured Cross proclaimed in any other way. For from the emperor Augustus, when Christ was born in the flesh, until Constantine the great, there were thirty-five emperors; likewise from James the brother of God until the same reign there were thirty-five bishops of Jerusalem. By imperial command the Fathers determined to celebrate the revered day of the exaltation of the honoured Cross and of the consecrations, annually on the fourteenth of the month of September, which is the eighteenth day before [4072B] the Kalends of October to the glory of the Father, Son and Holy Ghost.

Since by the grace of God we have arrived in our account at the famous day of our festival which is the revelation of the life-giving Cross, consider as far as possible, and by hailing the Cross a little, let us end our account. So hail, honoured Cross. Hail because on you the Lord Jesus Christ was raised up, in which are all the treasures of joy and grace. Honoured Cross, for because of you everlasting joy is being prepared in heaven and on earth. Hail, honoured Cross, because from above and from the beginning the Creator depicted your image in all creation.

---

[78] Cf. Theophanes, *Chronographia*, AM 5847, ed. de Boor, 41–42.

[79] 7 May.

[80] For the full text of Cyril's letter see E. Bihain, 'L'Épître de Cyrille de Jérusalem à Constance sur la vision de la Croix (BHG³ 413)', *B* (1973), 264–296.

Hail, glorious Cross, [4072C] because at your exaltation all the powers of the Heavens are sending up remarkable hymns to God. Hail, Cross, for on account of you the churches of the Orthodox have been established in the cities and in the islands and in every nation. Hail, Cross, for on account of you all the mouths of the faithful have been opened to the story of God. Hail, blessed Cross, for on account of you angels dancing with men on earth are hymning Christ. Hail, Cross, for on account of you men along with angels are standing before God in heaven, glorifying the Maker with ineffable joy. Hail, Cross, for on account of you Adam was released from the curse, leaping and exulting as he was released into paradise and regained his own self-esteem. Hail, Cross, for the entire power of the devil was overthrown by you and [his] entire demonic operation was trampled under foot. [4072D] Hail, holy Cross, for on account of you the holy and consubstantial Trinity is believed in every region, is sung, is hymned, is glorified and is known. Hail, Cross, for on account of you every soul who believes in Christ is saved.

Hail, Cross, for on account of you good things have been given to mankind which cannot be taken away. And what should we say [4073A] or what might we overlook? How might we praise the power of the Master's Cross in song? O name of the Cross, in which the splendours of the mysteries of Christ were hidden, [name] venerable to angels and revered among men. For what is more beloved than the name of the Cross, what is sweeter to Christians? What is more effective than it at effecting miracles? The Cross is the foundation of the Church. The Cross is the proof of God's power. The Cross is the joy of angels and the pain of demons. The Cross is the destroyer of demons. The Cross is the ever-shining and shining-everywhere luminary of the entire universe. The Cross is a wall, unshaken, unbroken, and invincible for the whole world. The Cross is the glory and strength of priests. The Cross is the complete armour of armies. The Cross is the safeguard of a city. The Cross is the total destruction of the devil.[81] The Cross is the good cheer of the people. The Cross is the hope of Christians. [4073B] The Cross is the doctor of the sick. The Cross is the infallible health of the healthy. The Cross is the harbour of those tossed by storms. The Cross is the peace of those at war. The Cross is the exultation of exultations of the Orthodox. The Cross is the dissolution of idolatry and restoration of piety. The Cross is the teacher of virginity and the defence of prudence. The Cross is the security of the just and the repentance of sinners. The Cross is the ornament of monks and the glory of those living in holiness.

The Cross is the defence of infants and the prudence of the young and the staff of the old. The Cross is the inexhaustible wealth of beggars, the unwavering way for the wayward. The Cross [provides] repose in daily toil. The Cross is good order for the foreigners and serenity for the whole world. And what should I say or what should we overlook? Or how might we praise you in song, most holy Cross? Be-

---

[81] This sentence is omitted in the Latin translation in *PG*.

cause the King has chosen you alone from all creation and has proclaimed you as [4073C] the invincible weapon against the devil and death. Wherefore blessed are all those who have been deemed worthy to look upon your manifestation. You are the proclamation of the prophets. For daily they cry out aloud in exultation over you, saying to God, 'You have given to those who fear You a sign of the escape from the face of the bow.'[82] You are the glory of the apostles. For they continuously cry out through one holy proclaimer among them, 'God forbid that I should glory, save in the Cross of the Lord.'[83] You are the crown of martyrs. You are the glory of those in the mountains and the caves and in the holes of the earth who have crucified the flesh together with suffering and desire. Oh the ineffable joy of the Lord's Cross! Oh the incomprehensible mysteries in it, and so that I may say with the Apostle, [4073D] 'Oh the depth of the riches both of the wisdom and knowledge of God! How unsearchable are his judgements'.[84] For they, having died through the Wood, have through the Wood been brought from condemnation to life. Oh the immeasurable grace of Him who has given [it].

So it is appropriate for us 'to bind' this wholly-festal 'sacrifice with cords even unto the horns of the altar.[85] Those protecting the things [4076A] that have been polluted through neglect or age, as those skilled in these matters say, or the things which out of diligence have been modified back into a more precious state, – these [are being turned] for the happiness of those being guided in exultations. So let us do as we are ordered, and stripping the attendant unpleasantness from our laziness, let us celebrate this shining and all-holy day of the memorial of the life-giving Cross with [acts of] pity and faith, washing away our sins, just as Scripture says, and let us shout out with fear and with joy as follows: 'Holy God, holy Mighty, holy Immortal, have mercy upon us. Have mercy upon us, Holy Trinity consubstantial and sharing the same throne, in which belongs glory, power, majesty and magnificence for ever and ever, world without end. Amen.

---

[82] Cf. Psalm, 58:6.
[83] Galatians, 6:14.
[84] Romans, 11:33.
[85] Psalm 117 (118):27 which is an unsatisfactory translation of the Greek. Better: 'to put in order this wholly-festal feast among those giving shelter even unto the horns of the altar'. 'This wholly-festal' is not in the text of the psalm.

19

Paul of Monembasia, *Historia animae utilis* BHG 1449d, Cod. Vat. Gr. 57

Alastair Carroll

As an undergraduate faced with the intimidating task of learning the Greek language I could not have hoped for a better teacher than Bob Jordan. His patience and kind comments made learning the language more of a pleasure than a chore and made a mere beginner feel like an expert. Throughout my time in Queen's Bob's expertise and constant willingness to help, despite his numerous other commitments, have proved invaluable to me, particularly in my postgraduate research. Bob's ability to engage his students both in the classroom as a teacher and outside on a personal level have left many of us with a lasting fondness for him. So it is with great affection and gratitude that I present the following diplomatic edition and translation of a short text found in the Codex Vaticanus graecus 579, fol. 81r-83v and is catalogued as n. 1449d in the *Bibliotheca Hagiographica Graeca*.[1] It belongs to the literary genre of 'stories which benefit the soul', in Latin *narrationes animae utiles*, and in Greek ψυχωφελεῖς ἱστορίαι or ψυχωφελῆ διηγήματα, which came into existence in Late Antiquity and remained popular throughout the Byzantine period. The stories are short in length and, as the name indicates, were written for the edification of the audience. The specific purpose of this edifying tale is to convince the readers of the efficacy of prayers for the dead.[2]

---

[1] The edition represents the text as it appears in the manuscript. I have chosen not to regularise the orthography and punctuation in order to recreate the original reading experience.

[2] More on this genre and more of these tales can be found in *Les récits édifiants de Paul, évêque de Monembasie, et d'autres auteurs*, ed. tr. J. Wortley (Paris, 1987); *The spiritually beneficial tales of Paul, bishop of Monembasia and of other authors*, tr. J. Wortley (CS 159, Kalamazoo, 1996).

[Fol. 81r] Παύλ(ου) τοῦ ὁσιωτ(ά)τ(ου) ἐν μοναχοῖς καὶ ἐπισκόπ(ου) γενομ(έν)ου μονεμβασίας τῆς πελοποννήσ(ου) διηγήματα διάφορα ὁσίων ἀνδρῶν πάνυ σύντομα καὶ ὠφέλιμα·

μοναχός τις διηγήσατο ἡμῖν λέγων, ὅτι παραβαλόντος μου ποτὲ τῷ ἁγίῳ θεοδωρίτῳ π(ατ)ριάρχῃ ἀντιοχείας· καὶ προτρα[Fol. 81v]πέντος μου παρ᾿ αὐτοῦ εἰς ἑστίασιν, διηγήσατο τῇ ἐμῇ ταπεινώσει ταῦτα· ὅτι πρὸ ὀλίγων ἡμερῶν, παρεγένετό τις ξένος ἐνθάδε· ἀλουσία καὶ πολυτριχία· καὶ ῥάκεσι τριχίνοις κοσμούμενος· καὶ τοῦτον προσκαλεσάμενος γεύσασθαι μετ᾿ ἐμοῦ· ἐλθόντος αὐτοῦ καὶ συγκαθεσθέντος, βλέπω αὐτὸν ἐσθίοντα τῇ ἀριστερᾷ αὐτοῦ χειρὶ· ἡ γὰρ δεξιὰ ἦν ἐντετυλιγμένη ῥακίῳ ἕως τοῦ ἀστραγάλου· λέγω οὖν αὐτῷ· διατί ἀδελφὲ οὐκ ἐσθίεις τῇ δεξιᾷ χειρί σου, ἀλλὰ τῇ εὐωνύμῳ· καὶ γὰρ ὁ μέγας βασίλειος ἐν τοῖς ἠθικοῖς αὐτοῦ διδάγμασι, λέγει· ἵνα ἡ μὲν δεξιὰ χεὶρ καθυπουργῇ τῷ σώματι ἀπὸ ὀσφύος ἕως κεφαλῆς· ἡ δὲ ἀριστερά, ἀπὸ ὀσφύος ὁμοίως ἕως κάτω· ὁ δὲ λέγει μοι· συγχώρησόν μοι ἁγιώτατε δέσποτα, πάθος τί ποτέ μοι ἐστί, καὶ διατοῦτο οὐ δύναμαι· καὶ πολλὰ βιασάμενος εἰπεῖν αὐτὸν καὶ μὴ θέλοντα ἑωρακὼς, ὥσπερ χαριεντιζόμενος τῷ ἀν(θρώπ)ῳ, δραξάμενος τοῦ ῥακίου τοῦ ἐπὶ τῆς χειρὸς αὐτοῦ καὶ ἐπὶ ἓν μέρος ῥίψας αὐτὸ, ἔδωκεν ἡ χεὶρ λοιπὸν ἀμύθητον καὶ δεινὴν δυσωδίαν· ὥστε πάντας κρατεῖν τὰς ἑαυτῶν ὀσφρήσεις καὶ ἀποφεύγειν· ἕως οὗ πάλιν τῷ ἁγίῳ ἐκείνῳ ῥακίῳ ἐνείλησε τὴν δύσωδη χεῖρα αὐτοῦ· καὶ οὕτω κατέπαυσεν ἡ ἀφόρητος ἐκείνη καὶ δεινὴ δυσωδία· ἐγὼ δέ φησιν ἐκπλαγεὶς ἐπὶ τούτοις, ἠρξάμην βιάζεσθαι τὸν ἄνδρα, εἰπεῖν μοι τί ἂν εἴη τοῦτο· ὁ δὲ στενάξας μέγα, ἤρξατο διηγεῖσθαι λέγων· ἐγὼ ἁγιώτατε πάπα, ἔσχον μ(ητέ)ρα εὐειδῆ πάνυ· καὶ σφόδρα νέα οὖσα, ἐχήρευσεν· ἐμὲ μόνον ἔχουσα νήπιον· τελευτήσαντος δὲ τοῦ ἐμοῦ π(ατ)ρ(ὸ)ς ὡς εἴρηται, ἐξέδωκεν ἑαυτὴν τῇ σπατάλῃ καὶ μέθῃ καὶ ἀσωτίᾳ· ὥστε ἐκ τῆς πορνείας αὐτῆς, συνάξαι πάμπολα χρήματα· ἐμοῦ δὲ τῆς ἐννόμου ἡλικίας ἤδη γεγονότος· καὶ αὐτῆς χρονισάσης τῇ τοιαύτῃ αἰσχρότητι, συνέβη καὶ αὐτ(ὴν) τελευτῆσαι· ἐγὼ δὲ εἰς αἴσθησιν ἐλθὼν· καὶ ἐννοήσας πόθεν ὁ τοσοῦτος πλοῦτος συνῆκται, ἐκδεδωκὼς ἑαυτὸν λοιπὸν τῇ ἀποταγῇ τῶν γηΐνων πραγμάτων· πολλῶν ὄντων τῶν π(ατ)ρώων καὶ [Fol. 82r] μητρώων μου χρημάτων, ἐθέμην ἐν τῇ καρδίᾳ μου λέγων, μὴ γένοιτό μοι δέσποτα κ(ύρι)ε ὁ θ(εὸ)ς, ἐκ τοῦ ἀσεβοῦς τούτου καὶ ἀκαθάρτου πλούτου χρήσασθαι, ἀλλὰ πάντα διαδώσω ἐκκλησίαις καὶ πένησι, ὑπὲρ τῆς ψυχῆς τῆς ἐμῆς μ(ητ)ρ(ὸ)ς· καὶ οὕτω ποιήσας, δίδωμι καὶ τὰ ἐμὰ πάντα, μὴ καταλείψας ἐμαυτῷ τί, πλὴν ὧν ἐφόρουν ἱματίων·

Translation[3]
[Fol. 81r] Various very brief and beneficial tales of holy men by Paul the most holy amongst monks who was bishop of Monembasia in the Peleponnese.

A monk once told this tale saying, 'Once when I visited the holy Theodoritos, patriarch of Antioch, and I was invited [Fol. 81v] by him to a meal, he told my humbleness this story: "A few days ago a stranger came here whose adornment was to be unwashed, [to have] lots of hair and [to wear] hair rags; and when I asked this man to eat with me, and he came, and sat down beside me, I saw that he was eating with his left hand, for the right was wrapped in a rag up to the wrist. So I said to him, 'Brother, why do you not eat with your right hand but with the left? For the great Basil in his *Teachings* says, 'the right hand shall administer to the body from the loins up to the head, and the left administers in like manner from the loins down.' And he said to me, 'Forgive me most holy lord I have some disease and therefore I can't.' And when I had pressed him repeatedly to explain and saw that he was unwilling, I grasped the rag on his hand, as if joking with the man, and threw it to one side, and the hand then gave off such an unspeakable and awful stench that all held their noses and ran away until he had again wrapped up his stinking hand in that holy rag. And that unbearable and awful stench stopped. And I,' he said, 'was astonished at these things and so began to force the man to tell me what that [smell] was. He sighed deeply and began to tell his tale, 'I, most holy father, had a very beautiful mother and she was widowed when very young, with me as her only baby, and she gave herself over to wantonness and drinking and wastefulness, after my father died, as has been said, so that she amassed a lot of money from her whoring, and when I had already become of legal age and she had spent years in this kind of shamelessness, it happened that she also died. And when I realised, and thought about from where this great wealth had come together, I gave myself over from then on to the renunciation of earthly things. Since I inherited much money from my father and [Fol. 82r] mother I decided in my heart and said, "may it not happen to me O master, lord God, that I use any of this impious and unclean wealth, instead I will distribute it all to churches and to the poor for the soul of my mother." Having done this I also gave all that was mine, and did not leave anything for myself, apart from the clothes that I wore.

---

[3] I would like to express my gratitude to Dirk Krausmüller who has helped me with the edition of the Greek text. Thanks must also go to Anthony Hirst whose help in 'cleaning up' the translation was invaluable.

καὶ ταῦτα ποιήσας ὑπὲρ τῆς ψυχῆς τῆς ἐμῆς μ(ητ)ρ(ὸ)ς μετὰ πάσης προαιρέσεως καὶ πίστεως ἀδιστάκτου, ἔλεγον· ἆρα πόθεν γνώσομαι, ἢ τίς με πληροφορήσει, ὅτι προσεδέξατο ὁ θ(εὸ)ς τὰ δοθέντα τοῖς πένησι· καὶ μάλιστα ὅτι ἀπὸ αἰσχρῶν ἦσαν συναχθέντα προφάσεων· καὶ ὅτι ἔτυχεν ἀνέσεως ἡ μ(ήτη)ρ μου, ἢ ὠφελείας οἱασοῦν, ἕνεκεν τῶν τοιούτων ἐλεημοσυνῶν τε καὶ προσφορῶν· ἀπλῆθον οὖν δέσποτα εἰς ἱεροσόλυμα πρὸς τὸν π(ατ)ριάρχην· ὅστις ἀκούσας τὰ συμβάντα, λέγει μοι· καλῶς ἐποίησας πάντα ὦ τέκνον, μεριμνήσας τὴν τῆς μ(ητ)ρ(ό)ς σου σ(ωτη)ρίαν· ταῦτα γὰρ ποιῶν, σαυτὸν εὐεργετεῖς καὶ σ(ωτη)ρίας ἀξιοῖς τὴν σὴν ψυχήν· πλὴν οὐδεὶς δύναται ἀκριβῶς τὸ τέλειον τοῦ πράγματος πιστώσασθαί σοι· ἀλλὰ πορεύθητι εἰς σκῆτιν καὶ εἰς θηβαΐδα· κἀκεῖ εὑρήσεις ἄνδρας θεοφόρους καὶ διορατικοὺς, οἳ δύνανταί σοι περὶ τούτου δι' εὐχῆς καὶ ἀποκαλύψεως πληροφορῆσαι· εὐθέως οὖν πορευθεὶς εἰς σκῆτιν καὶ εἰς θηβαΐδα, ἤκουσα παρὰ τῶν ὁσίων ἐκείνων καὶ ἀοιδίμων π(ατέ)ρων· λεγόντων πάντως ἐκ τῆς ἄγαν ταπεινώσεως, ὅτι οὐκ ἔστι τέκνον ἐν ἡμῖν σήμερον, οἷον αὐτὸς ἐπιζητεῖ ὁ σκοπός σου· ἀλλ' εἰ θέλεις ἀκοῦσαι τῆς ἡμ(ῶν) συμβουλείας, εἴσελθε εἰς τὴν ἐσωτέραν ἔρημον· κἀκεῖ εὑρήσεις ἄν(θρωπ)ον τοῦ θ(εο)ῦ τέλειον· δυνάμενόν σε περὶ τούτων πληροφορῆσαι· μὴ οὖν τὸν κόπον ἀκηδιάσῃς ὦ τέκνον· ἀλλὰ θαρρῶν πορεύου· ὁ κ(ύριο)ς μετα σοῦ· λαβὼν οὖν ἄρτους καὶ εὐχὴν καὶ ὕδωρ, ὥδευσα ἡμέρ(ας) τριάκοντα· καὶ εὗρον σπήλαιον μῖκρὸν· καὶ ὀλίγον ὕδωρ· καὶ περὶ τὸ ὕδωρ, ἴχνη ἀν(θρώπ)ου· καὶ περιχαρὴς γενόμενος, ἔκρουσα [Fol. 82v] κατὰ τὸ ἔθος· ἀπεκρίθη δὲ ἔνδον ὁ ἅγιος γέρων· ἐξελθὼν οὖν καὶ γενομένης τῆς συνήθους τοῖς μοναχοῖς εὐχῆς, ἐκαθέσθημεν· καὶ λέγει μοι ὁ δοῦλος τοῦ θ(εο)ῦ· καλῶς ἐλήλυθας τέκνον· τί τοσοῦτον κόπ(ον) ὑπέμεινας ἐλθεῖν ἕως ἡμῶν· εἰπέ μοι πῶς τὸ τῶν χριστιανῶν φῦλον πολιτεύεται σήμερον· πῶς οἱ βασιλεῖς· πῶς ἡ πίστις ἥδρασται· [in margine: κ] ἐμοῦ δὲ φήσαντος ὅτι εὐχαῖς ὑμῶν ὁσίαις τῶν ἰσαγγέλως βιούντων, πάντα εὐσεβῶς καὶ εἰρηνικῶς τὰ καθημᾶς βεβαιοῦνται· ἀλλ' εἰς ὃ παρεγενόμην δέσποτα, εἰς τοῦτο με φώτισον δέομαι τοῖς ἁγίοις σου ἴχνεσιν· αὐτοῦ δὲ εἰπόντος· καὶ τίς ἡ αἰτία τῆς πρὸς ἡμᾶς ἀφίξεως· καὶ ἐξηγησαμένου μου πάντα ὡς εἴρηται καὶ εἰπόντος, τὰ τῆς πληροφορίας ὦ δέσποτα λαβεῖν δέομαι, διὰ τῆς εἰς θ(εὸ)ν πεπαρρησιασμένης καὶ εὐπροσδέκτου σου δεήσεως, εἰ ἔτυχε τινὸς ὠφελείας ἡ ταπεινή μου μή(τη)ρ, ἢ οὔ, ὅπερ ἀπεύχομαι· ἀπεκρίθη δὲ ὁ ἀληθὴς δοῦλος τοῦ θ(εο)ῦ· ὑπὲρ τὴν ἐμὴν δύναμιν καὶ ἀξίαν ὦ τέκνον ἡ τοιαύτη αἴτησις· πλὴν παρακαλέσωμεν ἀμφότεροι τὸν θ(εό)ν· καὶ ὃ θέλει καὶ βούλεται ἀποκαλύπτει ἡμῖν· καὶ ποιήσας τῇ βαΐνῃ αὐτοῦ ῥάβδῳ ἔξωθεν τοῦ σπηλαίου γραμμὴν κυκλοειδῆ, ἔστησέ με μέσον· παραγγείλας, ἕως ἡμέρας ἓξ, μήτε καθεσθῆναι ὅσον εἰς δύναμιν, μήτε φαγεῖν μήτε πιεῖν,

And having done this for the soul of my mother very willingly and with unwavering faith I said, "How will I know, or who will fully assure me, that God has accepted what was given to the poor, especially since it was brought together by shameful means, and whether my mother gained remission or any kind of benefit because of such alms and offerings?" Then, lord, I went to Jerusalem to the patriarch who, when he heard what had happened to me, said, "You have done well, O child, to have cared about the salvation of your mother, for in doing this you benefit yourself and you render your soul worthy of salvation, but no-one is able to prove to you how the matter stands exactly. But go off into Sketis and the Thebaid and there you will find a divinely-inspired and clairvoyant man who can fully assure you about this through prayer and revelation."

I then immediately went to Skete and the Thebaid, and I heard the pious and famous fathers there make a statement that without doubt was a reflection of their utmost humility saying, "There is not among us today, child, such a one as you require for your purpose. But if you want to hear our counsel go into the inner desert and there you will find a perfect man of God who can assure you about these matters. Do not tire of the effort, o child, but go forth courageously. The lord be with you." And taking bread and prayer and water, I then travelled for thirty days and found a small cave and a little water, and around the water the footprints of a man, and, overjoyed, I knocked, [Fol. 82v] as one does. And the holy elder answered from within. Then after he had come out and we had said the prayer that is customary among monks, we sat down. And the servant of God said to me, "Welcome child. Why have you endured such toil to come so far to us? Tell me how the Christian people live today. How are the emperors? Does the faith stand firm?" And I said, "All our affairs are secured in piety and peace, through the pious prayers of you whose lives are equal to the angels. But enlighten me in the matter for which I have come, this I beseech at your holy feet." And he said, "What is the reason for your coming to us?" And I explained everything, as has been told, and said, "I beseech you, O lord, that I may receive assurance through your entreaty which is frank and well received before God, whether my humble mother gained some benefit, or whether she did not, which I pray is not the case." And the true servant of God answered, "Such a request is above my power and worth. Nevertheless, let us both beseech God and whatever he wants and wishes he will reveal to us." And having drawn a circle outside the cave with his palm-rod staff, he made me stand in the middle, and ordered me, as far as possible not to sit down nor to eat or drink for six days,

ἀλλὰ δέεσθαι τοῦ θ(εο)ῦ νυκτὸς καὶ ἡμέρας, ὅπως φανερώση ἡμῖν τοῦ ζητουμένου τὴν ἀποκάλυψιν· κἀγὼ δὲ ἔνδον τοῦ σπηλαίου τὸ αὐτὸ ποιήσω· καὶ δυνατός ἐστιν ὁ τῶν ἐννοιῶν κριτὴς καὶ τῶν νεφρῶν καὶ καρδιῶν ἐξεταστὴς· ὁ τῶν ἀδήλων γνώστης, καὶ φανερωτὴς τῶν ἀγνοουμένων ἀποκαλύψαι ἡμῖν τοῖς ἀναξίοις κατὰ τὸ θέλημα αὐτοῦ· καὶ ποιήσας εὐχὴν ἐκτενῆ, εἴασέ με ἔνδον τῆς γραμμῆς καὶ εἰσῆλθεν εἰς τὸ σπήλαιον αὐτοῦ· καὶ ποιήσαντός μου τὰ ἓξ νυχθήμερα, ὡς ἦλθεν ἡ ἑβδόμη νὺξ, γίνομαι ὡς ἐν ἐκστάσει· καὶ ὁρῶ κατὰ τὸ εὐώνυμον μέρος, λίμνην βορβορόδους δυσωδίας ἀμετρίτου· καὶ κεφαλὰς τινῶν ἀνιόντων καὶ κατιόντων ἐν τῷ βυθῷ τῆς λίμνης [Fol. 83r] καὶ σὺν αὐτοῖς, τὴν μ(ητέ)ρα μου ἀνιοῦσαν καὶ κατιοῦσαν ἑωρακῶς ἕως τραχήλου, καὶ γνωρίσασάν με καὶ κράζουσαν· τέκνον μου καλὸν ἐλέησόν με· καὶ πάλιν καταδύσασαν ἐν τῷ βυθῷ τοῦ βορβόρου, καὶ πάλιν ἀνελθοῦσαν ἕως τοῦ στήθους καὶ κράξασαν, τέκνον μου γλυκύτατον ἐλέησόν με· τέκνον μου βοήθει μοι· καὶ πάλιν βυθισθεῖσαν· καὶ τὸ τρίτον ἰδὼν αὐτὴν ἀνελθοῦσαν· καὶ ἔτι πλεῖον βοῶσαν μετὰ οἴκτου· καὶ πολλῶν δακρύων καὶ οἰμωγῶν, τέκνον ἐμὸν, βοήθει· τέκνον μου σπλαγχνίσθητι· τέκνον μου μὴ καταλίπης με εἰς τὴν ἀνάγκην ταύτην· ἐγὼ δὲ τοῦ κινδύνου ὥσπερ ἐπιλαθόμενος, ἐκτείνας τὴν δεξιὰν χεῖρα· καὶ δραξάμενος τῆς κόμης τῆς κεφαλῆς αὐτῆς· αὐτῆς δὲ πάλιν εἰς τὰ κάτω βρυθούσης, ἐβάφη ἡ χείρ μου ἐν τῷ βορβόρῳ τῆς δυσωδίας ἐκείνης, ἕως τοῦ ἀστραγάλου· ταύτην δὲ ἀνασπάσας· καὶ εἰς τὰ δεξιὰ περιβλεψάμενος, ὁρῶ κολυμβήθραν ὕδατος καθαροῦ, καὶ διειδεστάτου καὶ εὐώδους· ἐκεῖ οὖν ἐμβαλὼν αὐτὴν· καὶ ἀποπλύνας τοῦ δυσώδους ἐκείνου βορβόρου, τοῖς ἐκεῖσε λευκοφοροῦσι καὶ λαμπροῖς λαοῖς, κατέμιξα· δοξάζουσαν καὶ αἰνοῦσαν σὺν αὐτοῖς χ(ριστὸ)ν τὸν θ(εὸ)ν ἡμῶν· ἡμέρας δὲ λοιπὸν γενομένης, φωνήσας με ὁ δοῦλος τοῦ θ(εο)ῦ, ἐπυνθάνετο, τί ἂν εἴην ἑωρακῶς· ἐμοῦ δὲ διηγουμένου, αὐτὸς ἐπεσφράγιζε τὰ λεγόμενα· τὰ γὰρ αὐτὰ ἦν καὶ αὐτὸς ὡς ἔλεγε θεασάμενος· ἐμοῦ δὲ τὴν χεῖρα προβαλλομένου· καὶ τὴν ἄμετρον δυσωδίαν μὴ ὑποφέροντος, ἔφη ὁ ἅγιος· περὶ τούτου μή σοι μελέτω· τοῦτο γὰρ σφραγίς ἐστι τῆς ἀληθείας, τοῦ πιστεύειν ἡμᾶς, καὶ πάντας τοὺς ἀκούοντας καὶ ὁρῶντας, ὅτι ἀληθὴς ἡ ὀπτασία, καὶ οὐδὲ φάσμα, οὐδὲ φαντασία· καὶ ὅτι δυνατός ἐστιν ὁ θ(εὸ)ς, καὶ μετὰ θάνατον ποιεῖν ἔλεος καὶ οἰκτιρμοὺς, μετὰ τῶν ἐξ ὅλης καρδίας ποιούντων προσφορὰς καὶ ἐλεημοσύνας, ὑπὲρ τῶν προεκδημησάντων, καὶ αὐτοῖς παρέχειν ἔλεος· ὅτι οἱ οἰκτιρμοὶ αὐτοῦ, ἐπὶ πάντα τὰ ἔργα αὐτοῦ· καὶ ὅσα θέλει, καὶ δύναται· περὶ δὲ τῆς χειρός σου [Fol. 83v] ταύτης, ἐγώ σοι πληροφορῶ, ἠδύνατο μὲν ὁ θ(εὸ)ς παντελῶς αὐτ(ὴν) τῆς τοιαύτης ἀπαλλάξαι δυσωδίας· ἀλλ' ἵνα μὴ ὡς εἴρηται δύσπιστον δόξη εἶναι καὶ ἀμφίβολον τοῖς πολλοῖς, οὕτω ταύτην ἔχειν

but to beseech God day and night to reveal to us the answer to my question. And he would do the same inside the cave. He who judges thoughts and examines kidneys and hearts, who knows what is hidden and discloses that which is unknown, has the power to reveal to us the unworthy ones what he wills. He made an extended prayer and then he left me within the circle and went into his cave. After I had spent six days and nights, and the seventh night had come, I entered into a state of trance and saw on my left a lake of immeasurable muddy stench and the heads of some people going up and down into the depths of the lake [Fol. 83r] and I saw among them, my mother going up and down up to her neck. And she recognised me and called out, "My good child have mercy on me," and she again dived into the depths of the mud and again came up to her chest and called out, "My sweetest child have mercy on me, help me my child," and afterwards I saw her sink again and come up a third time and cry out even more pitifully and weep with many tears and wailings, "My child help, my child have mercy, my child don't leave me in this distress." And I, as if having forgotten the danger, stretched out my right hand and grabbed the hair of her head and when she was again weighed down, my hand was dipped into the mud of that stench up to the wrist. And after I had pulled her up and looked around to the right, I saw a pool of pure, clear, and fragrant water. Then after I had put her in there and washed off the stinking mud, I placed her among the people there who were dressed in white and shone brilliantly, and with them she was praising and glorifying Christ our God. And then, when it had become day, the servant of God called me and asked me what I had seen. And while I was telling him, he himself confirmed what I said to him. For he himself, as he said, had seen the same things. And when I held out my hand and I could not endure the immense stench, the holy man said, "Don't let this concern you. For it is a confirmation of the truth, so that we and all those who hear and see may believe that the vision is true and neither an illusion nor a figment of the imagination, and that even after death God is capable of bestowing mercy and compassion on those who wholeheartedly make offerings and give alms for the sake of those who have already departed, and that he is capable of giving them mercy. Because his compassionate acts are over all his works and whatever he wills of that he is also capable. And about this hand of yours, [Fol. 83v] I assure you that God could completely rid it of such stench. But in order that it does not appear to the many to be difficult to believe and doubtful, as has been said, it pleased him that it should be thus."

εὐδόκησεν· οὕτως οὖν εἰπών μοι ὁ δοῦλος τοῦ θ(εο)ῦ· καὶ μικρ(ὸν) ῥάκος τοῦτο ὅπερ ὁρᾶς, ἐκ τοῦ ἁγίου αὐτοῦ παλλίου ἀποτεμὼν, περιέθηκέ μου τῇ χειρὶ· καὶ εὐθὺς κατέπαυσε πᾶσα ἡ δυσωδία· προσεγένετο δὲ μᾶλλον δι' αὐτοῦ, εὐωδία· ἥτις καὶ ἐπιμένει τοῦ ῥάκκους ἐπικειμένου· εἰ δὲ τις ἄρῃ αὐτὸ· ὡς καὶ σὺ ἀρτίως ἐποίησας, οὐκ ἄν τις ὑποφέρει τῆς δϋσωδίας τὸ ἄμετρον· μετα δὲ ταῦτα λέγει μοι ὁ ὄντως δοῦλος τοῦ θ(εο)ῦ ἐκεῖνος· ἰδοὺ τέκνον τοσαύτην ὁδὸν ὁδοιπορήσας, σφόδρα ἐκοπίασας· καὶ τὰ πρὸς δαπάνην οὐχ ὑπάρχει σοι· ἢ πῶς ἀπελεύσῃ ἐν τῇ χώρᾳ σου ἀκόπως καὶ ὡς ταῦτα διελέγετό μοι, ἰδοὺ ἔπνευσεν ἄνεμος νότος· καὶ νεφέλη χαλάζης ἀνεσπάσθη ἐκ δϋσμῶν· ὁ δὲ ἅγιος γέρων ἔφη· σοὶ προστάσσω τῶ ἀγγέλω τῶ τὴν νεφέλην ἐπέχοντι· ἐν ὀνόματι ἰ(ησο)ῦ χ(ριστο)ῦ· τοῦ τὰς νεφέλας ἡνιοχοῦντος, καὶ τὰ πάντα οἰακίζοντος τῇ παντοδυνάμω παλάμῃ, λάβε τὸν ἀδελφὸν τοῦτον διὰ τῆς νεφέλης, καὶ ἀπόσωσον αὐτὸν εἰς τὰ ἴδια αὐτοῦ· ὅπως πᾶσι διηγεῖται τὰ μεγαλεῖα τοῦ θ(εο)ῦ· καὶ ὅτι δυνατός ἐστι τοῖς ὀρθῶς καὶ ἀδιστάκτως αἰτοῦσι, παρέχειν τὰ αἰτήματα αὐτῶν· διά τε προσφορῶν καὶ ἐλεημοσυνῶν, ὑπέρ τε νεκρῶν καὶ ζώντων· ὅτι οἱ οἰκτιρμοὶ αὐτοῦ ἐπὶ πάντα τὰ ἔργα αὐτοῦ εἰς γενεὰν καὶ γενεὰν ἕως τοῦ αἰῶνος· ἄρασα οὖν με ἡ νεφέλ(η) παρέστησέ με τῶ οἴκω μου· ὥσπερ τὸν ἀββακοὺμ ἐν τῶ λάκκω τοῦ δανιηλ, καὶ ἑτέρους· δοξάζοντα καὶ αἰνοῦντα χ(ριστὸ)ν τὸν θ(εὸ)ν ἡμῶν, ἐν πάσῃ σωφροσύνῃ τε καὶ ἁγνείᾳ· ὅτι αὐτῶ πρέπει δόξα εἰς τοὺς αἰῶνας τῶν αἰώνων· ἀμήν· παύλ(ου) τοῦ ὁσιωτ(ά)τ(ου) ἐν μοναχοῖς· καὶ ἐπισκόπ(ου) γενομ(έν)ου μονεμβασίας τῆς πελοποννήσ(ου) διηγήματα διάφορα ὁσίων ἀνδρῶν, πάνυ σύντομα καὶ ὠφέλιμα.

The servant of God, having spoken thus to me, cut off from his holy pallium this little rag which you see and put it around my hand and all the stench ceased immediately and instead a good smell resulted from this, which remains the case even now while the rag is covering it. But when somebody lifts it, as you too have just done, no-one can bear the immeasurable stench. And after this that true servant of God said to me, "Behold child, you have toiled greatly, having travelled such a long road, and you have nothing left to spend. What must you do? Or how will you go into your country without toil?" And when he said this to me, behold, a south wind blew and a cloud of hail was drawn up from the west. And the holy elder said, "I order you the angel who controls the cloud, in the name of Jesus Christ, the one who holds the reins of the clouds and who steers everything through his almighty palm, take this brother by means of the cloud and get him safely to his own place so that he may speak to all of the greatness of God and of how he is able to grant requests to those who make them correctly and without doubt, through offerings and almsgiving, for the sake of the dead and the living; for his compassionate acts are over all his works from generation to generation in eternity." Then the cloud, lifted me up and placed me at my house, just as Habbakuk into the den of Daniel, and others. And I glorified and praised Christ our God in every manner of temperance and purity because glory befits him in the ages of the ages. Amen.

20

The tale of Daniel's sister: text, translation and commentary De sorore Danielis, *BHG* 1438hb

Evangeli Skaka and John Wortley

The Abba Daniel dossier

Among the rich tradition of the 'spiritually beneficial tales' which, together with their sayings (*apophthegmata*) constitute the folklore of the desert fathers (fourth to the eighth centuries AD) the group of around fifteen stories associated with Daniel of Skete (see Appendix) stands out in a number of ways. There are many complex problems arising concerning these stories, at least some of which it may be possible to solve with the forthcoming publication by Tim Vivian[1] of all their extant versions (which are many).

For the most part the tales purport to be the work of an unnamed disciple of Abba Daniel whose activities appear more or less to have coincided with the reign the Emperor Justinian I, 529–567. The tales fall into three categories. Seven of them narrate experiences shared by the Abba and his disciple, such as his caring for a leper and their joint visit to a women's monastery (No 2, No 3; also No 5, and Nos 10.1, 3, 4, 5). Then there are stories which Daniel and his disciple hear conjointly, for instance from Palladios (No 8) or Abba Peter, the disciple of Abba Isaiah (No 9). Finally, there are a few tales which Daniel himself is said to have narrated: No 4, No 6, possibly No 10.2 and (partly) No 10.3; these last tend to be the stories which put the greatest strain on one's credulity. Of all these tales, only a few items (those in the third category) can really be called 'Tales *of* Daniel of Skete,' for most of them are, in truth, rather tales *about* him, or rather tales in which he is somehow involved. Thus the title Τὰ κατὰ τὸν ἀββᾶν Δανιήλ, 'The Abba Daniel dossier,' is by no means misleading. Not all the pieces are of equal value for learning about Daniel for, as the reader will quickly discover, his part in these miniature dramas is, in some cases, rather a minor one.

Dramas, however, they most certainly are; tales, sometimes even complex tales, in which colourful events succeed each other in rapid succession. In this respect they have far more in common with the *récits tardifs* of the tenth century rather than

---

[1] *Witness to holiness: Abba Daniel of Scetis*, ed. T. Vivian (forthcoming).

with the somewhat static tales found (for instance) in the two great sixth-century collections of *Apophthegmata*, the Alphabetic and the Systematic.

The tale of Daniel's sister

The tale presented here is no exception. The question arises however of whether it is indeed to be included in the Daniel dossier. For one thing, it fits into none of the three categories mentioned above; for another, there is no mention of the otherwise ubiquitous anonymous disciple and author here. Furthermore, the critical edition of the Greek text (almost certainly the basis of the versions) makes no mention of the name of the monk, yet it is widely assumed that the story is about Daniel, and not without good reason.

The tale of Daniel's sister survives in four versions: the *BHG* 1438hb edited here,[2] the *BHG* 1438h,[3] the *BHG* 2102e,[4] and a Syriac translation.[5] The silence kept in the first two versions as to the involvement of Daniel in the story is broken in the two latter ones. In *BHG* 2102e the monk referred to in the story is firmly identified as Daniel whereas, in the Syriac version, Daniel appears to be only the narrator of a story that concerns an anonymous monk. The following table registers the information given by each version:

BHG 1438hb	*BHG* 1438h	*BHG* 2102e[6]	Syriac version
Ἀδελφήν τις οἰκείαν καταλιπὼν ἐν Ἀλεξανδρείᾳ ἐξῆλθε καὶ ἐμόνασεν ἐν τῷ Ὄρει. Ἡ δὲ καταλειφθεῖσα ἐξ αὐτοῦ τῇ ἀσωτίᾳ	Ἀδελφός τις ἐκάθητο εἰς κελλίον τῆς Αἰγύπτου ἐν πολλῇ ταπεινώσει διαλάμπων. Ὑπῆρχε δὲ αὐτῷ ἀδελφὴ πορνεύουσα ἐν τῇ	Ἦν τις μοναχὸς ἐν Ἀλεξανδρείᾳ ὀνόματι Δανιὴλ ἔχων ἀδελφήν· καὶ καταλιπὼν αὐτὴν ἐν Ἀλεξανδρείᾳ ἐξῆλθεν εἰς τὰ Ὄρη. Ἡ δὲ ἀδεφλὴ αὐτοῦ	Abba Daniel used to relate how there was a certain brother who was living in the city of Alexandria, and he had a sister in the flesh. He left her behind in

---

[2] *Bibliotheca Hagiographica Graeca*, ed. F. Halkin, 3rd ed. (SubsHag, 8a, Brussels, 1957); and *Novum auctarium Bibliothecæ Hagiographicæ Graecæ* (SubsHag, 65, Brussels, 1984).

[3] *BHG* 1438h was edited by F. Nau, *ROC*, 12 (1907), No 43, 174–175. This version is also found in Paul of Evergetis's *Synagoge*, I.1.4.6, and Nikon of the Black Mountain's *Interpretations*, 52, Atheniensis 496, fourteenth century, ff. 185v-186v.

[4] For *BHG* 2102e we are using the Parisinus Coislin. 369, eleventh century, ff. 54v-57r, and Parisinus Suppl. gr. 147, fourteenth century, ff. 208r-209r.

[5] See S.P. Brock, 'A Syriac narratio attributed to Abba Daniel of Sketis', *AnalBoll*, 113 (1995), 269–290.

[6] The manuscript Paris. suppl. gr. 147 adds the following title: Περὶ τοῦ ἀββᾶ Δανιὴλ καὶ τῆς ἀδελφῆς αὐτοῦ.

BHG 1438hb	BHG 1438h	BHG 2102e[6]	Syriac version
τῆς πορνείας ἑαυτὴν ἐκδέδωκε...	πόλει...	ἐξέδωκε αὐτὴν τῇ ἀσωτίᾳ...	Alexandria and went out and having made himself a cell in the mountain, was dwelling there...

If the statement that he embraced the monastic profession 'on the mountain' (which usually means the mountain of Antony the Great) is true, he must have moved on, as there could be no question of walking there from Alexandria. Skete however was within walking distance of Alexandria, – for a good strong walker, which clearly the sister was not. Daniel is however described as having moved around a great deal in tales in which he is named; he could have been conducting his sister to a nearer location. Taking into consideration the extraordinary things which happen to him in the course of the other tales, one realises that a tale in which he has a sister no better than she ought to be, who dies on his hands, is not by any means *hors série*. The colourful descriptions of the sister's former life ('disporting herself with her lovers') and of her profound penitence employ phrases which came easily to the anonymous disciple who claims to have written the rest of the Daniel stories; phrases which are rarely found in contemporary tales, even in the rather more vivid narratives of John Moschos. On balance then it might be permissible to accept the tradition which presents this as a tale *de sorore Danielis*, about Daniel's sister.

All the Daniel tales are outstanding in one way or another, but this one has something about it which is very rare and valuable. There are over a thousand 'spiritually beneficial tales' of the Desert Fathers in existence but, unlike most bodies of folklore, they appear to have no identifiable forbears. (This is written by one who has spent over twenty years searching for their antecedents.) Many years ago Wallis Budge suggested that Coptic Christians were far more in touch with their Egyptian religious heritage than one might imagine, and that it would be in the folklore associated with hieroglyphics, sphinx and pyramids that we would find the sources of many of their ideas.[7] Nobody seems to have taken him very seriously at the time; one has to admit that the evidence of the tales does not overwhelmingly confirm his hypothesis. But there are indications from time to time that he might have been right. One of the most striking of those indications is to be found in the story now under consideration.

In the vision which Daniel experiences while sleeping on his sister's fresh grave, he witnesses the *psychomachia*, the tussle between the powers of light and darkness/good and evil for possession of the departing soul of his sister. The *psychomachia* is a *topos*, a frequently recurring feature, in beneficial tales and in

---

[7] E.A. Wallis Budge, *Egyptian ideas of the future life* (London, 1899), 72.

hagiography generally.[8] It is however not a native feature of Judaeo-Christian lore; the present tale may well indicate where it comes from. In the course of the struggle for the sister's soul, 'Bring me a pair of scales and weigh her impurity against her repentance' says 'the ruler.' Her tears and the blood from her feet are weighed against the accusations of wrong-doing and she is saved.

What are we to make of the scales and of this weighing? They are no more germane to the Judaeo-Christian tradition than is the *psychomachia*,[9] but they may indicate a clear connection with ancient Egyptian folklore. For the *psychomachia* used to figure very prominently in the religion of the ancient Egyptians. Weigh-scales moreover featured (and were often portrayed) in the Egyptian *psychomachia*. They were used as a means of testing the departing soul when it came into the judgement hall of Osiris, virtues being weighed against vices, so to speak. There too was Horus 'who leads the deceased into the presence of Osiris and makes an appeal to his father that the deceased may be allowed to enjoy the benefits possessed by all who are "true of voice" and justified in the judgement.'[10] The tales often feature an intercessor at the judgement scene, often the Blessed Virgin Mary (compare the appearances of the female deity Maat in the Egyptian judgement-scenes).

Another tale in which the same theme occurs tells of a dangerous arch-brigand in Thrace whom the Emperor Maurice (d. 602) finally managed to capture, but who fell ill within days of his arrest. He lay dying in the Sampson hospital at Constantinople and there he repented of his evil ways. He wept and wept for his sins, asking God to receive his tears, which he repeatedly wiped away on a handkerchief. The doctor in attendance had a vision about him. He saw certain 'burnt-faced-ones' [*aithiopes*], black devils in other words, who were casting accusations in one side of a pair of scales, weighing it down. But two bright angels cast the brigand's tear-soaked handkerchief in the other scale, tipped it and, by so doing, gained his soul. The good doctor found his patient dead next morning. On hearing of his good confession from the other patients, he took the handkerchief to the Emperor and told him of the matter.[11]

---

[8] See *s.v.* 'Psychomachia', *ODB*, ed. A. P. Kazhdan and A.-M. Talbot, 3 vols (New York and Oxford, 1991), III, 1755–1756.
[9] Scales are mentioned from time to time in the Judaic tradition; Nebuchadnezzar had been 'weighed in the balance and found wanting' (Dan 5:27); Job prays: 'Let me be weighed in an even balance' (Job 31:6) and there is the enigmatic mention in Ps 61:10, but there is no suggestion of the use of scales at a final judgment, nor is there any mention of them in the Gospels.
[10] R.A. Armour, *Gods and myths in ancient Egypt* (Cairo, 1986), 164.
[11] W863 (W= J. Wortley, *A repertoire of Byzantine beneficial tales,* http://home.cc.umanitoba.ca/~wortley/index.html), *BHG* 1450m: *de latrone converso [bis]*, Anastasios the Sinaite, *In Ps. vi, PG*, 89, 1112A–1116B. All abstracts and translations are J. Wortley's own work except where stated otherwise.

In a word, the two tales in which scales are used may confirm what Wallis Budge suspected. The search for the roots of psychophelitic literature must now be concentrated on Egyptian folklore.

The exemplar of the story

In his edition of the Syriac *Tale of Daniel's sister*, Brock argued that 'the Syriac version… happens to be (probably) the earliest witness to the story' and brought to our attention the fact 'that the Syriac is considerably fuller at both the beginning and especially the end'[12] when compared with the text of *BHG* 1438h, the only other Greek version available to him. Even though the length of both the beginning and the end of this story still remains the main criterion determining the superiority of a certain version against the others, there should be some qualification of Brock's argument in the light of the evidence provided by the two new versions we now have at our disposal. In what follows, we will try to show that the version used as the basis for all known versions, and thus the earliest witness to the story, is *BHG* 1438hb and not the Syriac version. All the examples quoted are deliberately taken from the end of the story, that being the most interesting part of it.

1. *BHG* 1438hb and the Syriac version

A comparison of the Syriac version with the text of *BHG* 1438hb indicates that the latter is in all probability the basis for the Syriac. The Syriac follows the Greek text closely, using exactly the same vocabulary and imagery. Their only difference is that the author/translator of the Syriac has in many cases expanded the simple phrases of the Greek or felt the need to give a detailed description of what might have been happening at the scene. From the short excerpts quoted below one can get a glimpse of the translator at work. The phrase 'And the ruler said' (Καὶ λέγει ὁ ἄρχων) is expanded into 'The official immediately gave orders saying', the garments (στολὴν) become 'dirty garments and ugly clothes' and the luminous place (τόπῳ φωτεινῷ) is the 'glorious and luminous region' in the Syriac. The sentence 'God's love for mankind had triumphed', the most powerful and moving pronouncement in the whole story, is omitted. However, there are some additions which either function as fillers ('When they have done as he had commanded them', 'whereupon the Ethiopian and those with him fled in great shame'), or give some further information, as in the case of the last sentence that brings into the story the holy fathers of Skêtê, who are totally absent from *BHG* 1438hb.

---

[12] Brock, 'A Syriac narratio', 269.

BHG 1438hb	Syriac version
Καὶ λέγει ὁ ἄρχων· «Ἀγάγετέ μοι τρυτάνην καὶ στήσατε τὴν ἀκαθαρσίαν αὐτῆς σὺν τῇ με[f. 69v]τανοίᾳ.» Καὶ εὑρέθη ἡ μετάνοια αὐτῆς βαροῦσα καὶ <u>ἐνίκησεν ἡ φιλανθρωπία τοῦ Θεοῦ</u>.	18. <u>The official immediately gave orders saying</u>, 'Bring before me the scales, and weigh her sins against her repentance'. When they have done as he had commanded them, her repentance was heavier and weighed down the balance, <u>whereupon the Ethiopian and those with him fled in great shame</u>.
Τότε κελεύει ὁ ἄρχων ἀποδυθῆναι αὐτὴν τὴν <u>στολὴν</u> ἣν ἐφόρει. Καὶ ἐνέδυσαν αὐτὴν στολὴν βυσσίνην καὶ παρέδωκεν αὐτὴν τῷ ἀγγέλῳ τῆς μετανοίας καὶ κατέστησεν αὐτὴν ἐν τόπῳ <u>φωτεινῷ</u>.	19. The official straightaway gave orders that her <u>dirty garments and ugly clothes</u> be taken off her, and he bade them clothe her in a luminous robe, whereupon they handed her over to the angel of repentance and put her in a <u>glorious and luminous</u> region.
Καὶ διυπνισθεὶς ὁ ἀδελφὸς αὐτῆς ἐχάρη λίαν καὶ ἀναστὰς ἐπορεύετο χαίρων. (see the edition below at lines 64–71)	20. When her brother woke up he rejoiced exceedingly and gave thanks to God. <u>He related all these things to the holy fathers in Sketis</u>, and when they heard them they gave glory to God who does not spurn those who repent, but glorifies those who glorify him –to whom glory, honour, worship and exaltation is befitting for ever and ever, amen. (ed. S. Brock, *AnalBoll*, 113 (1995), 280.

2. *BHG* 1438hb and *BHG* 2102e

A comparative study of *BHG* 2102e and *BHG* 1438hb shows clearly that the former is a slightly abridged version of the latter. The author of *BHG* 2102e for the most part copies *BHG* 1438hb word for word. However, a number of changes can be traced in *BHG* 2102e: a) The high style and carefully selected vocabulary of the original is often simplified (eg. ὁ μέλας becomes ὁ διάβολος, the ἀνὴρ χαρίεις becomes ἄγγελος τῆς μετανοίας, the τρυτάνην becomes ζυγόν). b) Whole phrases are occasionally omitted or summarised, like the description of the sister being clothed in a linen robe and handed over to the angel of repentance who puts her in a luminous place, something that is only hinted at in the concluding paragraph (κατέστησεν αὐτὴν ὁ ἄρχων ἐν τόπῳ φωτεινῷ). c) Two new elements are introduced in the final paragraph. The first is the exhortation of the narrator to his audience to imitate the example of the repentance of Daniel's sister (Διό, ἀδελφοί μου, κτισώμεθα καὶ ἡμεῖς τὴν θερμὴν αὐτῆς μετάνοιαν). The second is the reference to the brother's prayers and ascetic labours that, together with God's help, have been conducive to his sister's salvation (Συνήργησαν γὰρ αὐτῇ μετὰ Θεὸν οἱ κόποι καὶ ἡ εὐχὴ τοῦ γέροντος). Neither of these elements is of any direct importance to the story; both are common remarks that could have been added by anyone.

BHG 1438hb	BHG 2102e
Ὁ δὲ μέλας ἀντεμάχετο λέγων ὅτι τοσοῦτον χρόνον μετ᾽ ἐμοῦ ἦν τὸ θέλημά μου ποιοῦσα καὶ ἵνα μικρὰς ἡμέρας ἀκολουθήσῃ σοι θέλεις ξενῶσαί με ἐξ αὐτῆς; Καὶ ἐκτείναντες τέσσαρες ἄνδρες τὰς χεῖρας - οἱ μέλλοντες παραλαμβάνειν αὐτὴν ἐπὶ τῇ κολάσει - ἐπελάβοντο τῶν τριχῶν αὐτῆς καὶ ἤρξαντο αὐτὴν σπαράσσειν. Καὶ λέγει ὁ ἄρχων· «Μὴ ἐγγίσητε αὐτῇ, ἕως οὗ ἔλθῃ καὶ ἡ μετάνοια αὐτῆς.» Καὶ εἰσῆλθεν ἀνὴρ χαρίεις ἔχων ἐν τῇ χειρὶ αὐτοῦ κάμπτραν χρυσῆν, ἔνθα ἦσαν τὰ δάκρυα αὐτῆς καὶ τὸ αἷμα τῶν ποδῶν αὐτῆς. Καὶ λέγει ὁ ἄρχων· «Ἀγάγετέ μοι τρυτάνην καὶ στήσατε τὴν ἀκαθαρσίαν αὐτῆς σὺν τῇ με[f. 69v]τανοίᾳ.» Καὶ εὑρέθη ἡ μετάνοια αὐτῆς βαροῦσα καὶ ἐνίκησεν ἡ φιλανθρωπία τοῦ Θεοῦ. Τότε κελεύει ὁ ἄρχων ἀποδυθῆναι αὐτὴν τὴν στολὴν ἣν ἐφόρει. Καὶ ἐνέδυσαν αὐτὴν στολὴν βυσσίνην καὶ παρέδωκεν αὐτὴν τῷ ἀγγέλῳ τῆς μετανοίας καὶ κατέστησεν αὐτὴν ἐν τόπῳ φωτεινῷ. Καὶ διυπνισθεὶς ὁ ἀδελφὸς αὐτῆς ἐχάρη λίαν καὶ ἀναστὰς ἐπορεύετο χαίρων. (see the edition below at lines 56–71)	Ὁ δὲ διάβολος ἀντεμάχετο τῷ ἄρχοντι ὅτι τοσοῦτον χρόνον σὺν ἐμοὶ ἦν, τὰ ἐμὰ θελήματα ποιοῦσα, ἐν τοῖς ἐμοῖς ἀναστρεφομένη πάντοτε, καὶ ἵνα μικρὰς ἡμέρας ἀκολουθήσει σοι θέλεις με ξενῶσαι αὐτῆς; Καὶ ἔμελλεν παραλαμβάνειν αὐτήν. Καὶ λέγει ὁ ἄρχων· «Μὴ ἐγγίσητε αὐτὴν ἕως ἂν ἔλθῃ ἡ μετάνοια αὐτῆς. Καὶ ἦλθεν ὁ ἄγγελος τῆς μετανοίας καὶ ἦν ἐν τῇ χειρὶ αὐτοῦ κάμπτρα χρυσῆ ἔνθα ἦσαν τὰ δάκρυα καὶ τὰ αἵματα τῶν ποδῶν αὐτῆς. Καὶ ἐνέγκαντες ζυγὸν ἔβαλλον εἰς τὸ ἓν μέρος τὰ ἁμαρτήματα αὐτῆς καὶ τὴν μετάνοιαν εἰς ἕν. Καὶ εὑρέθη ἡ μετάνοια αὐτῆς βαροῦσα ὑπὲρ τὴν ἁμαρτίαν καὶ ἰδόντες οἱ δαίμονες ἔφυγον. Διό, ἀδελφοί μου, κτισώμεθα καὶ ἡμεῖς τὴν θερμὴν αὐτῆς μετάνοιαν. Πολλὰ γὰρ ἰσχύει τὸ δάκρυον καὶ μάλιστα τοῦ μετ᾽ ἐξομολογήσεως χέοντος αὐτό. Διὰ γὰρ τῶν δακρύων κατέστησεν αὐτὴν ὁ ἄρχων ἐν τόπῳ φωτεινῷ ἐν μοναῖς ἁγίων. Συνήργησαν γὰρ αὐτῇ μετὰ Θεὸν οἱ κόποι καὶ ἡ εὐχὴ τοῦ γέροντος. (Coisl. 369, ff. 56v-57r and Suppl. gr. 147, ff. 208v-209r)

3. *BHG* 1438hb and *BHG* 1438h

BHG 1438h is the shortest of all versions. Taking into consideration that in it all the events of the story are summarised in a few lines, we can argue that *BHG* 1438h is an abbreviated version of *BHG* 1438hb, even though it is rather doubtful that the latter was its basis. The most striking difference between these two versions is the absence of the brother's dream from *BHG* 1438h. Nor is the fact that the sister's repentance has been accepted by God revealed to her brother but to one of the holy fathers to whom the brother related the incident and sought their advice. As one can see from the text quoted below, the colourful narrative of the brother's dream, which covers almost one page in *BHG* 1438hb, has been replaced by the rather dry and succinct verdict of the holy fathers in *BHG* 1438h that hardly extends to four lines:

BHG 1438h
Μετὰ δὲ ταῦτα, λέγει αὐτῇ· Ἀπέλθωμεν τὴν ὁδὸν ἡμῶν, ἀδελφή. Ὡς δὲ οὐκ ἀπεκρίθη αὐτῷ, ἐκνεύσας εὗρεν αὐτὴν νεκράν· θεωρεῖ δὲ καὶ τὰ ἴχνη τῶν ποδῶν αὐτῆς ᾑμαγμένα, ἥν γὰρ ἀνυπόδετος. <u>Ὡς δὲ ἀπήγγειλε τοῖς γέρουσι ὁ ἀδελφὸς τὸ συμβάν, ἀντέβαλον εἰς ἀλλήλους. Ἀπεκάλυψε δὲ ὁ θεὸς ἑνὶ γέροντι περὶ αὐτῆς ὅτι ἐπειδὴ ὅλως οὐδενὸς ἐμερίμνησε σαρκικοῦ, ἀλλὰ καὶ τοῦ ἰδίου σώματος κατεφρόνησε μὴ στενάξασα ἐν τῇ τοσαύτῃ πληγῇ, τούτου χάριν προσεδεξάμην αὐτῆς τὴν μετάνοιαν.</u> (ed. F. Nau, *ROC*, 12 (1907), 174.30–175.2)

To sum up, it is evident from the brief analysis of the four different versions that *BHG* 1438hb (or a text that belongs to the same branch of the manuscript tradition of this story) must have been the exemplar of the Syriac version *BHG* 2102e and, to some extent, of *BHG* 1438h. However, it is more likely that the narrator of the latter did not have in front of him any particular text, but he was recording this story from memory.

The Greek text

The text edited below (*BHG* 1438hb) belongs to the first part of the *Ekloge Kephalaion*, a monastic florilegium compiled by John the Oxite at the end of the eleventh century and the beginning of the twelfth century.[13] However, the story itself should have been written much earlier than the eleventh century. The year AD 935/936,[14] the year when the Syriac version that is based on *BHG* 1438hb was written, can safely be considered as the terminus ante quem for the composition of *BHG* 1438hb.

The story is to be found in the following manuscripts:
1. Athos Lavra I 56 (**I**), fourteenth century, paper, ff. 19v-20v
2. Athos Lavra K 111 (**K**), fourteenth century, paper, ff. 5v-8r
3. Meteorensis Metamorphoseos 143 (**M**), fourteenth century, paper, ff. 52v-53v
4. Meteorensis Metamorphoseos 394, thirteenth century, paper, f. 337v. This manuscript contains only a summary of the story: Μνήσθητι καὶ τοῦ γέροντος τοῦ τὴν αὐταδέλφην αὐτοῦ ἐκ τοῦ πορνείου ἐκβαλλόντος καὶ καθ' ὁδοῦ κρίμασι Θεοῦ διὰ τῆς ἐκροῆς τῶν αἱμάτων τῶν ποδῶν αὐτῆς τῆς σωτηρίας ἀπολαβούσης.

---

[13] For John the Oxite, the *Ekloge Kephalaion* and a discussion of its complex manuscript tradition see: E. Skaka, 'John Oxeites' *Ekloge Kephalaion*, Part III: prolegomena and critical text' (DPhil thesis, Oxford University, 2004).

[14] See Brock, 'A Syriac narratio', 270.

5. Vindobonensis theol. gr. 276 (**V**), thirteenth to fourteenth century, parchment, ff. 43r-46r
6. Sinaiticus gr. 461 (**T**), ca. 1425, paper, ff. 184r-185r
7. Hierosolymitanus S. Sabas 633 (**S**), fourteenth century, paper, ff. 65v-69v
8. Athos Zographou 19, 1599, paper, ff. 44v-47r
9. Athos S. Anne 10, second part seventeenth century, paper, ff. 27v-29r
10. Athos Xenophontos 42, 1605, paper, pp. 130-137
11. Athos Lavra Ω 83, 1612, paper, ff. 55v-58r
12. Athos Lavra Λ 52, 1648, paper, ff. 173r-176r
13. Patmiacus 288, 1609, paper, ff. 43r-45v

The edition presented here is based on the collation of the earliest available manuscripts, namely the manuscripts I, K, M, V, T, and S.

[S: f. 65v] Ἐκ τοῦ Γεροντικοῦ

Ἀδελφήν τις[15] οἰκείαν[16] καταλιπὼν ἐν Ἀλεξανδρείᾳ ἐξῆλθε καὶ ἐμόνασεν ἐν τῷ Ὄρει.[17] Ἡ δὲ καταλειφθεῖσα ἐξ αὐτοῦ τῇ ἀσωτίᾳ[18] τῆς πορνείας ἑαυτὴν ἐκδέδωκε[19] καὶ πολλῶν ψυχῶν[20] πρόξενος ἀπωλείας[21] ἐγένετο. Καὶ
5   ὃς[22] μαθὼν ταῦτα καὶ ἀπαρεσθεὶς ἀπηρνήσατο αὐτὴν[23] ἐπὶ χρόνοις πολλοῖς.[24] Ὕστερον δὲ ὑπὸ[25] τῶν γνωρίμων καταγνωσθεὶς ὡς αὐτὸς ὢν[26] αἴτιος τῆς[27] ἀπωλείας[28] αὐτῆς καὶ τῶν συμφθειρομένων αὐτῇ, προ[f. 66r]σευξάμενος τῷ Θεῷ συνάρασθαι αὐτῷ, ἐπορεύθη εἰς[29] Ἀλεξάνδρειαν.

---

[15] Ἀδελφήν τις] Ἀδελφός τις ἀδελφὴν M
[16] οἰκείαν post καταλιπὼν trsp S
[17] ἐν τῷ Ὄρει om S
[18] ἀσωτείᾳ K MT
[19] ἐκδέδωκε] ἐξέδωκε M] δέδωκε S
[20] ψυχῶν] ψυχαῖς IK MV
[21] ἀπολείας S
[22] Καὶ ὃς] Ὁ δὲ S
[23] αὐτὴν] ἑαυτὴν M
[24] χρόνοις πολλοῖς] χρόνους πολλοὺς S
[25] ὑπὸ] ἀπὸ M
[26] ὢν] ἦν S
[27] τῆς om V
[28] ἀπολείας S
[29] εἰς] τὴν add V S

Καὶ ἐλθὼν εἰς τὸν πυλῶνα τῆς ἀδελφῆς αὐτοῦ ἀπέστειλε τινὰ λέγοντα
10 αὐτῇ· «Ὁ ἀδελφός σου ἥκει ἐκ τῆς ἐρήμου καὶ φωνεῖ σε[30].» Ἐκείνη δὲ ἦν
ἀκατακάλυπτος τὴν κεφαλὴν καὶ ἀνυπόδετος τοῖς ποσὶ μετὰ τῶν ἐραστῶν
αὐτῆς παίζουσα, καὶ ἅμα τῷ[31] ἀκοῦσαι τὸ ὄνομα τοῦ ἀδελφοῦ αὐτῆς ὅλη
παρελύθη.[32] Ἐξελθοῦσα δὲ εἰς ἀπάντησιν αὐτοῦ[33] ἠσπάσατο αὐτόν. Ὁ δὲ
ἰδὼν αὐτὴν ἐν τοιούτῳ σχήματι τύψας τὴν ἑαυτοῦ ὄψιν λέγει αὐτῇ·
15 «Κυρία μου ἀδελφή, τί σοι [f. 66v] γέγονεν; Ἱνατί κατεφρόνησας τοῦ Θεοῦ
καὶ ἐμίσησας[34] τὴν ἀθλίαν ψυχήν σου[35] καὶ ἀπώλεσας καὶ σεαυτὴν καὶ
ἄλλους πολλοὺς καὶ ἐλύπησάς μου[36] τὸ γῆρας;» Ἡ δὲ δακρύουσα εἶπεν·
«Οὐαί μοι τῇ ἀθλίᾳ ὅτι ἀπωλόμην[37] εἰς τέλος! Ἀλλὰ παρακαλῶ σε, ἅγιε
τοῦ Θεοῦ, εἰ ἄρα οἶδας ὅτι μετανοοῦσαν ὁ Θεὸς δέχεταί με[38] τὴν πόρνην
20 καὶ ἀκάθαρτον, μὴ μὲ ἐγκαταλίπῃς ἐνταῦθα. Ἔσομαι γὰρ ὑπακούουσά
σου διὰ παντὸς καὶ δουλεύουσα τῷ Κυρίῳ ἐξ ὅλης μου[39] τῆς καρδίας.» Ὁ
δὲ ἀκούσας ἐχάρη καὶ λέγει αὐτῇ· «Στραφεῖσα λάβε τὴν καλύπτραν τῆς
κεφαλῆς σου καὶ τὰ [f. 67r] ὑποδήματα τῶν ποδῶν σου, ὅτι τραχεῖα[40] ἡ
ὁδὸς ἦν μέλλομεν ὁδεύειν.» Ἡ δὲ εἶπε· «Ζῇ Κύριος, ὅτι[41] ὃν τρόπον
25 παρέδωκέ με[42] ὁ Θεὸς[43] εἰς τὰς χεῖρας σου, οὕτως[44] πορεύσομαι μετὰ σοῦ
καὶ οὐ λήψομαι[45] μεθ᾽ ἑαυτῆς τὶ ἐκ τῆς προσόδου τοῦ διαβόλου. Ἄγωμεν,
κῦρι ἀδελφέ. Συμφέρον[46] γάρ μοι τὴν κόμην ἀσχημονεῖν[47] ἢ[48] εἰς τὸ
ἐργαστήριον τοῦ διαβόλου εἰσελθεῖν.» Ὁ δὲ ἀκούσας ταῦτα πλειόνως[49]

---

[30] φωνεῖ σε] φωνεῖσαι V
[31] τῷ] τὸ MV S
[32] παρελύθη] καὶ add T
[33] εἰς ἀπάντησιν αὐτοῦ om M
[34] ἐμήσησας V] ἐμίσισας M
[35] ψυχήν σου] σου ψυχὴν M
[36] μου post γῆρας trsp M
[37] ἀπολόμην S
[38] ὁ Θεὸς δέχεταί με] δέχεταί με ὁ Θεὸς I K
[39] μοῦ post καρδίας trsp M S
[40] τραχεῖα] ἐστὶν add T
[41] ὅτι om S
[42] με] μοι T S
[43] ὁ Θεὸς post χεῖρας σου trsp M
[44] οὕτω K
[45] λήψομε V
[46] συμφέρει S
[47] μοι τὴν κόμην ἀσχημονεῖν] μοι τὴν κόμην ἀσχημονὴν (-νεῖν supra lin) S] με τὴν κόμην ἀσχημονεῖν MV] γυμνὴν ἀσχημονεῖν με τὴν κεφαλὴν IK
[48] ἢ] καὶ μὴ K
[49] πλειόνως] πλεῖον V] πλειοτέρως S

ἐχάρη καὶ παραλαβὼν αὐτὴν⁵⁰ ἐξῆλθεν⁵¹ ἐπὶ τὴν ἔρημον ὁδὸν μακράν.
30 Ἐρράγησαν⁵² οὖν⁵³ οἱ πόδες αὐτῆς ἐκ τῆς τραχείας ὁδοῦ καὶ χείμαρροι αἱμάτων ἐξήρχοντο ἐξ αὐτῶν.⁵⁴ Αὐτὴ⁵⁵ δὲ ἠκολούθει⁵⁶ [f. 67v] τῷ ἀδελφῷ αὐτῆς δάκρυσι ῥαίνουσα πᾶσαν τὴν ὁδόν, τύπτουσα τὸ στῆθος αὐτῆς καὶ λέγουσα· «Κύριε,⁵⁷ δέξαι μου τὴν μετάνοιαν ὥς ποτε τῆς πόρνης.»

Ἐν ὅσῳ δὲ περιεπάτουν τὴν ὁδόν, βλέπει ὁ ἀδελφὸς αὐτῆς τινὰς
35 ἐρχομένους καὶ λέγει αὐτῇ· «Κυρία μου ἀδελφή, ἐπειδὴ οἱ ξένοι οὗτοι οὐ γινώσκουσιν ὅτι ἀδελφή μου⁵⁸ εἶ, ἔκνευσον μικρὸν καὶ κρύβηθι, ἕως ἂν παρέλθωσιν.⁵⁹ Ἡ δὲ ἐκνεύσασα ἐκρύβη καὶ καθίσασα⁶⁰ εὐθέως παρέδωκε τὸ⁶¹ πνεῦμα αὐτῆς τῷ Κυρίῳ. Μετὰ δὲ τὸ παρελθεῖν τοὺς ὑπαντήσαντας αὐτοῖς⁶² ἐφώνει⁶³ αὐτὴν⁶⁴ ὁ ἀδελφὸς αὐτῆς⁶⁵ λέγων· «Ἀ[f. 68r]δελφή μου,
40 ἀνάστα. Δεῦρο ὀδεύσωμεν⁶⁶ τὴν ὁδὸν ἡμῶν.» Μὴ ἀποκρινομένης⁶⁷ δὲ ἐκνεύσας καὶ⁶⁸ κατακολουθῶν τοῖς αἵμασιν⁶⁹ αὐτῆς,⁷⁰ εὗρεν αὐτὴν κειμένην νεκρὰν⁷¹ καὶ στενάξας εἶπε· «Πάντως ἀνάξιος ἤμην εἰς τὸ σῶσαι αὐτήν.»

Ἀπὸ δὲ τῆς πολλῆς ἀθυμίας ἐκοιμήθη ἐπάνω τοῦ τάφου αὐτῆς καὶ ὁρᾷ τινὰ κατ᾽ ὄναρ ἐν ὑπεροχῇ καθήμενον καὶ⁷² πλῆθος⁷³ δορυφόρων
45 παρισταμένων αὐτῷ κύκλῳ καὶ⁷⁴ κρίνοντα. Καὶ ἀκούει⁷⁵ τοῦ ἄρχοντος

---

⁵⁰ αὐτὴν] ταύτην S
⁵¹ ἐξῆλθον S
⁵² ἐράγησαν V
⁵³ οὖν om V
⁵⁴ αὐτῶν] αὐτῆς V
⁵⁵ Αὕτη V
⁵⁶ ἠκολούθη MVS
⁵⁷ Κύριε om S
⁵⁸ ἐπειδὴ οἱ ξένοι – ἀδελφή μου om V
⁵⁹ παρέλθωσιν] διέλθωσιν IK MV
⁶⁰ καθήσασα M
⁶¹ τὸ] τῷ V
⁶² αὐτοῖς] αὐτῷ M
⁶³ ἐφώνησεν S
⁶⁴ αὐτὴν om S
⁶⁵ αὐτῆς] αὐτὸς S
⁶⁶ ὀδεύσομεν M
⁶⁷ ἀποκριναμένης I K
⁶⁸ καὶ om S
⁶⁹ τοῖς αἵμασιν] τὰ αἵματα S] τῶν ποδῶν add M
⁷⁰ αὐτῆς] αὐτοῖς V
⁷¹ κειμένην νεκρὰν] νεκρὰν κειμένην S
⁷² καὶ add om IK
⁷³ πλῆθος] πολλῶν IK
⁷⁴ καὶ om T

ἐκείνου λέγοντος «Ἀγάγετέ μοι ὧδε τήνδε[76] τὴν πόρνην,» περὶ τῆς ἀδελφῆς τοῦ ἀββᾶ λέγων.[77] Καὶ ἠνέχθη. Καὶ ἰδοὺ ἀνὴρ μέλας τὸ εἶδος ἔστη κατηγορῶν αὐτῆς, κρατῶν χάρτην καὶ λέγων τὰς πορνείας αὐτῆς[78] καὶ ἀκαθαρσίας, καὶ ἐπληρώθη ὁ τόπος[79] δυσωδίας πολλῆς. Ἡ δὲ ἵστατο
50 ἐλεεινῷ[80] σχήματι κάτω νεύουσα. Κελεύει οὖν ὁ ἄρχων ἐνεχθῆναι τὸν ἄγγελον τῆς μετανοίας. Καὶ εἰσῆλθεν ἀνὴρ χαρίεις[81] τῷ[82] προσώπῳ κρατῶν [f. 68v] χάρτην ἐν τῇ χειρὶ αὐτοῦ. Καὶ λέγει αὐτῷ[83] ὁ ἄρχων· «Ἀνάγνωθι καὶ σὺ τί εἶδες τῆς πόρνης ταύτης.» Καὶ ἤρξατο ἀναγινώσκειν τὴν ὑπακοὴν[84] τὴν πρὸς[85] τὸν ἀδελφὸν αὐτῆς καὶ ὅτι ἠκολούθησεν αὐτῷ[86] ἐν
55 τῇ[87] μετανοίᾳ ἀκατακάλυπτος[88] τὴν κεφαλὴν καὶ ἀνυπόδετος τοῖς ποσὶν[89] αὐτῆς,[90] τῇ ῥύσει[91] τῶν αἱμάτων[92] τὴν γῆν φοινίξασα.[93] Ὁ δὲ μέλας[94] ἀντεμάχετο[95] [f. 69r] λέγων ὅτι τοσοῦτον χρόνον μετ' ἐμοῦ ἦν τὸ θέλημά[96] μου ποιοῦσα καὶ ἵνα[97] μικρὰς[98] ἡμέρας[99] ἀκολουθήσῃ[100] σοι θέλεις[101]

---

[75] ἀκούῃ V
[76] τήνδε post πόρνην trsp S] om T
[77] περὶ τῆς ἀδελφῆς τοῦ ἀββᾶ λέγων] τὴν ἀδελφὴν δηλαδὴ τοῦ γέροντος S
[78] αὐτῆς post ἀκαθαρσίας trsp M
[79] τόπος] ἐκεῖνος add T
[80] ἐλεεινῷ] τῷ add S
[81] χαρίης M
[82] τῷ] τὸ V
[83] αὐτῷ] αὐτῶν T
[84] ὑπακοὴν] αὐτῆς add MV
[85] τὴν πρὸς] ἣν ἐνεδείξατο εἰς M
[86] αὐτῷ] αὐτὸν M] μοι S
[87] τῇ om T
[88] ἀκατάλυφος S
[89] τοῖς ποσὶν] τοὺς πόδας IK
[90] αὐτῆς] προστιθέμενος add M
[91] τῇ ῥύσει] τῇ ῥύσσει V] τὴν ῥύσιν M
[92] αἱμάτων] αὐτῆς, ὧν ἐκ τῶν ποδῶν ἐξ... add M
[93] τὴν γῆν φοινίξασα T] τὴν γῆν... S^mg (legi nequit)] φοινίσουσα τὴν γῆν V] βεβαμμένους ἔχουσα τοὺς πόδας IK
[94] μέλας] ἐκεῖνος add M
[95] ἀντεμάχετο] αὐτῷ add S] αὐτῶν add T
[96] τὸ θέλημα] τὰ θελήματα S
[97] ἵνα] ἐκ τοῦ T
[98] μικρὰς] μικρὸν IK MV
[99] ἡμέρας om M
[100] ἀκολουθήσῃ] ἀκολουθήσει M] ἀκολουθῆσαι T
[101] θέλης T

ξενῶσαί[102] με ἐξ[103] αὐτῆς; Καὶ ἐκτείναντες[104] τέσσαρες[105] ἄνδρες[106] τὰς χεῖρας
- οἱ μέλλοντες παραλαμβάνειν αὐτὴν ἐπὶ τῇ κολάσει - ἐπελάβοντο τῶν
τριχῶν[107] αὐτῆς καὶ ἤρξαντο αὐτὴν[108] σπαράσσειν.[109] Καὶ λέγει[110] ὁ ἄρχων·
«Μὴ ἐγγίσητε[111] αὐτῇ,[112] ἕως οὗ ἔλθῃ καὶ[113] ἡ μετάνοια αὐτῆς.» Καὶ εἰσῆλθεν
ἀνὴρ χαρίεις[114] ἔχων ἐν τῇ χειρὶ αὐτοῦ κάμπτραν[115] χρυσῆν, ἔνθα ἦσαν τὰ
δάκρυα αὐτῆς καὶ τὸ αἷμα τῶν ποδῶν αὐτῆς.[116] Καὶ λέγει ὁ ἄρχων·[117]
«Ἀγάγετέ[118] μοι[119] τρυτάνην[120] καὶ στήσατε τὴν ἀκαθαρσίαν αὐτῆς σὺν τῇ
με[f. 69v]τανοίᾳ.» Καὶ εὑρέθη ἡ μετάνοια αὐτῆς βαροῦσα καὶ ἐνίκησεν ἡ
φιλανθρωπία τοῦ Θεοῦ. Τότε κελεύει ὁ ἄρχων ἀποδυθῆναι αὐτὴν τὴν
στολὴν ἣν ἐφόρει. Καὶ ἐνέδυσαν αὐτὴν στολὴν βυσσίνην[121] καὶ παρέδωκεν
αὐτὴν τῷ ἀγγέλῳ τῆς μετανοίας καὶ κατέστησεν αὐτὴν ἐν τόπῳ φωτεινῷ.
Καὶ διυπνισθεὶς ὁ ἀδελφὸς αὐτῆς ἐχάρη λίαν καὶ ἀναστὰς[122] ἐπορεύετο
χαίρων.[123]

---

[102] ξενῶσαι] ἐξῶσαι IK
[103] ἐξ] ἀπ' T
[104] ἐκτείναντες] οἱ add V
[105] τέσσαρεις M
[106] ἄνδρες om T
[107] τρυχῶν V
[108] αὐτήν post σπαράσσειν trsp IK
[109] σπαράσσειν] σπαράσσην S[ac]] ταράσσειν IK
[110] λέγει] αὐτοῖς add S
[111] Μὴ ἐγγίσητε] Ἄφετε T
[112] αὐτῇ] αὐτὴν MT
[113] καὶ om M
[114] χαρίης M
[115] κάμπτραν] καλύπτραν T
[116] καὶ τὸ αἷμα τῶν ποδῶν αὐτῆς om M
[117] «Μὴ ἐγγίσητε - ἄρχων om S
[118] ἀγάγεται S
[119] μοι om T S
[120] τρυτάνειν V
[121] βυσίνην V
[122] ἀναστὰς] εὐχαριστῶν IK
[123] χαίρων] ἐν τῇ ὁραθείσῃ ὀπτασίᾳ κατ' ὄναρ αὐτῷ add S

Translation

There was a man who abandoned his sister in Alexandria, left the town and embraced the monastic way of life on the Mountain. Deprived of his support, she abandoned herself to a profligate life of promiscuity, becoming the agent of destruction for many souls. He was displeased when he heard about this and, after some considerable time, disowned her but, later on, he was accused by some acquaintances of being himself the cause of her ruin and of those who were being destroyed with her. Praying to God that he might please Him, he went into Alexandria and, coming to the gate of his sister ['s residence], sent someone to tell her: 'Your brother has come from the desert and is asking for you.' She who was disporting herself with her lovers, with her head and her feet exposed, desisted completely the moment she heard her brother's name. Out she came to meet him and embraced him, but when he saw what a state she was in he struck himself on the forehead and said to her: 'My lady sister, what happened to you to make you look with contempt upon God and hate your wretched soul? Why have you destroyed yourself and many others, why have you afflicted my old age?' [c.f. Genesis 44:29.] With tears in her eyes she declared: 'Ah, what a wretch I am, for I am utterly ruined! But I beg of you, holy one of God, if you know that God will receive me as a penitent, me the prostitute, the polluted one, do not leave me here. For I will be subject to you for ever, serving the Lord with all my heart.' He rejoiced on hearing this and said to her: 'Go back and get the covering for your head and shoes for your feet, for the way is rough by which we are about to travel.' *'As the Lord lives* [I Kings 1:29], I shall go with you just as the Lord God delivered me into your hands' she replied. 'I shall take nothing with me from my involvement with the devil. Let us be gone, my lord brother; it is fitting for me to suffer the disgrace of showing my hair rather than to [re-]enter the devil's place of work.' Rejoicing even more at these words, he took her with him and set out on the long road into the desert. Here her feet were torn by the rough trail and they bled profusely, but she followed her brother, sprinkling the entire route with her tears, striking her breast and saying: 'Lord, receive my repentance as you did the prostitute's.'

As they were walking along the road her brother saw some people coming. He said to her: 'My lady sister, since these strangers are unaware that you are my sister, go aside and hide yourself until they have gone by.' She went aside to conceal herself but, as soon as she sat down, she surrendered her soul to the Lord. When the people they encountered had passed by he called to her saying: 'Get up, sister; let us travel our road again.' When she did not answer he turned aside, followed her blood-stains and found her lying dead. 'Alas, I was altogether unworthy to save her' he sighed. [He presumably now buries the corpse.]

Exhausted, he now lay down on her grave to sleep; he dreamt that he saw a person seated on high, sitting in judgment, with a host of guardsmen standing around him, He heard that ruler [*archon*] saying: 'Bring that prostitute here to me' (meaning the Abba's sister) and in she was led. Now, behold: a black-looking man was standing there, accusing her. With a paper in his hand, he was rehearsing her promiscuities and impurities; the place was suffused with a disgusting stench. As for her, she just stood there, a miserable sight, with her eyes cast down. Then the ruler ordered the angel of repentance to be brought in, and there entered a pleasant looking man holding a paper in his hand. To him the ruler said: 'Declare what you know of this prostitute,' at which he began to make known her obedience to her brother, how she followed him in repentance, her head uncovered and her feet unshod, her feet reddening the earth with the blood which was flowing [from them]. The black one retaliated saying: 'Do you mean to alienate me from her, the one who was with me, doing my will, for so long, just because she followed you for a few days?' At this four men (the ones who were about to bear her off to punishment) put out their hands, grasped her hair and began to tear her away. The ruler said: 'Do not come near to her until her repentance arrives.' At that point a cheerful-looking man came in with a golden casket in his hand. This contained her tears and the blood from her feet. 'Bring me a pair of scales and weigh her impurity against her repentance' said the ruler. Her repentance was found to be the heavier; God's love of mankind [*philanthropia*] had triumphed. The ruler ordered her to be stripped of the garment she was wearing; then they put a linen robe on her and handed her over to the angel of repentance, setting her in a place suffused with light. Her brother awoke in great gladness, got up and went his way rejoicing.

Appendix

Texts: Most of the 'Daniel dossier' can still only be read in 'Vie et récits de l'Abbé Daniel de Scété,' edited by Léon Clugnet, *Revue de l'Orient Chrétien*, 5 (1900), 49–73 and 370–391. The known tales are (using Halkin's classification):

BHG No	Title	Edition	W No
2099z	1. *Vita*=*BHG* 2254-5, item 10.4 below		
2100	2. *Narratio de homicida*	Clugnet No 8	W460
2101	3. *de virgine quae ebrietatem simulabat*	Clugnet No 7	W461
2101a	4. *de coenobita in iudicem delato*	Clugnet No 1	W462
2102	5. *de mendico cæco*	Clugnet No 4	W463
2102a	6. *de monacho qui in monumento dormiebat*	Clugnet No 1	W464
2102b	7. *de muliere casta*= *BHG* 2453, item No 10.5 below		
2102c	8. *de balneis*	*Synagoge* III.16.7 and (ending) ed. Nau in *ROC*, 8 (1903), 99	W465
2102d	9. *de moniali in balneis*	Mioni No 11; *OCP*, 17 (1951), 92–93	W466

79, 80	10.1) *Anastasia patricia*	Clugnet No 2	W047
121, 122	10.2) *Andronicus et Athanasia*	Clugnet No 10	W470
618	10.3) *Eulogius latomus*	Clugnet, *ROC*, 5 (1900), 254–61	W474
2255	10.4) *Marcus salus*	Clugnet No 3	W468
2453	10.5) *Thomaïs Alexandrina*	Clugnet No 5	W469
2102e	11. *de sorore Danielis*	Cf. *AnalBoll*, 113 (1995), 269–280 (Syriac version)	W467[124]
	'The life of Abba Daniel, the Egyptian'	*The Spiritual Meadow* c. 114	W315

---

[124] This and most of the other Daniel tales are to be found in the Latin collection edited by M. Huber, *Johannes Monachus, 'Liber de Miraculis'*, Sammlung mittellateinischer (Texte, 7, Heidelberg, 1913).

21

Ælfric of Eynsham's *Letter to Sigeweard*
(*Treatise on the Old and New Testaments*)

Hugh Magennis

The present contribution is a translation of a text by an early medieval monk, not from the world of Byzantium, which is the area of particular expertise of this volume's honorand Bob Jordan, but from the opposite end of Christendom. It is a text, however, in which Bob will find much that is familiar as its author was drawing upon exegetical and doctrinal traditions deriving ultimately from the East. In accordance with the theme of *metaphrasis*, I am delighted to have it included in a volume in appreciation of Bob, a man (to quote from the beginning of my text) 'swiþe wis, se þe mid weorcum spricð': 'very wise, who speaks through his works'.

The text translated below from the Old English of Ælfric of Eynsham (c.955–c.1010) is the earliest extended discussion of the Bible, considered as a whole, in a western vernacular language and is one of the major discussions of the Bible in medieval English. Ælfric is celebrated as the most prolific Old English writer and a man of extensive learning, producing homilies, biblical translations and adaptations, saints' lives, letters, and other works, all forming part of his concerted project of providing sound Christian teaching for the English people, based on Latin scholarship and in line with the principles of the 'Benedictine reform' of which he was a product and a leading light.[1] Written in the period after 1005 when he went to the new monastery at Eynsham as abbot, the *Treatise on the Old and New Testament* is one of Ælfric's latest works and like other writings of the same period is addressed to a prominent layman. In it Ælfric presents an outline of the contents of the Bible, specifying the books of the canon and providing an overview and a basic commentary on important scriptural events and figures. In the course of the work he refers to many of his previous biblical translations and homilies, so that the *Treatise* presents something of a retrospective overview of his own biblical writings, as well as being an overview of the Bible itself.

In the commentary which Ælfric integrates into his summary of the Bible in the *Treatise*, he draws attention to the spiritual significance of key episodes and people,

---

[1] On the Benedictine reform, see J. Hill, 'The Benedictine reform and beyond', *A companion to Anglo-Saxon literature*, ed. P. Pulsiano and E. Treharne (Oxford, 2001), 151–169.

pointing out the meanings of names and numbers but particularly being guided by the principles of typological exegesis (interpreting the Old Testament as foreshadowing and being fulfilled by the New), as inherited from the fathers of the church and further elaborated in the early medieval period. He uses the Old English words *getacnian*, 'to signify' (cf. Modern English *betoken*), and *getacnung*, 'sign, type, significance' (cf. *betokening*), to emphasise spiritual meaning, and he further heightens the sense of the overall unity of biblical history by grounding his account within the structural framework provided by the concept of the 'six ages' of the world.

The writing in the *Treatise* shifts between the personal (as reflected in the direct address to an individual and use of the second person singular pronoun) and the general (with the plural pronoun). As Ælfric says at the beginning, 'The text was composed for one person but can benefit many'. The 'one person' is the layman Sigeweard, who lived (it is thought) at what is now Asthall, about eight miles from Eynsham, and had evidently been importuning Ælfric for suitable reading material for some time. The *Treatise* is in the form of a letter to him, and a particularly personal note is struck at the end of it, when the monk firmly upbraids the layman for giving him too much to drink when he visited him. Ælfric obviously has a wider audience in mind as well, however; the final sentence assumes that copies of the book will be made and Ælfric expresses his anxiety that scribes should copy it accurately, a recurring concern in his writing. And we can envisage not only a general audience but also 'live' performance audiences for this work, as for Ælfric's works generally: there is a strong 'aural' aspect to the prose, which is written in Ælfric's distinctive rhythmic-alliterative style, a style crafted surely with a view to oral performance.

It is clear that the audience that Ælfric has in mind is an intelligent but unlearned one, whether Sigeweard himself or the wider audience we can postulate. These are people who do not know Latin and who require a somewhat simplified account of hermeneutic questions. What we find in the *Treatise* is basic knowledge about the Bible, as represented in the late Anglo-Saxon period. By reading this *libellus* [little book], Ælfric tells Sigeweard, he will not be 'altogether deprived' of the meaning of the Bible, 'even though you cannot grasp fully all the contents of this true Scripture'. He adds, 'You will nevertheless be advanced somewhat in your understanding through these little samples.' For Ælfric, full knowledge of the Bible is available only to those who can study it in Latin and with access to scholarly commentaries on it. In his *Treatise*, as elsewhere, he provides for the uninitiated a guided introduction to this knowledge, not pursuing subtler points of interpretation but nonetheless basing his exposition firmly on the most respected and orthodox sources and painstakingly explaining the Bible in terms of the essentials of Christian belief. Thus he interprets biblical history by reference to the doctrines of the Trinity, the Fall and Atonement, and so on. He is particularly anxious, wherever possible, to stress the unity of the two testaments.

The *Treatise on the Old and New Testament* is concise but comprehensive in its coverage. As typical of medieval treatments, it incorporates into its account of Genesis the story of the fall of the angels. It also includes information about the missionary work and deaths of the apostles, based not only on the canonical Acts of the Apostles but on apocryphal acts and passions. Particularly notable is a long anecdote about the apostle John in his old age, an anecdote that covers more than three pages in the present translation.[2] For Ælfric, the edifying message of this hagiographical episode (in which a young man is converted, lapses, and then is reconverted by John) must justify the extended attention he gives to it; it is the only piece of detailed narrative in the whole text.

The *Treatise on the Old and New Testament* is a summary of the Bible, with some additions, but it is also a kind of sermon with a moral theme for its audience. The theme is that of the necessity of works as well as words for those who would serve God. It is a theme that Ælfric traces throughout biblical history, developing it with growing urgency and with evident application to Sigeweard and his wider audience (thereby bringing out the 'tropological', or moral, interpretation of biblical events). Ælfric is known to have a tendency to be 'additive' in his sermonising, but in the *Treatise* it is the theme of words and works that accounts for the extended *exemplum* of John and the young man; this theme also helps to explain Ælfric's apparent digressions near the end on the three orders of society and on the regrettable prevalence of bribes in the justice system that he sees in operation in the world around him.

At the end of the *Treatise* Ælfric also presents a graphic depiction of the destruction of the Jews, who were punished for their works in rejecting Christ. His tone of hostility is particularly striking in the context of the text as a whole, in which the Old Testament Jews were presented insistently as the people of God. Ælfric's tirade reflects a persistent anti-Semitic strain in Christian thought, of which he was the most notable exponent in Anglo-Saxon England.[3] In the scheme of the *Treatise*, as well as providing a stark conclusion to the epic story of the Jews, this section functions as another *exemplum* offering a warning to the audience that they will be judged by their works, as the Jews were. Anglo-Saxons had little knowledge of real Jews but, as Ælfric and others taught them, this distant people

---

[2] This episode is taken from the Latin translation of the *Ecclesiastical History* of Eusebius of Caesarea, a translation that Ælfric attributes in the *Treatise* to Jerome but which was in fact done by Jerome's contemporary Rufinus. For an English translation of the episode as it appears in Eusebius's original, see *Eusebius: the history of the church from Christ to Constantine*, ch. 23, tr. G.A. Williamson (Harmondsworth, 1965), 128–131 (Book III).

[3] See A.P. Scheil, 'Anti-Judaism in Ælfric's *Lives of Saints*', *Anglo-Saxon England*, 28 (1999), 65–86.

were to blame for crucifying Christ. Later generations of Christians also believed this, as we know only too well.

The present translation makes available for readers who do not have Old English an important document from late Anglo-Saxon England. The document is one of the most extensive English vernacular treatments of the Bible from the Middle Ages and it encapsulates the essentials of early medieval spiritual interpretation of the Bible as taught to congregations by the best-informed church leaders of the time; it also presents something of an epitome of an important part of its author's life's work, as a teacher of the Bible. The *Treatise* was translated once in the past but that was as long ago as 1623, by William L'isle, who produced a fluent rendering but was working without access to the scholarly resources that modern Anglo-Saxonists have at their disposal.[4] The present translation is based on the text of the two surviving manuscripts of the work, as published by S.J. Crawford in his 1922 edition,[5] the manuscripts being Oxford, Bodleian Library, Laud Misc. 509 (which is complete), and Oxford, Bodleian Library, Bodley 343 (which contains part of the treatise on the Old Testament only).

It is fruitful to read the *Treatise* in the context of other works by Ælfric, especially his *Preface to Genesis*, in which he expresses considerable disquiet about the enterprise of translating the Bible into English (although he himself was the most prolific such translator before Wyclif), and his prefaces to his homilies.[6]

Translation

Incipit libellus de veteri testamento et novo [Here begins a little book on the Old and New Testament.] The text was composed for one person but nonetheless can benefit many.

Abbot Ælfric greets Sigeweard at Asthall [in Oxfordshire] in a friendly manner. I tell you in truth that he is very wise who speaks through his works, and he has success before God and in the world who adorns himself with good works. It is

---

[4] *A Saxon treatise concerning the Old and New Testament, written about the time of King Edgar (about 700 yeares agoe) by Ælfricus Abbas, thought to be the same that was afterward Archbishop of Canterbury, whereby appeares what was the canon of Holy Scripture here then received, and that the Church of England had it so long agoe in her mother-tongue*, ed. and tr. W. L'isle (London, 1623).

[5] *The Old English version of the Heptateuch, Ælfric's Treatise on the Old and New Testament and his Preface to Genesis*, ed. S.J. Crawford (Early English Text Society, Original Series, 160, London, 1922), 15–75.

[6] For translation of the former, see D.W. Robertson, *The literature of Medieval England* (New York, 1970), 165–167; for the latter, see *Ælfric's Prefaces*, ed. J. Wilcox (Durham Medieval Texts, 4, Durham, 1994) (with translations of Latin prefaces). An excellent discussion of Ælfric's biblical translations and his thinking about translation is provided by R. Stanton, *The culture of translation in Anglo-Saxon England* (Cambridge, 2002).

made very plain in holy writings that the holy men who were diligent about good works were honoured while in this world and now are saints in the bliss of the heavenly kingdom, and memory of them continues now for ever because of their constancy and their faithfulness towards God. The memory of the heedless people who passed their lives in complete vanity and so ended them is forgotten in holy Scriptures, except that the Old Testament tells of their evil deeds and that they are damned.

You have asked me very often for writings in English, and I was not so quick about supplying them for you before you entreated me for them with your deeds, when you eagerly asked me for the love of God that I should speak to you in your own house; and when I visited you, you lamented that you were unable to obtain my writings. Now I wish you to have at least this little amount, since wisdom is so pleasing to you and you wish to have it – so that you are not altogether deprived of my books. God loves good deeds and wishes to have them from our hands, and it is clearly written of him that he himself rejoices in his own works, just as the Psalmist sang about him: *Sit gloria Domini in seculum seculi; letabitur Dominus in operibus suis*; that is in English, 'May the glory of the Lord be for ever and ever; the Lord will rejoice in his own works'.[7] Thus spoke the prophet.

The almighty Creator manifested himself by the great works which he performed in the beginning, and he wished that creation should see his glory and should dwell with him in eternity, always obedient to him in its service. For it is very wrong that creation should be disobedient to him who created it. This world did not exist at first, but God himself made it, who was ever without beginning in his great glory and who in his majesty was as mighty as he now is, and also as great in his light: for he is light itself, and life and truth. And the plan was always in his intended thought that he would make these wonderful creatures, because he wished through his great wisdom to create them, and by his true love to quicken them into life, which they have.

The Holy Trinity is in these three persons: the almighty Father, who came from no other being; the great Wisdom ever begotten by that wise Father from him alone, without beginning, who redeemed us afterwards from our bondage with his incarnation, which he received from Mary; the love of both of them, which is ever common between them, is the Holy Spirit, who endows all things with life. He is so great and so mighty that by his grace he gives light to all the angels who dwell in heaven and to the hearts of all the people living on earth who believe rightly in the living God; and truly he forgives the sins of all the people who freely repent of their sins, and there is no forgiveness except through his grace. He spoke through the prophets who made prophecies concerning Christ, for he is the will and truly

---

[7] Psalm 103 (104):31.

the love of the Father and the Son, just as we said before. He gives yet a sevenfold gift to humankind, concerning which I have written already in a certain other treatise in English, just as the prophet Isaiah set it down in the book of his prophecy.[8]

The almighty Creator when he created the angels made through his wisdom ten hosts of angels of great beauty on the first day. He created many thousands of them in the first creation, in order that they might honour him in his glory. They were incorporeal, light and powerful, living in blessedness completely without sins, of such a beautiful nature that we cannot express it. As yet there was no evil among the angels, nor did any evil come through God's creation, for he himself is entirely good and every good thing comes from him; and the angels dwelt then in that glory with God.

Well then, within the six days in which the true God created the world, which he willed to create, an angel that was most splendid there saw how beautiful he himself was and how shining in glory. He perceived his strength and how mighty he was created. His sense of dignity also pleased him then. He was called *Lucifer*, that is, 'light-bearing', because of the great brightness of his form. Then he thought it too base for him to obey any lord, since he was himself so splendid. He was unwilling to worship his creator and thank him for what he had received, unwilling to submit himself very eagerly in recognition of the great glory that was bestowed upon him. He would not have his creator as his lord, nor was he willing to continue in the righteousness of the true Son of God, who had created him beautiful. Instead he intended in his arrogance to win the kingdom and through his pride to make himself God. He got comrades for himself against the will of God, firmly committed to his treachery. As a result he ended up with no throne where he could sit, for heaven would not endure him: there was no kingdom that could be his against the will of God, who made all things. Then the proud one discovered what kind of powers he really had, when his feet could no longer stand anywhere, but he fell down, changed into a devil, and all his comrades, from the household of God to the pains of hell, in accordance with their desert.

Then on the sixth day, after this happened, almighty God created a human being from the earth, Adam, with his own hands, and he gave him life, and Eve then afterwards from Adam's rib, so that they and their offspring with them might enjoy the fair dwelling place that the devil lost, if they properly obeyed their creator. Then afterwards the devil deceived these people, so that they broke the command of God very quickly; and they both became mortal and both were driven out of that place of joy to this middle-earth. Here they and all the offspring

---

[8] cf. Isaiah 11:1–3.

that came from them lived in sorrow and toil afterwards, until our Saviour Christ atoned for our evil, just as this account tells us later.

We will start off with the series of books that the great leader Moses wrote, just as God himself dictated in their private meetings when he remained with God on Mount Sinai for forty days at once and received his teaching. He did not desire food in all that time because of the great example of the teaching of the books.

He wrote five books in his wonderful composition. The first is Genesis, which contains this story right from the creation, and tells about Adam's sin, and how he lived nine hundred years in the first age of this world and had children with his wife, Eve, and afterwards departed with sorrow to hell. Cain was his son, who killed his brother Abel, an innocent man, because of his own envy which he bore towards him. And Cain's offspring that came from him were afterwards all drowned in the deep flood, which in the days of Noah destroyed all humankind, except for the eight people that were in the ark; and from that evil race nothing came afterwards. But Adam begot another son after the slaying of Abel, who was called Seth, from whose procreation came all who remained alive, Noah, and his wife, and their three sons, Shem, Ham, and Japheth, with their wives.

We will now discuss this narrative briefly – for we have already often written about this in greater detail, which you can look up – and also about its significance: namely that Adam, who was created by God on the sixth day, signified our Saviour Christ, who came into this world and restored us to his likeness. Eve, whom God himself made out of Adam's side, signified God's church, which afterwards was born from Christ's side. The killing of Abel most truly signified the killing of our Saviour, whom the Jews slew, evil brothers like Cain. Seth, Adam's son – who was also the third – is called 'Rising', and he undoubtedly signified Christ, who rose from death on the third day. The seventh man from Adam was called Enoch. He carried out God's will and God received him up with sound body out of this life, and he is living still, just as is Elijah the noble prophet, who was also taken to the other life, and they will both come against Antichrist, in order that they may put down his deceit through God; and they will be slain then by that same enemy and will then arise, just as all men will do.

Noah, who was in the ark while the great flood drowned all the world except for eight people, means *requies*, that is 'rest' in English; and he signified Christ, who for this reason came to us, that he might bring us from the waves of this world to rest and happiness with him. And so forth to the end: every holy patriarch by word or deed truly gave testimony to our Saviour and his life.

This was the first age of this world. The second age of this world was from then to the time of the patriarch Abraham. Now the book tells us about Noah's descendants that his sons begot seventy-two sons, who began to build the wonderful stronghold and the high tower that in their folly was supposed to ascend up to heaven. But God himself came there and looked upon their work and gave each of them their own separate language, so that to each of them what the other said was incomprehensible. And thus they stopped the building at once, and they then dispersed to distant lands, with as many languages as people.

In that same age idolatry was raised up widely throughout this world, just as we have written previously in another treatise intended to strengthen the faith. In this age too the evil people of five townships of the region of the filthy race of Sodomites were suddenly all burnt up with a fire of brimstone, and their strongholds also, all of them except for Lot alone, whom God led away from there with three members of his family, because of his righteousness.

From Noah's eldest son, who was called Shem, came the race of the Hebrews, who believed in God. They were the forefathers of Abraham, and his father was Terah, who lived first in the kingdom of Chaldea until Abraham travelled at God's command to the land of Canaan, where his kinspeople afterwards dwelt. The patriarch Abraham had two sons, Ishmael and Isaac, and he honoured God with all his heart, and the heavenly God spoke to him often because of his great faith, for he had been willing to offer his own son to God, his beloved Isaac, as a gift on his altar in the old manner, if God had so wished it. God then blessed him, and his child was safe, and God himself promised him that through his offspring all humankind was to be blessed, because of his great faith and because of the obedience he had shown to God. Abraham, who was willing to sacrifice Isaac at God's command, had signification of the heavenly Father, who sent down his Son to his death for us; and Isaac signified the Saviour Christ, who was put to death for us.

The third age lasted until David, the famous king of Abraham's lineage; from him came Christ afterwards, who redeemed all humankind. From Ham, the son of Noah, came the Canaanite people, and from Japheth, his youngest son, who was blessed by Noah, came the northern races along the north sea – because there was a division into three parts through them, Asia in the eastern realm for the eldest son, Africa in the south for the race of Cham, and Europe in the northern part for the offspring of Japheth. And almighty God after Noah's Flood gave to all humankind in common out of his great generosity the species of fish and birds and four-footed animals and clean cattle; he forbade them, however, to consume blood.

Isaac then begot Esau and Jacob, two twins, which has great meaning. But the younger brother, who was called Jacob, was dearer to God because of his good virtues, and he was blessed because of his moral purity. He begot twelve sons; they were the patriarchs, famous men. And there was a great famine lasting seven years in all, and they all travelled to the land of Egypt, where they found food. The second youngest son was called Joseph, who became a lord there in the land of Egypt under the king, much favoured by him, and he kept his father there in complete honour, together with all his brothers and their children. Joseph lived in splendour in that land to one hundred and ten years. And thus the Book of Genesis ends here.

The second book is called Exodus, which Moses wrote concerning the great signs and the ten plagues which were visited upon king Pharaoh and his people by almighty God in the time of Moses. He and his brother Aaron, sons of Amram, were born, as this book reveals to us, in Pharaoh's time; they were very dear to God, exceedingly powerful men who performed many wonders. Then it was that God wished to take his people, the race of Abraham, out of that land to their own country again. But Pharaoh did not wish the people to depart from him, until God sent to him, to his immense terror, ten kinds of plague because of his malicious attitude. And Moses then afterwards led that race from the bondage of Pharaoh, four hundred years after Jacob arrived there with the Hebrew people. In the host that travelled from Egypt there were six hundred thousand men, not counting women and children and not counting the tribe of Levi, which was not added in. Moses led them then through the power of God right across the Red Sea, as we read in books; and king Pharaoh went on after them with a greater army, intending to return the people to his land, back to hateful bondage with him. Then the sea opened in front of Moses and the water stood up above their heads like walls of stone, and they went along the sea bed until they came ashore completely safe, praising the heavenly God in song. Moses then struck the sea with his rod and the water fell upon Pharaoh's army, on top of his numerous chariots and his splendid horsemen, and it drowned them all, so that not a single man survived.

This book tells us next that God afterwards fed the whole host with heavenly food. The food came to them anew every day from heaven for the period of forty years that they travelled in the wilderness; and from hard stone there came running water. And God established laws for them, that is, plain ordinances for the guidance of the people, in five books, which Moses wrote, as God directed him: the two books we have mentioned; *Leviticus* is the third; *Numerus* [Numbers] the forth; the fifth is called *Deuteronomium* [Deuteronomy], that is, 'second law'. These three books tell us how afterwards they travelled through that broad wilderness, where no one had lived before, and about the great wonders that God worked for them during the forty years of this whole episode.

We have translated these books into English. In them one can hear how the heavenly God spoke to Moses through his works and his wonders, and he also committed those works to writing for people's remembrance, with profound meanings. And the great Moses when he was a hundred and twenty years of age departed from this life, and God himself buried him. And he set Joshua in Moses' place as leader of the people. Moses had blessed him beforehand, and God himself promised that he would be with him, just as he had been with Moses, in his great wonders.

The book that he composed, *Liber Ioshue* [Book of Joshua], tells how he travelled with the people of Israel to the land of Abraham and how he conquered that land and how the sun stood still until he gained victory, and how he divided all the land. This also I translated into English once, for ealdorman Æthelweard; in it one may see God's great wonders carried out with deeds. His father's name was Nun, and he lived a hundred and ten years and then passed away after his great victory; and the race there afterwards inhabited the land under the law of Moses. Joshua symbolised the Saviour when he led the people to the land that had been promised to them, just as the Saviour does, who leads to the kingdom of heaven those who believe in him, if they please him with good works.

After this there were in the same land judges among the race of Israel, who guided the people, as it is written in the *Liber Iudicum*, that is, the Book of Judges. This book tells us clearly about the people, that they lived in peace as long as they honoured the heavenly God zealously in worship of him; but as often as they abandoned the living God, then they were oppressed and treated with insult by the heathen tribes that lived around them. Again when they called earnestly to God with true repentance, then he would send them help through some particular judge, who resisted their enemies and delivered them from their misery; and so they lived in that land for a long time. People can read about this, if they are interested in hearing it, in the book in English which I translated concerning this: I thought that you would through this wondrous narrative wish to turn your minds diligently to the will of God. At this point this book ends.

There was a woman called Ruth, who was from the people of the Moabites, but she was married to the grandfather of Jesse, and Jesse was the father of David. The book that tells about this is called *Liber Ruth* [Book of Ruth], and it is included in the canon of our Bible. After these judges the people of Israel chose for themselves kings, as the narrative reveals to us, in the time of Samuel, the faithful prophet. Concerning these, four books are written, which are called in Latin *Liber Regum*, that is, the Book of Kings, as they are referred to collectively, and the *Verba Dierum* [Words of the Days], which is the fifth book, appended to them because of the many instructions that this book has over and above the others; and Samuel and Malachi wrote these books. In these books it tells us that Saul was first chosen as king among the people of Israel, because they wished to have someone to defend them, who would protect them against the heathen people. They informed the prophet Samuel about their wish to have a king for their race, just as other nations had in all lands. Well then, Samuel told this to God, and God granted to him that they should make Saul the son of Kish their king; and he reigned afterwards for a period of forty years and bravely defended the people against the heathen tribes with weapons, though he transgressed in many other respects.

David, son of Jesse, the worthy psalmist from the first tribe, which was called Judah, was afterwards chosen by God's will as king among the people of Israel, to defend them; and he reigned strongly and defended the people against the heathen tribes that fought against them, and he always had the victory and slew the heathens in every battle, because he honoured almighty God with all his heart and he adorned his kingdom with good works. He ruled the kingdom for forty years altogether, and his fame is celebrated in faith-inspiring books.

The fourth age of this world lasted from David to the prophet Daniel. David means *fortis manum*, of which the sense in English is 'strong of hand', because he overcame the wild bear and tore apart its jaws without any weapon and overcame also the wild lion, breaking its jaws with his bare hands; and he went in single combat against the giant called Goliath when he was a boy and with his sling he fired a stone at that faithless giant, so that he lay senseless, and he struck off his head and put to flight all the Philistines who fought against Saul, thereby gaining victory. He signified the Saviour Christ, who is strong of hand: he easily overcame the hateful devil and won from him all the faithful into his church, just as David took the sheep from the wild beasts. He is a holy prophet and he prophesied much concerning our Saviour Christ, as the psalms show us, which he through the spirit of God sang in praise to God. The Psalter is one book among others in the Bible that he composed through God.

In his old age he appointed his son as king, the wise Solomon, who then reigned for forty years, always in complete peace; and kings honoured him because of his great wisdom, and people sought his wisdom from distant countries, and from every land came gifts in his honour; and he preserved his people without any war. He built a splendid temple to God inside Jerusalem of astonishing artistry, so beautifully constructed, so firmly fortified and so spacious a building overlaid with gold and bright silver, that we cannot describe it.

He composed three books in his wisdom; one is *Parabole*, that is, the Book of Proverbs, not in our sense, but sayings of wisdom, warning to the foolish as to how one can best avoid sin and travel the road that leads to God. His second is called *Ecclesiastes*, that is in English, 'counsel for all people', fittingly to be heard at an important assembly. The third is called *Cantica Canticorum*, which means in English 'foremost of all songs', which he sang concerning Christ and Christ's church, that is, the whole congregation that believes in Christ. These books now have their place in our Bible. Solomon means 'peace-loving' in English, and he signified our Saviour Christ, who brought us peace and is the Lord of peace, he who has joined us to the hosts of angels and established a church for us, which is his holy congregation.

Now many kings appear in the Books of Kings, concerning which I have also composed a book in English. Some of them were righteous and worshipped God always, as Hezekiah was and then Josiah and also some others, who were victorious and preserved their kingdom bravely through God, whom they worshipped; and they dwelt in peace. Some were impious and acted very badly, taking no notice of God, and God did not help them. They defiled their people through their evil doings and lived in shame because of their lack of belief, and they ended badly in their infamy; thus did Zedekiah, that wretched king, who was led in fetters to the city of Babylon, and his two sons were slain before his eyes; afterwards he was blinded and put into prison.

And in those lands further misery took place later. Nebuchadnezzar, the famous king in the land of the Chaldeans, came to Jerusalem with a great army and slew the people and destroyed the city; he demolished the temple that had stood for four hundred years since it was built. This was because of the faithlessness of their kings, who abandoned their Lord, and because of the people's heedlessness, who did not pay attention to God. He led the king, called Jehoiachin, to Chaldea with him, very ignominiously, so that he could acknowledge his wicked deeds against the heavenly God, at least in captivity. The king of Chaldea came then to his land with the plunder and the remains of the host, among whom were Daniel the worthy prophet and the three boys Shadrach, Meshach and Abednego, otherwise called Hananiah, Azariah and Mishael. The king ordered these three boys to be thrown into a burning oven, but their fetters were at once burnt off and they went about unharmed, praising with song the heavenly God who protected them in the hot oven to such an extent that even their hair was not burnt; and the king ordered them then to come out of the oven.

At this stage the fifth age of this world began, which lasted right until Christ himself came into this world in the sixth age in human nature from the womb of Mary, he who ever was God with his almighty Father. The remains of the host of this conquered people dwelt in the Chaldean land under the king, acknowledging their sins against almighty God. They dwelt there in bondage for seventy years, until king Cyrus sent them back to the Jewish land and ordered them to build again the splendid temple, just as almighty God put it into his mind, that he might show pity towards his people after their great misery. And they remained there afterwards until Christ himself was born.

Now there are two famous books arranged in order with Solomon's books, as though he composed them. People have attributed them to him, because of their likeness to his style and because of their eloquence; but Jesus son of Sirach composed them. One is *Liber Sapientiae*, that is, the Book of Wisdom, the other *Ecclesiasticus*, great books indeed, which by accepted custom are read in church for their great wisdom.

We consider the prophets now, who prophesied about Christ through the Holy Spirit, concerning the coming of the Saviour into this middle-earth in true humanity, as we intend to write below. Isaiah was the name of a holy prophet in the time of the kings, as his book informs us. He prophesied concerning Christ as truly and most accurately as if he were an evangelist. He said in his works just as we quote here: *Ecce virgo concipiet et pariet filium et vocabitur nomen eius Emmanuel, et reliqua*: 'Behold a maiden shall conceive and bear a son, and his name will be called "God himself is with us" '.[9] Again the same prophet wrote in his works, *Puer natus est nobis et filius datus est nobis, et reliqua*: 'Unto us a child is born and to us a son is granted, and his dominion is upon his shoulder, and his name will be called wonderful, counsellor, and indeed strong God and father of the future world, truly Lord of peace; and his kingdom will be manifold, and there will be no end to his eternal peace'.[10] His book is very great and it is manifold in its reference to Christ, the glory of God and all humankind, who are, in spiritual meaning, in God's congregation. He preached the faith in the land of the Jews, speaking out against injustice, until the cruel king called Manasseh, son of Hezechiah, split him apart and so killed him.

The prophet Jeremiah was a very holy prophet in that land from his childhood, because God himself said to him, 'Truly I knew you before I fashioned you in your mother's womb, and I made you holy before you were born; and I have ordained you as a prophet to the races'.[11] He lived in purity and he wrote a book through the Holy Spirit in his prophecy, great and wide-ranging for the teaching of men, and of spiritual significance also with reference to the Saviour. He was often shackled and put in prison because of his holy teaching, and he lamented greatly the sins of the people, as his book tells us; and in the end he was stoned to death in the land of Egypt because of his faith. The philosopher Plato, the wisest man among the heathen people, debated with him and the prophet guided him, so that he knew to believe in the living God, as Augustine has put it down in his books. Jeremiah is especially our prophet.

The prophet Ezechiel was also captured with the people when the Chaldean king slaughtered the Jews and drove the remainder of the host to his own land, when the prophet Daniel was also seized. Ezechiel dwelt there in bondage and prophesied there, and he wrote a book, a great work, about humankind and about our Lord, very profound in its meaning, until the governor of the captive people killed him, as an authoritative writer informs us.

The prophet Daniel lived in Chaldea, honoured by the kings, and he wrote a book of his prophecy, which God himself revealed to him. He referred clearly in his work to Christ's birth, just as he came to humankind, when it was four hundred and ninety years from the time of king Darius until our Lord came in true incarnation from the womb of Mary. His book is a very great one with many special meanings, too long to recite their details here, including how he was thrown in with the wild lions. We wrote about this in a discourse in English some

---

[9] Isaiah 7:14.
[10] Isaiah 9:6–7.
[11] Jeremiah 1:5.

time ago. He was not put to death but passed away naturally when he was a hundred and ten years old, and he was buried in Babylon.

There are twelve prophets in addition to these, who wrote twelve books of their prophecies, somewhat smaller in scale, but great in meaning with reference to Christ's incarnation and to the people of God, just as God revealed to him. We will record their names in this treatise: Hosea, Joel, Amos, Obadiah, Jonah (who spent three days inside the whale, and the whale brought him to the city of Niniveh: this experience signified the death of our Lord, who lay for that long a time in the grave, before he arose from death through his divine power), Micah, Nahum, and Habakkuk. The latter referred to the Saviour by his name when he wrote, *Ego autem in Domino gaudebo et exultabo in Deo Iesu meo*, that is in English, 'I will rejoice in the Lord and I will exult in God my Saviour'.[12] Our Saviour was called Jesus, and this prophet said so before he had been born, just as the archangel did in the gospel. He is also called Christ; another prophet spoke about this many hundred years before he had been born: *Adstiterunt reges terre et principes convenerunt in unum adversus Dominum et adversus Christum eius*, 'Earthly kings and rulers rose up against our Lord and the Saviour Christ'.[13] That referred to king Herod and the ruler Pilate, just as the apostles understood by it. Then Zephaniah, Haggai, Zechariah and Malachi.

There were also other prophets, who did not write any books, such as Elijah and Elisha, but their miracles are recorded nonetheless in the Books of Kings in illustrious remembrance. There were ten maidens living at various times among the heathen peoples, who were called *Sibyllae*, that is, 'prophetesses', who prophesied all concerning our Saviour Christ. Very plainly they composed their books inspired by the true God, writing with complete faith about the course of his life. However, their books are not in the canon of our Bible, as these others are.

The scribe Ezra wrote a book, telling how the people returned from the land of Chaldea to the land of the Jews, and they rebuilt the city of Jerusalem, and the temple within it, as king Cyrus gave them permission after seventy years to dwell in their own land. And that book is included in this Testament, with its profound meaning and hidden significances.

An important servant of God in the land of Uz was called Job, a man of great faith and wealthy in possessions. He was tested by means of the false devil, as the book tells us that he himself composed after his tribulations. I once did a version of this in a homily in English. This book is also certainly a prophecy about Christ and his church, as teachers tell us, and it is included in this Testament. A certain Jewish man called Tobit was also tested, a very charitable man and very much

---

[12] Habakkuk 3:18.
[13] Psalm 2:2.

believing in the living God. He was taken as a captive to the land of Syria, but he kept his faith there nonetheless and carried out good works. God tested him, so that he became blind and remained so for ten years; God healed him again, however, through his archangel called Raphael, as the narrative of his own book tells us, which he himself wrote; and that book is counted with this number, because in it also there is such special meaning.

Queen Esther, who saved her people, also has a book among this number, because God's glory is to be found in it. I translated it into English in our style, in an abbreviated version. The widow Judith, who overcame the Syrian leader Holofernes, has her own book about her own victory among these books. This one is also put into English according to my manner, as an example to you our people, to defend your land with weapons against the invading army.

Two books are included among these books according to ecclesiastical tradition, which have to do with God's glory, called *Machabeorum* [Maccabees], because of the intense warfare in which they engaged, when they fought fiercely with weapons against the heathen army that contended fiercely against them with the intention of destroying them and obliterating them from the land God had given them, thereby putting an end to the glory of God. Behold then, Mattathias, the illustrious servant of the Lord, along with his five sons, fought against that army in more battles than you will believe, and they had the victory through the true God in whom they believed according to the law of Moses. They did not wish to fight only with fair words, speaking well but going back on that afterwards; they feared that the heavy sentence would come upon them about which the prophet spoke concerning a particular generation of people: *Et iratus est furore Dominus in populo suo et abhominatus hereditatem suam, et cetera*: 'The Lord was angry with his people and in a rage, and he rejected his inheritance; he committed them into the hands of heathens and their enemies truly had power over them; the ravaging enemy oppressed them grievously, and they were humiliated at their hands'.[14] Machabeus, the illustrious warrior of the Lord, was unwilling to have this judgement through the anger of the Lord but preferred zealously to call upon God with faith in this other saying: *Da nobis, Domine, auxilium de tribulatione, quia vana salus hominis, et cetera*: 'Give us, dear Lord, your true help in our distress, and make us strong, for human help is powerless and futile. But let us seek power in the powerful God and he will bring to nothing the enemies that harm us'.[15] Machabeus then fulfilled these previous words of his with brave deeds and overcame his enemies. For this reason his victorious deeds are set down in these two books of the Bible to the glory of God. And I translated them into English. Read them if you wish, for your own benefit.

---

[14] Psalm 105:40–3.
[15] Psalm 59:13–14.

Explicit de Veteri Testamento [Here ends 'On the Old Testament']

Incipit de Novo Testamento [Here begins 'On the New Testament']

I tell you now Sigeweard that I have set down here these few illustrations from the ancient books of the Old Testament under the law of Moses, and that if you desire all the wisdom that these books contain, then you would believe that I did not deviate from truth in this writing. I will now further speak to you briefly about the New Testament after the coming of Christ, in order that you be not altogether deprived of its meaning, even though you cannot grasp fully all the contents of this true Scripture; you will nevertheless be advanced somewhat in your understanding through these little samples.

Lex et prophete usque ad Iohannem, sicut legitur in Evangelio [The law and the prophets lasted until John, as is read in the gospel]:[16] the law of Moses and of the prophets was truly in existence until the birth of John, who baptised Christ. He is the end of the Old Law, and from him began the preaching of the gospel, and he was born with the coming of Christ. Just as the day-star rises in the morning before the sun, so John shone in his holy preaching before the Saviour, and he was his precursor in his preaching, and with his baptism he revealed the coming baptism of Christ. Christ himself said of him that there was no greater man than he was among the children of women – but Christ himself was not counted in this comparison, who was born from a pure virgin. John wrote no book himself, but his deeds are written in the gospel of our Lord, whom he baptised and whose precursor he was in life and also in death, and his fame is now celebrated everywhere that Christendom exists and wherever the books of Christ are known.

There are four books written about Christ himself. One of these Matthew wrote, who was with the Saviour and was his own disciple going about in this life, and he saw his miracles and wrote them in his book in the Hebrew language, as they came into his mind, after Christ's passion, in the land of the Jews, for the benefit of those who believed in God. And he is the first evangelist in this Testament. The evangelist Mark, who was with Peter in his teaching and was his godson in fact, distinguished in divine teaching, wrote the second book, based on Peter's teaching, which he learned by means of his instruction in the city of Rome, and he wrote it at the entreaty of the faithful people from among the townspeople there who believed in God through Peter's preaching. The evangelist Luke wrote the third book. He followed the apostles from childhood and afterwards accompanied Paul on his travels and learned the evangelical teachings from him,

---

[16] Matthew 11:13; Luke 16:16.

living in purity. He wrote the book of Christ in the land of Achaia in the Greek language, according as he had learned by the instruction of Paul and that of the other apostles. In Asia, at the entreaty of the bishops there, the apostle John began to write, in Greek, the fourth book, concerning Christ's divinity and concerning the deep mysteries that the Lord revealed to him, when he leaned on his beloved breast, in which was hidden the heavenly treasure.

These are the four streams from the one wellspring which flows from paradise over the people of God, and these four evangelists were symbolised beforehand, as Ezechiel saw them:[17] Matthew in the form of a man, Mark of a lion, Luke of a calf, John of an eagle. This was in accordance with what they each signified: Matthew wrote of Christ's becoming man; Mark like a roaring lion called on the wildness of humankind as in a wilderness; Luke began in the manner of Zachariah the priest, who offered a calf to God in sacrifice; and John, like an eagle, with his sharp eyes eagerly surveyed the lofty mysteries and set down his gospel about Christ's divinity.

These four books reveal how Christ came among men, from the virgin Mary, to redeem middle-earth in the sixth age of this world, according as the prophets had written in their books, in Bethlehem, a city in Judea, in the time of the noble emperor Augustus; and many thousands of angels announced his birth with heavenly singing. Then three kings came to Christ with gifts from distant parts in the east; and Herod killed all the little children who were in that land. He intended to kill Christ, but he did not get to him at all, since he searched for him so treacherously; and that evil king died in torment. The books speak very plainly concerning Christ, how he worked miracles, how he was baptised, how he chose his apostles, that is, his messengers, twelve in number, when he first began to preach. They are called by the following names in the books: Peter, Andrew, James, John, Thomas, Matthew, the other James, Philip, Bartholomew, Thaddeus, Simon the Canaanite, and Paul; Paul was chosen after Christ's ascension, and Matthias was also chosen in place of Judas, who betrayed Christ and was doomed. After these he chose seventy-two as his disciples in his work of teaching, whom he sent abroad to every city which he intended to visit, so that people might know of his coming. He lived among humankind in this middle-earth for just over thirty-three years. He established Christianity and revealed through his miracles, as his gospel says, that he is the Son of God, since he raised up the dead by his power and easily healed every infirmity; and he turned water into wine, walked on the sea with completely dry feet, calmed the winds by the command of his word, drove devils out of people afflicted with madness, and restored their reason after madness. Afterwards he suffered death voluntarily, hanging on the cross for our

---

[17] Ezechiel 1:4–11.

redemption, and he arose from death on the third day and ascended into heaven to his heavenly father, having won the victory; and he rules all things. And he will come to judge all human kind on the great day, each person according to their works. I deal with this briefly here, for I have composed in English about forty homilies, or just over, based on these four books, in which you can read about this story with greater understanding than I provide here.

The apostles also composed works of instruction for the peoples who converted to the faith, so that by means of their admonition they might strengthen their minds throughout Christendom in Christ's faith, which had newly sprung up with the great new revelation. The apostle Peter wrote two epistles – but they are larger than the parts read at mass – which have a strong effect in strengthening the faith, and they are counted as books in the Bible. James the just wrote one great epistle to teach understanding to people who observe Christianity in their life to any degree. The evangelist John, to the honour of God, wrote three epistles, which are three books filled with love for the instruction of the people. The apostle Judas [Jude] wrote one epistle, not the lost Judas who betrayed the Saviour, but the holy Judas who always followed him. Thus there are now seven books in this series.

The apostle Paul wrote many epistles, for Christ appointed him to be teacher to all peoples, and in true piety he ordained the ways that the faithful should keep to in their life, when they devoted themselves and their life to God. This one apostle wrote fifteen epistles to the peoples that he converted to the faith. They are great books in the canon of the Bible and they benefit us in their guidance of us, if we follow the precepts of this teacher of the people. He wrote one epistle to the Romans, two to the Corinthians, another one to the Galatians, one to the Ephesians, one to the Philippians, two to the Thessalonians, one to the Colossians, one also to the Hebrews, two to his own disciple Timothy, one to Titus, one to Philemon, and one to the Laodiceans, fifteen in all, as loud as thunder to the faithful people.

I will say a few words on this subject, first about the Saviour and how in his holy gospel he taught us who love him: *Si diligitis me, mandata mea seruate, et cetera*: 'If you love me, keep my commandments';[18] 'He who loves me keeps to my word, and my father will love him, and we will come to him and truly will remain with him afterwards; he who does not love me does not keep to my word'[19]. Here we can hear that the Saviour loves deeds more than smooth words. Words pass away, while works remain. As the righteous apostle James said, *Estote factores verbi et non auditores tantum fallentes vosmet ipsos*: 'Fulfil truly your words with deeds, and do not mislead yourselves so that you listen to the words alone without the works'.[20] John

---

[18] John 14:15.
[19] John 14:23–4.
[20] James 1:22.

also taught us, with these words: *Filioli mei, non diligamus verbo neque lingua, sed opere et veritate*: 'My dear children, let us not love, I beg you, with words and with language but with work and fidelity to truth'.[21] On this same subject the apostle Paul said, *Qui dicunt se nosse Dominum, factis autem negant*: 'They say that they know the true God but with their works they deny it'.[22] The person who promises repentance from sin and gives his pledge on the matter, and goes back on that afterwards, how can he then have the help of the Saviour, who sees and perceives in his heart that he will go back on his word to him again? But a person must deal seriously with his Lord, who wishes that we should speak to him with works; for he who speaks well and does not carry out his words does nothing but doom himself.

The evangelist Luke, who was a physician in life, composed two books for the salvation of our souls: one is his book about Christ, the other is called *Actus Apostolorum*, that is, in the English language the Acts of the Apostles, about the acts that they performed together and how afterwards they travelled to distant countries, just as the Saviour had commanded them in his holy gospel, telling them that they should teach all nations and convert them to the faith with their teaching.[23] Peter preached in the city of Antioch and it was through him that they were first called 'Christians' there; and he travelled afterwards very speedily to Rome and preached the faith to the citizens there for twenty-five years with miracles and signs, until the emperor Nero put him to death on a cross. Paul travelled widely throughout the world preaching to many peoples, until eventually he reached the city of Rome, where he also preached; and Nero had him beheaded on the same day that he hanged Peter. Andrew preached in the land of Achaia and in Scythia, and afterwards he was hanged on a cross for the name of the Saviour. James the younger, who was John's brother, preached to the twelve tribes of the Jews, which were dispersed, working signs, until king Herod beheaded him; and John his brother preached in Asia, in the east of the world, and he was not slain at all but departed to Christ after working many miracles, when he was ninety-nine years old. Philip preached to the heathen people along the sea and then departed to Herapolis, where his life was ended. Thomas preached among the Parthians and Medes and in Hyrcania, until he came to India and was slain there for the true faith. Bartholomew preached in a remoter part of India and was slain there. Matthew preached in the land of the Ethiopians, that is, the 'sun-people', and the king, who was not a believer but an unbeliever, put him to death. James the just remained in his country, preaching the faith within Jerusalem, until the Jews killed him. Simon and Judas were martyred together in the land of the Persians for the faith of Christ, where they preached and consecrated bishops in twelve districts,

---

[21] 1 John 3:18.
[22] Titus 1:16.
[23] Matthew 28:19.

until they were slain. Matthias, who was chosen in place of Judas to complete the number of the apostles, preached in the land of the Jews. I have written about the deaths of all the apostles, except for Matthias alone, about whom I could not find out. You could read these and edify yourselves by them, if you were true to your own souls.

John lived in this life the longest of them and he wrote in his exile the book called *Apocalipsis*, that is, the 'Revelation', which Christ revealed to him in a spiritual vision, about the Saviour himself and his church and about doomsday and the diabolical Antichrist and about the resurrection to eternal life. And this is the last book in the Bible.

I can tell you something more about John, so that you will believe that, as the story tells us, he spoke through his deeds to a certain youth whom he loved and also helped. Jerome, the worthy and wise scholar who translated our Bible into Latin from the Greek and Hebrew books, wrote about the holy evangelist John, the son of Christ's mother's sister, in the ecclesiastical book *Ecclesiastica Hystoria* [*Ecclesiastical History*], speaking about him in these words: *Audi fabulam, non fabulam sed rem gestam de Iohanne apostolo, et cetera*: 'Hear this narrative not as a fictitious tale but as something actually done by the apostle John in his old age, and worth remembering for all the faithful.' Domitian was the name of the diabolical emperor who succeeded Nero and instigated persecution against the Christians and killed them with tortures. He ordered the holy apostle to be seized and put into a bath of boiling oil, because hot oil goes right into the bone; and the oil was prepared for the bath. Then they brought John and put him in the vat in the boiling oil, but he was preserved by the power of God and came out from the bath with his body unharmed, just as he was unblemished by bodily lusts and filthy wantonness.

Later, because John would not stop his preaching, the evil emperor ordered him to be sent far into exile to an island called Patmos, and he remained there until the emperor's counsellors slew their lord, as they were pleased to do because of his savagery and madness. The counsellors then decreed that all should be annulled and changed that he had wished to bring about through his wicked policy. Then the faithful apostle was summoned back home from the island to the city of Ephesos, where he had his dwelling-place, working God's miracles and instructing the people always in the faith. After a time the apostle travelled, as he had been invited by the faithful, to neighbouring towns to preach the faith and set up churches in every district, where there had been none before, and he appointed ordained priests for them, concerning which the Holy Spirit constantly guided him, according to the narrative. He arrived then, as he had been requested, at a town near Ephesos, where he consecrated a bishop and himself entrusted the ecclesiastical usages to the ordained priests whom he installed there; and with great solemnity he instructed the population there to faith in God with joyous heart.

Then John saw a particular youth among the people. He was young in age, striking in appearance, strong of stature, handsome of face, of very cheerful disposition and quick in understanding, and he began in his own gentle disposition to love the young boy and want to gain him for Christ. Then John looked up towards the bishop who had newly been consecrated and spoke to him as follows: 'Bishop, it is my wish that you should have this young man at your house to receive your teaching. I entrust him to you with particular diligence, with Christ and this congregation as witnesses.' Well now, the bishop gladly accepted the afore-mentioned youth and said that he would look after him carefully in his dwelling, just as he had asked him. John re-emphasised his words afterwards and often told the bishop as an instruction that he should guide the young boy towards the true faith. He then departed back to Ephesos to his own bishopric.

That bishop then took in the young boy, just as he had been asked, and instructed him in Christ's teaching every day and looked after him worthily, finally baptising him in full confidence that he was a believer. Thus he stayed with him reverently, until the bishop allowed him to go voluntarily, thinking that he would persevere in his spiritual ways through the grace of God. The youth, however, unused to freedom and unsteady in his principles, realised at once that he was his own master, and began to be inordinately drawn to vices and various kinds of bad ways with youths of the same age, who thoughtlessly went on in their vain desires with their acts of defilement and their depraved behaviour. He and his companions started to take to excessive drunkenness on their nightly travels; and they encouraged him to steal, in accordance with their own practice, and he habituated himself completely to their sinful ways and to even greater crimes with that wicked troop. Through their influence he hardened himself in his mind to engage in terrible acts, and just as a spirited horse that has not been tamed and will not obey the person riding it, so this youth behaved in his wicked deeds, stiffened by the enormity of his crimes into hopelessness of his own salvation, so that he despaired of the mercy of the Lord and ignored the baptism he had received. It seemed to him too feeble to commit minor sins, but he kept advancing more and more in his wickedness and did not permit anyone to be his equal in evil. He did not put up with being inferior to the evil companions who had led him astray but wanted to be top in that evil troop; he even got his companions to become robbers out in the wide countryside in all weathers.

After a time the apostle went back to the afore-mentioned city, where the bishop lived who had taken the youth into his care, just as John had asked; he had entrusted him to him, and he had been very joyful at the bishopric, since he had fulfilled his Lord's service and done everything he had been called upon to do. Then the apostle said firmly, 'Now, bishop, bring before me that which I entrusted to you on the pledge of my Lord, witnessed, as you must acknowledge, in the presence of this congregation.' Then the bishop was struck with fear, thinking that he was being asked for some payment or some money, which he had not received from the apostle; but then he bethought himself and realised that the blessed John would not lie to him nor ask him for something he had not entrusted to him; and so he hesitated nervously. John saw that he was sitting there in dismay and spoke to him again, as follows: 'I ask you now to produce the young boy whom I entrusted to you, for the soul of that brother is dear to me.' Then the old man began to sigh strangely and was overwhelmed with weeping. He said to John, 'My dear friend, he is dead now.' Then John asked immediately, 'How is it that he is dead, or by what kind of death?' The bishop spoke to him again in answer: 'He is dead to God, for he has run off full of vice as an unbeliever and become a robber of travellers and the head of a gang of thieves that he assembled himself; he lives in the hills with a lot of thieves, of whom he is now the chieftain and commander.'

Well then, John shook his head in intense sorrow and said to the bishop, 'I left you as a good shepherd, so that you would keep watch over your brother's soul. Anyway, get a harnessed horse ready for me now and a guide who knows the way that leads to those thieves.' What he had asked for was immediately provided and he at once travelled with all speed, until he spotted the gang of thieves and came right to their watchmen. Then the watchmen firmly seized his guide, so that he could in no way escape in flight. John, however, had no intention of fleeing and did not take flight at all, but he shouted out, 'I came to you voluntarily; lead me now to your chieftain without delay.' Thereupon they quickly called for him the youth who was their leader; and he then appeared, bearing weapons, and he was immediately overcome with shame when he recognised Christ's apostle, and he began to flee from his presence. John then spurred his horse and went after him, paying no attention to his age, and he called out loudly, addressing the one who was fleeing, 'O my son, why are you fleeing from your father? Why do you flee from this old and unarmed man? Don't be afraid, you poor wretch – you still have hope of life. I wish to render an account to Christ for your soul and I will gladly give my life for you, just as the Saviour gave himself for us, and I will give my soul for yours. Wait now and hear these words, and believe that the Saviour has sent me to you.'

The robber stopped when he heard these words and bowed down to the ground with all his body, and he threw away his weapons and wept most bitterly. Trembling he fell at John's feet in sorrow and lamentation, overwhelmed with tears, asking for mercy as best he could; and he hid his right hand, greatly ashamed of the crimes and killings he had committed with that hand. Then the apostle swore that he would truly obtain mercy for him from the merciful Saviour, and he himself also bowed to him and took his right hand, because he feared for his crimes; and he led him away weeping to the church and prayed for him constantly to the Saviour with brotherly love, as he had promised him, fasting also for many days at once, until he obtained mercy for him from the merciful Christ. He comforted him also with his beautiful teaching and calmed his troubled mind gently with his words of comfort so that he should not despair; and he did not stop at all until his soul was inwardly gladdened through the Holy Spirit and he had received mercy for all his misdeeds.

He ordained him also into the service of the Saviour. This narrative does not tell us what role he gave him, but that youth gave true example to all who amend their deeds and turn to the Lord, showing that, if they are resolute, they can arise from the death of their soul and from the fetters of their sins and can bring joy to their Creator with true repentance and have eternal life with the beloved Saviour who reigns for ever in eternity.

We have now spoken of the ecclesiastical books of the old law and also the new. These are the two testaments concerning Christ's incarnation and concerning the Holy Trinity in its true oneness, just as Isaiah saw in his spiritual vision that God sat accompanied by *duo seraphin*, that is, 'two hosts of angels', singing around about him, *Sanctus, sanctus, sanctus, Dominus Deus Sabaoth*, that is in English, 'Holy, holy, holy, Lord God of hosts; all the breadth of earth is filled with his glory'.[24] These two seraphim truly refer to the Old Testament and the New, which ever praise with words and with works almighty God, who alone reigns in one Godhead, without beginning or end. Teachers who do not wish to take their teaching and examples from these holy books are like those teachers of whom Christ himself said, *Cecus si ceco ducatum prestet, ambo in foveam cadent*: 'If the blind man guides the blind man, then they will both fall into a blind pit'.[25] Teachers who do wish to take their teaching and examples from these holy books, both from the Old Testament and from the New, are like the teachers of whom Christ himself again said, *Omnis scriba doctus in regno celorum similis est homini patrifamilias, qui profert de thesauro suo nova et vetera*: 'Each learned scholar in God's congregation is like the lord who constantly gives from his own gold-hoard old things and new things'.[26]

There are seventy-two books in the Bible – for some of them are split into two in the church of the faithful because of their length, as anyone can see who knows their order. And peoples were divided into that number at the wondrous stronghold that the giants boastfully wished to build after Noah's Flood, before they dispersed; and our Saviour sent the same number of disciples to preach to humankind the teachings of these books with the message of Christianity that came into this world through the Saviour himself and his heralds. There are other books, however, composed by holy teachers, which people widely cherish everywhere throughout Christendom to the glory of Christ.

---

[24] Isaiah 6:3.
[25] Matthew 15:14.
[26] Matthew 13:52.

The sixth age of this world stretches from Christ right to doomsday, the time of which is unknown to all men, though the Saviour knows it. The seventh age is that which runs along with these six, from the righteous Abel to the end of this world, and it is an age not of living people but of departed souls in the other life, where they rejoice awaiting the eternal life, when they will arise sound from death, as we all must, to face our Lord. The eighth age is the one eternal day after our resurrection, when we will reign with God in soul and body in eternal happiness; and there will be no end to that one day, when the holy will shine as the sun does now.

How can that person do well who turns his mind away from all these books and is so wilful that he would rather live by his own judgement free from association with them, as if knowing nothing of the Scriptures of Christ? The famous prophet Moses taught us in his writings, saying to all, *Interroga patrem tuum et adnuntiabit tibi, maiores tuos, et dicant tibi, et cetera*: that is in English, 'Ask your father about the true God and he will inform you about him; enquire of your elders and they will tell you'.[27] If you are unwilling to understand and be guided here, you will learn in a place where it will be more painful for you, in eternal torments, so that you will understand then who it was that you rejected and whose Scriptures.

Counsellors should consider with wise deliberation, when there is too much evil among the people, which of the supports of the throne is broken, and they should repair it at once. The throne rests upon these three supports: *laboratores, bellatores, oratores*. *Laboratores* are the ploughmen and unfree labourers who provide our means of sustenance for us and are devoted only to this. *Oratores* are those who intercede with God for us and promote Christianity among Christian people, serving God in the spiritual fight; they are devoted to that alone for the benefit of all of us. *Bellatores* are those who protect our strongholds and also our land against the approaching army, fighting with weapons, just as Paul, teacher of nations, said in his teaching: *Non sine causa portat miles gladium, et cetera*: 'The soldier does not bear his sword without cause; he is God's minister appointed for your own benefit to avenge those who do evil'.[28] The throne rests on these three supports, and if one of them is broken it falls down at once to the certain damage of the other supports. But what concern is it of ours to consider this? They should consider it whose responsibility it is.

The righteous God loves just judgements, but bribes too often wrongfully pervert just judgements contrary to the will of the Lord, and this evil becomes widespread among the whole people, where that abuse reigns unhindered. The person who wishes to be God's minister, should judge justly in faithfulness to the

---

[27] Deuteronomy 32:7.
[28] Romans 13:4.

truth, without any bribe; then he would honour God with good morality and his reward would be great before God, who lives and reigns for ever and ever. Amen.

I wanted to discuss that unhappy people the Jews, who executed our Lord, but I wanted first to say what I have said. Many from that race believed in Christ but the majority of them would not believe in him and perished for that reason. Many miseries came upon them after the passion of Christ in all kinds of misfortunes, and many from that people were slain in sudden attacks. They killed Christ's apostles James the younger and James the just, and they stoned Stephen to death with hard stones; they increased their wickedness, to their own detriment, being unwilling to repent of the killing of the Saviour or to ask for his mercy with any penitence. Then he sent strange signs to them and afterwards invasion by the Romans. Vespasian was emperor at the time; he sent his son Titus against them with a great army of the Roman people, and he besieged their city until they died from hunger; and because of the terrible smell people threw the bodies out over the walls, and they could not defend the multitude because of their lack of strength. They chewed on their belts and gladly ate grass, and one person took from another what little the other had, even the food from someone's mouth, completely without restraint. Robbers rampaged over the city searching eagerly for food hidden in secret stores and threatening people with violence; and they beat anyone who had anything, if that person was willing to resist their madness. It is not for us to go into the shameful abominations that were perpetrated there, but many hundreds of people from that wretched race perished because of the intense hunger, more than we wish to say. The robbers eventually killed each other and the city was conquered and razed to the ground, as the Saviour said before his passion. The young children who survived the famine were taken away in all that country to make fine clothes, just as they had been trained, and from these children that race still survives everywhere. So this was the recompense for their evil deeds, as was the torment of hell, which is more oppressive for them.

Now you can properly understand that works speak more strongly than naked words, which have no effect. But there is nonetheless good work in good words, when one person teaches another and strengthens that other in the faith with truthful teaching and when one speaks wisdom for the benefit and correction of many, so that God may be praised, who reigns for ever. Amen.

You wished to persuade me, when I visited you, that I should drink, as though for enjoyment, rather above my custom; but know, dear friend, that whoever gets another person to drink more than he is capable of, must bear the sin of both of them, if any harm comes from the drinking. Our Saviour Christ in his holy gospel forbade drunkenness to all believers: let him who wishes keep his law. And the holy teachers after the Saviour have condemned that vice through their teaching, and have taught that people should drink so as not to harm themselves, for too much drinking certainly destroys their soul and health, and illness comes from drinking.

Let whoever copies this book write it according to the exemplar and for God's love correct it, so that it does not end up being too deficient, to the peril of the writer and to the blame of me.

22

Symeon the New Theologian
Epistle 2

Concerning repentance, and what a person who has recently confessed should do

John Turner

Symeon the New Theologian (949–1022) was born to an aristocratic family and served in the bureaucracy. He became a novice at Stoudios under Symeon Eulabes, then *hegoumenos* of St Mamas, and then the founder of monastic communities at Chrysoupolis and St Marina after he was expelled from the City. His cult was promoted in the later eleventh century by Niketas Stethatos, and he is regarded as a significant saint and mystic of the Orthodox Church. He was the author of hymns, catecheses, chapters and treatises, and of ten letters, edited in the doctoral thesis of Fr J. Paramelle, SJ. This translation is based, with the editor's permission, on that hitherto unpublished text.

As a tribute and εὐχαριστήριον to Dr R.H. Jordan, who taught me a great deal by his kindly corrections of my attempts to translate *Synagoge II*, I dare to offer this translation, for which he is in no way responsible. He will perhaps be glad that there is only one footnote.

We are taught by the Holy Scriptures, my spiritual brother, that neither ought we ever to despair as regards the multitude of our sins, nor ought we to have confidence in the performance of our penances, and therefore neither must he who is standing have confidence, nor he who has fallen give up hope. On the contrary, even he who has sinned much must have confidence in his repentance, and he who has erred, but not excessively, must not think to obtain forgiveness for his wrong-doing simply through works. Rather, he must display repentance and penitence, displayed not by words or through abstaining from food, drinking only water, having his pallet on the floor, and practices of this kind, but that which is created by a disposition of the soul, and which blessed David demonstrated, encompassed as he was by the world and the cares of this life. For he always remembered and weighed up within himself how good and compassionate a master he had provoked to anger, by being a transgressor of his commandments and a man revealed as unmindful of his many and countless gifts and graces and not thankful for them, and so – as he himself wrote – he always went mourning and with a sad countenance. Nor was he ill-treated by another person, but he afflicted himself and humbled himself exceedingly, roaring by reason of the lamentation of his heart, and doing all those things which one after another the psalms teach us as we sing them day by day.

And this David did, king though he was and entrusted with the care of his people, and also both of his wife and his children and his house. And what of Manasses? And what of those of a later date, of whom you yourself, I suppose, are not ignorant? I mean Peter the chief of the apostles, the tax-collector, the thief, the prostitute – and why do I speak at length? – the prodigal son who squandered his father's property with prostitutes and tax-collectors. Through what kind of actions did these gain pardon for their wrong-doings? Consider! Was it through fasting, through keeping vigil, through having their pallet on the floor, through emptying themselves of their possessions to give them to the needy, or through any other laborious activity performed by the body? Certainly not! But it was through repentance by itself, and through tears from their soul and through being condemned by their conscience. For having come to the perception of their own sins, and having condemned themselves and lamented from their very souls, each of them gained pardon for their lapses. And now too this comes about for all of us who genuinely and fervently come to our master, Christ, by the way of repentance and tears. And the good Lord, who loves mankind, does not close his undefiled heart of benevolence to us, nor would he ever do so, for it is not by means of works of the Law – lest any man should boast –, but by God's love for mankind and his grace that the forgiveness of sins is given. And what is sought is not just this, but that we may no more fall into the same wickednesses, nor like a dog, return to our own vomit. It is impossible to guard against this, unless, by all means and with all earnestness, we provide ourselves with guards and helpers, and we ourselves take spiritual armour, by which we shall be enabled to withstand our enemies and opponents.

For since we have been captured by the Enemy, enslaved by our pleasures, and through our passions have become both subjects of, and bound by treaty to, the Foe, we are inevitably hauled and dragged around by passions, pleasures and desires of this kind. Inevitably, too, we are led away by force in a pitiable condition as bondsmen to serve, and be the slaves of, our Adversary and Enemy, we fall away from being the slaves of our master Christ, and we display ourselves as being in breach of his commandments and of our pledges to him. That we may not suffer this, let us, in opposition to each of the enemies that attack us, get a helper on our side and an ally, being taught by the divinely inspired Scripture, *For this reason I ordered my life by all thy commandments; I hated every unjust way.* (Ps 118:128, LXX) And in opposition to the remembrance of shameful thoughts let us set the remembrance of God and of the awe-inspiring judgement and of those unbearable torments; against sluggishness, zeal and earnestness; against gluttony, fasting; against love of pleasure, self-control; against much drinking, drinking little; against the kindling [of the lusts] of the flesh, remembrance of the eternal flames and persistency in entreating God, together with vigil and thirst For if we act thus against each passion – that I may not be prolix through wishing to enumerate all of them – and if we set against each single passion the opposite virtue, we shall by such actions be guarded on all sides as if by soldiers, and shall keep ourselves unhurt and unwounded, because the mere extirpation of evil habits and of atrocious deeds and actions, supposing it possible to achieve this without hardships and toil, is enough for the salvation of those who repent.

Besides this, we are writing to give you a brief reminder of the things you ought to do and observe, which are these:

When the Divine Mystery is being celebrated, you must go out of the church when 'As many as are catechumens, go forth' is said by the priest or the deacon. Do not, however, go away nor get into conversation with anyone at that time, but stand in the narthex in front of the doors and recollect your faults and bewail them. Then after the elevation of the divine mystic elements, go inside again. In the evening after compline, get into some private place and recite the Trisagion, and also Psalm 50, 'Lord, have mercy' fifty times, 'Lord, pardon me a sinner' fifty times, then Psalm 6, 'Lord, rebuke me not in thine anger', 'Lord, pardon me for whatever I have sinned by deed and word and in thought' fifty times, and perform twenty-five prostrations.

On Wednesday and Friday abstain from meat, cheese, eggs, and wine and fish, but if this makes you dispirited, partake of fish and wine, and partake of them in moderation. During the Lents of the holy apostles and of Christmas, keep from meat, cheese and eggs, but partake of the remaining things in moderation. And double your prayer, that is the previously specified psalms and the prostrations. During Great Lent, on Wednesday and Friday you will have neither wine, nor oil, nor fish, while on other days bruise your body and bring it into bondage by being satisfied with little and by abstinence to the extent that your natural constitution allows, in the manner that befits Christians wishing to be saved; and also during this season double your prayer as in the same way as was previously specified.

You ought also to abstain from the divine and awe-inspiring gifts. I mean the undefiled body and blood of our master and lord Jesus Christ – I also advise you to abstain from even his blessed bread, what is called *kataklaston* –, until you have your will in an unchangeable state in regard to the ugly deeds of sin, and until you acquire a disposition that will not be turned away from good and as regards sin holds fast absolutely to hatred. But when you perceive that you yourself have thus entered into this state, then, brother, draw near with faith unwavering, not as about to partake of mere bread and wine, but as about to partake of God's body and blood, indeed of God himself. And so you will become a participant in his glory, and through the consecrated elements will gain purification and complete forgiveness for your own sins, and will have eternal life within yourself, and will become a son of light and of the day. But if you do not first become someone of this kind before receiving Christ, then the demons will have more animosity against you as one who despises God, will see that you are drawing near unworthily and will converge upon you violently. Having mercilessly tumbled you into the mire of licentiousness, they will afterwards cast you aside. And moreover instead of being a Christian you will become a Christ-slayer, and you will be condemned with those who crucified him, as Paul says, 'For he who eats and drinks the Lord's body and blood unworthily, will be guilty of profaning the Lord's body and blood.'

These then are all the orders we are giving you, for fear of over-burdening you, but if you on your own account do something by way of adding to them, you will benefit yourself and will procure for yourself good things in the future. For we do not write to tell you to do the things spoken of, as if they conferred purification of soul and forgiveness of sins, but as things which lead to merely remembering your own sins. If indeed we knew that you are not grieved [by your sins], we would not write even this much to your Charity,[1] but would demand of you only the extirpation of your evil habits and most atrocious deeds and actions. And we do entreat you to keep to that, and if keeping to it is something you can do without toil and hardship, we shall be satisfied merely by this.

Write to us without delay about your health, so that as we perceive your faith in us and your [kindly] disposition towards us, we may remember you more fervently and persistently when, unworthy as we are, we stretch forth our hands towards God. The grace of God be with your spirit.

---

[1] 'Your Charity' (τὴν σὴν ἀγάπην) sounds unEnglish, but there is no other suitable equivalent. In *ep. 3* it recurs both in the singular and also in the plural form, 'your Charities' (τὴν ὑμετέραν). Although not common in the *Catecheses*, in the plural form it is found in *Cat, IV*. 47f. (SC 96, 318).

23

The Liturgy of the Minor Blessing of the Water according to Cod. Paris. Coisl. 213

Jeffrey C. Anderson and John W. Nesbitt

The authors are undertaking a study of the bathing ritual conducted under patriarchal auspices at the Blachernai church of Constantinople. Documentation for the ritual occurs in the *Euchologion* of Strategios in the Bibliothèque Nationale (Coislin 213), where it is found in the next to last chapter. The final chapter in the manuscript contains the sung and spoken passages used when the priest performed the monthly blessing of the water, creating what we would call 'holy water'. The ritual is not to be confused with either the service conducted by the patriarch at the Blachernai or the one associated with baptism on the occasion of the Feast of Lights (Epiphany).[1] There are nonetheless common points as well as the differences that give each its distinctive character, and for the sake of its comparative value we here publish the *Euchologion* text. Since the manuscript contains no directions within this chapter, readers may wish to refer to the reconstruction made by Panagiotos Trempelas, who used the *Euchologion* of Strategios as one of his nearly seventy-five manuscript sources.[2] In the reconstruction, the *Euchologion* plays a minor role in the apparatus.

The manuscript that is our source was written, in 1027, for a priest at Hagia Sophia named Strategios.[3] It therefore represents patriarchal practice at a precise moment in Byzantine history, and for this reason is an uncommonly important witness. The text was edited in part by Aleksej Dmitrievskij,[4] who was apparently the source used by Trempelas. Dmitrievskij relies on another manuscript (Cod. Sinai. gr. 959) for the final prayer, and publishes a small number of readings not supported by the manuscript,

---

[1] Major Blessing of the Water: J. Mateos, *Le typicon de la Grande Eglise*, I, *Le cycle des douze mois* (OCA, 165, Rome, 1962), 183–187. P. Trempelas, Μικρὸν Εὐχολόγιον, II, Ἀκολουθίαι καὶ τάξεις ἁγιασμοῦ ὑδάτων, ἐγκαινίων, ὄρθρου καὶ ἑσπερινοῦ (Athens, 1955), 1–44.

[2] P. Trempelas, 'Ἀκολουθία τοῦ μικροῦ ἁγιασμοῦ', *Theologia*, 22 (1951), 226–241, 402–415; Trempelas, Εὐχολόγιον, 45–74.

[3] R. Devreesse, *Le fonds coislin* (Paris, 1945), 194. M. Arranz, *L'eucologio Costantinopolitano agli inizi del secolo XI* (Rome, 1996), 12–15, with the subscription. The dissertations on the *Euchologion* written by J. Duncan and J. Maj are unavailable to us.

[4] A. Dmitrievskij, *Opisanie liturgičeskich rukopisej chranjaščichsja v bibliotekach pravoslavnago vostoka*, II, *Euchologia* (Kiev, 1901), 1051–1052.

which we know from a microfilm. We reproduce the text in diplomatic style: parentheses enclose letters represented by standard abbreviation signs as well as those commonly omitted when writing the nomina sacra. Angle brackets surround letters that must be supplied without the benefit of symbols; also in angle brackets are words inadvertently omitted by the scribe and ones added to facilitate a contemporary reader's identification of passages. We follow the scribe's use of initial letters to signal the beginnings of new readings, but start each on a new line. A brief discussion of the ritual follows the text.

Cod. Paris. Coisl. 213, Chapter 142 (fols. 209v-210v)

Ἑτέρα ἀκολουθ<ία>(καὶ) τάξις ἁγιασμοῦ γινομέ<νη> εἰς διαφόρους ἐκκλη<σίας> ταῖς κυριακαῖς (καὶ) ἑορταῖς ἐν τῷ νάρθηκι ἢ (καὶ) ἑτέρ(ῳ) μέρει τῆς ἐκκλη<σίας> φιάλης οὔσ<ης> ἢ καὶ λεκα<νίου>, ἔχουσα εὐχ<ὴν> α' γίνετ(αι) δὲ μετὰ τὴν ἔναρξιν τῆς θεί(ας) λειτουργίας· ψαλλομέν(ων) τῶν ἀντιφών(ων)(καὶ) μ<ε>τ<ὰ> τὸ τέλος τοῦ ἁγιασμοῦ γίνετ(αι) ἡ εἴσοδο(ς) καὶ ἀκολούθ<ως> τὰ ἐπίλοιπα τῆς θείας μυσταγωγίας.

Ἄρχετ<αι> ὁ ἱερε<ύς>, Εὐλογητὸς ὁ Θ(εὸ)ς ἡμῶν πάντοτε, νῦν κ(αὶ) ἀεὶ (καὶ) εἰς τ<οὺς> αἰῶ<νας τῶν αἰώνων>. Καὶ ἄρχονται ψάλλειν τὰ τροπά<ρια> ταῦτ<α>, ἦχ<ος> π<λάγιος> β',

Ἡ τὸ χαῖρε δι' ἀγγέλου δεξαμένη (καὶ) τεκοῦσα τὸν κτίστ(ην) τὸν ἴδιον, Παρθ(έ)νε, σῷζε τοὺς σὲ μεγαλύνοντας.

Ἡ τὸν κτίστην τῶν ἁπάντων ἐν γαστρί σου συλλαβοῦσα, Παρθ(έ)νε, (καὶ) τέξασα αὐτὸν δυσώπει ὑπὲρ τῶν τιμώντων σε.

Ῥῆξον πάντων ὀφλημάτ(ων) τὰς σειρ(άς) μ(ου), Θ(εοτό)κε, βραβεύουσα ἄφε<σιν> (καὶ) τὴν εἰρήνην τοῖς πόθῳ τιμῶσί σε.

Σῶσον πάντ(ας), παναγία Θ(εοτό)κε, τοὺς κειμένους πταισμάτ(ων) ἐν βάθεσι, (καὶ) μὴ παρίδῃς ἐν ὥρᾳ κρίσε(ως).

Τῇ πρεσβείᾳ τῆς ἐνδόξου Θ(εοτό)κου, ζωοδότα Χ(ριστ)ὲ ὁ Θ(εὸ)ς ἡμῶν τὴν πίστιν ἡμῶν ἀσάλευτον φύλαττε.

Τίς προστρέχων τῷ ναῷ σου, Θ(εοτό)κε, οὐ λαμβάνει ταχέ(ως) τὴν ἴασιν ψυχῆς ὁμοῦ τε (καὶ) σώματος, Ἄχραντ<ε>; | 210

Χαῖρε ὄρος, χαῖρε βάτε, χαῖρε πύλη, χαῖρε κλίμαξ, χαῖρε θεία τράπεζα, ἡ πάντων χαῖρε βοήθεια, Δέσποι<να>.[5]

Θ(εοτό)κε, ἡ τεκοῦσα (διὰ)...[6]

Δό(ξα)...

Τῇ πρεσβείᾳ τ(ῶν) ἁγίων ἀπ(οστόλων)...[7]

---

[5] The scribe leaves two lines empty following this *troparion*.
[6] Fol. 202v: Θ(εοτό)κε, ἡ τεκοῦσα διὰ λόγου, ὑπὲρ λόγον τὸν Λόγον, παύμνητε, κινδύνων ῥῦσαι (καὶ) ἡμ(ᾶς) τοὺς δούλου<ς> σου.
[7] Fol. 202v: Τῇ πρεσβείᾳ τῶν ἁγίων ἀποστόλ(ων), ζωοδότα Χ(ριστ)ὲ ὁ Θ(εὸ)ς ἡμῶν τὴν

Τὸν Π(ατέ)ρα (καὶ) Υ(ἱὸ)ν δοξολο<γοῦμεν>[8], ζήτ<ει> ταῦτ<α> εἰς τ<ὸν> ἁγιασμ<ὸν> τοῦ λού<ματος>[9] τ(ῶν) Βλαχ<ερνῶν>[10].

Παναγία Θ(εοτό)κε ἡ τεκοῦσα τ(ὸν) Σ(ωτῆ)ρα, κινδύν(ων) διάσωσον (καὶ) πάσ(ης) βλάβης τοὺς δούλους σου, Ἄχραντε.

Τῆς εὐσπλαγχνί(ας) τ(ὴν) π<ηγὴ>ν…[11]

Ἕτε<ρα> τροπ<άρια>, Νῦν ἐπέστη ὁ κ(αι)ρὸ<ς> ὁ π(άν)τ(ας) ἁγιάζ(ων)…[12] στίχ<ος>, Μεγαλύ<νει> ἡ ψυχ<ή μου> τ(ὸν) Κ(ύριο)ν[13].

Νάμασ(ιν) ἐπομβρίσ(ας) Χ(ριστ)έ, π<ηγὴ>ν…[14]

Δό(ξα)…

Παρθ(έ)νο(ς) ἔτεκ(ες) ἀπειρό<γαμε>…

(Καὶ) νῦ(ν)…

Παναγία <παρθένε> Θ(εοτό)κε, τ(ῶν) χειρῶν ἡμ(ῶν) τὰ ἔργ<α>…[15]

Ἐπέστη ὁ βασιλεὺς τ(ῶν) βασι<λευόντων>,[16] ζήτ<ει> ταῦτ<α> εἰς τ<ὸν ἁγιασμὸν τοῦ> λού<ματος> τ(ῶν) Βλαχ<ερνῶν>.

Εἶτα, μετὰ τοῦτο, ὁ διάκο<νος>,

Ἐν εἰρ<ή>ν<η> τοῦ Κ(υρίο)υ δε<ηθῶμεν>.

Ὑπ<ὲρ> τῆς ἄνωθ<εν> εἰρ<ή>ν<ης>…

Ὑπ<ὲρ> τῆς εἰρ<ή>ν<ης> τοῦ Σ<ωτῆρος>…

Ὑπ<ὲρ> τοῦ ἁγίου οἴκου τ<ούτου>…

Ὑπὲρ τοῦ εὐλογηθῆν(αι) τὸ ὕδωρ τοῦτο τῇ ἐπιφοιτήσει (καὶ) δυ<νάμει> (καὶ) ἐνεργείᾳ τοῦ ἁγίου Πν(εύματο)ς τοῦ Κ(υρίο)υ δε<ηθῶμεν>.

Ὑπ<ὲρ> τοῦ καταφοιτῆσαι τ(ῷ) ὕδατι τούτ(ῳ) τὴν καθαρτικὴν τ(ῆ)ς ὑπερουσίου Τριάδο(ς) ἐνέργειαν τοῦ Κ(υρίο)υ δε<ηθῶμεν>.

πίστιν ἡμῶν ἀσάλευτον φύλαξο(ν). MS: ἁγία.

[8] Fol. 202v: Τὸν Π(ατέ)ρα (καὶ) Υἱὸν δοξολογοῦμεν καὶ τὸ Πν(εῦμ)α τὸ ἅγιον λέγοντες, Τριὰς ἁγία τὸν κόσμον εἰρήνευσον.

[9] As it is consistently spelled in the MS.

[10] Referring to the entries on fol. 202v given in the preceding notes.

[11] Fol. 202v: Τῆς εὐσπλαγχνί(ας) τ(ὴν) πηγὴν ἄνοιξον ἡμῖν, εὐ<λ>ο<γη>μέ<νη>…

[12] Fol. 203: Νῦν ἐπέστη ὁ καιρὸς ὁ πάντ(ας) ἁγιάζων, καὶ ὁ δίκαιος ἡμᾶς ἀναμένει κριτής, ἀλλ' ἐπίστρεψον ψυχὴ πρὸς μετάνοιαν ὡς ἡ πόρνη κράζουσα σὺν δάκρυσι, Κ(ύρι)ε ἐλέησόν με. MS: ἡμῶν.

[13] Luke 1:46.

[14] Fol. 203: Νάμασιν ἐπομβρίσας, Χριστέ, πηγὴν τῶν ἰάσεων ἐν τῷ <παν>σεπτῷ ναῷ τῆς Παρθ(έ)νου σήμερον τὴν σὴ(ν) εὐλογίαν καὶ ῥαντισμῷ φυγαδεύεις τὰς νόσους τ(ῶν) ἀσθενούντων, ἰατρὲ τ(ῶν) ψυχ<ῶν> ἡμ(ῶν), Κ(ύρι)ε.

[15] Fol. 203: Παναγία παρθ(έ)νε Θ(εοτό)κε, τῶν χειρῶν ἡμῶν τὰ ἔργα κατεύθυνον, (καὶ) συγχώρησιν πταισμάτων δώρησαι ταῖς ψυχαῖς ἡμῶν τῇ πρεσβείᾳ σου ἐν τῷ ψάλλειν ἡμᾶς τῶν ἀγγέλων τὸν ὕμνον, Ἅγιος ὁ Θ(εό)ς, ἅγιος ἰσχυρός, ἅγιος ἀθάνατος ἐλέησον ἡμᾶς.

[16] Fol. 202: Ἐπέστη ὁ βασιλεὺς τ(ῶν) βασιλευόντων, ὁ Κ(ύριο)ς καὶ Θ(εὸ)ς ἡμῶν, παραγέγομεν ἰάμενο(ς)| 202v τὰς νόσους ἡμῶν καὶ τὰ πταίσματα συγχωρῶν.

Ὑπ<ὲρ> τοῦ γενέσθαι αὐτὸ πηγὴν ζωῆς (καὶ) ἀφθαρσία<ς> τοῦ Κ(υρίο)υ δε<ηθῶμεν>.
Ὑπ<ὲρ> τοῦ καταπέμψαι Κ(ύριο)ν τὸν Θ(εὸ)ν ἡμῶν τὴν χάριν[17] τῆς ἀπολυτρ(ώ)σεως τὴν εὐλο<γίαν> τοῦ Ἰορδά<νου> (καὶ) ἁγιάσαι τοῦ Κ(υρίο)υ δε<ηθῶμεν>
Ὑπ<ὲρ> τοῦ δωρηθῆν(αι) ἡμῖν τὸν ἁγιασμὸν τοῦτον πρὸ<ς> καθαρισμ(ὸν) ψυχῆς (καὶ) σώματος (καὶ) πρὸς πᾶσαν ὠφέλειαν ἐπιτήδειον τοῦ Κ(υρίο)υ δε<ηθῶμεν>.
Ὑπ<ὲρ> τοῦ ῥυσθῆν(αι) ἡμ(ᾶς)...
Ἀντιλα<βοῦ, σῶσον, ἐλέησον καὶ>...
Τῆς παναγί(ας) <ἀχράντου, ὑπερευλογημένης, Δεσποίνης>...

Ὁ ἱερε<ὺς> ἐπεύχ<ε>τ(αι) τὴν εὐχ<ὴν> ἔχουσαν οὕτως, Κ(ύρι)ε ὁ Θ(εὸ)ς ἡμῶν, ὁ μέγας τῇ βουλῇ καὶ θαυμαστὸς τοῖς ἔργοις, ὁ πάσης τῆς φαινομένης κ(αὶ) νοουμένης | [210v] κτίσεως δημιουργός, ὁ φυλάσσων τὴν διαθήκην σου (καὶ) τὸ ἔλεός σου τοῖς ἀγαπῶσί σε καὶ τηροῦσι τὰ σὰ προστάγματα, ὁ πάντων τῶν ἐν ἀνάγκαις ἐλεεινὰ προσδεχόμενος[18] δάκρυα· τάχα γὰρ διὰ τοῦτο παραγέγονας ἐν δούλου μορφῇ, οὐ φάσμιν ἡμᾶς ἐκδειματούμενος,[19] ἀλλ᾽ ὑγείαν τῷ σώματι ἀληθῆ ὀρέγων καὶ λέγων, Ἴδε ὑγιὴς γέγονας, μηκέτι[20] ἁμάρτανε·[21] ἀλλὰ (καὶ) ἐκ πηλοῦ ζῶντος ὀφθαλμοὺς εἰργάσω καὶ τούτων νίψασθ(αι) κελεύσας,[22] τὸ φῶς ἰδεῖν παρεσκεύασας λόγῳ· τὰς τῶν ἐναντίων παθῶν σπιλάδας,[23] ταραττούσας, τὴν τοῦ βίου τούτου ἁλμυρὰν θάλασσαν καταστείλας, τὰ ἀχθοφόρα τῶν ἡδονῶν κατεσβέσας κύματα. Αὐτὸς οὖν, φιλάνθ(ρωπ)ε Δέσποτα, ὁ δοὺς ἡμῖν χιονόφεγγον[24] φορέσαι στολὴν ἐξ ὕδατος καὶ Πν(εύματο)ς, ἀπόσμηξον ἡμῶν διὰ τῆς τῶν ὑδάτων τούτων καταδύσεώς τε (καὶ) ῥαντισμοῦ τὴν σὴν εὐλογίαν τοὺς ῥύπους καθήρω(ν) τῶν παθῶν. Ναί, Δέσποτα, τὴν ταπείνωσιν ἡμῶν ἐπισκεπτόμενος τῇ μεσιτείᾳ (καὶ) ἱκεσίᾳ τῆς παναγίας, ἀχράντου, ὑπερενδόξου, εὐλογημένης Δεσποίνης ἡμῶν, Θ(εοτό)κου καὶ ἀειπαρθένου Μαρίας, τῶν ἁγίων (καὶ) ἐπου(ρα)νίων δυνάμεων[25] (καὶ) τιμίων ἀρχαγγέλων, τοῦ ἁγίου (καὶ) ἐνδόξου προφήτου, προδρόμου κ(αὶ) βαπτιστοῦ Ἰωάννου, τῶν ἁγίων κ(αὶ) πανευφήμων ἀποστόλων, τῶν ἁγίων καὶ δικαίων Ἰωακεὶμ

---

[17] MS: χάρην.
[18] MS: πρὸς δεχόμενος.
[19] MS: ἐκδηματούμενος.
[20] MS: μὴ κέτι.
[21] John 5:14.
[22] Cf. John 9:1–11.
[23] MS: σπηλάδος.
[24] MS: χοονόφεγγον.
[25] MS: δυνάμεως.

καὶ Ἄννης, τῶν ἁγίων ἀναργύρων καὶ θαυματουργῶν ἰατρῶν Κοσμᾶ (καὶ) Δαμιανοῦ, Κύρου κ(αὶ) Ἰωάννου, Παντελεήμονος καὶ Ἑρμολάου | [Text ends incomplete: two leaves missing.[26] For the last lines from Cod. Sinai. gr. 959, see Dmitrievskij, *Opisanie*, 51.]

As the introductory sentences explain, the blessing took place in various churches of the city and would be conducted on Sundays and feast days. The celebration was not, we learn from other sources, discretionary throughout the year but was confined to the beginnings of the months.[27] The priest, deacon and choirs required for singing the troparia gathered around a basin in the narthex or in another part of the church where there was a fountain (phiale, in the atrium or baptistery). Finally, the Blessing was integrated into the liturgy – hence the stipulated days of celebration – where it was inserted after the Enarxis and before the First Entrance. The priest officiating signalled the start of the ritual with 'Blessed is our God, always, now and forever and ever', to which the assembled would have responded 'amen'. Invocations and a series of troparia were then sung. The text for a block of these appears in the earlier bathing ritual of the Blachernai, so the scribe simply gives incipits and refers the priest back to the previous chapter, where the passages are copied out in full. Following the troparia, the deacon pronounced a *synapte* that begins with the customary 'In peace let us beseech the Lord', then continues with a series of supplications specific to the blessing of the water (those written out in full) before returning to the familiar closing, 'Protect, save, have mercy...' followed by 'Commemorating our most holy, undefiled...'.[28] The Blessing ends with the priest offering a prayer that is cut short by the loss of two leaves following fol. 210. A substantial part of the ending of the prayer as well as the final portion of the ritual have been lost.[29] Fortunately, the beginning of the prayer with its invocations as well as the body, offering words specific to the occasion, survive intact. When transcribing this last chapter, the scribe omitted a considerable amount of supporting material that is found elsewhere in the manuscript, in, for example, the service at the Blachernai. Only once does he indicate the versicule(s) that accompanies a *troparion*, and he may not always supply the 'Glory to the Father and the Son and the Holy Spirit / both now and always and forever and ever' that regularly punctuates troparia. He gives no reference to a reading from Scripture, and does not indicate what actions the priest and deacon might perform during the service. Such directions appear in other sources for the blessing, but there is insufficient stability among them to allow a confident reconstruction of the ritual as celebrated in the early

---

[26] Devreesse, *Fonds coislin*, 194.
[27] With the exception of September and January: Trempelas, *Εὐχολόγιον*, 47–49.
[28] Compare the *synapte* in the liturgy: P. Trempelas, *Αἱ τρεῖς λειτουργίαι κατὰ τοὺς ἐν Ἀθήναις κώδικας* (Athens, 1935), 25–26.
[29] Different versions are published: *Εὐχολόγιον τὸ μέγα* (Athens, 1927), 257–258; Trempelas, *Εὐχολόγιον*, 64–67; Dmitrievskij, *Opisanie*, 51.

eleventh century.

The absence of directions for priest and deacon fortuitously invites our considering the text as a literary composition, a drama with a beginning, middle and end, and from this standpoint then to look at the surrounding context. The opening parts of the ritual, mainly short hymns, are conventional in sentiment with one exception; this is the *troparion* addressed to the Theotokos: 'Who has hastened to your church, O Theotokos, and not quickly received healing of the soul as well as the body?' Otherwise, the hymns might be sung on any occasion, though the references to their use compiled by Enrica Follieri suggest limited popularity beyond the occasion of the blessing.[30] As the service nears the point at which the deacon begins the *synapte*, two hymns further adumbrate themes relevant to the blessing. The popular *troparion* 'Open to us the gate of compassion, O blessed Theotokos...' has the expected word 'gate' altered to read 'spring'. Following this *troparion* is another that evokes the story of the woman who washes Christ's feet;[31] her tears are the cleansing agent of her repentance. The subsequent hymn fully sounds the overall theme. Christ is addressed as the physician to our souls who rains down in streams a source of healing and who banishes through its purification the afflictions of the weakened. The *synapte* assigned to the deacon comes before the priest's long prayer as its preface. It invites the assembled to pray to the Lord to bless the water through the power of the Holy Spirit, to send down the redeeming grace that consecrated the Jordan river, to make the water a source of eternal life, and to give the assembled its blessing to cleanse body and soul. Absent are direct references to sin, wickedness or unworthiness. The assembled focus entirely upon the cathartic power of the water and its efficacy to heal body and soul through a transformation that will be effected by the Holy Spirit; the only biblical image summoned is appropriately that of Christ's baptism. The *synapte* represents a concentrated expression of the substance of the service and does so through a series of short statements unembellished by the poetry of the troparia or the discursive and referential quality of the priest's prayer that follows it. Each statement in the litany ends with 'let us beseech the Lord' and thus introduces the final prayer delivered by the priest, the critical moment in the ritual when according to other sources the priest, holding a cross, performs the blessing.[32]

During the divine liturgy the priest sometimes concludes his prayers by invoking a series of intercessors. Here he begins with the Virgin, the heavenly powers and archangels, and John the Baptist (in a sequence that, as in most other prayers, calls to mind the topmost row of icons on the templon). Immediately following are Joachim and Anna, then the sainted physicians Kosmas and Damian, Kyros and John, Panteleimon and the priest who converted him, Hermolaos.[33] Naming the physicians so promi-

---

[30] E. Follieri, *Initia hymnorum ecclesiae graecae* (Studi e testi, 211–215bis, Vatican City, 1960–1966).
[31] Luke 7:37–50.
[32] Trempelas, Εὐχολόγιον, 70.
[33] The sequence is identical to that found in the eleventh-century *euchologion* Cod. Sinai. gr. 959 (Dmitrievskij, *Opisanie*, 51) but not the versions published by J. Goar, *Euchologion sive rituale graecorum*

nently among the intercessors underscores how the Church viewed the consecrated water. It was a medium for the divine spirit and therefore a curative for illness. The hymns and prayer make this conclusion unremarkable, but all that goes before this point in the service links spiritual healing with physical, whereas the invocation of the sainted physicians puts the matter more one-sidedly. Still, the mention of St Hermolaos may leave the reader wondering how so obscure a saint may relate to the linkage between spiritual and physical healing. According to the brief biography we encounter in the *Synaxarion* of Constantinople under 26 July, the saint's feast day, Hermolaos served during the reign of Emperor Maximian as a priest in the city of Nikomedeia. He was acquainted with St Panteleimon, and he was beheaded about the same time as St Panteleimon suffered martyrdom, in 305.[34] In this same source, under 27 July, St Panteleimon's feast day, we are informed that initially a prominent physician named Euphrosynos instructed Panteleimon in the medical arts, but that later the priest Hermolaos taught Panteleimon faith healing: effecting cures by invoking Christ's name.[35] In the passio of St Panteleimon written by Symeon Metaphrastes Hermolaos is quoted as saying to the megalomartyr that the 'teachings of Hippokrates and Galen are of little value', that the pagan gods are empty stories, that 'the one true God is Christ' and that if one believes in Christ one may dispel all diseases by the simple expedient of invoking him. In this way one may restore sight to the blind, breath to the dead, and clear skin to the leper.[36] It is through his espousal of faith healing that Hermolaos holds a prominent place in joining belief with physical cures.[37] The privileged position of Joachim and Anna is less easy to pin down. They are the aged couple whose conception of a child was the miraculous result of divine intervention. One wonders if another, unspecified use for consecrated water might not have been in seeking to combat infertility.

The blessing ritual unfolds outside the nave of the church. It made the atrium or

---

complectens ritus et ordines... (Venice, 1730, repr. Graz, 1960), 361, or Trempelas, Εὐχολόγιον, 65–66.

[34] *Propylaeum ad Acta Sanctorum Novembris. Synaxarium Ecclesiae Constantinopolitanae e codice Sirmondiano*, ed. H. Delehaye (Brussels, 1902), 843.

[35] *SynaxCP*, 847, ed. Delehaye: τὴν δὲ κατὰ Χριστὸν ἰατρικὴν καὶ πίστιν παρὰ Ἑρμολάου τοῦ πρεσβυτέρου μανθάνει (lines 18–20).

[36] *PG*, 115, 2, 449.

[37] Susan Boyd has pointed out that the earliest extant depiction of St Hermolaos dates from c.900. On icons and in frescoes he is regularly depicted in company with St Panteleimon. A major exception is a copper votive plaque of the late tenth or early eleventh century. Here he is shown alone holding his right hand in blessing and a gospel book in his left hand. It is noteworthy that as a physician-saint he is not represented holding a scalpel. The manner of his depiction is consistent with his teachings to rely on faith and to heal through a 'bloodless' procedure. The plaque is engraved with an inscription (only a portion is visible) reading: 'For the health and salvation and the remission of sins [of]... [this was presented]'. The plaque establishes that by 1050 a cult of St Hermolaos had sprung up and that his help was implored for maintaining or restoring good health. See 'Ex-voto therapy. A note on a copper plaque with St Hermolaos', *Aetos: studies in honor of Cyril Mango presented to him on April 14, 1998*, ed. I. Ševčenko and I. Hutter (Stuttgart and Leipzig, 1998), 15–27.

narthex a site for a solemn liturgical function, and one that required some specific support in the form of a supply of water that would be accessible to the congregation. In some instances the source would be a fountain in the atrium,[38] but the requirements for a phiale could not have been met in every Byzantine church. Those lacking a supply of water under pressure would presumably have had a simple basin installed in the narthex.[39] Examples of church decoration arguably refer to either the ritual or simply the presence of blessed water. Among the subjects depicted in the narthex of the church at Daphni is the annunciation to Anna.[40] The grand fountain in Joachim and Anna's garden occupies a prominent part of the composition at Daphni. By locating within the narthex at least a representation of a phiale like the one at Hagia Sophia, the designer has created an appropriate backdrop for either the ritual or the presence of consecrated water. Interpreting the image in this way – as a reference to contemporary architecture, a well-known apocryphon and a liturgical ritual – is made more difficult, though not entirely implausible, by the place of the annunciation in a series of three episodes from the life of the Virgin. There are, of course, much deeper associations of gardens, fountains and fertility, but they operate on the mind at another level.

---

[38] L. Bouras, 'Some observations on the Grand Lavra phiale at Mt Athos and its bronze strobilion', *Deltion tes Christianikes Archaiologikes Hetaireias*, 8 (1975–1976), 85–96.
[39] Possibly like the basin published in *Treasures of Mt Athos* (Thessalonike, 1997), 243 (item 6.7). St Sophia had both a phiale and a baptistery: G. Majeska, *Russian travelers to Constantinople in the fourteenth and fifteenth centuries* (DOS, 19, Washington, DC, 1984), 201–202; the patriarchal blessing of the water prior to baptism took place in the latter location: Mateos, *Typicon*, 182.
[40] E. Diez and O. Demus, *Byzantine mosaics in Greece: Hosios Loukas and Daphni* (Cambridge, 1931), fig. 109. The group of Kosmas and Damian, Kyros and John appears in facing pairs in one the vaults of the north bay of the narthex at Hosios Loukas: Diez and Demus, *Byzantine mosaics*, 119.

24

A feast for the senses

Patricia Finlay

This short scribal poem in twelve-syllable verse is found on folio 247v of the Barberini Psalter (Vat. Gr. 372), a *deluxe* eleventh-century Byzantine psalter with over 300 marginal illustrations. Carefully located opposite a full-page image of David as Orpheus, the poem seeks to heighten the contemporary viewer's experience of that image. At the same time, its myriad references to sight, sound and taste provide a timely reminder for the modern reader that turning the pages of such manuscripts was and is a highly sensual experience.

With his customary kindness and patience, Bob Jordan taught me the rudiments of Greek and indeed helped me to translate this poem. I hope that the few changes I have made will not offend his sensibilities.

Ὅρα, θεατά, τὴν ὁρωμένην θέαν
Πρὸς τὸν καθ'ἡμᾶς ἀτενίζων Ὀρφέα.
Δαβὶδ γὰρ οὗτος ὃς θεωμένῃ λύρᾳ
ᾠδὴν μελιχρὰν αἰσθητὴν πέμπειν θέλει
Τῇ δ'αὖ νοητῇ κρουσμάτων μελῳδίᾳ
Τὸν νοῦν τελειοῖ· δέλτον οὗπερ ἀρτίως
Εὐτερματώσας τῷ θεῷ λέγω · Χάρις.

See, o spectator, the sight being seen,
Gazing intently towards our Orpheus;
For this is David, who with a looked-at lyre
Wishes to send a honey-sweet ode perceived by the senses
And on the other hand, with a spiritual melody of notes
Makes the mind perfect. Having just now brought
To a good end his book, to God I say 'Thanks'.

25

Philip of Oxford, On preaching the Holy Cross in England

Edward Moss

It is not without a certain amount of trepidation on the part of its translator that an obscure thirteenth-century crusading sermon has found itself included in the present volume alongside renderings of some more celebrated works. The *Brevis Ordinacio De Sanctae Crucis in Anglia* is a remarkable and neglected text in so far that it provides us with a rare insight into the rhetorical strategies employed by professional preachers to persuade congregations to accept the *votum crucis*, an oath enforced by excommunication that offered the remission of sins in return for military service on an armed pilgrimage.

The text itself was first edited by Reinhold Röhrich, a century and a quarter ago and his version is based on two manuscripts. The first was Balliol College MS 167, folios 212v-215r, the second is sadly no longer extant. Authorship remains a contested matter due to the lack of any definitive evidence, but the most likely candidate, as Röhricht suggested, was a Master Philip of Oxford. Although such associations must remain slightly tentative, Philip was a Paris-trained theologian and preacher, teaching at Oxford who is mentioned as a recipient of Innocent III's bull of May 1213, *Pium et Sanctam*. This text was intended as a follow-up to the militant encyclical *Quia Maior* promulgated in the April of the same year. Taken together, these texts reflect the consolidation of Innocent's political ambitions and worldview that were to culminate in 1215 with the canons of the Fourth Lateran Council. As a named recipient of one of these texts, Master Philip remains an important vector linking the official discourses of the Crusading Movement with the provincial English congregations at whom such preaching was to be directed. An internal reference to the Albigensian crusade of 1209 locates the composition of the text after this date, and as it does not draw directly on the canons of 1215, we may assume the *Ordinacio* was composed between these dates, probably around 1214.

Rather than a stand-alone read, the *Ordinacio* needs to be appreciated not only as part of a wider series of discourses such as the papal documents mentioned above, but also in conjunction with the descriptions provided in texts such as *The Journey Through Wales* of Giraldus Cambrensis. Although describing events taking place in the late 1180s, this account of a preaching tour through the Welsh valleys, accompanying Baldwin the archbishop of Canterbury, supplies a unique insight into the sociology of the crusading movement as well as the reception and influence of its promotional discourses on the 'home front'.

It is perhaps the rareness of the *Ordinacio* as well as the factors mentioned above that make it such an significant text, and I was surprised to find that no version of it existed in English although historians of the crusading movement like Penny Cole and Christopher Tyerman provide wide ranging discussions of the text in their respective works.[1]

Having said that, its erstwhile inaccessibility makes it a most fitting tribute in a volume designed to celebrate the career of Dr Robert Jordan, someone who has dedicated a significant portion of his life to hauling information from the darkest idiomatic recesses of Byzantine monastic manuscripts and restoring them to the corpus of information available to a grateful academic community. Furthermore, an equally significant portion has been devoted to teaching classical languages to fledgling Byzantinists. Learning the rudiments of Greek with Dr Jordan was simply a delightful experience, as with tremendous patience and gentle erudition, the most complicated of grammatical devices were explained in digestible and often amusing terms to the least complicated of undergraduates.

It is no exaggeration to state that after a few months of studying the *Apophthegmata* and the *Chronographia* of *Theophanes the Confessor* with Bob, Messrs Keegan and Beardsley had been permanently replaced in my affections by Messrs Liddell and Scott. Similarly, no-one was more willing to help me as a PhD student investigate and prepare translations of obscure medieval Latin works such as the *Gesta Herewardi* or the polemical writings of Petrus Cluniacensis, works that many classicists would consider beyond the scope of their expertise. It remains only to express my most profound gratitude and wish a long and happy retirement to a magnificent teacher with few metaphrastic peers, and perhaps most importantly of all, to the truest of gentlemen.

---

[1] P. Cole, *The preaching of the crusades to the Holy Land, 1095–1270* (Cambridge, MA, 1991). C. Tyerman, *England and the Crusades 1095–1388.* (Chicago, 1988).

Here begins a brief prescription concerning the preaching of the Holy Cross to lay people, which does not look to the embellished arrangement of words, but rather to the clear and obvious display of truth, and let facility of the tongue, moderated by the guidance of reason and the pen gathering only material for preaching, compensate for its brevity.

Human weakness beset by pressures often looks at the smallness of its own powers and perceives in itself nothing except the darkness of defiles and the waves of attacking enemies. But when it raises its mind to the light of heavenly protection and the gifts of eternal reward, steadily cleaving to God, it gathers through him successively more and more strength and powerfully destroys the disquiets of the threefold enemy, that is, what is bitter according to the flesh it transforms into what is sweet according to the spirit, and rejecting private vanity and worldly display, it chooses the shortest route to reach him 'from whom comes all salvation, who is the way, the truth and the life'[2] in order that the death of worldly life should be like a gateway and entrance to the heavenly kingdom and eternal life. When therefore the more something is good and delightful, the more it is to be sought after and the greater is the haste with which we should run to it, that is, to him than whom on the cross, which is the shortest way to heaven, nothing is better or more delightful, we must flee delay and hurry with burning desire. Therefore do not seek delay in coming to him by not observing through the evidence of its effect the commandment, 'Thou shall love the Lord thy God with all thy heart etc',[3] on which depend all the law and prophets',[4] and follow him who says 'The servant is not greater than his lord'[5] and 'Where I am (namely on the cross) there shall my servant be'[6], because let him who serves me follow me, namely on the cross, by dying on which the Lord redeemed the human race, for he says in the Gospel, 'Except an ear of wheat fall upon the ground and die, it abides alone.'[7] Christ is said to be a grain of wheat because we shall enjoy him, and he is said to be a grain because just as the grain of wheat is white on the inside and red on the outside, so Christ on the inside was white through his integrity and virginity, and on the outside red on the cross through his own blood. In the grain of wheat there is a certain cleft as it were, between two which are joined; so there are in Christ two natures, namely God and Man, which are joined in him. For Christ is truly God and truly Man because he is a giant of dual substance. Just as a grain of wheat is ground between two millstones, so was Christ on the cross between two peoples, namely the Jewish

---

[2] John 14:6.
[3] Matthew 22:37.
[4] Matthew 22:40.
[5] John 13:16.
[6] John 12:26.
[7] John 12:24.

and the gentile, because the Jews condemned Christ to death, and the Romans, who were gentiles, slew him. 'A grain fell to earth': so did Christ fall into the womb of the virgin Mary. 'Except it die it abides alone': so unless Christ had died, he would have remained alone in glory without the company of man because in his death he redeemed mankind on the cross and opened the gates of heaven in accordance with 'You overcoming the sting of death.' The grain however is divided when the inside pith leaves and the grain sprouts and it ceases to be a grain, whence in a certain way it dies in this drying up: so also Christ was divided in a certain way into two, namely body and soul, when his soul left his body and opened the gate of heaven and he ceased to be a man, whence in that division of body and soul Christ died. Appropriately therefore Christ is called the grain, and not simply the grain, but the grain of wheat. *Item:* Life entered through Christ and Mary, just as death did through Adam and Eve. Moreover, Mary was on the cross, because she was in the greatest torment when she saw her son hanging on the cross, whence Isaiah in the last chapter: 'Before she travailed, she brought forth; before her pains came, she was delivered of a man child.'[8] Who ever heard of such a thing? Who ever saw anything like this? A woman now gives birth when she labours and has the utmost pains before the child emerges from the womb. It was not so with the Blessed Virgin Mary, who gave birth without pain, but afterwards when she was distressed seeing her only son, innocent, placed on the cross without cause, and despised and abandoned by his disciples, then she suffered the pains of labour. Therefore Isaiah said correctly of her: 'Before she travailed she brought forth; before her pain she was delivered of a man child.'[9]

Item: Just as through a woman, namely Eve, who was made from a man, namely Adam, without union with a man, men had to die, so conversely through a man, namely Jesus Christ, who was made from a woman, namely Mary, without union with a man, we ought all to live through God's grace and have eternal life. *Item:* There is another argument. Death entered through a rib as if through Eve 'who was made from the rib of Adam.'[10] Conversely life came through the side because it came through the blood of Christ, which issued from his side. *Item:* Through an action there came death, because it came through the act of eating whereas on the other hand life came through suffering because the suffering of Christ on the cross brought life.

Item: Through the pleasure of Adam and Eve in eating of the apple there was death: conversely through the bitterness for Christ and Mary on the cross there was life. *Item:* Adam and Eve ate the apple in order that they might keep together body and soul because men eat in order to live. Therefore since things are cured by

---

[8] Isaiah 66:7.
[9] Isaiah 66:7.
[10] Genesis 2:21.

their opposites, the treatment had to be through death, because death takes place through the separation of body and soul. Therefore our salvation had to be through death. *Item:* Death was brought about through a man with sin: therefore life had to be brought about through a man existing without sin.[11] That man therefore from whom through himself had to be the restoration of the human race could not have been the offspring of Adam and a sinless man, because all of Adam's offspring, who were simply men, were born with original sin. He had therefore to be God and man, and he had to be of the race of Adam, for from the time that Adam sinned, it was necessary for the human race that either he himself or one of his descendants should atone for that sin, because if a new man should be created by God to redeem the human race, the human race would not be restored to its former liberty because this human creature would be bound to obey and serve him; he had therefore to be God and man and of the offspring of Adam.

Item: It was said in Genesis 15, 'Abraham and your seed would be subjected to slavery and return here in the fourth generation' because there was a generation from neither man nor woman (Adam), a generation from man and not from woman (Eve), one from man and woman (the rest of mankind), and one from a woman and not from a man (Christ).[12] The three generations first named preceded the incarnation. But in the nativity of Christ God brought about the fourth generation, and it was impossible that there should be more as is evident from the fourfold division that was foretold. Therefore what was said was accomplished: 'They return here in the fourth generation' because Christ freed the seed of Abraham from slavery. *Item:* He who bleeds himself in order to be cured of pain does not take blood from a sick part, but from a healthy part; so since human nature was sick, it did not draw blood from a sick part in order to heal it, but from a healthy part, namely from the body of Jesus Christ on the cross because it was healthy and free from sin, and thus the human race was cleansed from sins and eternal death. Whence John in the first chapter said, 'The blood of Christ cleanses us from all sin.'

Item: Through a man and a woman, Adam and Eve, death entered a delightful place, beautiful and enjoyable, namely Paradise; so conversely through a man and a woman, namely Christ and Mary, life entered a place wearisome, ugly and loathsome. *Item:* Death was in a beautiful tree, and life in a tree that is the ugly cross. *Item:* Death is beneath the bounds of Paradise, and life is outside the stronghold, whence in the last chapter to the Hebrews: 'Let us go forth to him outside the camp, bearing his reproach. For we have no abiding city.'[13]

---

[11] Romans 5:14, 1 Corinthians 15:22–25.
[12] Genesis 15:13–18.
[13] Hebrews 13:13–14.

Item: In the beautiful tree of Paradise under the cover of life was concealed death, and conversely, in the ugly and loathsome tree under the cover of death life was hidden, just as for those marked with the sign of the cross life lies hidden under the cover of work, which is a kind of death. *Item:* Death comes through a man made from virgin earth, namely Adam; so through a man made from virgin woman, namely Christ, comes life. *Item:* Just as Adam and Eve wrought death in the middle of Eden, and Lucifer did the same in the midst of heaven, so God our king wrought salvation in the midst of earth, namely in Jerusalem, which is the middle of the earth. 'On mount Zion and in Jerusalem will be salvation,'[14] where the lamb on the cross overcame 'the roaring lion that is the devil, who goes about etc.'[15] *Item:* Just as water coming in with a rush cleanses and scours the ditches, so the cross cleanses the hearts of sinners. May you be on the cross therefore, that we 'may be cleansed of all filthiness of the flesh and the spirit' as the apostle Paul says.[16]

Item: Just as in chapter four of the second Book of Kings it is said that some men were cutting wood beside the Jordan in order to build a house for themselves: 'One man's axe-head fell into the water, and he cried and said to the prophet Elisha "Alas master, I had borrowed it" and the prophet Elisha said "Where did it fall?" and he showed him the place. And Elisha cut down a stick and sent it there, and the iron swam to the wood. And he said, "Lift it." And he put out his hand and took it.' By Elisha Christ is indicated, by the wooden stick the cross, and by the iron, which was hard and cold, is signified the coldness in love of sinners and their persistence in sins. And just as the iron axe-head was moved up from the muddy waters and towards the wooden stick, and in this way to Elisha, so the sinner from the depths of his evil, which is at one time gluttony and at another lechery and other things, is moved to the cross, and cleaves to it and thus reaches Christ, whence 'This is the ladder of sinners' and in the Gospel 'If I shall be lifted up from earth.'[17]

He who fights is in fear of death and should not be burdened, but ought to have the burden taken away from him so that he may be mobile. Deservedly therefore the Church should unburden its fighter who fights for it and support his weight, and therefore from those marked with the cross our lord the pope rightly takes away the punishment due to their sins, and puts the whole Church under an obligation on their behalf who can be cleansed by means of their own contrition, devotion, confession, toil and effort, through the prayers and almsgivings that are made by all Christians for pilgrims to the Holy Land.

---

[14] Joel 2:32.
[15] 1 Peter 5:8.
[16] 2 Corinthians 7:1.
[17] John 12:36.

Item: If a man should be burdened by several stones, and someone should take one stone away from him, and a different person another, and a third person a third stone, and so forth, he would be relieved entirely of his burden; similarly one marked with the cross is relieved from punishment for his sins through our lord the pope and the whole church. 'And whomsoever you shall loose over earth, he will be loosed in heaven also.'[18] It is to be noted that it says 'over earth', not 'below earth' or 'in earth'. He is over earth who neglects earthly matters, he is in earth who attaches his heart to earthly matters and of such persons the Apostle says: 'Their glory is confusion who taste of earthly things.'[19] That is, they take pleasure and relish in earthly things, just as John in the Apocalypse says, 'Woe, woe, to the inhabitants of the earth.'[20] 'The woman,' namely Eve, 'saw that the tree was good to eat and pleasant to the eyes and delightful to behold. She took of its fruit and ate and gave to her husband and he ate.'[21] But earlier God commanded Adam: 'Eat of every tree in the garden, but of the tree of the knowledge of good and evil do not eat.'[22] Wherefore Eve answered the serpent, 'Of the fruit of the tree which is in the middle of the garden God has commanded us not to eat or touch lest we die.'[23] Therefore by the right judgement of God the bodies of Adam and Eve were divided from their souls because against the command of God they divided the apple with a bite, whence death is derived from a bite. They had to die therefore and all of us through them, and the blame and the punishment were involved in the same action because blame lay in the division of the parts of the apple and punishment in the division of body and soul.

Item: Whoever eats a poisonous thing must die, and Adam and Eve ate fruit poisonous to them and because it was God's command to them, it was necessary for them to die.

Item: In the division of the apple Adam and Eve had delight; conversely in the division of body and soul they had bitterness as had in like fashion those who followed them.

Item: Just as Eve seduced Adam and it was necessary for him to die, so the flesh seduces the spirit sometimes, and so it is necessary for it as it were to die because it was in eternal death.

Item: Just as Eve offered the forbidden fruit to Adam, so the flesh offers different forbidden things to the soul. Whatever is forbidden to man is represented by the aforesaid fruit, and the spirit by Adam and the flesh by Eve.

---

[18] Matthew 16:19.
[19] Philip 3:19.
[20] Revelations 8:13.
[21] Genesis 3:6.
[22] Genesis 2:16–17.
[23] Genesis 3:3.

Item: Just as through the fruit, which was food, the command of the Lord was breached and death entered, so through food, which is the flesh and blood of Christ and was made at the command of the Lord, life entered and enters daily. John VI, 'The bread of God who comes down from heaven and gives life to the world.' So they said to him, 'Lord, always give us this bread', and Jesus said to them, 'I am the living bread; he who comes to me will not hunger, and he who believes in me will not thirst.'[24] 'And so everyone who sees the Son and believes in him has eternal life.'[25] And below in the same chapter, 'Unless you eat the flesh of the Son of Man and drink his blood you will have no life in you. My flesh is truly meat and my blood is truly drink. He that eats my flesh and drinks my blood dwells in me, and I in him.'[26] And he who is in him is in a strong fortress, surrounded on all sides by such a strong wall that the devil is not able to approach him, and therefore John in the Apocalypse says 'Write "Blessed are the dead who die in the Lord."'[27] But the flesh of Christ is not food of the belly, but food of the soul. For Augustine says, 'Believe and eat', and the Lord says, 'Everyone who sees the Son and believes in him has eternal life.'[28] And so in Habbakuk, 'The just man lives by faith.'[29] and below in the same chapter, 'Who eats my flesh and drinks my blood has eternal life.'[30] Therefore each of these, both eating and having eternal life, leads to belief, but he who consumes unworthily eats and drinks judgement to himself.'[31] And so the priest remaining unrepentant in mortal sin takes the body of Christ to his own damnation, but to the salvation of his faithful parishioners who are not in mortal sin; also he consumes the body of Christ only as minister of the sacrament; but they do so spiritually. If indeed the priest were not in mortal sin, he would then take the body of Christ as minister of the sacrament and spiritually. Now a declaration about the sacrament is above human understanding. Nevertheless let one be stated however it may be. A man sometimes goes out of his house to meet his master and facilitate his entering his place. So in a way it is with the bread because there, where there was bread in perishable substance, that substance of the bread is through the power of the sacred words true God and true man, but there remain there the accidents of bread, which were as it were lodgings and place, namely the whiteness of the bread, the roundness, taste, amount, and hardness, and these accidents are ground by the teeth, and the body of Christ, which is there, is under those accidents food of the soul and not of the body. And those accidents miracu-

---

[24] John 6:33–34.
[25] John 6:40.
[26] John 6:53–56.
[27] Revelations 19:13.
[28] John 6:40.
[29] Habbakuk 2:4.
[30] John 6:54.
[31] 1 Corinthians 11:29.

lously remain in the absence of the original substance. Therefore God provided an effective remedy against the cause of death, namely food for the soul, against food for the belly.

Concerning the circumstances of the cross
When soldiers are in war, they have their stronger armour on the outside, such as the breastplate, and the weaker on the inside; Christ on the contrary had his weaker armour on the outside, namely the flesh, and the stronger inside, namely his godhead, which lay hidden beneath the flesh.

Item: When Eve took the fruit from the tree, she closed her hand towards the tree, but conversely Christ on the cross turned his hands away from the tree, and had them open in order to indicate that we should turn our hands away from forbidden things; by the fruit then is signified any forbidden thing.

Item: Christ on the cross bends to kiss, offering peace to the sinner, and stretches open his arms on the cross to an embrace. For he says, 'I came not to call the righteous, but sinners,' and elsewhere he says, 'Joy shall be greater in the kingdom over one sinner.'[32] His side was opened in order to conceal his secret.

Item: A single nail was driven in and pierced the feet of Christ because the body is represented by the feet since it turns now this way and now that just as the feet bear the body now this way and now that. And the love of one, namely God, ought chiefly to be in the heart, and therefore there was a single nail in his feet, which signifies the heart, where there is one love, in which all other virtues should be blended. For just as many branches come forth from one root, so also many virtues come from the one love that is rooted in the heart. Therefore the single nail in the feet represents a single love.

Item: By the hands works are signified because we perform works with our hands. Hence there were two nails in his hands to signify that our works should be twofold, in the active and in the contemplative life.

Item: The threefold number of nails signified the Trinity.

Item: The Lord on the cross leaned towards the earth and directed his gaze there to signify that he himself was on the cross for that which was on the earth, namely for man, the sinner. But Peter on the cross directed his gaze upwards to signify that he was on the cross for him who was above in Heaven, namely for Christ.

Item: The Lord on the cross leaned towards the north to signify that he was on the cross for the sinner, who is signified by the north, because just as the north is cold, so the sinner is cold in the love of God, whence Isaiah, 'From the north stretches forth all evil.'[33]

---

[32] Luke 5:32.
[33] Isaiah 1:14r.

Item: Mary, mother of the Lord, stood by the cross to the north, between the north and Christ on the cross, to signify that she mediates between sinners and Christ; for she receives those who flee to her in sorrow and devotion, and she intercedes for them as a mother with her son. For whom the world rejects, and who is worthless in the eyes of the world (such as inveterate harlots are), God accepts his coming to him.

Item: The Lord on the cross delineates our whole life to us, so that we may imitate him since every action of Christ is our instruction. Hence from Isaiah, 'Behold I have delineated you upon my palms,'[34] that is, your life. And in the Gospel he says, 'Where I am etc'[35] Because 'the servant is not greater than his master.'[36] Therefore let us not stretch our hands or our feet or our heart or any limb to anything forbidden, but for Christ let us restrain all our limbs from unlawful things, and then we follow Christ.

Item: God had the holes of the nails for us so he might in this way have an eternal memorial of us, whence Isaiah says, 'Can a woman forget her child etc?'[37] and 'Behold I have delineated you upon my hands.'[38] And further 'What is man that you remember etc?'[39] God does not wish therefore that you should perish, whom for his own life he redeemed. He is mindful of you, who so often after baptism have fallen into the snares of the devil through your sins, both fleshly and of the spirit. Hence he sends to you here a cleansing and scouring of your sins, that you may take up the cross to help the Holy Land, and thus by means of the cross you will enter into the kingdom of heaven, and so you will see it desirable to view and inexpressibly enjoyable, whence Matthew, 'Blessed are they with pure hearts etc.'[40]

Item: Just as a piece of cloth is first washed with bitter lye, and afterwards in sweet and warm water, so the soul is first washed in bitter tribulation and later in tears which follow tribulation, and then is made warm through contrition for sin and the remembrance of past events. For through motion born in an embrace heat is naturally aroused, and tears through true remorse of the heart will be sweet and delightful in the sight of God. A clear example is blessed Mary Magdalen. It can also be clear that tears proceeding from true penance please God less because the Lord seeing Jerusalem, wept over it and said, 'If you also had known'.[41] For the Lord was lamenting over sinners who rejoice in the worst things, who if they foresaw their own damnation, would scarcely cease to lament, but they pass their days

---

[34] Isaiah 49:16.
[35] John 17:24.
[36] John 13:16.
[37] Isaiah 49:15.
[38] Isaiah 49:16.
[39] Psalms 8:4.
[40] Matthew 5:8.
[41] Luke 19:41.

in wickedness because they repose their peace in an abundance of worldly goods, which is not peace, since the more richer that abundance is, the more disturbances of the heart it causes to flow in, and it more and more alienates the soul from God. So let us flee the treasury of temporal things so that we may soar to eternal things, recalling that passage in Gregory, 'He is estranged enough from the faith who waits for the time of his old age to do penance; for it must be feared that while he hopes for mercy, he may fall into judgment.

Concerning the flesh and its pleasures

It is said in the Book of Kings that two women, overwhelmed by hunger, ate the child of one of them. Afterwards, the other was unwilling to hold to the agreement that her child should be eaten. And the king of that land threatened Elisha with death because he was unwilling to intercede with God that the famine should cease.[42] By the first woman, whose child is eaten, is signified the flesh. That is, men's works perish, namely through gluttony, lechery or another sin of the flesh. By the other woman is signified any faithful soul who is unwilling to agree that her son should be eaten, that is, that her works should perish on account of the pleasures of the flesh. By Elisha is signified Christ.

Item: The meal of the body is threefold, food for the soul and both sacraments in heaven, where nothing fails. Let them therefore be restored in this world both with food for the body and sacraments for the soul in accordance with the teaching of God in order that we should be restored to the heavenly meal forever with unfailing glory.

Item: A sick rich man at the onset of his illness refuses a doctor while it is possible to be cured and puts him off until, with death rapidly approaching, it is not possible to be cured, and then the doctor refuses him; thus it is with the sinner who follows the flesh. For he refuses the medicine of God when God offers himself to him and calls him to his service, and the sinner puts it off until with death approaching, judgement comes, and then the Lord rejects him.

Item: The nails in the cross were warm with the blood of Christ; so sinners ought to be inflamed with love to the service of Christ through the blood of Christ. For by the nails are signified sinners, by reason of their coldness and lack of feeling, and the nail is driven into the cross by means of a hammer; so through the weight of guilt, the sinner is driven into the excruciating punishment of Gehenna.

Item: In the Gospel it is read that certain pigs had been afflicted by demons and ran into the sea; thus it is with certain men who live according to the flesh through the suggestion of demons because they live like pigs and run into the bitterness of Hell, which is signified by the bitterness of the sea. 'So take up thy bed,'[43] that is,

---

[42] 2 Kings 6:26–33.
[43] John 5:5.

your flesh, upwards from worldly matters because the pleasures of the flesh are like the tail of a snake which escapes while it believes that it is held, and understand what the commentary says about the passage in the Gospel mentioned above, namely unless someone has lived like a pig, the devil does not have power over him, except to test him out, but not to destroy him.

Item: The more you press water between your hands, the more it runs out and the less it is retained; so it is with the pleasures of the flesh and of the world.

Item: A wandering traveller who always follows the force of the wind rarely has an agreeable lodging; so whoever follows every motion of the flesh rarely has lodging in heaven.

Item: The dove does not eat flesh; so neither does the good man follow the pleasure of the flesh.

Item: The dove with its beak separates the grain of wheat from the chaff; so does the good man separate those things which are of God, who is the grain of wheat, from those which are of the flesh.

Item: Wood which is often ignited and often extinguished is easier to set on fire than green wood which was never burnt; so it is with the carnal man, who has more often practised lust than he who was always chaste.

Item: Concerning the rich, the lustful and whoever follows the pleasures of the flesh: Cain slew Abel, that is ownership slew grief and penitence. Cain stands for ownership and Abel for grief.

Item: Death entered on a Friday because of the pleasures of the flesh, in the eating of the apple, which was done against God's command. And on the same day, namely Friday, through the bitterness of the flesh and on the cross, life entered and the gate of heaven was opened.

Item: A country glutton ate the skin of the stomach from the entrails of a cow and because of the adherence of the skin, a great part of the skin remained between the teeth of that countryman, and he was not able to remove the skin from his teeth and sought aid from his wife. And wishing to help him, she cut off his upper lip with a sharp knife. Similarly carnal pleasure cuts off the upper lip of a lecherous man, that is, his attention to higher things, and makes it so that the man does not think of God, but of those things which please the flesh: 'For the flesh lusts against the spirit.'[44]

Item: A knowing cook places as little as he can in a dirty and smelly jar; so also does the experienced man put as little in his stomach as he can because all food and drink gets worse in the stomach.

Item: When the fish called the pike, which is to water what the wolf is to land, sees the net, it drives itself into the mud and though it is pierced, it will not go towards the net; so the rich and pleasure-seeking man, when he sees the cross, dives

---

[44] Galatians 5:17.

into worldly and fleshly pleasures as if into the mud, and though he is pierced by the sermons of preachers, he does not go to the net of God, namely the cross.

Item: Big fishes do not pass through the middle of the net, but when caught remain there; so rich men do not pass through the net of the devil, but remain caught in it. However, small fish pass through the net and escape to safety; and thus poor men pass through the temptations of the devil and come to the cross and so to God, who is the author of salvation. The nets of the devil are gluttony and lechery, pride, envy, greed, anger, perjury, false witness and a lying tongue etc.

Item: Many give the whole flower of their life to the devil, and in the end give the dross to God, for the Lord in his mercy accepts the coming to him of the inveterate harlot who is despised by the world.[45] For the Lord says, 'At whatever hour the sinner', and in Ezekiel, 'I do not want the death of the sinner etc. I do not want the death of one who dies, but I do want that he should be converted and live.'[46]

Item: Just as an ear of wheat, struck by lightning, reeks and is of no account, so also a man, struck by the lightning of lechery, is hidden in sin and empty of the grace of God and light of God just like the blackened and empty ear.

Item: A man in winter sees his own breath, but in summer not at all; so a man in adversity and misery sees himself, but never in the prosperity of riches and the pleasure of the flesh.

Item: Just as water falling to the ground does not return to the vessel whence it came, so neither does the impertinent sinner return to God, from whom he departed after baptism.

Item: A needle is compared to the penitent because it pierces, and to the person confessing his sins because it has an open hole, and to the person rising again from his sins because it penetrates and sews up the skin, which is made from a dead animal.

Item: The sinner is torn into as many parts as are those forbidden things to which his mind is distracted by consenting to them. Salvation is the opposite when his whole attention is concentrated on love for God and is sewn up for him by the needle of penitence.

Concerning the calling of men to the cross

Just as our Lord Jesus Christ, when he was on earth in the body, went about his Galilee, seeking the sick in order to heal them, so now does the Holy Spirit, calling the sick to the cross that again he may heal them because the Holy Spirit always advises inwardly that you should rise to the cross. But the flesh, the world and the devil also advise that you should rise. The devil knows that the Holy Spirit is oppo-

---

[45] Luke 6:37–50.
[46] Ezekiel 18:23.

site to him. Cut the snare of the devil, the flesh and the world dragging you down to Hell, and rise through the virtue of the Holy Spirit to the cross and thus to heaven.

Item: Our Lord, hanging on the cross, said, 'I thirst.'[47] He thirsted then for that on account of which he suffered, but he suffered on account of the salvation of sinners, for he says, 'I have not come to call the righteous, but sinners.'[48] Therefore he thirsted for the salvation of sinners, and thirsts for it still. So let someone arise and give him to drink, that is, let him offer body and soul to Christ; for that man is greatly wretched and greedy who refuses to give Christ a drink when he is thirsty and begging for a drink. Let him take on his shoulder the sign of the holy cross and say in his heart, 'O Lord I entrust myself to you, who cry out on account of me!'

Item: 'They gave him wine mixed with gall, and when he tasted, he did not drink.'[49] Through wine there is designated any pleasure whatsoever, 'for wine make glad the heart of man.'[50] So it is given to be understood that if fleshly or secular pleasures are given to you either from the birth of the world or from the devil, bitterness follows and is also mixed with them. When you have tasted them, you ought not to drink or wallow in them, like a fat pig in the stinking mire. But abandon them and follow Christ your redeemer, rise then from pleasures and run to the cross, whence you will receive the bread of life. Rise, you who are sleeping etc.[51]

Item: A pig devours the acorn and never looks up to the oak tree from which it gets the acorn, but always fixes its eyes and face on the earth. So also the wicked man, although he has all his benefits from the cross, never looks up to the cross, but fixes himself completely on worldly feelings. All our good things are from the cross because baptism is from the blood and water that flowed from the side of Christ, and also our redemption and salvation and particularly the goodness of clerics. You must not be the pig therefore, but rise and elevate the eyes of your heart to him crucified and hanging on the cross for you, and follow me! Eustace and Godfrey, Flemish knights and brothers, came in turn to the Holy Land, and in the process Godfrey received a serious wound and before he could be healed, the Christians began a campaign against the Saracens. Godfrey himself, weighed down with weakness from the wound, was not able to take part and therefore begged his brother Eustace not to enter the war, but to wait fifteen days until by the grace of God he had got his health back so that they might enter the war with strength re-

---

[47] John 19:28.
[48] Matthew 9:15.
[49] Matthew 27:34.
[50] Psalms 103.16.
[51] Although not quoting directly, the *Ordinacio* here alludes to John 6:48 and Ephesians 5:15.

newed. Wishing 'to be dissolved and be with Christ'[52], Eustace answered like a true soldier of Christ, 'I don't want to delay attacking the enemies of the cross because great advantage will be had by coming to God fifteen days sooner than you.' And he entered the war and became a martyr of God. When she heard this, their mother praised God that she had brought forth such a son who was obedient to him. The companions of the knight James of Avesnes said, 'All our friends are dying. Let us retreat from the Saracens', but James said, 'I will go there more willingly, and let no man restrain me.' Since therefore you are going to die, you must rise so that in death and through death we may find life!

Item: If someone with a treasure could not keep it always, but had perforce to be without it, and he in return for this treasure could justly and peacefully have some good town or greater good, surely he would be foolish to give it away utterly for nothing or doubtfully keep it in the hope of losing it. You have the treasure entrusted to you, namely earthly life, which you must go without because death is unavoidable for you. Since however you can have instead of it eternal joy and God, who is better than anything, you are foolish if you refuse it – therefore die on the cross for Christ, and you will have him! 'Rise therefore and take my cross etc.'[53] He became man in order to be partaker in eternal glory. The Lord calls you through the apostles and prophets and through us preachers in order that you may have, through taking up the cross, that which you were made for. Rise therefore etc.

Item: Anyone who is faithful seeks from the Lord forgiveness of sins and eternal rest. Our Lord offers you who are faithful what you seek of him provided that these come through contrition and confession. Rise therefore etc.

Item: What will you say to the Lord on that fearful day of judgement when he asks, 'Why were you unwilling to come to me when I ordered you? Beware lest he should say to you: "Amen, Amen I say to you I know you not." And lest he should say to you this horrible thing, "Go, accursed one, into everlasting fire."'[54] In order that you should be an obedient servant to your Lord, and secure on that dreadful day, obey the commandment which says, 'Follow me', and I warn you by the authority of him whose messenger I am that you should follow him. Break therefore the snares of falsehood, and arise in true faith and take the cross so that you can say on the day of judgement, 'Lord you have been on the cross for me, and I on the cross for you! You died for me, and I for you!' Arise therefore, servant of God, and because you are his servant, you are bound to obey him.

Item: God has known the secrets of our hearts. Therefore if anyone of us is such that he would wish to take up the cross for a time on behalf of the temporal kingdom of England or France, I call on him by the spilling of the blood of Jesus

---

[53] Matthew 16:24.
[54] Matthew 25:12.

Christ that he should take up the cross for the kingdom of heaven, which is eternal and infinitely better. Understand that 'the Lord is the examiner of hearts' and will be our judge. See that he does not say to you in judgement, 'You have preferred worldly things and for them you have put aside heavenly things.' Let this not be, and let him not say in reproach that which is in the canticle, 'Let our riches rise up and help you etc.'[55] Rise therefore etc.

Item: Zachariah says, 'Let him return to Jerusalem with mercy, and my house will be built on it.'[56]

Item: Our Lord complains through Micah that the devil snatches away so many in great numbers to hell, that Our Lord has few and collects them like one who 'collects bunches after the vine-pickers.' Micah says in the seventh chapter, 'Alas, that I have become like one who gathers bunches of grapes in the autumn.'[57] For the devil snatches away to himself in hell the proud, the envious, the covetous, the wrathful, the slothful, gluttons, lechers, perjurers, false witnesses, detractors, murderers, who die impenitent, and so many false Christians whom the Lord values little. Therefore to be otherwise with Christ and to elude the snares of the devil, rise with true contrition and devotion, and receive the sign of the cross upon you, and you will be the heir of Christ, confirmed to him by the cross as if by contract. In you he will live as if in his temple. For the apostle Paul says, 'the temple of God, which is you'.[58] And on Sundays we ask in prayer, 'Our Father, let thy kingdom come.' Namely let it come to you. If therefore men are his kingdom, he will reign in them. In order therefore that he himself should reign in you and that you should have him and eternal life, take up the cross and follow Jesus!

Item: In the final chapter of the Song of Solomon it says, 'Set me as a seal upon your heart, as a seal upon your arm, for love is strong like death.' Our Lord Jesus Christ here invites you to take the cross in both heart and deed. For he says, 'Set me,' namely crucified with three iron nails, pierced by a lance, scourged, derided by men, above your heart as a sign in compassion and faith. For the cross is the seal of the Lord, which the devil most fears because he was conquered and is still conquered in the cross, but 'because faith without works is dead,'[59] it is therefore added 'as a seal upon your arm', that is upon your work. Therefore be a pilgrim, follow, 'for love is strong like death.'[60] For the Lord says 'So strong is and was the love I had for you, O sinner, that it separated my soul from my body,' and death does not do anything except precisely that, because in order to redeem you to life

---

[55] Cf. Deuteronomy 32:38.
[56] Zachariah 1:16.
[57] Micah 7:1.
[58] 1 Corinthians 3:16.
[59] James 2:17.
[60] Solomon 8:6.

he destroyed death. In this we have known the love of God because he laid down his life for us.'[61] Therefore so great does your love for Christ become that it separates your soul from carnality and the pleasures of the flesh, just as death separates the soul from the body. Arise then, follow the Lord's command and assume the seal of the Lord, namely the cross, in both heart and work, and offer to God your body and soul which he gave you.

Item: Although vinegar is bitter, still it makes good the flavour of a sauce; so also the passion of the Lord, although it is bitter, sweetens our thoughts, conversations and works with compassion and gives them taste, which is love. And just as vinegar is penetrative and piercing, so the passion of the Lord penetrates the hard hearts of men and pierces them through compassion. Therefore you share the suffering of Christ on the cross and sweeten your works through the bitterness of the cross in order to have eternal life!

Item: It was said to Joshua after the destruction of Jericho, 'Raise the shield that is in your hand against the city of Hai.'[62] A shield is round; so also any faithful man will have a crown in heaven, which is signified by the crown of Christ. A shield has four corners and so does the cross. The highest corner is the faith by which we aspire to God, who is 'the fire consuming'[63] sins just as the fire destroys the tow. And because it is above, for that reason it says, 'Lift up your hearts.'[64] The lowest corner is the fear of the Lord, experienced for sins. 'I have always feared the Lord just likes the waves swelling above me.'[65] If the earth were to open at the approach of an earthquake, anyone would be afraid of being swallowed by it; much more greatly should the sounding of the trumpets of the Lord and the opening of hell be feared. The third corner is abstinence in face of prosperity lest a man should live in the earth like a mole. The fourth corner is patience in tribulation 'according to the multitude of my pains' and 'if I spoke, my foot was moved.'[66] In order therefore to be safe from Hell, lift up your shield that is the cross! Let these be in your hands for action, namely 'in work against the city of Hai.'[67] Cleave to the cross. The Lord says in the Gospel, 'Blessed are you that when they shall revile you etc., rejoice and exult since plentiful is your reward in heaven.'[68]

Item: Amos, 'The Lord built his ascension to heaven' with stone in the sepulchre, with iron and wood in the cross, by his wounds and blood. Whence in chapter five

---

[61] 1 John 3:16.
[62] Joshua 8:18.
[63] Deuteronomy 4:24.
[64] Joshua 2:2.
[65] Job 21:23.
[66] Psalm 93:18–19.
[67] Joshua 8:18.
[68] Matthew 5:11ff.

of the Song of Songs, 'Just like thy beloved, my beloved is white and ruddy', because he is white through innocence and red through blood.'[69]

Item: Further examples also may be invoked not only to make listeners pay more attention with the removal of boredom, but also so that they may be more moved by the example of others to contrition and may hold in greater contempt the deceitful emptiness of the world or something of this kind, for example. Three knights, who were brothers, were in the war against the Albigensians, and many of the faithful were being slain. So in tears two of them said to the third, 'Alas and alack, we shall all die today.' The third said to comfort his brothers, 'Let us die for him who died for us, for I should not be better prepared than by a day of penance.' Rise boldly therefore, and take the cross. A knight was captured by the Saracens and hung from a wall at which the Christians were firing stones to destroy it. And the Christians ceased fire because they were afraid of killing him as he hung there. Seeing this, the knight besought the Christians by the shedding of Christ's blood that they should not cease on his account, and therefore they did not cease, but fired a stone, which by the grace of God struck the ropes and bindings by which he was hanging from the wall, and broke them. And he was freed and ran safely towards the Christians. Do not despair of Christ, but having a firm faith in Christ and a desire to come to him, rise through the sprinkling of blood which he shed for us, and follow him on the cross. A knight in the war against the Saracens, who had been wounded by four men, heard, because the doctors were saying so, that his wounds were mortal. He took the arms which he had laid down and said, 'My Lord Jesus Christ suffered five wounds for me. I shall return to the war and suffer a fifth wound for him because I have suffered four times.' When he had put on his armour, he went back into the battle and killed many Saracens, and falling after a fifth wound, yielded up his spirit to Christ. So rise, you who wish to yield up your spirit to Christ. Another knight in the war against the Saracens, said to his horse, 'Blackie, Blackie, many times have you carried me into war with glory and victory, but never like today, because today you will carry me into eternal life.' And having slain many, he became a martyr in the Lord. Rise therefore and be a martyr of Christ since you should be what is necessary for you, namely that you should die. A knight, Hugo de Beauchamp by name, in the war against the Saracens was killed while carrying the true cross. He said: 'I was never in a *beau champ* until today although my name is Beauchamp. Rise so that you may arrive in the Beau Champ!' It was Ingerranus de Boves whom the knight addressed, saying, 'It is a cowardly knight who allows his feet sooner than his head to carry him from battle.' Ingerranus rose and took the cross; and many knights from among his kin and also others, seeing and hearing about this, likewise took the cross.

---

[69] Song of Solomon 5:9f.

26

Two catecheses on the office of monastic tonsure

Angela Constantinides Hero

Robert Jordan has translated five of the longest and most important *typika* in the Dumbarton Oaks translation of the Byzantine monastic foundation documents.[1] These texts, whose language I have described elsewhere as interesting to the philologist but a bitter cup to the translator,[2] certainly 'gained in translation'. In appreciation, therefore, of his outstanding contribution to the Dumbarton Oaks project I offer here a translation of two short catecheses on the meaning of the office of monastic tonsure by Neophytos *Enkleistos*, the founder of the monastery of the Holy Cross, known as the *Enkleistra* in Cyprus.[3]

The author

According to his *Testament*,[4] Neophytos was born in the village of Lefkara in Cyprus in 1134. At the age of eighteen he ran away from home seeking to avoid an arranged marriage and entered the monastery of St John Chrysostom on Mt Koutzovendis, where he was tonsured in 1152. Six years later, in pursuit of spiritual guidance, he travelled to the Holy Land and afterwards made an unsuccessful at-

---

[1] These are the *typika* of the monasteries of Evergetis, Kecharitomene, Pakourianos, Pantokrator and Phoberou.
[2] See A.C. Hero, 'A brief commentary on the language of the Byzantine monastic foundation documents', *Work and worship at the Theotokos Evergetis*, ed. M. Mullett and A. Kirby (BBTT, 6.2, Belfast, 1997), 262.
[3] My translation is based on Βίβλος τῶν κατηχήσεων, ed. B.K. Katsaros, Ἁγίου Νεοφύτου τοῦ Ἐγκλείστου Συγγράμματα, ed. I.E. Stephanes, P. Soteroudes and B.K. Katsaros, 2 vols (Paphos, 1998), II, 357–364. The pagination of the Greek text of the edition is indicated by square brackets in the English text of the translation, but the division into paragraphs is mine. Words that I have added to the translation to clarify the meaning have been placed in square brackets also. Scriptural passages follow the L.C. Brenton translation of the *Septuagint* (London, 1844) and the *Revised standard version* translation of the New Testament (New York, 1973).
[4] See '*Testamentary Rule* of Neophytos for the hermitage of the Holy Cross near Ktima in Cyprus', tr. C. Galatariotou, *Byzantine monastic foundation documents*, ed. J.P. Thomas and A.C. Hero, 4 vols (DOS, 35, Washington, DC, 2000), IV, 1349–1352; also Galatariotou's essential study, *The making of a saint: the life, times and sanctification of Neophytos the Recluse* (Cambridge, 1991).

tempt to visit the monastic community on Mt Latros, northeast of Miletos in Asia Minor. Upon his return to Cyprus in 1159, he withdrew to a cave on the mountains near Paphos where he carved out a cell, an altar and a tomb, intending to live in total isolation as a recluse (ἔγκλειστος). However, as his reputation for piety spread, he was joined there by a companion and later by other followers, and in time his hermitage (ἐγκλείστρα) developed into a monastery which is still in existence.[5]

Despite his lack of formal education,[6] Neophytos was a prolific writer.[7] Among his works that have come down to us is a collection of fifty-five catecheses, that is, short homilies addressed to the monks of his monastery and those in the monastery of St John Chrysostom on Mt Koutsovendis where his brother was the superior. As noted by their recent editor, [8] these texts attest to Neophytos's familiarity with the Scriptures, ascetic and patristic literature and the canons of the church councils. His language is a mixture of words, forms and constructions borrowed primarily from biblical Greek and occasionally from both classicising models and the vernacular. There is, however, a certain charm and freshness to his straightforward style and he demonstrates his exceptional understanding of the importance of conciseness and clarity in a sermon when he remarks that 'a short speech capable of holding a listener's attention is better than a fancy, long one.'[9]

In the two catecheses translated here he succeeds in presenting a succinct, step-by-step exegesis of the Byzantine rite of monastic tonsure which is still capable of holding the attention of the reader.

---

[5] For the history of the monastery after its founder's death and pertinent bibliography, see Thomas, Introduction to *'Testamentary Rule'*, BMFD, ed. Thomas and Hero, IV, 1339 and 1347. On the restoration of the monastery's wall-paintings conducted in 1963, see C. Mango and E.J.W. Hawkins, 'The hermitage of St Neophytos and its wall-paintings,' *DOP*, 20 (1966), 119–206.

[6] He writes in his *Testament* (Galatariotou, *'Testamentary Rule'*, BMFD, ed. Thomas and Hero, IV, 1350) that when he arrived at the monastery of St John Chrysostom on Mt Koutzovendis he did not know the first letters of the alphabet and was assigned to menial labour at the vineyard. But before his departure six years later, having mastered the elements of grammar, he was working in the church as assistant ecclesiarch.

[7] For a complete list of his works, see Galatariotou, *Making of a saint*, 251–281. A critical edition of his surviving works is being prepared by a team of scholars under Professor Demetrios G. Tsamis at the university of Thessalonike. Two volumes have appeared already; see *Neophytou Syngrammata*.

[8] See Katsaros's excellent introduction to Βίβλος τῶν κατηχήσεων, *Neophytou Syngrammata*, II, 113–118; 150–174.

[9] See the conclusion of the second catechesis below.

Translation
[p. 357] Catechesis 13
By the same a catechesis concerning the office of monastic tonsure and the renunciation of the world

Father, pronounce the blessing.

Fathers and brothers, the divine David says: 'Give heed, O my people, to my law; incline your ear to the words of my mouth. I will open my mouth in parables; I will utter dark sayings which have been from the beginning. All which we have heard and known and our fathers have declared to us.'[10]

I am not eager to 'utter dark sayings unknown to you from the beginning,' though I can myself say much from [the sayings and acts] of our most holy fathers of old about virtues high as heaven, supernatural achievements, divine and truly heavenly spirit, a life in the flesh equal to that of angels, a source of miracles such as that dwelling in Christ Himself and how through Him and according to His precepts they performed all the miracles that He performed. When I look at their angelic life and achievements and the divine grace inherent in them, I think of these men as earthly angels or heavenly men or most precious stones of the heavenly Jerusalem, while I consider myself a beast or a piece of wood or stone or clay or any other useless and unprofitable thing.

Therefore, I will bypass their divine achievements as old and hasten to bring to your attention new and recent [p. 358] and unforgettable achievements concerning, that is, your tonsure and renunciation of the world and profession of allegiance to Christ.

For this reason 'give heed' to my God-given sermon; 'incline your ear' to the words of God's grace and we shall recall to mind and inquire after and search for the meaning of our tonsure and our vows. We must, however, for the sake of clarity write some of what is said in the form of question and answer.

[Question]: Why does he who is being tonsured stand with his head uncovered and without girdle and shoes?[11]

[Answer]: The Fathers did not make these rules simply and without consideration, but following the Apostolic traditions. For [the Apostle] says: 'A man who prays must not cover his head, for he dishonours his head, since the head of man is Christ.'[12] and it is obvious to everyone that he who is to be tonsured comes to pray to Christ. For this reason he stands with his head bare, expecting to receive the helmet of salvation.

He stands without girdle because he has untied and removed the girdle of lust and desire and is about to be girded with the strength of chastity and self-control.

---

[10] Psalms 77 (78): 1–3.
[11] See Ἀκολουθία τοῦ μικροῦ σχήματος, *Euchologion sive rituale Graecorum*, ed. J. Goar (Venice, 1730; repr. Graz, 1960), 406.
[12] I Corinthians 1:3–4.

'Let your loins be girded' with the girdle of chastity and self-control, he says, and 'let your lamps be burning' and illuminating and driving away any work of darkness and be yourselves 'like a man who is waiting [for his master to come home]'[13] and so forth.

He stands barefoot because he must walk without wavering the clear road of God and by his good works proclaim the good news of peace. This is also a symbol of a humble and poor and modest way of life because Christ came in poverty and humility and 'had nowhere to lay his head.'[14] This is why [p. 359] he who is to be tonsured stands with his head uncovered, without girdle and without shoes in order to proclaim the humility and simplicity of the [monastic] life.

[Question]: Why does he not approach quickly the holy sanctuary, but [proceeds] little by little?[15]

[Answer]: This signifies that after removing the worldly girdle and renouncing the desires of the flesh, he proceeds spiritually little by little from strength to strength until he reaches the holy of holies[16] and enters as a 'faithful servant into the joy of his master.'[17]

[Question]: And why does he prostrate himself before the holy doors and rises again?

[Answer]: His prostration signifies two benefits: his escape from sin and his longing for the ascetic and angelic life. His rising also signifies two benefits: his rise above all sin associated with man's fall and his profession of a life according to God.

Let us now stop at this question and let us on the following Sunday recall to mind and consider exactly the rest of the topic concerning the secret meaning and the treasures of our monastic tonsure. And let us hasten to lead a life worthy of our habit and do nothing low and unworthy of such sublimity and dignity. Let us not by our deeds dishonour such honour and appear lacking in understanding. For he says: 'Man that is in honour understands not'[18] Created in 'God's image and likeness,'[19] he did not understand such honour and having done things unworthy of that great honour, he was then 'compared to the senseless cattle and is like them.'[20] And the fact that he was created [p. 360] in the image of God did not benefit him at all for he rendered it useless and betrayed the honour.

Let us, therefore, pay attention and understand the honourable dignity of our angelic habit and not dishonour it, for its dignity will be of no avail to us, just as

---

[13] See Luke 12:35–36.
[14] Matthew 8:20.
[15] See Goar, *Euchologion*, 389.
[16] Exodus 26:35.
[17] See Matthew 25:21.
[18] Psalms 48 (49). 21.
[19] Genesis 1:26.
[20] Psalms 48 (49):21.

the fact that our forefather was created in the image of God was of no avail to him after his transgression.

May the 'Lord of hosts'[21] give us a hand of assistance and strength and save us. 'To him be glory' and power 'for ever. Amen'[22]

[p. 361] Catechesis 14
By the same a catechesis continuing what was said last Sunday concerning the meaning [of the office] of monastic tonsure

Father, pronounce the blessing.

Brothers and fathers, with the help of God I wish to continue what I discussed last Sunday, which was the third question concerning the fact that he who is to be tonsured must prostrate himself [before the holy sanctuary] and then rise. The fourth question is as follows: What is the intent of questions and answers?[23]

[Answer]: They signify that we make vows to God regarding a second life and a second baptism because we sullied our former life and baptism through our sins. At the asking of him who baptised us at that time, we renounced Satan and all his works, all evil, that is, and impurity and swore allegiance to Christ the pure, to worship Him in purity and sincerity. But seeing that we made our vows at that time through some sponsors because we were infants and as we grew up we sinned, we are asked at the holy altar the same questions we were asked then at the sacred baptismal font. [p. 362] Through them we renounce the world, our parents, our brothers, our wives, our children, our relatives, our associates, our friends and simply everything associated with this world, and we vow to lead the monastic and virtuous life in Christ. We vow to remain in the monastery and persevere in the practice of asceticism until our last breath. We vow to preserve ourselves in chastity and abstinence and sanctity and to obey the superior and the entire brotherhood in Christ and 'to be patient in tribulation and distress'[24] for the love of Christ and eternal life.

While he who is being tonsured makes these and other vows, the superior addresses him. 'You see', he says, 'my brother, to whom you swear allegiance and whom you renounce! You see what promises you gave to Christ the Lord! For there are angels present who write down invisibly this profession of yours for which you will be held accountable at Christ's second coming.'

A fearsome threat, my brothers; a great danger for those who are not careful. The trial is frightful for those who do not lead an upright life. Great is the security of the vows because their violation is also a great, steep precipice.

---

[21] Psalms 58 (59):5.
[22] Romans 11:36.
[23] See Goar, *Euchologion*, 383.
[24] Romans 2:9; 12:12.

'Do not imagine,' says [the superior], 'that these professions of yours are mere words nor that they are delivered before men only, but before God, the angels and the holy altar.' You see whom you renounce: it is the devil, the world and all evil. And you vow to do good works before God for which you will render account at the second coming of Jesus Christ the Lord.

[Question]: Why does he who is being tonsured offer the scissors to the superior with his own hands?[25] [p. 363]

[Answer]: In order to make clear by this [gesture] that his decision is voluntary; that he was not prompted by force or necessity but chose willingly the benefit of monastic life which he desires.

[Question]: What does the cutting of hair signify?[26]

[Answer]: [It signifies] the severance of ties to the world and all evil and the change of life and allegiance to God through a second baptism. Because he was first baptised in the name of the Father and the Son and the Holy Spirit and failed to observe these vows, it is necessary for him to have his head shorn again in the name of the Father and the Son and the Holy Spirit and make second vows. If he observes these, he will re-invoke the first through the second; and if he preserves this second baptism unsullied, he will purify the first [baptism] through the second.

[Question]: Why is a lighted candle handed to him?[27]

[Answer]: Because at the holy baptism they light up candles and because the candle given to him is a symbol of chastity and prudence. And since the wise maidens will meet Christ the bridegroom[28] with candles of divine light, the candle is given to him who is being tonsured as a prefiguration of the divine light that he may emulate and attain the conduct of the wise maidens and enter with them into the joy of the bridechamber of Christ the bridegroom.

[Question]: Why do all the monks embrace him after he has received the monastic habit?[29]

[Answer]: This kiss is a most clear sign of joy and love. Of joy because the father of the prodigal son who came back after a sojourn in a far country [p. 364] received him and embraced him with genuine [affection] and kissed him tenderly. He put on him the robe he wore before and the entire household celebrated with joy,[30] for he says 'there is joy in heaven over one sinner who repents.'[31]

For these reasons they embrace him and because he has forsaken the world and the desires of the flesh and joined them in the monastic habit and practice of monasticism. And just as, according to the gospel, a woman rejoices after childbirth

---

[25] Goar, *Euchologion*, 407.
[26] Goar, *Euchologion*, 407.
[27] Goar, *Euchologion*, 411.
[28] See Matthew 25:1–13.
[29] See Goar, *Euchologion*, 386; 408.
[30] See Luke 15:11–24.
[31] Luke 15:7.

'because a child is born into the world,'[32] they too rejoice that a man came to them from the world, seeking regeneration through tonsure and being of one mind, one voice and one spirit with them. They are delighted and they kiss him because the kiss, as I said before, is a symbol of love and joy.

We shall again cut this sermon short and stop here. I like to make short, not long speeches, lest some in the audience weakened by standing grow weary and let their mind wander. For a short speech capable of holding the listener's attention is better than a fancy, long one. What we discussed today is sufficient profit for those who seek to profit. Next Sunday,[33] we shall finish weaving together the rest of these [instructions] and like a small web divided into many parts we shall complete [the explanation] of the meaning of [the office of] tonsure.

And let those who are in need of [spiritual] garments take from there and put on 'the robe of salvation and the garment of joy,'[34] for he says 'as many of you as have been baptised into Christ have put on Christ.'[35] You are, therefore, bearing Christ.

---

[32] John 16:21.
[33] The sermon for that Sunday has not survived.
[34] Isaiah 61:10.
[35] Galatians 3:27.

27

The liturgical *typikon* of Symeon of Sinai

Nancy P. Ševčenko

One of the relatively few liturgical *typika* to have survived from the Byzantine period is the one composed in 1214 by Symeon, archbishop of Sinai, for the use of his monastery. The original manuscript, still on Sinai, has not been edited, but sections of it were transcribed by Dmitrievskij, in volume III of his monumental collection of Byzantine liturgical texts.[1] Symeon's *typikon*, which is based on that of St Sabbas of Jerusalem, contains some information relevant to the history and topography of the monastery of Sinai. I will translate only those particular passages, thereby reducing the text even further, but with hopes that before too long someone will undertake an edition of the entire text.

This translation should be based not on Dmitrievskij's transcription but on the original manuscript, as was done by Robert Jordan for his translation of the *typikon* of the Evergetis monastery in Constantinople.[2] But the translation of a *typikon*, however partial and premature, was a tempting, if challenging, way to honour Dr Jordan, whose meticulous publication has brought welcome clarity to the Evergetis *typikon*. In this case, imitation should be seen as the sincerest form of flattery.[3]

---

[1] Sinai Ms. 1097. A.A. Dmitrievskij, *Opisanie liturgičeskich rukopisej*, 3 vols (Kiev and St Petersburg, 1895–1917, repr. Hildesheim, 1965), III, 394–419. According to Dmitrievskij, the codex has 134 folia, and measures .255 x .173 m. Sinai 1101, a manuscript dated 1311, and Sinai 1103 are later copies.
[2] R.H. Jordan, *The Synaxarion of the monastery of the Theotokos Evergetis. September to February* (BBTT, 6.5, Belfast, 2000).
[3] I have not inserted into my translation the helpful system of references to the various offices that are provided by Jordan in his volume. I have attempted to be consistent with his liturgical terminology, but have not always followed to the letter his translation of other phrases. For definitions of the liturgical terms used here, see the Glossary in Jordan, *Synaxarion of the monastery of the Theotokos Evergetis*, 571–583. Useful too is the 'Index liturgique' found in M. Arranz, *Le typicon du monastère du Saint-Sauveur à Messine* (Rome, 1969), 376–449. Sections in italic type here are based on Dmitrievskij's summaries of the parts he did not transcribe, or refer to sections of no apparent relevance to Sinai. Not all of the information provided by Dmitrievskij has been included. I wish to thank Dirk Krausmüller for his kind help with some of the more obscure lan-

Translation

Typikon after the model of the lavra of our saintly father Sabbas, of the monastery in Jerusalem, intended <for> and dedicated to the all-sacred and holy monastery of the supremely holy Theotokos, established on the holy mountain Sinai, wherein is also honoured the great God-seeing prophet Moses. It was newly acquired at the behest of its bishop, our most holy father the citizen of heaven and monk, lord Symeon. The month of February, the second indiction, the year 6722 (= a.d. 1214).[4]

Concerning the Θεὸς Κύριος [Ps. 117:27].... (At the end of **Vespers**), then we go to the grave of the saint, chanting the sticheron of the saint, and the priest says a prayer.[5]

Concerning **Apodeipna**. At **Apodeipnon**, when the sun is setting, twelve strikes of the heavy <hammer> give the signal, and the iron <one>, and the priest gives the Glory, and we begin the Trisagion[6]....

Concerning **Orthros**. At **Orthros**, forty strikes of the heavy <hammers> give the signal, then the iron <one>, and, once the candles are lit, the great semantron gives the signal, and the priest takes the censer and giving the Glory, he censes, chanting the Hexapsalmon and when it is finished, the synapte.[7]...

Concerning the **Liturgy**, *this is how it should....*[8] *Concerning the Allelouia, when we do not say the* Θεὸς Κύριος.[9] *Concerning* **Apodeipna**, *when we chant the Allelouia.*[10] *Concerning* **Orthros**, *when we chant the Allelouia.*[11]... *Concerning the akolouthia for Saturday, when we chant the Allelouia.*[12]... *Akolouthia of Great Lent: Cheese Sunday.*[13]...

Monday of the First Week (of Lent). At **Orthros**, toward the 10th hour or later, the heavy <hammers> and the iron <one> give the signal, and the lamps are lit, then the great <semantron> is sounded, and the priest gives the Glory and, with a censer, says the Trisagion.... The interval between the <great> semantron and the

---

guage of this text, though he should not be held responsible for any errors in translation that may remain.

[4] Dmitrievskij, III, 394. Regarding the date, see note 50 below.
[5] Dmitrievskij, III, 394–395. This final sentence was evidently taken over from the Sabbas typikon: it must refer to the tomb of St Sabbas in his monastery, not to anything at Sinai.
[6] Dmitrievskij, III, 395. I wish to thank Sysse Engberg for helping to clarify the various different sounds involved here. The missing feminine noun after 'heavy' was probably sphyra, a large iron hammer.
[7] Dmitrievskij, III, 395.
[8] Dmitrievskij, III, 395.
[9] Dmitrievskij, III, 395.
[10] Dmitrievskij, III, 395.
[11] Dmitrievskij, III, 395–396.
[12] Dmitrievskij, III, 396.
[13] Dmitrievskij, III, 396.

heavy <hammers> should be as long as <it takes> for the brothers to chant the Amomos [Ps. 118] in their cells.[14]

Akolouthia of **Vespers**. *Akolouthia of the* **Pre-sanctified**.... *Akolouthia of* **Apodeipna**.[15]

Concerning **Agrypnia**/The Procedure for **Agrypnia**.[16]... And we begin stichera of the prophet in the mode of the day, and we form a procession with censer and candles, the priest going first. After the end of the sticheron, the priest says aloud, so all can hear, Σῶσον, ὁ Θεός, τὸν λαόν σου [cf. Ps. 27:9],[17] the Kyrie Eleeson fifty times. Then the priest says aloud, 'Let us pray for the remission of sins of the servant of God, our archbishop Symeon...'. Fifty Kyrie Eleesons. After this, he says aloud, Ἐπάκουσον ἡμῶν ὁ Θεὸς ὁ Σωτὴρ ἡμῶν [Ps. 64:5]. And with us on bended knee, the priest prays aloud, Δέσποτα πολυέλεε.[18]... (After the brothers say Θεοτόκε παρθένε three times), the kandelaptes lays out three breads, from which the brothers eat, in the basket over the library. ... Note that from Easter to the feast of All Saints, it is the Acts (of the Apostles) that are read at this reading, while on the remaining Sundays of the year, it is the seven catholic (Epistles) and the fourteen Epistles of the holy apostle Paul, and the Apocalypse of the Theologos, if the abbot sees fit.[19]... When we have finished the morning prayer, the priest says out loud, Εἰρήνη πᾶσι, and we begin to chant in the customary way, and we go into the Holy Bush, and when we are inside the church of the Holy Bush, heads uncovered: Δέσποινα, πρέσβευε τοῦ σωθῆναι ἡμᾶς, ὅτι σὺ ἡ ἐλπὶς τῶν ἀπηλπισμένων καὶ καταφυγὴ τῶν ψυχῶν ἡμῶν. The priest <says> the ektene, 100 Kyrie Eleesons, and the priest makes the commemoration and dismisses.[20]...

Note that on 1 May we are to celebrate the remembrance of the great earthquake that took place through the loving kindness of our Saviour Jesus Christ, the one that crushed and crumbled up to no small extent not only the fortification walls of the monastery, but also the cells inside the monastery, levelling some to the foundations, crushing the others into pieces, lasting as though for days and days, so that we all forsook the monastery, and stayed in the desert, where we also raised the songs of thanksgiving to God the lover of mankind, Ὁ ἐπιβλέπων τὴν

---

[14] Dmitrievskij, III, 397.
[15] Dmitrievskij, III, 397–398.
[16] Dmitrievskij, III, 398–402. Here Dmitrievskij puts in parallel columns the information about the Agrypnia gleaned from fols. 7f and 16f respectively.
[17] Here, according to Dmitrievskij, the priest remembers Moses, Aaron and Elisha.
[18] Here, according to Dmitrievskij, the priest remembers Moses, Aaron, Elijah and Elisha and the megalomartyr Catherine.
[19] Dmitrievskij, III, 401–402.
[20] Dmitrievskij, III, 402.

γῆν καὶ ποιῶν αὐτὴν τρέμειν.[21] He did not neglect the appeal of us sinners, through His ineffable compassion and incomparable goodness, moved to pity by the entreaties of His servant the prophet Moses, and not rejecting the prayers of His supremely glorious and all holy Mother. On 1 May we are to hold for her an all-night **Agrypnia**. We keep a fast on that day until evening. If it happens that Pentecost falls on this day, let the **Divine Liturgy** be held at its (regular) time, and let the brothers take up their consecrated bread, and go to their cells, eating nothing else, but let them pray with a contrite heart and a clear conscience and to give thanks to our holy God. When evening comes, we are to eat the dry food, and perform the **Agrypnia**, and recite the whole Psalter, with the akolouthia of the prophet Moses, and on the morrow let there be a festive meal (agape) for the brothers.[22]...

Rule for the church service of our saintly father Theodosios the koinobiarch.[23] Procedure for the **Agrypnia**... we perform the usual processions in the Holy Bush, chanting stichera of the prophet.[24]...

Short ekphrasis of the church procedure of the monasteries in Jerusalem.[25]

Akolouthia of Great Lent.... Here we pray for the servant of God, our archbishop Symeon the monk, and for our entire brotherhood in Christ, as it is the custom to do always at His holy **Liturgy**... (on the fourth week of Lent), the encaenia of <the chapel of> the holy apostles Peter and Paul.[26]... Easter.[27]...

Note that on Thursday of this week (the week of Thomas, the second week after Easter), we are to celebrate our saintly father John of the Ladder, and on his behalf hold a festive meal (agape) for the brothers. Similarly, on 15 July we are to celebrate the encaenia of his church at the Phoukara, and to make a special meal (paraklesis) there, and to console the brothers who have gone there.[28] Similarly, on the feast of the great holy Forty Martyrs, we are to do the same at Ligaia, and we are to do it this way also at the encaenia of the church of those holy Forty Martyrs,

---

[21] The text of this *troparion* is given in full in the notice for 1 May below, Dmitrievskij, III, 416.
[22] Dmitrievskij, III, 402–403. Cf. 281–284 below.
[23] 11 January.
[24] Dmitrievskij, III, 403.
[25] Dmitrievskij, III, 403.
[26] Dmitrievskij, III, 403–404.
[27] Dmitrievskij, III, 406.
[28] This is probably the Fucra guaranteed to Sinai by Pope Honorius III in his bull of 1217 and by a succession of later popes. The bull of 1217 is addressed to our abbot Symeon of Sinai: A.C. Tautu, *Acta Honorii III (1216–1227) et Gregorii IX (1227–1241)* (Vatican, 1950), 35 (no.17); cf. 195 (no.148).

which is on the twelfth of the month of September.[29] We are to celebrate our saintly fathers this way as well.[30]...

Pentecost.[31] *Akolouthia of those Saturdays of the whole year on which there is the commemoration of a great saint and we chant the* Θεὸς Κύριος. ...*Akolouthia of the ecclesiastical psalmody of the whole year.*[32]

2 September. Contest (athlesis) of the holy priest-martyr Mamas and of our saintly father John the Faster, patriarch of Constantinople. Forefeast of the holy and great prophet Moses.[33]...

4 September. Contest (athlesis) of the holy priest-martyr Babylas, archbishop of Antioch, and of the three children with him, and of the holy priest-martyr Babylas, who became a teacher in Nikomedeia, along with his eighty-four children. This commemoration we are to chant the following day, on the fifth, after the commemoration of the prophet Zacharias. On this day itself we celebrate the great and God-seeing Moses. A **Great Agrypnia**. If it should be a Sunday, recitation of the continuous psalmody; but if it is not, we say the Μακάριος ἀνήρ [kathisma 1][34] in plagal mode 4, only the first antiphon. At the Κύριε ἐκέκραξα [Ps. 140:1], we intercalate eight stichoi and we chant the stichera in mode 4 to Ὡς γεννατον ἐν μάρτυσιν from his own akolouthia, another in plagal mode 1, and that too from the same akolouthia, three others <namely> those in the Menaion, *Glory*..., idiomelon in plagal mode 2. The all-sacred feast now follows. The Entrance, the prokeimenon of the day, the readings, the first from Exodus [Ex. 2:5] the second [cf. Ex. 3:1] <and> from Exodus [Ex. 33:11], the ektene, and the procession takes place, and during it we chant stichera in mode 3, from his akolouthia to Μεγάλη τοῦ σταυροῦ σου, Κύριε, ἡ δύναμις, idiomelon in plagal mode 2, Σήμερον ἡ οἰκουμένη πᾶσα. Both now..., theotokion in the same mode to Ἡ ἀπεγνωσμένη· Ἄκανθαν ἐπετρύγησεν ὁ προπάτωρ and we go to the larnax of St Catherine and there we chant stichera of the saint in plagal mode 2, at *Glory*, the Despotikon(?) Προτυπῶν τὴν ἀνάστασιν. *Both now*... theotokion, ektene, and deesis. And then we go into the church of the venerable Prodromos,[35] and, once we are inside, we chant stichera in plagal mode 4 Πρόδρομε τοῦ Σωτῆρος, *Glory*... in the same mode Ὅσιοι πατέρες, *both now*... theotokion Τὴν πάσεπτόν

---

[29] This is probably the Liiah which comes directly after Fucra and before Raython (Raithou) in the document of 1217 (see previous note).
[30] Dmitrievskij, III, 406–407.
[31] Dmitrievskij, III, 407.
[32] Dmitrievskij, III, 408.
[33] Dmitrievskij, III, 408; cf. 417.
[34] Μακάριος ἀνήρ, the opening words of Psalm 1, begin Kathisma 1, which consists of Psalms 1–8.
[35] This chapel contained the relics of the holy fathers of Sinai and Raithou: cf. p. 281 below.

σου κοίμησιν Παναγία Παρθένε, and then we go through the Beautiful Gate chanting stichera prosomoia of the prophet, at *Glory* Χαίρετε προφῆται τίμιοι, *both now*... theotokion Χαῖρε Μαρία Θεοτόκε, and then ektene Σῶσον, ὁ Θεὸς, τὸν λαόν σου [cf. Ps. 27:9] and so on, and after that we go into the Holy Bush, chanting the stichera Ἀνοιγέσθω ἡ πύλη τοῦ οὐρανοῦ σήμερον. Once we are in the chapel, we chant stichera in plagal mode 2, special to it, the first Δεῦτε ἀναβῶμεν and another, a second, to Ἡ ἀπεγνωσμένη. And when we have finished these, we chant another Δέσποινα, πρέσβευε. While we are all chanting the Despoina, we are all to stand with our heads uncovered until the ektene, and the 100 Kyrie Eleesons, and then the priest <says> the prayer Δέσποτα πολυέλεε and we begin stichera prosomoia of St Moses from his akolouthia, and chanting we return to the naos, *Glory* of the saint, *both now*... theotokion and apolytikion Καὶ ἐν πυρὶ παραδειχθεὶς καὶ ἐν σαρκὶ φανερωθεὶς τὸ Μωυσέως ἐδόξασας πρόσωπον τῆς ἐννόμου ἱερατείας τὸν Ἀαρὼν τύπον τῆς καινῆς ἀνέδειξας χάριτος, ταῖς αὐτῶν ἱκεσίαις Χριστὲ ὁ Θεὸς ἐλέησον ἡμᾶς.[36] And the dismissal takes place. If **Great Vespers** is to be chanted, we say Θεοτόκε παρθένε three times, and the blessing of the bread with the wine takes place, and we say the psalm Εὐλογήσω τὸν Κύριον [Ps. 33:1] and there is a reading.

Note that if this feast falls on a Sunday, it is preceded by the resurrection (stichera). At **Orthros** the usual recitation of the continuous psalmody, and the polyeleos [Ps. 134–35], the anabathmoi. If it is not a Sunday, the first antiphon of the 4th mode, prokeimenon of the Gospel, the Gospel for the fourteenth Saturday, the Gospel of Matthew, two canons of the saint in mode 1 Χριστὸς γεννᾶται, another in mode 3, another in the fourth, Θαλάσσης τὸ ἐρυθρατον πέλαγος, after the third ode a poetic kathisma, after the sixth the kontakion, and if there is time, a reading, exaposteilarion. At Ainoi, stichera prosomoia, *Glory* in plagal mode 4 Τῶν προφητῶν θεόπτα, *both now*... theotokion, Great Doxology, and dismissal. At the Liturgy, prokeimenon in mode 4 Σὺ ἱερεὺς εἰς τὸν αἰῶνα [Ps. 109:4], second stichos Εἶπεν ὁ Κύριος τῷ Κυρίῳ μου [Ps. 109:1], stichos Ῥάβδος εὐθύτητος [Ps. 44:7], the Apostle [cf. Hebr. 11:24]. Alleluia Μωυσῆς καὶ Ἀαρὼν ἐν τοῖς ἱερεῦσι [Ps. 98:6], second stichos Ἐπικαλοῦντι τὸν Κύριον [Ps. 98:6]. The Gospel according to Matthew (exact passage unidentified), koinonikon Ἀγαλλιᾶσθε δίκαιοι [Ps. 32:1].[37]...

---

[36] Text and translation in J. Mateos, *Le Typicon de la Grande Église*, 2 vols (Rome, 1962–1963), II, 20–21 (for the first Sunday of Lent).
[37] Dmitrievskij, III, 409–410. For other *troparia* in honour of Moses, see 417.

24 November. <Commemoration> of the holy martyr Aikaterine and of the holy martyr Merkourios.[38] The **Agrypnia** should follow its (own) procedure: After the recitation of the continuous psalmody Μακάριος ἀνήρ [kathisma 1], the Κύριε ἐκέκραξα [Ps. 140:1], we intercalate eight stichoi, and we chant stichera of the saint in mode 2, to Πανεύφημοι μάρτυρες. Another stichera in plagal mode 2, Ἡ ἀπεγνωσμένη διὰ τὸν βίον, and another of St Merkourios from the Menaion, to Κύριε ἐκέκραξα. *Glory* of the saint, *both now...* of the feast. At the stichon, stichera of the feast, *Glory* of the saint, *both now...* of the feast, and the procession takes place, and we go to the larnax of the saint, chanting the stichera of the Menaion. But if by chance the stichera of the Menaion are sung at the Κύριε ἐκέκραξα, we chant at the procession one of the two katabasia. *Glory* of the saint, *both now...* of the feast. Returning to the naos, we chant other stichera of the saint, *Glory* of the saint, *both now...* of the feast, apolytikion Ἡ ἀμνάς σου. And the ektene takes place. If we chant **Great Vespers**, the psalm Εὐλογήσω τὸν Κύριον [Ps. 33:1] and the consecrated bread is given out and there is a reading from the Acts of the Apostles. At **Orthros**, three kathismata of the continuous psalmody are recited, and the polyeleos [Ps. 134–35]. We read the martyrion of the saint. After <the> third <ode>, the kontakion of St Merkourios, after the sixth, the kontakion of the saint, canons of the saint, of the martyr and of the feast, <after> the ninth <odes>, the candles are given to the brothers.[39] At Ainoi, stichera of the saint, *Glory* of the saint, *both now...* of the feast, Great Doxology, and dismissal.[40]...

11 January: (an all-night vigil for St Theodosios) and the ektene takes place at the reliquary (theke) of our saintly father.[41]

14 January. <Commemoration> of our saintly and God-bearing fathers, those who were massacred at Sinai and Raithou. At this holy feast we celebrate a **Great Agrypnia** as follows: If it falls on a Sunday, we recite the continuous psalmody Μακάριος ἀνήρ [kathisma 1] preceded by the resurrection <stichera>; if it is not a Sunday, we do not recite the continuous psalmody, but after the psalm of **Lychnikon**, Κύριε ἐκέκραξα [Ps. 140:1] in the mode (of the day?), *Glory... both now...* theotokion. The Entrance with censer and two large candles, the prokeimenon of the day with a pair (of verses), readings <for> saintly <ones>, the first Δικαίων ψυχαί [Wisdom of Solomon 3:1], the second Δίκαιοι εἰς τὸν

---

[38] In the paragraph which follows, references to 'the saint' will automatically refer to St Catherine. References to Merkourios will be noted as such.
[39] The order is a bit confused here: it is the canons that are interrupted by *kontakia*, not the reading.
[40] Dmitrievskij, III, 411. For other *troparia* in honour of Catherine, see 417 and 418.
[41] Dmitrievskij, III, 412.

αἰῶνα [Wisdom of Solomon 5:15], the third Δίκαιος ἐὰν φθάσῃ [Wisdom of Solomon 4:7].[42] Then the Καταξίωσον and the procession goes out, we chant *Glory... both now....* The ektene takes place at the container for the candles in the church of the Prodromos, where rest the venerable and holy relics of our holy fathers, and from them there we go into the Holy Bush, chanting stichera of the Holy Bush, whichever seem best to the abbot, and from them there we return to the naos, we chant three stichera of the prophet Moses, *Glory... both now...* theotokion, a troparion of our holy fathers Ὁ Θεὸς τῶν πατέρων ἡμῶν the same one both at the Θεὸς Κύριος and at the end of **Orthros**. And the distribution of the bread takes place, then there is a reading, the martyrion of our holy fathers, then the Hexapsalmos, the usual recitations of the continuous psalmody, the polyeleos [Ps. 134–35], the anabathmoi, if it is not a Sunday, the first antiphon of the 4th mode, prokeimenon in plagal mode 2 Εὐφράνθητε ἐπὶ Κύριον [Ps. 31:11] a second stichos Μακάριοι ὧν ἀφέθησαν [Ps. 31:1], a third stichos Μακάριος ἀνήρ, ᾧ οὐ μὴ λογίσεται [Ps. 31:2], the Gospel <for> saintly <ones>, the 50(th Psalm), canons of the saints and of the Holy Bush, after the third ode, a poetic kathisma, after the sixth, the kontakion. The exaposteilarion. At **Ainoi**, stichera, *Glory* idiomelon, *both now...* theotokion, then the Doxology loudly, the Trisagion, the apolytikion, ektene, and we fortify ourselves according to custom, and <say> also the prayer loudly, and we go out in procession into the storeroom of the holy oil, which was made miraculous by our saintly father George,[43] chanting stichera of our saintly father George himself, *Glory... both now...* theotokion, then we return to the naos, and the ektene takes place and the final dismissal. At the **Liturgy**, typika, odes four and six of the canon of the saints, then the Entrance, apolytikion, *Glory... both now...*, the kontakion, prokeimenon Εὐφρανθήσονται δίκαιοι [Ps. 63:10],[44] the stichos Εἰσάκουσον ὁ Θεός [Ps. 63:1], the Apostle to the Galatians [Gal. 5:22, here preceded by 'Brothers'], allelouarion in mode 4 Ὁ Θεὸς ἐν τοῖς ὠσὶν ἡμῶν, [Ps. 43:1], Ἔσωσας γὰρ ἡμᾶς ἐκ τῶν θλιβόντων ἡμᾶς [Ps. 43:7], the Gospel for the saintly <ones>, koinonikon Εἰς μνημόσυνον αἰώνιον [Ps. 111:6]. Regarding the end of the feast period (apodosis),[45] it is as the abbot thinks best, if he thinks it best to do the apodosis along with the akolouthia and the **Agrypnia** of the fathers, if not, it will be done on the following day.[46]...

---

[42] These readings are found in the Menaia at Vespers for the feast of St Theodosios, 11 January.
[43] Dmitrievskij (III, 413, note 1), on the basis of Uspenskij, identifies this figure as George Arsilaites, a figure mentioned by John Climacus as his spiritual advisor (*PG*, 88:1112).
[44] Note there is a difference in wording: the Psalter has: Εὐφρανθήσεται δίκαιος (singular).
[45] The term refers to the end of an eight-day period of the celebration of a feast, in this case, the feast of the Baptism on 6 January.
[46] Dmitrievskij, III, 412–413. For other *troparia* in honour of the saints, see 418.

25 March: Annunciation; 30 March: John Climacus; 23 April: George.[47]

1 May. <Commemoration> of the holy prophet Jeremiah. At the **Lychnikon**, the usual akolouthia of the continuous psalmody, Κύριε ἐκέκραξα [Ps. 140:1], the stichera of the saint and of the day. On this day we are to give up the Octoechos and to chant the akolouthia of the saint and of the earthquake – see 26 October – the canons, a troparion in mode 2 Τοῦ προφήτου σου, Κύριε.[48] At **Orthros** the usual akolouthia. At the **Liturgy**, prokeimenon in mode 4 Σὺ ἱερεὺς εἰς τὸν αἰῶνα [Ps. 109: 4], stichos Εἶπεν ὁ Κύριος [Ps. 109:1], <for> the Apostle: the Catholic Epistle of James [5:10], allelouarion in mode 4 Μωυσῆς καὶ Ἀαρὼν ἐπεκαλοῦντο τὸν Κύριον [Ps. 98:6], The Gospel according to Luke, koinonikon Εἰς μνημόσυνον [Ps. 111:6].[49]

The same day we are to celebrate the memory of the terrible earthquake, which took place through <God's> love of mankind. It started in the morning, that is, of the first day of the present month, and went on all day long demolishing our monastery to no small extent and obliterating the cells, the towers and the wall. This earthquake happened in the year 6719 (a.d. 1211), the ninth indiction.[50] And we are to keep a fast from the thirtieth of the month of April, but the liturgy of the apostle is celebrated at its time,[51] and the brothers take their pieces of blessed bread (antidora) and go in their cells, keeping them until evening. In the evening they partake of them, and eat dry food. They are to perform a canon as well, all <of them> in their cells, each according to his own ability, giving thanks to the all-good and merciful God, the lover of mankind, on whose behalf He absolved us from his wrath. When the sun sets, the kandelaptes gives the sign, and we all assemble in the church, not a single brother absent, and the priest says Εὐλογητόν. And we begin the Trisagion and the rest, and then we begin the Μακάριος ἀνήρ [kathisma 1], and we say three kathismata, and then we begin the canons and first we chant the canon of the earthquake. If there is no canon of the earthquake, we chant a parakletikos <canon> to Christ, then <one> of the God-seeing prophet Moses, then of the Theotokos, and we say the first and third odes, then poetic kathismata from the canons, and then comes the reading. And once again we begin the Psalter and we say three kathismata and again the canons, odes four, five and six, and we say the kontakion of the Theotokos Τῇ ὑπερμάχῳ and the oikos, and

---

[47] Dmitrievskij, III, 413–414.
[48] The text is given in full, with translation, in the *Typikon of the Great Church*: Mateos, *Typicon*, I, 278, for 1 May.
[49] Dmitrievskij, III, 414.
[50] This date, as the ninth indiction, does not fit if the date of the typikon, 1214, is the second indiction, since an indiction is a fifteen-year period. For mysterious reasons Dmitrievskij has calculated the year 6619 as 1201, instead of 1211.
[51] The feast of St James, the brother of the Lord, celebrated on 30 April.

there is a reading. And again the last four kathismata of the Psalter and the remaining three odes of the canons, the priest <says> the ektene, and the procession takes place. And it goes into the Holy Bush, we chant stichera of the Holy Bush, and after the completion of the stichera, we say Δέσποινα, πρέσβευε τοῦ σωθῆναι ἡμᾶς, all of us standing with our heads uncovered. Then the deesis is made by the priest, 'That this holy monastery and every city and town may be spared from famine and pestilence, earthquake and flood, fire, foreign invasion and civil war: and that our all-good and merciful God may be gentle, benevolent and placable with respect to the multitude of our sins, and that the Lord God may avert from us every wrath and harm that comes to threaten us,' we say. And we start the 100 Kyrie Eleesons. The priest makes the commemorations, and we say *Glory* and sticheron of the prophet, *both now...* theotokion, and chanting stichera such as these, we come into the naos and the priest makes the synapte and dismisses.[52]

And the kandelaptes goes away and gives the signal, and we, having rested a bit, rise, and the priest says Εὐλογητόν, and we begin the Hexapsalmon in the usual way, the Θεὸς Κύριος [Ps. 117:27], and we do the akolouthia of **Orthros** in the usual way. We say at the **Agrypnia** a troparion of the earthquake in plagal mode 4 Ὁ ἐπιβλέπων τὴν γῆν καὶ ποιῶν αὐτὴν τρέμειν, ῥῦσαι ἡμᾶς τῆς φοβερᾶς τοῦ σεισμοῦ ἀπειλῆς, Χριστὲ ὁ Θεός, καὶ κατάπεμψον πλούσια τὰ ἐλέη σου πρεσβείαις τῆς παναχράντου Μητρός σου, ὡς μόνος φιλάνθρωπος.[53] Another in the same mode Ὑπερύμνητος εἶ, Χριστὲ ὁ Θεὸς ἡμῶν, ὁ σαλεύων τὴν γῆν εἰς τὸ ἐπιστρέψαι καὶ σωθῆναι τοὺς κατοικοῦντας ἐν αὐτῇ καὶ πάλιν στερεῶν αὐτὴν δι' ἀγαθότητα καὶ ἄφατον εὐσπλαγχνίαν, πρεσβείαις τῆς Θεοτόκου ἐλέησον ἡμᾶς.[54] At the **Liturgy** the akolouthia of the day and of the earthquake, allelouarion in plagal mode 1 Ὁ Θεὸς ἀπώσω ἡμᾶς [Ps. 59:1], stichos Συνέσεισας τὴν γῆν καὶ συνετάραξας αὐτήν [Ps. 59:2], and koinonikon. And when the **Divine Liturgy** has been celebrated, we go into the refectory <where> the festive meal (agape) takes place. This model is to be kept inviolate each and every year, and not to be impeded by anyone.[55]...

11 May: the anniversary of the city, and (commemoration) of the priest-martyr Mokios...; 31 July: Procession of the Cross.[56]

(At the end of the notice for 1 August): Note that after the completion of **Orthros** we perform the veneration of the precious and holy wood, following the

---

[52] Dmitrievskij, III, 415–416.
[53] Cf. Mateos, *Typicon*, I, 78–80 (text and translation), for 26 October.
[54] Cf. Mateos, *Typicon*, II, 50–52 (text and translation) for Friday of the fifth week of Lent.
[55] Dmitrievskij, III, 416.
[56] Dmitrievskij, III, 416.

order of the Third Sunday of Lent. After the dismissal, the precious cross goes in procession round the interior of the monastery, that is, to the abbot's quarters, the refectory, the cellars, the granary, the storehouse and all the cells of the brothers, then, when we return, the dismissal. At the **Liturgy** the water is blessed and we partake of it. After the dismissal of **Vespers**, the precious wood is brought back again to its container.[57]...

15 August: Koimesis... On this day we eat grapes which have been blessed by the priest, as is the custom; we celebrate this feast for nine days.[58]

Observations

The observations made here are preliminary and will need to be revised once the text of the entire *typikon* becomes available. The composition of the various offices, and their potential significance for liturgical history, will therefore not be treated here.[59]

Topography

The only sites outside the monastery that are mentioned are Phoukara, where there was a church of John Klimakus, and Ligaia, where there was a church of the Forty Martyrs. The Phoukara church celebrated its dedication (encaenia) on 15 July. At the Ligaia church, the feast of the Forty Martyrs was presumably celebrated on 9 March, and its encaenia surely on 12 September. At least some monks travelled to these sites on these feastdays. For mention of these sites, as Fucra and Liiah, in other contemporary sources, see notes 28 and 29 above.

Events

The earthquake of 1 May 1211 affected the perimeter wall of the monastery, including its towers, as well as the cells of the monks.[60] No deaths are reported, but the damage seems to have been considerable, and the liturgical response developed for the anniversary of this date is one of the most elaborate of all the akolouthiai described in the *typikon*. To my knowledge, this destruction has not been registered in the architectural history of the monastery.

Monastic areas

Mention is made of the abbot's quarters, the refectory, the cellars, granary, storehouse and monastic cells. These areas were visited one by one in the course of the

---

[57] Dmitrievskij, III, 416–417.
[58] Dmitrievskij, III, 417.
[59] One element is worth noting: the statement that, at the discretion of the abbot, the Apocalypse can be read at the Agrypniai on Sundays following the feast of All Saints, in place of the Epistles.
[60] For the problem of the date, see n.50 above.

procession of the True Cross on 1 August. Mention is also made of several sounds calling the monks to service: the heavy <hammer>, the iron <hammer or semantron?> and the great semantron.

The location of the chapel of saints Peter and Paul, whose encaenia was celebrated during the fourth week of Lent, is not given. There is no evidence that it was inside the monastery walls.

Church spaces and relics

Besides the naos of the church, mention is made of the larnax or tomb of St Catherine (located in the bema), of the chapel of the Prodromos, and of the chapel of the Burning Bush. The larnax is visited on the feast-day of St Catherine (24 November), and also on 4 September, the feast-day of Moses. On this day, 4 September, it would appear that the monks visited their various relics in sequence, including the relics of the Sinai and Raithou martyrs which were housed in the adjacent chapel of the Prodromos.[61] The latter relics were visited again, in the same place, on the feast-day of these holy fathers, 14 January. On this same day, 14 January, the monks also stopped by the place (unidentified) where oil was kept which had been made miraculous by a certain holy man George (possibly a monk of the sixth century). Mention is also made of a reliquary of St Theodosios the koinobiarch.

The chapel of the Burning Bush was certainly the most important of all these sites. A visit to it formed part of every Agrypnia, and to judge by the prayers offered there, it served as a chapel in which to address not only Moses, but the Virgin as well. The monks stood there with their heads uncovered.

Special venerations

Besides the Virgin, to whom the monastery was dedicated, the saints particularly venerated on Sinai were Moses, the Martyrs of Sinai and Raithou, and Catherine. The feast of Moses, on 4 September, was preceded by at least two days of forefeast, and the saints usually celebrated on that day, two priests by the name of Babylas, were shifted to 5 September. As was said above, the celebration of the feast of Moses included a visit to relics of the other special saints of Sinai as well. The feast of St Catherine on 24 November is less elaborate than that of the others: she shares the day with St Merkourios, and though there is an Agrypnia in her honour, it is not the Great Agrypnia awarded Moses and the Sinai martyrs. This may be the earliest evidence we have for the presence of her relics inside the monastery.

---

[61] The chapel, a pastophorion to the right of the apse and the chapel of the Burning Bush, is now dedicated to the holy fathers themselves, no longer to the Prodromos. For a plan of the church and its chapels, see *Sinai: treasures of the monastery of Saint Catherine*, ed. K.A. Manafis (Athens, 1990), 37.

The commemoration of the earthquake on 1 May was a major element in the liturgical calendar of this *typikon*, and was one of the longest services of all.

Symeon, the author of the *typikon*

Symeon wrote this *typikon* in 1214, but was active on behalf of Sinai even earlier. His energetic efforts to acquire Venetian and papal assurances that the monastery's possessions in Crete, Cyprus, Syria, etc., and the economic privileges once enjoyed by the monastery, would be protected by these authorities in the face of the Crusader occupation means that a number of Latin documents were addressed to Symeon in his capacity as archbishop of Sinai.[62] His exact dates are unknown. The damage caused by the earthquake must have made the protection of Sinai's income-producing Mediterranean possessions all the more vital.

---

[62] On Symeon, see N.P. Ševčenko, 'The monastery of St Catherine on Sinai and the cult of St Catherine', *Byzantium: faith and power. The symposium*, ed. S. Brooks (New York forthcoming), with bibliography. The earliest of these documents is one addressed to him in 1212 by the Doge of Venice, Pietro Ziani: G.L.F. Tafel and G.M. Thomas, *Urkunden zur älteren Handels- und Staatgeschichte der Republik Venedig mit besonderer Beziehung auf Byzanz und die Levante*, 3 vols (Vienna, 1856–1857, repr. Amsterdam, 1964), II, 146–150, no.233. See also n.28 above. This Symeon is not to be confused with the monk Symeon who travelled to Normandy from Sinai and ended his life in Trier, in 1035.

28

Politian's ode to Horace

Michael McGann

The works of Horace were first printed in the early 1470s, probably in Venice. In 1482 Cristoforo Landino published in Florence an edition with commentary, to which was prefaced an ode by Politian, a Latin and Italian poet of considerable talent. He was also like our *laudandus* a man of formidable learning. The ode celebrates the poet's rejuvenation, after long neglect, in the new edition. Horace has been given, in to-day's language, a makeover ('young... with pampered skin', *curata iuvenem cute*).

TO HORATIUS FLACCUS

Poet better than Thracian Orpheus
at stopping mobile streams
or leading wild beasts *and* their lairs
    with strumming thumb;

poet master of the lyre of Lesbos,
first to rouse Latin strings and
quick to label the guilty
    with black song:

who frees you from the barbarous fetter?
who has driven the cloud from your brow,
scraped the mould and brought you young to the dance
    with pampered skin?

Not long ago the clouds of old age
veiled you, but here you are now,
face bright and learned brow wreathed
        with fragrant flowers!

Just as the mild spring after chilly snow
restores to the glorious sun
the snake and her young
        with old skin sloughed:

So *Landino* rivalling the ancients
has restored you to the dance
for which you once played in damp Tivoli
        with sweet strings.

Now you can luxuriate in delight and
carefree sport. Now you can join bands
of boys or play among the girls
        with chattering lyre.

29

Alexandros Papadiamandis, *Love in the snow*

Kathryn Baird

Alexandros Papadiamandis (1851–1911) is one of Greece's most highly regarded writers of prose fiction. Born on the Aegean island of Skiathos, then on the geographical fringe of the newly founded Greek nation,[1] he spent most of his adult life in Athens, where he supported himself by translating fiction for newspapers and periodicals and by writing. His translations (of which there are over eighty) include Dostoevsky's *Crime and punishment* (1889), and works by European and American authors ranging from Alexander Dumas and Emile Zola to Mark Twain.[2] He also produced some one hundred and seventy of his own stories and sketches, which vary in length from two to one hundred pages.[3] Most are set on Papadiamandis's native Skiathos. Perhaps his best known work is the novella *Η φόνισσα* (*The murderess*, 1903), in which a troubled grandmother reviews her life of servitude to others. Concluding that all women in her traditional community must inevitably follow the same path, she commits a series of murders of little girls, believing that her deeds are acts of mercy.

Papadiamandis's stories often portray in some detail the traditional community of Skiathos. Depiction of such communities, a feature of most of the fiction published in Greece during the last two decades of the nineteenth century, came to be called *ethography*. Though Papadiamandis is often associated with this strand of realism, he was daring in his exploration of its possibilities and tended to emphasise the harsher aspects of the lives he was depicting, rather than sentimentalise his material, as some others did.[4] Among his admirers have been generations of writers, including Kostis Palamas and the Nobel Prize winning poet Odysseus Elytis, who

---
[1] A. Papadiamandis, *Tales from a Greek island*, tr. E. Constantinides (Baltimore and London, 1987), ix–xx.
[2] Th. G. Stavrou, 'Alexandros Papadiamantis: a Greek writer against the current', *A Greek diptych: Dionysios Solomos and Alexandros Papadiamantis*, by L. Coutelle, Th. G. Stavrou and D. R. Weinberg (Minneapolis, 1986), 63–97.
[3] A. Papadiamandis, *Άπαντα*, ed. N.D. Triandafyllopoulos, 5 vols (Athens, 1981–1988).
[4] R. Beaton, *Introduction to Modern Greek literature*, 2nd ed. (Oxford, 1999), 76–79.

wrote a long essay paying tribute to the 'magic' of his work.⁵ And he has been revered as the 'saint of modern Greek letters'⁶ whose work is imbued with the spirit of Greece and the Greek Orthodox tradition. Churches feature prominently in his work and the events of many of the stories (like those described in 'Love in the snow') take place against the background of religious festivals. His writing is rich in biblical allusion and through his diachronic use of Greek (embracing its ancient, biblical, Byzantine and contemporary forms) Papadiamandis turns to beautiful effect its wide range of vocabulary and linguistic register. For he wrote in a mixture of the archaising *katharevousa* and of demotic, his dialogue especially reflecting the language of the people, often the dialect spoken on Skiathos. The oral tradition is also reflected in his use of folk tale and song, as in the songs which are a feature of this story.

'Love in the snow' (1896) conveys a vivid sense of a small, traditional and tightly-knit community against the background of which Papadiamandis offers his readers an acute insight into the sufferings of Uncle Iannios. But the story is set at Christmas, a season of hope and salvation amidst the darkness of winter, and the symbolism with which it ends points to compassion and redemption.

I am fortunate enough to have been taught by Bob both at school, where he guided me through Homer, and at Queen's, where his sensitive direction of a rather rusty mature student opened a window on some of the joys of Byzantine literature, especially the writings of the sixth-century hymnographer Romanos the Melodist, also an inspiration to Papadiamandis.⁷ Bob's patient teaching has nurtured in me a love of Greek and influenced my encounter with the modern form of the language, including my reading of Papadiamandis. In this translation for him of a story considered to be one of Papadiamandis's greatest, I have tried to follow the original as closely as I can. On those occasions where long rhythmic sentences, lavish sound patterning, elaborate word order and change of register are difficult to render exactly I have made concessions to English and readability. I have attempted to achieve a consistency of tone and to catch both the mood and something of the exquisite use of language of a man who, for his biographer George Valetas,⁸ was none other than ὁ ποιητής, 'the poet'.

---

⁵ O. Elytis, *Η μαγεία του Παπαδιαμάντη* (Athens, 1978).
⁶ P. Charis, *Nea Estia*, 355 (Christmas 1941), 1.
⁷ N.A. Bees, 'Ῥωμανὸς ὁ Μελῳδὸς καὶ Ἀλέξανδρος Παπαδιαμάντης', *Nea Estia*, 355 (Christmas 1941), 29–33.
⁸ Valetas also prepared the first complete edition of Papadiamandis. See G. Valetas, *Ἀλέξανδρου Παπαδιαμάντη, Ἅπαντα*, 6 vols (Athens, 1972).

* * *

The heart of winter. Christmas. New Year. Epiphany.

And he'd rise in the morning, throw round his shoulders his old reefer jacket – the one garment still surviving from past years of good fortune – and go down to the market on the sea front. He'd be muttering as he trudged from the ramshackle house, loud enough for a neighbour of his – a woman – to hear him:

'He's all desire, not watery soup – a lover boy, not old and stooped.'

He said it so often that in the end all the local girls who heard him gave him the nickname, 'Uncle Iannios the lover boy'.

Of course he was no longer young, or handsome, and he had no money. He'd squandered it all many years ago, with the boat, at sea, in Marseilles.

That jacket had been with him at the beginning of his career, when he'd first enlisted as a sailor on his cousin's cargo boat. He'd bought a stake in that boat with his share of the journeys' profits, and then he'd bought his own boat, and made many fine voyages. He'd dressed in English felts, velvet waistcoats, top hats; he'd sported golden watch chains, he'd made money. But he went through it all in time with the Courtesans of Marseilles, and all that remained was the old reefer jacket, which he wore thrown round his shoulders, as he went down to the shore in the morning to enlist as a hand on some lugger, hired for a pittance, or go with some foreign boat to catch octopus in the harbour.

He had no one in the world. He was alone. He'd been married and become a widower, he'd had a child, and become childless.

And late in the evening, night-time, midnight, when he'd downed a few glasses to forget, or warm up, he'd return to the old ramshackle house, pouring out his pain in song:

> *My long and narrow alley,*
> *may your steep and slippery street*
> *lead me there where I will dally*
> *and my lovely neighbour meet.*

Sometimes he'd complain cheerfully:

> *Charming neighbour, lovely neighbour, chatterbox and liar,*
> *I've never heard you say the words 'It's Iannios I desire'.*

* * *

Deep winter, the sky overcast by day. Up on the mountains snow; sleet down on the plain. The mornings would put you in mind of the folk song:

It rains, it rains and soon will freeze,
and the priest's at the handmill if you please.

But it wasn't the priest who was turning the handmill, it was the neighbour, that chatterbox and liar of Uncle Iannios's song. Because this was the fact of the matter: the miller's wife worked with her hands, turning the handmill. At that time, you see, the local gentry thought it harmful to eat bread made with flour from a water or windmill and preferred it to be ground by hand.

And she had a great trade, that Chatterbox. She glowed, she had big eyes, and she had rouge on her cheeks. She had one husband, four children and a little donkey for carrying the flour. She loved them all – her husband, her children, her little donkey. It was only Uncle Iannios she didn't love.

Who would ever love him? He was alone in the world.

* * *

And he'd abandoned himself to love – love of his neighbour the Chatterbox – to forget his boat, the Ladies of Marseilles, the sea and her billows, his troubles, his extravagances, his wife, his child. And he'd abandoned himself to wine to forget his neighbour.

Often when he was coming back in the evening, night-time, midnight, and his long shadow – tall and thin, with the jacket coming loose and slipping off his shoulders – would reach forwards in front of him into the long, narrow alley, and the snow flakes – like white flies, like wisps of cotton – would be borne aloft in flurries and fall to the ground, he'd see the mountain turning white in the darkness and his neighbour's window, shuttered and mute, with a soft dim glow from the upstairs window. And he'd hear the handmill still turning, and the mill would stop, and he'd hear her tongue grind on and then he'd remember her husband, her children, her little donkey. She loved them all, yet she wouldn't give him a second look. And he'd get angry like a bee, spit like an octopus, and give way to philosophical thoughts and poetic images.

'If only love had arrows!... if only love had snares... if only love had flames... to pierce those windows with its arrows... to warm hearts... to set up snares in the snow... An Old Pheretzelis catching thousands of blackbirds in his nets.'

He imagined love as a sort of Old Pheretzelis, spending all day up there on the high, pine-shaded hill, busy setting traps in the snow, to catch innocent hearts, like the half-frozen blackbirds which search in vain for some last windfall left in the olive grove. The little, longish fruits have vanished from the wild olive trees on Varantas's mountain, the myrtles have vanished from the fragrant trees in Mamos's gully, and now the little singing blackbirds, with their dark plumage, and those sweet merles and the cheerful thrushes all end up as victims in Old Pheretzelis's traps.

* * *

One evening he'd be returning, not too much the worse for wear, and gazing at the Chatterbox's windows as he haunched his shoulders and mumbled:

'One God will judge us… and one death will part us.'

And then with a sigh he'd add:

'And one cemetery unite us.'

But before he headed off for sleep he couldn't help murmuring his usual song:

> *My long and narrow alley,*
> *may your steep and slippery street*
> *lead me there where I will dally,*
> *and my lovely neighbour meet.*

* * *

Another evening the snow had spread out like a sheet, all over the long and narrow little street.

'A white sheet… may it whiten us all in the eyes of God… and whiten us within, so that our hearts are free from evil.'

Dimly he was conjuring up an image, a vision, a waking dream. In which the snow would smooth out and whiten everything, all the sins, all of the past: the boat, the sea, the top hats, the watches, the golden chains and the iron chains, the whores of Marseilles, the extravagance, the bad luck, the shipwrecks. In which the snow would cover and purify and shroud them all, so that they wouldn't appear naked, with their throats exposed, like people coming out of orgies and Frankish dances, before the eye of the Judge, the Ancient of Days, the All Holy. In which it would whiten and shroud that little street, long and narrow, with its slippery slope and its foul smell, and the old tumbledown cabin, and the filthy, ragged jacket. It would shroud and cover the lovely neighbour, that chatterbox and liar, her hand mill, her friendly ways, her airs and her graces, her prattle and glow, her powder and rouge, her smile, her husband, her children, her donkey. Everything, let everything be covered, whitened and purified.

And another evening, the last, night-time, midnight, he came home drunker than ever.

He could hardly stand on his feet, or move, or get a breath.

The depth of winter, a tumbledown house, a broken heart. Loneliness, boredom, a wearisome, evil, uncaring world. Health ruined. His body battered, wasted, withering inside. He was no longer able to live, or feel, or know joy. He could find no solace, no warmth. He drank to get on his feet, he drank to take a step, he drank to fall over. He could hardly put one foot in front of the other.

He found the road. He recognised it. He tripped on a stone. He stumbled. He fell on his back with his legs in the air. He muttered:

'If only the fires had love!... if only the traps had snow...'

He could no longer form a logical sentence. He was confusing words and meanings.

He stumbled again. He steadied himself on a doorpost. Accidentally he touched the knocker. The knocker made a loud noise.

'Who is it?'

It was the door of his neighbour, the Chatterbox. Someone would probably think he'd been planning to get into her house, by fair means or foul. What else could they think?

Up above, lights and people moving about. Preparations were in hand it seemed. Christmas, New Year, Epiphany. The heart of winter.

'Who is it?' the voice asked again.

The window creaked. Uncle Iannios was just under the balcony, invisible from above. There's no-one there. The window was slammed shut. If only it had been a moment later.

Uncle Iannios was holding himself upright against the doorpost. He tried to recite his song, but the words appeared like scuppered ships in the waters of his mind.

'Chatterbox neighbour, long, narrow alley! ...'

He could hardly get the words out and they were almost inaudible. Lost in the bluster of the wind and the swirling of the snow.

'And I am an alley,' he muttered ... 'a living alley.'

He let go. He stumbled, teetered, keeled over and fell. He was spread out on the snow, and the length of his body took up the whole width of the long, narrow alley.

He tried once to get up, but then the stupor took over. He was finding a terrible warmth in the snow.

'The fires had love! ...the traps had snow!'

But the window had closed a moment before. A moment later and the Chatterbox's husband would have seen the man fall down in the snow. But he didn't see him. Not he, not anyone.

Snow fell on snow. And the snow piled up, lay two spans high, and formed a mound. And the snow became a sheet, a shroud.

And Uncle Iannios turned white, and fell asleep under the snow, so that he would not appear naked with his throat exposed – he and his life and his deeds – before the Judge, the Ancient of Days, the All Holy.

30

C.P. Cavafy: fourteen Byzantine texts and translations

Anthony Hirst

The fourteen poems on Byzantine themes presented here do not all have the same status in Cavafy's oeuvre. Six are from the 154 'acknowledged' poems of the 'Canon' – poems which Cavafy included in his own privately printed collections – and the titles of these six poems will be familiar to any reader of Cavafy: 'Byzantine Archon, exiled, versifying', 'Anna Dalassena', 'Anna Comnena', 'Manuel Comnenus', 'John Cantacuzenus prevails', and 'Of coloured glass'. The rest are poems which were never published by Cavafy himself. Three of these ('Fugitives', 'Theophilus Palaeologus', and 'It's taken') come from the late George Savidis's edition of the *Unpublished poems* (Ἀνέκδοτα ποιήματα, 1968), republished in augmented form as *Hidden poems* (Κρυμμένα ποιήματα, 1993) – a large and diverse group of more or less completed poems which Cavafy, for various reasons, withheld from publication. The other five ('From the *Secret history*', 'In the sixth or seventh century', 'The emperor Conon', 'The Patriarch', and 'At Epiphany') are from Renata Lavagnini's edition of the *Unfinished poems* (Ἀτελῆ ποιήματα, 1994), an important collection of thirty poems which Cavafy was actively working on in the last years of his life but never brought to the point where they satisfied his own exacting standards.

The Greek texts of the 'acknowledged' poems are not quite the same as those you will find in the current standard two-volume 'new' edition of George Savidis (*Τὰ ποιήματα*, 1991 and reprints). They are taken instead from Cavafy's own last printings of the poems and differ from Savidis's texts in certain details of orthography. With the 'unfinished' poems I have made some changes to Lavagnini's 'final texts', which are, in most cases, based on the latest near-complete version of the poem. I have been more adventurous than she was in incorporating later variants where they fit both the syntax and the metrics of the earlier draft. In the case of 'The Patriarch', the second paragraph is largely an addition to Lavagnini's text, constructed from a number of overlapping variants which appear, out of sequence, in the poet's notes. My alternative versions of the Greek texts of these 'unfinished' poems would not have been possible without Lavagnini's meticulous transcriptions and careful analyses of all the manuscripts. In the Greek texts of both the 'unpublished' and 'unfinished' poems I have rejected all of Savidis's and Lavagnini's modernisations or standardizations of what I know to be Cavafy's preferred orthographic practices.

I have published translations of some of these poems before in the context of critical articles, but here those translations have been thoroughly reworked. In the reworking, as in the translations that are new, I have striven for the 'impeccable iambics' (ἰάμβους ὀρθοτάτους) of Cavafy's exiled Byzantine Archon and, of course, of Cavafy's own Greek texts. My iambics, like Cavafy's (though less frequently) rely on synizesis: the running together, as one metrical syllable, of the vowel sounds of two syllables, either within a word or between words. In addition, mine sometimes rely on the variable syllabic count of many English words when spoken ('unnatural', for example, may be reduced to three syllables, 'blathering' to two), or allow a diphthong to count as two syllables (like the emphatic 'our' in the last line of 'Fugitives').

I am afraid that my use of Latin forms of Byzantine and ancient Greek personal and place names will strike Byzantinists as odd and retrogressive. My reason for preferring Latin spellings in the translation of poetry is that they fit more naturally into English, not only because of their long-established use, but also because of the greater affinity in the distribution of stress patterns between English and Latin (at least as pronounced by English speakers) than between English and Greek. In Cavafy's Byzantine poems, for example, there are many polysyllabic oxytone Greek names, such as 'Kantakouzenos' and 'Dalassene', which do not integrate well into English when (as in these translations) naturalness and the minimisation of foreignness are objectives.

These are by no means all of Cavafy's Byzantine poems (a matter, in any case, of definition), but they are the ones that deal most closely with issues of Byzantine polity and imperial power; the fruits, for the most part, of a major twentieth-century poet's critical engagement with various Byzantine (and later) historians. They include two poems ('In the sixth or seventh century' and 'Fugitives') which reflect the fading Greek culture of Cavafy's own city, Alexandria, in the Byzantine period, the first before the Arab conquest, the second after.

The fourteen poems are arranged here in historical sequence, from the reign of Justinian to the Fall of Constantinople, following Cavafy's observable practice in the historical portions of his thematic collections. Happily, in offering such texts and translations to Bob Jordan, historical annotation would be superfluous.

* * *

Τῆς ἀνεκδότου Ἱστορίας

Συχνὰ τὸ βλέμμα τοῦ Ἰουστινιανοῦ
φρίκην καὶ βδελυγμίαν ποιοῦσε στούς θεράποντάς του.
Κάτι ὑποπτεύονταν αὐτοὶ ποῦ δὲν τολμοῦσαν νὰ τὸ ποῦν·
ὅταν τυχαίως μιὰ νύχτα βεβαιωθῆκαν
πῶς ἦταν ἀπ' τὴν Κόλασι βγαλμένος δαίμων:
βγῆκεν ἀπ' τὸ δωμάτιό του ἀργά, καὶ περπατοῦσε
ἀκέφαλος στοῦ παλατιοῦ τοὺς διαδρόμους.

Τοῦ ἕκτου ἢ τοῦ ἑβδόμου αἰῶνος

Τὶ συγκινητικὴ ποῦ εἶναι ἡ Ἀλεξάνδρεια
τῆς τελευταίας ἐποχῆς. Τοῦ ἕκτου
αἰῶνος, ἢ στοῦ ἑβδόμου τὴν ἀρχὴ
πρὶν ἔλθει ὁ κραταιὸς ἀραβισμός.
Ἑλληνικὰ ὁμιλεῖ ἀκόμη, ἐπισήμως·
ὄχι πολὺ αὐθορμήτως, καὶ χωρὶς
ζωντάνια βέβαια, πλήν, ὡς κόσμιον,
τὴν γλῶσσα μας ἀκόμη ὁμιλεῖ.
Ἀπὸ τὸ Ἑλληνικὸν μοιραίως θὰ σβυσθεῖ·
μ' ἀκόμη ἐντὸς αὐτοῦ βαστιέται ὅσο μπορεῖ.
Δὲν εἶν' ἀφύσικον ἂν ἔτσι αἰσθηματικὰ
τὴν ἐποχή της ἀτενίζω αὐτὴν
ἐγὼ ποῦ Ἕλλην ποιητής, – κ' Ἕλλην δικός της
τὸ ἑλληνικόν μου ἔργον κάμνω στὸ ἔδαφός της.

Ὁ αὐτοκράτωρ Κόνων

Ἄ πατριάρχη ἀγαθέ, ἄ πατριάρχη ἐνάρετε
μὴ βαυκαλίζεσαι ποῦ εἶναι ἀδύνατον
καθαίρεσις νὰ γίνει τῶν ἁγίων εἰκόνων,
ἀφοῦ δὲν φάνηκεν ἀκόμη ὁ αὐτοκράτωρ Κόνων.

Ἄ πατριάρχη δυστυχῆ μὴ βαυκαλίζεσαι·
ὁ ἀπαίσιος Λέων, νά, μπῆκε στὴν αἴθουσα
καὶ τ' ὄνομά του τώρα θὰ σοῦ πεῖ.

From the *Secret History*

Often Justinian's stare evoked
in his attendants horror and repugnance.
Already they suspected something that they dare not name;
and then by chance one night they saw the proof
he was indeed a demon out of Hell:
emerging from his chamber very late, he walked
the palace corridors without a head

In the sixth or seventh century

How moving Alexandria is
in that last period. The sixth
or early seventh century
before the advent of the Arab power.
She still speaks Greek, officially.
Hardly spontaneously, and, to be sure,
without vitality, yet decently enough
she does still speak our language.
In much of the Greek world it's destined to die out,
but in this place it still holds on as best it can.
It's not unnatural if with such emotion
I contemplate *this* period of hers,
I, who, as a Greek poet – and one of *her* Greeks,
compose my Greek work on her soil.

The Emperor Conon

Ah, my good patriarch, my virtuous patriarch,
do not delude yourself, supposing it's not possible
that the destruction of the holy icons should begin
because the Emperor Conon has not yet appeared.

Ah, my unhappy patriarch, do not delude yourself;
the hateful Leo – see! – has come into the chamber
and is about to tell you what his name is.

Φυγάδες

Πάντα ἡ Ἀλεχάνδρεια εἶναι. Λίγο νὰ βαδίσεις
στὴν ἴσια της ὁδὸ ποῦ στὸ Ἱπποδρόμιο παύει,
θὰ δεῖς παλάτια καὶ μνημεία ποῦ θ' ἀπορήσεις.
Ὅσο κι ἂν ἔπαθεν ἀπ' τοὺς πολέμους βλάβη
ὅσο κι ἂν μίκραινε, πάντα θαυμάσια χώρα.
Κ' ἔπειτα μ' ἐκδρομές, καὶ μὲ βιβλία,
καὶ μὲ σπουδὲς διάφορες περνᾶ ἡ ὥρα.
Τὸ βράδυ μαζευόμεθα στὴν παραλία
ἡμεῖς οἱ πέντε (μὲ ὀνόματα ὅλοι
πλαστὰ βεβαίως) κι ἄλλοι μερικοὶ Γραικοὶ
ἀπ' τοὺς ὀλίγους ὅπου μείνανε στὴν πόλι.
Πότε μιλοῦμε γιὰ ἐκκλησιαστικὰ (κάπως λατινικοὶ
μοιάζουν ἐδῶ), πότε φιλολογία.
Προχθὲς τοῦ Νόννου στίχους ἐδιαβάζαμε.
Τὶ εἰκόνες, τὶ ῥυθμός, τὶ γλῶσσα, τὶ ἁρμονία.
Ἐνθουσιασμένοι τὸν Πανοπολίτην ἐθαυμάζαμε.
Ἔτσι περνοῦν ἡ μέρες, κ' ἡ διαμονὴ
δυσάρεστη δὲν εἶναι, γιατί, ἐννοεῖται,
δὲν πρόκειται νἆναι παντοτεινή.
Καλὲς εἰδήσεις λάβαμε, καὶ εἴτε
ἀπὸ τὴν Σμύρνη κάτι γίνει τώρα, εἴτε τὸν Ἀπρίλιο
οἱ φίλοι μας κινήσουν ἀπ' τὴν Ἤπειρο, τὰ σχέδια μας
ἐπιτυγχάνουν, καὶ τὸν ῥίχνουμεν εὐκόλως τὸν Βασίλειο.
Καὶ τότε πιὰ κ' ἐμᾶς θἄρθ' ἡ σειρά μας.

Βυζαντινὸς Ἄρχων, ἐξόριστος, στιχουρῶν

Οἱ ἐλαφροὶ ἂς μὲ λέγουν ἐλαφρόν.
Στὰ σοβαρὰ πράγματα ἤμουν πάντοτε
ἐπιμελέστατος. Καὶ θὰ ἐπιμείνω,
ὅτι κανεὶς καλλίτερά μου δὲν γνωρίζει
Πατέρας ἢ Γραφάς, ἢ τοὺς Κανόνας τῶν Συνόδων.
Εἰς κάθε ἀμφιβολίαν του ὁ Βοτανειάτης,
εἰς κάθε δυσκολίαν στὰ ἐκκλησιαστικά,
ἐμένα συμβουλεύονταν, ἐμένα πρῶτον.
Ἀλλὰ ἐξόριστος ἐδῶ (νὰ ὄψεται ἡ κακεντρέχης
Εἰρήνη Δούκαινα), καὶ δεινῶς ἀνίων,
οὐδόλως ἄτοπον εἶναι νὰ διασκεδάζω

Fugitives

It *is* still Alexandria. Just take a stroll
along the central street that leads towards the Hippodrome,
and you'll see palaces and monuments that will amaze you.
And even though it's suffered damage in the wars,
and though it's shrunk a bit, it's still a marvellous place.
Besides, what with excursions and our books
and various themes for study, time goes by.
We gather in the evenings by the shore,
the five of us (all with invented names
of course) along with certain other Greeks
among the few who've stayed on in the city.
Sometimes we talk of church affairs (here people seem somewhat
inclined towards the Latin view), and sometimes literature.
The other day it was some lines by Nonnus we were reading.
Such images, such rhythm, such expression, and such harmony.
Enthralled, we were extolling the Panopolite.
And so our days go by; our sojourn here
is not unpleasant, for, you understand,
there is no question it could last forever.
We've had good news, and whether something happens now
in Smyrna, or in April
our friends advance from Epirus, our plans
are working out, and we can easily get rid of Basil.
And then it will be *our* turn at last.

Byzantine Archon, exiled, versifying

Well, let the frivolous now call me frivolous.
To serious matters I was always most
attentive. And I shall maintain
that no one knows more thoroughly than I
the Fathers, or the Scriptures, or the Canons of the Councils.
In every doubt Botaneiates had,
in every problem in ecclesiastical affairs,
he'd seek *my* counsel, mine before all others'.
But exiled here (may that malevolent
Eirene Doucaina be cursed), and so abominably bored,
it's hardly inappropriate that I amuse myself

ἑξάστιχα κι ὀκτάστιχα ποιῶν–
νὰ διασκέδαζω μὲ μυθολογήματα
Ἑρμοῦ, καὶ Ἀπόλλωνος, καὶ Διονύσου,
ἢ ἡρώων τῆς Θεσσαλίας καὶ τῆς Πελοποννήσου·
καὶ νὰ συνθέτω ἰάμβους ὀρθοτάτους,
ὅπως - θὰ μ' ἐπιτρέψετε νὰ πῶ - οἱ λόγιοι
τῆς Κωνσταντινουπόλεως δὲν ξέρουν νὰ συνθέσουν.
Αὐτὴ ἡ ὀρθότης, πίθανον, εἶν' ἡ αἰτία τῆς μομφῆς.

Ἄννα Δαλασσηνὴ

Εἰς τὸ χρυσόβουλλον ποῦ ἔβγαλ' ὁ Ἀλέξιος Κομνηνὸς
γιὰ νὰ τιμήσει τὴν μητέρα του ἐπιφανῶς,
τὴν λίαν νοήμονα Κυρίαν Ἄννα Δαλασσηνὴ -
τὴν ἀξιόλογη στὰ ἔργα της, στὰ ἤθη -
ὑπάρχουν διάφορα ἐγκωμιαστικά:
ἐδῶ ἂς μεταφέρουμε ἀπὸ αὐτὰ
μιὰ φράσιν ἔμορφην, εὐγενικὴ
«Οὐ τὸ ἐμὸν ἢ τὸ σόν, τό ψυχρὸν τοῦτο ῥῆμα, ἐρρήθη».

Ἄννα Κομνηνὴ

Στὸν πρόλογο τῆς Ἀλεχιάδος της θρηνεῖ,
γιὰ τὴν χηρεία της ἡ Ἄννα Κομνηνή.

Εἰς ἴλιγγον εἶν' ἡ ψυχή της. «Καὶ
«ῥείθροις δακρύων» μᾶς λέγει «περιτέγγω
«τοὺς ὀφθαλμούς..... Φεῦ τῶν κυμάτων» τῆς ζωῆς της,
«φεῦ τῶν ἐπαναστάσεων». Τὴν καίει ἡ ὀδύνη
«μέχρις ὀστέων καὶ μυελῶν καὶ μερισμοῦ ψυχῆς».

Ὅμως ἡ ἀλήθεια μοιάζει ποῦ μιὰ λύπη μόνην
καιρίαν ἐγνώρισεν ἡ φίλαρχη γυναῖκα·
ἕναν καϋμὸ βαθὺ μονάχα εἶχε
(κι ἂς μὴν τ' ὁμολογεῖ) ἡ ἀγέρωχη Γραικιά,
ποῦ δὲν κατάφερε, μ' ὅλην τὴν δεξιότητά της,
τὴν Βασιλείαν ν' ἀποκτήσει· μὰ τὴν πῆρε
σχεδὸν μές' ἀπ' τὰ χέρια της ὁ προπετὴς Ἰωάννης.

by making six- and eight-line verses –
that I amuse myself with legends
of Hermes, Dionysus and Apollo, or the heroes
of Thessaly and the Peloponnese;
nor yet that I compose impeccable iambics,
the like of which – if you'll forgive my saying so –
Constantinople's scholars never could compose.
It's this impeccability, no doubt, that is the cause of the reproach.

Anna Dalassena

The Golden Bull Alexius Comnenus issued
to honour most conspicuously his mother,
the very clever Lady Anna Dalassena –
remarkable both in her works and ways –
contains a number of encomiastic passages;
here, though, let us extract from them
a single sentence, beautiful and noble:
"Neither of those cold words 'mine' and 'thine' was ever uttered."

Anna Comnena

Anna Comnena, in the Prologue
to her *Alexiad*, laments her widowhood.

Her mind is reeling. "And
with floods of tears," she tells us, "do I bathe
mine eyes . . . . but oh what stormwaves" in her life,
"oh what rebellions." She is seared by grief
"unto the bones and marrow and the soul's undoing".

The truth, however, seems to be that only one
grave sorrow did this power-hungry woman know,
one single deep regret was all she had
(though she may not acknowledge it), this proud Greek Lady, who,
with all her ingenuity, had not contrived
to obtain the empire for herself, but almost from her very hands
it had been taken by that upstart John.

Μανουὴλ Κομνηνὸς

Ὁ βασιλεὺς κὺρ Μανουὴλ ὁ Κομνηνὸς
μιὰ μέρα μελαγχολικὴ τοῦ Σεπτεμβρίου
αἰσθάνθηκε τὸν θάνατο κοντά. Οἱ ἀστρολόγοι
(οἱ πληρωμένοι) τῆς αὐλῆς ἐφλυαροῦσαν
ποῦ ἄλλα πολλὰ χρόνια θὰ ζήσει ἀκόμη.
Ἐνῶ ὅμως ἔλεγαν αὐτοί, ἐκεῖνος
παληὲς συνήθειες εὐλαβεῖς θυμᾶται,
κι ἀπ' τὰ κελλιὰ τῶν μοναχῶν προστάζει
ἐνδύματα ἐκκλησιαστικὰ νὰ φέρουν,
καὶ τὰ φορεῖ κ' εὐφραίνεται ποῦ δείχνει
ὄψι σεμνὴν ἱερέως ἢ καλογήρου.

Εὐτυχισμένοι ὅλοι ποῦ πιστεύουν,
καὶ σὰν τὸν βασιλέα κὺρ Μανουὴλ τελειώνουν
ντυμένοι μὲς τὴν πίστι των σεμνότατα.

Ὁ Πατριάρχης

Ὁ αὐθάδης κι ὁ ἀχάριστος Ἰωάννης
ποῦ ἂν ἦταν πατριάρχης τὸ χρωστοῦσε
στὴν καλωσύνη ποῦ τοῦ εἶχε δείξει
ὁ κύρ Ἰωάννης Καντακουζηνὸς
(ὁ ἄξιος ἄνθρωπος ποῦ εἶχε ἡ φυλή μας τότε
σοφός, ἐπιεικής, φιλόπατρις, ἀνδρεῖος, ἱκανός)
τόν ἔξυπνον τάχα ἔκαμεν ὁ ἀσυνείδητος
ὁ πατριάρχης κ' εἶπε πῶς θὰ μεριμνήσει
γιὰ νὰ ξαναγίνει τὸ ἄδικο
τοῦ Ἰωάννη Λάσκαρη (μὴ νοιώθοντας
ὁ ἐλαφρός, τὶ προσβολὴ μεγάλη
ἦταν τὰ λόγια του γιὰ τὴν ἀρχὴ
τῶν Παλαιολόγων). Ἐγνώριζε
βεβαίως ὁ ἄθλιος ποῦ κίνδυνον
κανένα δὲν διέτρεχεν ὁ θρόνος κ' ἡ ζωὴ
τοῦ ἀνηλίκου κὺρ Ἰωάννη Παλαιολόγου
ἀπὸ τὸν τίμιον καὶ τὸν εὔορκον
κὺρ Ἰωάννη Καντακουζηνόν.

Τὤξερε ὁ ἄθλιος, μὰ γύρευε

Manuel Comnenus

The emperor Lord Manuel Comnenus
one drear September day
felt death nearby. The court
astrologers (well paid) were blathering on
about the many years he still had left to live.
But even as they're speaking, he
recalls old pious customs
and from the monks' cells he commands
ecclesiastical apparel to be brought,
and puts it on, rejoicing to present
the reverent aspect of a priest or monk.

Happy are all those who believe
and like the emperor Lord Manuel meet their end
dressed in their faith most reverently.

The Patriarch

The insolent and the ungrateful John,
who, if he was patriarch, owed it
to the kindness shown to him
by milord John Cantacuzenus
(the worthy man our race had at that time,
wise, clement, patriotic, brave and able) –
supposing he was being clever, the unscrupulous
patriarch announced that he'd take care
there was no repetition of the injustice
done to John Lascaris (not thinking,
the blockhead, what a huge affront
his statement was to the authority
of the Palaeologi). And of course
he was aware, the wretch, that the under-age
Lord John Palaeologus ran no risk
to either throne or life
from the honourable and loyal
John Cantacuzenus.

He knew it, the wretch, but sought

μέ κάθε τρόπο νὰ δημοκοπεῖ
κ' ἐδήλωσεν ὅτι θὰ προνοήσει
νὰ μὴ ξανακουστεῖ στὸ κράτος ὅσα ἐν
«τοῖς ἀνωτέρω γεγένηται χρόνοις δι' ἀφέλειαν
»καὶ ῥαθυμίαν τοῦ τηνικαῦτα πατριαρχεύοντος
»Ἀρσενίου. Ἐγὼ» (ἐ γ ώ ! ὁ καμπόσος)
«τοίνυν ἀντιλήψομαι τῶν κοινῶν
«ὁμοῦ τῇ βασιλίδι» (τὰ προκόψαμε!) «πραγμάτων
»ἐγὼ καὶ τῆς τοῦ νέου βασιλέως
προστήσομαι σωτηρίας».

Στὰ Φῶτα

Ὅταν στὰ Φῶτα ἑτοίμασαν τὰ ἴδια πάλι
ποῦ εἶχαν κάμει τὰ Χριστοῦγεννα,
ὅταν ξανάφεραν τὴν κανάγια τους,
σκοπεύοντες ἐκ νέου νὰ παρακινήσουν
στὸν δῆμο τὸ παιδὶ (ἀλοίμονο
τὸν Ἰωάννη τοῦ καλοῦ κὺρ Ἀνδρονίκου
ποῦ ἔπρεπε αὐτὴ κι ὁ γιός της νὰ τὸν ἔχουν)-

ὅταν στὰ Φῶτα ἑτοίμασαν τὰ ἴδια πάλι·
τοῦ ὄχλου πάλι τὲς χυδαῖες βρισιὲς
καὶ τοὺς ἀχρείους ὑπαινιγμοὺς γι' αὐτήν.
δὲν βάσταξε τὴν ἀγωνία γιὰ δεύτερη φορὰ
καὶ μὲς στὴν παληοκάμαρη ποῦ ἦταν φυλακισμένη
ξεψύχησε ἡ Καντακουζηνή.

Τὴν τελευτὴ τῆς Καντακουζηνῆς, τὴν τόσο οἰκτρά,
ἐπῆρα ἀπὸ τὴν Ἱστορία τοῦ Νικηφόρου Γρηγορᾶ.
Στὸ Ἱστορικὸν ἔργον τοῦ βασιλέως
Ἰωάννη Καντακουζηνοῦ κάπως ἀλλέως
γράφεται· ἀλλὰ ὄχι ὀλιγότερα λυπητερά.

by every means to play the demagogue
and made it clear that he'd ensure
the empire would not be disturbed again by such things
as had "in former times occurred through the naivety
and indolence of the then patriarch
Arsenius. I myself" (*myself* – oh what presumption!)
"shall, therefore, with the empress, take in hand
the affairs of state" (and we had made a mess of them!)
"and I shall make the safety of the young emperor
my first responsibility."

At Epiphany

When at Epiphany they set in train the selfsame things
that they'd already done at Christmas,
when once again they got their rabble out,
intending to parade the child
before the populace once more (alas
poor John, heir to the worthy Lord Andronicus,
whose care by rights would have been hers, hers and her son's) –

when at Epiphany they set in train the selfsame things,
again the vulgar insults of the crowd
and base insinuations touching her,
she did not face the agony a second time
but in the shabby chamber where they held her prisoner
Lady Cantacuzena breathed her last.

Lady Cantacuzena's sorry end
I took from the *Historiae* of Nicephorus Gregoras.
In Emperor John Cantacuzenus' work
of history, in somewhat different terms
it is described, but no less piteously.

Ὁ Ἰωάννης Καντακουζηνὸς ὑπερισχύει

Τοὺς κάμπους βλέπει ποῦ ἀκόμη ὁρίζει
μὲ τό σιτάρι, μὲ τὰ ζῶα, μὲ τὰ καρποφόρα
δένδρα. Καὶ πιὸ μακρυὰ τὸ σπίτι του τὸ πατρικό,
γεμάτο ροῦχα κ' ἔπιπλα πολύτιμα, κι ἀσήμικό.

Θὰ τοῦ τὸ πάρουν - Ἰησοῦ Χριστέ! - θὰ τοῦ τὰ πάρουν τώρα.

Ἄραγε νὰ τὸν λυπηθεῖ ὁ Καντακουζηνὸς
ἂν πάει στὰ πόδια του νὰ πέσει. Λὲν πῶς εἶν' ἐπιεικής,
λίαν ἐπιεικής. Ἀλλ' οἱ περὶ αὐτόν; ἀλλ' ὁ στρατός; -
Ἤ, στὴν κυρία Εἰρήνη νὰ προσπέσει, νὰ κλαυθεῖ;

Κουτός! στὸ κόμμα νὰ μπλεχθεῖ τῆς Ἄννας -
ποῦ νὰ μὴν ἔσωνε νὰ τὴν στεφανωθεῖ
ὁ κὺρ Ἀνδρόνικος ποτέ. Εἴδαμε προκοπὴ
ἀπὸ τὸ φέρσιμό της, εἴδαμε ἀνθρωπιά;
Μὰ ὡς κ' οἱ Φράγκοι δὲν τὴν ἐκτιμοῦνε πιά.
Γέλοια τὰ σχέδια της, μωρὰ ἡ ἑτοιμασία της ὅλη.
Ἐνῶ φοβέριζαν τὸν κόσμο ἀπὸ τὴν Πόλι,
τοὺς ρήμαξεν ὁ Καντακουζηνός, τοὺς ρήμαξε ὁ κὺρ Γιάννης.

Καὶ ποῦ τὸ εἶχε σκοπὸ νὰ πάει μὲ τοῦ κὺρ Γιάννη
τὸ μέρος! Καὶ θὰ τὄκαμνε. Καὶ θᾶταν τώρα εὐτυχισμένος,
μεγάλος ἄρχοντας πάντα, καὶ στεριωμένος,
ἂν ὁ δεσπότης δὲν τὸν ἔπειθε τὴν τελευταία στιγμή,
μὲ τὴν ἱερατική του ἐπιβολή,
μὲ τὲς ἀπὸ ἄκρου εἰς ἄκρον ἐσφαλμένες του πληροφορίες,
καὶ μὲ τὲς ὑποσχέσεις του, καὶ τὲς βλακεῖες.

John Cantacuzenus prevails

He sees the lands he still commands,
the grain, the animals, the orchard trees.
And in the distance his ancestral home,
well stocked with costly furniture and clothes, and silverware.

They'll take them from him – Jesus Christ! – they'll take them from him now.

Cantacuzenus would perhaps take pity on him,
were he to go and fall down at his feet. They say he's clement,
clement to a degree. But those around him? And the army?
Or should he fall before the Lady Eirene, plead with her?

Imbecile! – ever to have got mixed up in Anna's party –
would Lord Andronicus had never lived
to marry her. What benefits did we receive
from all her carryings on, or what consideration?
Not even the Franks respect her any more.
Her plans were laughable, her strategy was stupid.
While from inside the City they kept threatening all and sundry,
Cantacuzenus demolished them, demolished them, Lord John.

And to think that he had meant to side with Lord John's faction!
And would have done it. And been well off now,
still the great nobleman, his place secure,
if, at the last minute, that prelate had not swayed him,
with all the prestige of his sacred office,
with those disclosures, false from start to finish,
with all his promises and twaddle.

Ἀπὸ ὑαλὶ χρωματιστὸ

Πολὺ μὲ συγκινεῖ μιὰ λεπτομέρεια
στὴν στέψιν, ἐν Βλαχέρναις, τοῦ Ἰωάννη Καντακουζηνοῦ
καὶ τῆς Εἰρήνης Ἀνδρονίκου Ἀσάν.
Ὅπως δὲν εἶχαν παρὰ λίγους πολυτίμους λίθους
(τοῦ ταλαιπώρου κράτους μας ἤταν μεγάλ' ἡ πτώχεια)
φόρεσαν τεχνητούς. Ἕνα σωρὸ κομάτια ἀπὸ ὑαλί,
κόκκινα, πράσινα ἢ γαλάζια. Τίποτε
τὸ ταπεινὸν ἢ τὸ ἀναξιοπρεπὲς
δὲν ἔχουν κατ' ἐμὲ τὰ κοματάκια αὐτὰ
ἀπὸ ὑαλὶ χρωματιστό. Μοιάζουνε τουναντίον
σὰν μιὰ διαμαρτυρία θλιβερὴ
κατὰ τῆς ἄδικης κακομοιριᾶς τῶν στεφομένων.
Εἶναι τὰ σύμβολα τοῦ τὶ ἤρμοζε νὰ ἔχουν,
τοῦ τὶ ἐξ ἄπαντος ἤταν ὀρθὸν νὰ ἔχουν
στὴν στέψι των ἕνας Κὺρ Ἰωάννης Καντακουζηνός,
μιὰ Κυρία Εἰρήνη Ἀνδρονίκου Ἀσάν.

Θεόφιλος Παλαιολόγος

Ὁ τελευταῖος χρόνος εἶν' αὐτός. Ὁ τελευτῖος τῶν Γραικῶν
αὐτοκρατόρων εἶν' αὐτός. Κι' ἀλλοίμονον
τὶ θλιβερὰ ποῦ ὁμιλοῦν πλήσιον του.
Ἐν τῇ ἀπογνώσει του, ἐν τῇ ὀδύνῃ
ὁ Κὺρ Θεόφιλος Παλαιολόγος
λέγει «Θέλω θανεῖν μᾶλλον ἢ ζῆν».

Ἄ Κὺρ Θεόφιλε Παλαιολόγο
πόσον καϋμὸ τοῦ γένους μας, καὶ πόση ἐξάντλησι
(πόσον ἀπηύδησιν ἀπὸ ἀδικίες καὶ κατατρεγμὸ)
ἡ τραγικές σοῦ πέντε λέξεις περιεῖχαν.

Of coloured glass

One detail moves me greatly in the crowning at Blachernai
of John Cantacuzenus and Eirene,
the daughter of Andronicus Asan.
Because the precious stones they had were few
(great was the poverty of our unhappy empire),
they were adorned with artificial ones, a mass of little bits
of glass, red, green and blue. There's nothing
humiliating or improper,
in my opinion, about these little bits
of coloured glass. But rather they are like
some doleful testament against
the unjust ill-fate of those being crowned.
They are the symbols of what it was fitting they should have,
of what, above all, it was right that they should have
when they were crowned, a milord John Cantacuzenus, a milady
Eirene, daughter of Andronicus Asan.

Theophilus Palaeologus

This the last year. And he the last
of the Greek emperors. Alas
how dismally those round him talk.
In his despair, in his affliction,
milord Theophilus Palaeologus says,
"I'd rather die than live."

Ah, Lord Theophilus Palaeologus,
how much of the anguish of our race, and how much weariness
(how much attrition through injustice and oppression)
did those five tragic words of yours contain.

Πάρθεν

Αὐτὲς τὲς μέρες διάβαζα δημοτικὰ τραγούδια,
γιὰ τ' ἄθλα τῶν κλεφτῶν καὶ τοὺς πολέμους,
πράγματα συμπαθητικά· δικά μας, Γραικικά.

Διάβαζα καὶ τὰ πένθιμα γιὰ τὸν χαμὸ τῆς Πόλης
«Πῆραν τὴν Πόλη, πῆραν την· πῆραν τὴν Σαλονίκη».
Καὶ τὴν Φωνὴ ποῦ ἐκεῖ ποῦ οἱ δυὸ ἐψέλναν,
«ζερβὰ ὁ βασιληᾶς, δέξια ὁ πατριάρχης»,
ἀκούσθηκε κ' εἶπε νὰ πάψουν πιὰ
«πάψτε παπάδες τὰ χαρτιὰ καὶ κλεῖστε τὰ βαγγέλια»
πῆραν τὴν Πόλη, πῆραν την· πῆραν τὴν Σαλονίκη.

Ὅμως ἀπ' τ' ἄλλα πιὸ πολὺ μὲ ἄγγιξε τὸ ᾆσμα
τὸ Τραπεζούντιον μὲ τὴν παράξενή του γλῶσσα
καὶ μὲ τὴν λύπη τῶν Γραικῶν τῶν μακρυνῶν ἐκείνων
ποῦ ἴσως ὅλο πίστευαν ποῦ θὰ σωθοῦμε ἀκόμη.

Μὰ ἀλοίμονον μοιραῖον πουλὶ «ἀπαὶ τὴν Πόλην ἔρται»
μὲ στὸ «φτερούλν' ἀθε χαρτὶν περιγραμμένον
κι οὐδὲ στὴν ἄμπελον κονεύ' μηδὲ στὸ περιβόλι
ἐπῆγεν καὶ ἐκόνεψεν στοῦ κυπαρίσ' τὴν ῥίζαν».
Οἱ ἀρχιερεῖς δὲν δύνανται (ἢ δὲν θέλουν) νὰ διαβάσουν.
«Χέρας υἱὸς Γιανίκας ἐν» αὐτὸς τὸ παίρνει τὸ χαρτί,
καὶ τὸ διαβάζει κι ὀλοφύρεται.
«Σίτ' ἀναγνώθ' σίτ' ἀνακλαίγ' σίτ' ἀνακρούγ' τὴν κάρδιαν.
Ν' ἀοιλλῆ ἐμᾶς νὰ βάϊ ἐμας ἡ Ρωμανία πάρθεν».

It's taken

These last few days I have been reading some demotic songs,
about the exploits of the klephts, about the battles,
engaging matters, and our own, and Greek.

And I've been reading dirges for the ruin of the City.
"They took the City, took it; took Salonica as well."
And then that Voice, which, while those two were chanting
"the patriarch upon the right, upon the left the emperor",
was heard commanding them to cease,
"O priests, now put away your books, and close the Holy Gospels"
they took the City, took it; took Salonica as well.

And yet what moves me more than all the others is the song
from Trebizond with its peculiar language
and all the sorrow of those far-off Greeks,
who had perhaps gone on believing we might still be saved.

But no, alas! A bird of fate "from out the City came"
and in "its wing a little scroll and covered all in writing,
not in the vineyard would it sit, nor yet inside the garden,
it went and sat itself upon the ground beside the cypress."
The prelates can't – or else they will not read.
"A widow's son Yanikas is" and he takes up the scroll,
and reads it and then cries aloud.
"And now he reads, and now he weeps, and now he beats his breast.
Alack for us. Ah, woe is us. Byzantium is taken."

31

From the *Holy Mountain Journal* of Angelos Sikelianos

Anastasia Psoni

Angelos Sikelianos (1884–1951) was born in Lefkada, one of the Ionian Islands, which, since they had never been under the Ottoman rule, had become a cultural centre and a channel for western ideas and literary developments to filter through to independent Greece. A separate intellectual and artistic tradition developed in the Ionian Islands, so that we can speak of an Ionian School in literature. Sikelianos may be regarded as the last heir to this distinct tradition.

Angelos Sikelianos is one of the most enigmatic and least understood figures in Modern Greek literature, and it is only recently that his work has been the subject of serious research. He is generally considered to be a traditional poet, but there is more in his poetry than such a simple definition suggests: the lyrical element is strong and is often combined with a mystical intensity. The life force in Sikelianos's poetry appears abundant and inexhaustible; everything in the natural world, including humans, is seen as part of the cosmos celebrating in unison the sacredness of being alive. The poet is the seer and hierophant who can connect with a creative divine power. This visionary quality, though, makes much of his highly allusive and metaphorical poetry difficult to read, decipher or translate. In his poetry Sikelianos attempts a synthesis of ancient Greek religion and Byzantine Christianity. He believed that Christianity was a natural development of ancient Greek religion.

Deeply aware of the mystical aspects of Christianity, Sikelianos sought the experience of a spiritual retreat; and in 1914, with his friend Nikos Kazantzakis, the poet set out on a journey around Greece which ended on Mt Athos, where they stayed from 15 November to 25 December, that is, for the forty days of the Christmas Fast which ends with the Liturgy on Christmas Day.[1] Sikelianos's journey to Athos followed closely on the outbreak of First World War, and it is

---

[1] The rules of fasting are of a rigour that would astonish many western Christians, but we need to be aware of them if we are really to understand Sikelianos's spirituality. See T. Ware, *The Orthodox Church* (Harmondsworth, 1964), 306–307.

possible that the poet felt the urgent necessity of concentration and contemplation. Sikelianos was thirty years old at the time; Kazantzakis, thirty-one.

During his stay in the Holy Mountain, Sikelianos wrote down his thoughts, his impressions and his vision. It is interesting to note, that, while he stayed there during the winter months, both the printed dates in the German pocket diary he was using for his journal and some of his entries suggest that the visit took place in the spring and summer. Konstantoulaki-Hantzou, who edited the Greek text of the *Journal*, admits that his vision of Easter in the midst of winter and the celebration of life expressed in the journal entries is surprising.[2] It is possible that the poet may have wanted to indicate that this was a purifying experience leading to a creative rebirth, in line with the symbolism of spring.[3]

For this translation, I have selected those entries, beginning with the start of the journey to Athos, which I thought showed more clearly Sikelianos's philosophical and metaphysical attitude as well as his mystical nature. The journal contains dates printed in German which show the month and the day of the month, but not the day of the week or the year, though Sikelianos alludes to the year and gives actual dates in certain entries.[4] The printed dates may or may not have had some significance for Sikelianos.

In this journal Sikelianos makes references to various writers and poets that appealed to him. Most of these are writers who had developed a mystical view of life which they expressed in their work.[5] I have tried to locate the references when possible but certain writers, known to the poet at that time, have since faded away into obscurity.[6]

---

[2] See A. Sikelianos, *Το Αγιορείτικο Ημερολόγιο*, ed. I. Konstantoulaki-Hantzou (Athens, 1988), xvi.

[3] Under '30 März', for example, he writes: *Πάσχα. Αήττητοι και/ροί ήρξαντο*, and under '30 Juni', *αιώνια άνοιξη, οι μαργαρίτες, τ'αρώματα του χορταριού*.

[4] For example, under '11 Juli', he writes '6 Δεκ. 914' (i.e. 6 Dec. 1914).

[5] For more information, see Sikelianos, *Το Αγιορείτικο Ημερολόγιο*, vii–xvii.

[6] Editorial note: as mentioned above, Sikelianos's *Holy Mountain Journal* is written in a German pocket diary. The *Journal* begins on the page for '1. Januar' and ends on the page for '21. September'. In her published transcription, the Greek editor, Konstantoulaki-Hantzou, reproduced the German dates at the top of each page. They are retained here in numerical form and in square brackets as though they were folio numbers ('[25.2]' for '25. Februar', etc.). The diary appears to have included one or two undated pages at the end of some months. Here, the undated pages following 31.5 and 30.6 are numbered 31.5a and 30.6a.

Most of the *Journal* is in prose, ranging from the extremely prosaic (a reminder to buy a certain book, for example) to the highly poetic, but there are also a few short passages in verse. Verse is clearly distinguished in the text below, being indented and set in italics. In the remainder of the text, the layout seeks to represent, but not to imitate, the organisation of the published transcription of the Greek. The Greek editor reproduced not only the

From the *Holy Mountain Journal*

[25.2] On the boat to the Holy Mountain. The sunset through glasses and the light dim. We are leaving Thessalonike. Peace returns to my body.

[26.2] The Holy Mountain

Karyes. Tragos.[7]

The golden plane trees.

The streams – the waterfall; opposite – strawberry trees – blossoms and fruit; the stone-paved ascent. Thoughts coming from the crown of the race; from the crown of the individual. The senses all pure again.

[27.2] Karyes. Protaton. ... [1.3] The corridors through which they take us to gaze at the sea in the moonlight; outside on the veranda. The rattling of pebbles. The meadow extending to the sea.

[2.3] Easter. The sea. For the first time! The sea of the Lord. The holy dolphins.

The sea, full of sea monsters surrounds us.

The Serbian priest, so very [3.3] pale.

> *God's ocean, far and wide.*
> *Thunder battered the waves.*
> *Like the Holy Spirit, above it*
> *Hung the moon.*

[4.3] Tornikios (1025).[8] In the library of Iviron. The Portaïtissa[9] who was brought by the sea; Gabriel recovered her (829). [5.3] Her arrival; the foam

---

pagination but also all the line breaks of the original manuscript. While the translator would have preferred to follow this layout as closely as possible, including printing the German dates in full, I felt that this would make the translation unnecessarily difficult to read; besides, it would have spread the text over almost forty pages of this book.

Apart from the page and line breaks, and the indentation of the second part of lines of verse which break across two lines of text, the only other organisational feature in the Greek edition is the use of blank lines. These presumably correspond to spaces or other indications of discontinuity in the manuscript, and might be said to mark off paragraphs (though some of these 'paragraphs' consist of only a single word). These blank lines are the basis of the paragraph divisions in the translation below. The page breaks of the original are indicated by the parenthetic numerical dates, but line breaks are not observed, except in the passages of verse. Where text is omitted from the translation this is indicated either by ellipses within paragraphs or by wider gaps between paragraphs (AMH).

[7] Billy-goat. The monastic rules of Athanasios formulated in the first *Typikon* were written on goatskin. E. Tsigaridas, Ἅγιον Ὄρος, Λογοτεχνικά κείμενα για το Ἅγιον Ὄρος (Thessalonike, 1991), 7.

surrounding her. Gabriel is watching her from afar. Dolphins are playing all around her.

[6.3] The gold embroidery in the Sanctuary, the double-headed eagle; the heavy Gospel book.

Panagia[10]

Aphrodite

[7.3] The sword blade was well-crafted and flexing like the tail of a fish struggling inside the net.

[10.3] …Vigil of the Entry.[11] To the ringing of the bells we went down, as if angels were holding us [11.3] by the armpits. The courtyard in the moonlight.

The phiale.[12]

p[.]s. The armpit, a source of laughter. Chrism[13] in the joints etc. etc.

Frankincense with rose water.

[12.3] Synaxarion. The sky could not contain him, but a woman did.

O Pitcher![14]

---

[8] The name of an eminent Byzantine family. All known family members held important offices in the Byzantine state. The reference indicates the 'great Tornikios', who, with a wealthy Georgian, John the Iberian, founded the monastery of Iviron in the tenth century. See Tsigaridas, Ἅγιον Ὄρος, 7–8.

[9] Our Lady of the Portal, referring to a very old icon which had been thrown into the sea by its owner, a Byzantine lady, to protect it from destruction by iconoclasts. Floating, the icon reached the shores of Athos near Iviron monastery. Monks of the monastery were told in a dream to recover the icon from the waters and, led by a golden light, they found it and they placed it in the monastery church. But the icon left the church three times, taking up a position near the gate. In the end, the monks left the icon there, but built a little temple for her. According to tradition, a pirate struck the icon with his sword and the wound began to bleed. The stunned pirate repented and converted to Christianity. A red mark on the Virgin's face can still be seen on the icon. A Russian copy is kept in Agia Triada, Moscow, with the name Iverskayia (Mother of Iviron). See P.K. Chrestou, *Το Άγιον Όρος. Αθωνική Πολιτεία – Ιστορία, Τέχνη, Ζωή* (Athens, 1987), 423.

[10] The most common Greek name for the Virgin Mary, meaning 'All Holy'.

[11] The Feast of the Entry of the Theotokos into the Temple (21 November).

[12] Canopied stoup containing holy water.

[13] Holy oil for anointing in Catholic and Orthodox rites.

[14] An epithet of the Virgin.

In the night (vigil) I was given the wine in [13.3] a silver bowl. I bent down and drank. The stamped Eucharist bread. (The mosaic in Daphni with the Panagia as a little girl.)

The angels are curly-haired [14.3] and the smoke caught in their locks is steaming like dew drawn from sheep by the rising sun.

[26.3] Boiled wheat.[15] The summer night, blue through the church window panes. Remember the night in Xylokastro, as it appeared in your mind during the liturgy in the [27.3] Iviron church.

[30.3] Damaskenos.[16] When spring arrives the elements of the body turn back to be renewed.

Easter. Unsurpassable times have begun [31.3] to rise up.

(Pythia) Hera (she was kissed by great Helios).

And her name is Maria, who, like the ocean, carries in her womb a heavily laden vessel.

For it is in the waters of the spring that the spirit's spring slumbers having only one fish [1.4] (the divine one, caught with a fishing hook).

The Lament Singer.[17]

Our Lady of the Springs.

[5.4] The 10 bells of the Iviron monastery.

Portaïtissa. A miracle!

Eyes, lips. The whole ocean.

The crown.

Her golden garment. A golden suit of armour.

[6.4] The inner courtyard.

---

[15] Mixed with sugar, nuts and raisins, this is offered at memorial services.

[16] St John Damaskenos (675–749?) is thought of as a Greek forerunner of St Thomas Aquinas. He wrote a renowned summary of *Theology* and composed hymns still sung today.

[17] A reference to the Virgin and her lament at the Cross. The 'Virgin's Lament' is an established literary tradition in Greece; the earliest example is a sixth-century *kontakion* of Romanos the Melodist. See R. Beaton, *Folk poetry of Modern Greece* (Cambridge, 1980), 141–144; M. Alexiou, *The ritual lament in Greek tradition* (Cambridge, 1974), 63; M. Alexiou, 'The lament of the Virgin in Byzantine literature and Modern Greek folk song', *BMGS*, 1, (1975), 113–116.

Song of Songs. 'And my inner parts were stirred because of him.'[18]

a blend of winds

a blend of myrrh

[8.4] St Nicholas in Stavronikita monastery. The oyster between his eyebrows.[19]

The scent of pine-wood kindling in the corridors.

[9.4] Far below the window at Stavronikita a seagull was travelling. From high up you could see the birds hiding away in trees and shrubs by [10.4] the sea. Perched on dry branches they shook their little heads.

In the cemetery of Stavronikita.

Remember the transfiguration, the deep imitation of [11.4] your soul, before the twelve-year-old Jesus. The need for purity and dignity in front of him at the circular table.

[12.4] The two sights together, the Portaïtissa and the Twelve-Year-Old, in Stavronikita.

Evening birdsong on the mountains.

[13.4] The Twelve-Year-Old.

My prayer.

The fountain through the arches. In the background the stone slab with the cross at the base and the thin jet of water. Our Lady[20] of the Springs.

The Twelve Year Old.

[14.4] The snake that fell from the tower of Stavronikita. A black rat snake; it fell from a height and died instantly; very big (a house snake, I believe).

[15.4] St Nicholas, the Christian Glaucus.[21] The big oyster on his forehead. Only half has survived.

---

[18] Song of Songs 5.4, following the words 'my beloved put his hand upon the latch'.

[19] It is a well-known mosaic icon. According to tradition it was thrown into the sea during the Iconoclast movement where it remained until it was recovered 700 years later. Damage between the eyebrows was caused by an oyster (στρείδι) which stuck there and can still be seen. Hence the icon's name, St Nicholas the Streidas. See Chrestou, *Το Άγιον Όρος*, 425–426.

[20] He writes Δέσποινα, which in Modern Greek refers specifically to the Virgin Mary. (In Byzantine, the term, an imperial title, was used as a formal address to any woman of refinement. The Modern Greek word δεσποινίς ('miss') is a cognate.)

[16.4] The prayer rope. A spiritual prayer.

Breathing out: have mercy on me. Breathing in: Lord Jesus Christ.[22] This is the [17.4] monks' pure prayer from the time of waking to the moment the service starts.

[18.4] After burying their dead, the monks gather around the grave and repeat, with the rhythm [19.4] of the above pure prayer, 'Lord, grant rest to the soul of your servant.'

The concentration of the *nous* [20.4]on the heart.[23]

Contemplative fathers; those devoted to the inner prayer.

[21.4] Gregory Palamas,[24] the contemplative *par excellence* in his book, the *Philokalia*.

The notion of constantly praying.[25]

[25.4] Because relentless thinking does not allow the object of thought to be manifest.

And with the blue of the sky my mind slowly was imbued.

[26.4] An inner humming.

The inner humming of the song.

And it happens that, when the *nous* is praying, concentrating on the heart, and the mind slips into daydreaming, [27.4] pondering over other things; so it

---

[21] A fisherman in Boeotia. He pursued Scylla provoking the anger of Circe who turned the maiden into a sea-monster. After eating a magic herb, Glaucus was changed into a sea-god and grew old in the sea. See Ovid, *Metamorphoses* XIII and XIV. The story also appears in Keats' *Endymion*, Book III.

[22] The poet is referring to 'the prayer of silence' which is thought to allow the praying individual to listen rather than talk; one way to reach this stage is, what is called, the Invocation of the Name (of Jesus): 'Lord Jesus Christ, Son of God, have mercy on me.' It is connected with breathing in and out. The 'Jesus prayer' was favoured by hesychasts. See K.T. Ware, *The power of the name. The Jesus prayer in Orthodox spirituality* (Oxford, 1999), 1–17.

[23] According to the hesychasts, during the Jesus prayer 'the individual has to concentrate on the heart'. 'Heart' in this context is to be understood in the Semitic and biblical rather than the modern western sense; it signifies not only emotions and feelings but the totality of the individual as a human being. See Ware, *Power of the name*, 17.

[24] St Gregory Palamas (1296–1359), archbishop of Thessalonike, who took up the defence of the Hesychasts against Barlaam. See Ware, *Orthodox Church*, 76.

[25] The poet refers to the above prayer, which, being so simple, the monks repeat continually like a mantra, even when working. See Ware, *Power of the name*, 26.

submits to no one, save the beings perfect in the Holy Spirit, those who achieved tranquillity. X.I. 481 *Philokalia.*

[28.4] When the face of *nous* bows towards the heart, it can see the spiritual effulgence springing from it in an eternal flow, and then is an excellent time [29.4] to be silent.

I am setting out for my beloved (Prayer?)

The intellect can still easily recognise both the greatest and the smallest.

Pleasant, beseeching [30.4] soundless voices.

Inside me the whole ocean is singing.

A herd of oxen in front [1.5] of blood. My first night in Stavronikita monastery. The music I heard in my sleep. Waking up in the depth of [2.5] night, I thought of the song of the 'Twelve-Year-Old Jesus'.

Opening of the heart.

Inrush of the spirit.

[13.5] 1st) At Vespers, the wooden semantron;[26] the monk goes around the church with his cap. The poundings at first rhythmical, then fast, staccato; finally peaceful, solemn, deep. And suddenly just one strong beat, and the monk enters the sanctuary through the rear [14.5] door.

2nd) He returns. And this now is Jesus giving up his spirit at the end. And the final beat is the 'It is finished'! For him, in each sound of the hammer lies the whole drama of Jesus; the second [15.5] time around, he pounds twice; the third, three times.

Boiled wheat for Theia-Maria's memorial service; the memorial service.

At Stavronikita monastery. An old icon with Peter and Paul embracing each other, [16.5] cheek to cheek. Each one, separately, looks at Jesus.

The hand bell.

You must purchase the *Synagoge* of Evergetinos.[27]

---

[26] A wooden sounding board. See C. Cavarnos, *Anchored in God. An inside account of life, art and thought on the Holy Mountain of Athos* (Athens, 1959), glossary.

[27] Evergetinos, Paul (d. 1054). Compiler of an influential monastic florilegium, a selection of spiritual texts in four books. It was entitled *Synagoge*, and is usually referred to as the *Evergetinon*. The first volume in the Belfast series is translated by R.H. Jordan.

[17.5] *Song of Cana*

Oh companion of my soundless thoughts
Who open and close my sleepless eyes
To strengthen your cedar bed.

[22.5] The bell-shaped grapes of September.

The giant rosemary bush in the Pantokrator monastery.

Candlelight.

Orange trees and cypresses.

The ploughed earth is blackish (eros).

[27.5] Chrysostomos: his last words: Glory to God for everything.

My final good-bye to the monks at Stavronikita. I kissed the bishop, Gabriel's hand, and Synesios on the face.

[28.5] Eleutherios was deeply moved when I kissed him. He could not utter a word.

[29.5] At Karakalou monastery.

The communal supper. A long hall. Eight pillars – long tables on the right. The fathers eat in silence. In front of them small green jars. When we entered (the tables are slightly warped), [30.5] a male cat jumped and strode under the tables quietly. On the left a tripod stand. The reader is reading as they are eating while the male cats move around. The abbot sits at the top table [31.5] under the icon of Jesus. At the end of the hall, three altars. On the left a Panagia, in the middle, the iconostasis. On the right (where the abbot sits) Jesus. Suddenly the abbot pounds with a small hammer, and the supper ends.

[31.5a] Then the reader approaches the abbot and, kissing his hand, asks for his blessing. And the abbot gives him wine and bread. Then he pounds with the little hammer for a second [1.6] time (three times) and everyone stands up, the abbot first and then, one by one, all the fathers. At the back, though, near the right exit, the servitor, the reader and the cook are on their knees, [2.6] and while the others are passing by, they ask for absolution, to be forgiven if they have not worked well; walking past them, the abbot blesses them with his black pastoral crosier. The priest opposite, though, [3.6] blesses all the fathers.

When the eyes draw their power from *nous*. From *nous*, and from the pure knowledge of all things.

[5.6] The shiny-haired goats. Their shiny curls.

When the wheat ripens and its grain is milky, suddenly a hot wind starts blowing etc.

Sweet Compline [6.6] will come.

> *And the companion of soundless thoughts*
> *Had closed the blossom of your strength,*
> *Like bees on the honeycomb.*

[9.6] Sunday night at Karakalou (St Andrew's day).[28] During the supper I feel my soul and body so very full that I cannot take anything else in. At the sound of the bell I feel a lyrical warmth. The trumpet of St Pachomios[29] in the desert. We are setting out for Vespers. They wake us at dawn.

[11.6] …(The case of Silenus[30] in Vodena.)[31] Deacon Euthymios is longing to become a shepherd again.

The doves in Karakalou monastery. A cloud around [12.6] the tower. Their shadows on the walls of the tower. They move around, altogether, left first, then right, until they settle on the jetties.

[13.6] The little tree bent under the singing birds as if under the weight of fruit.

When the abbot pounds with the hammer for the first time he knocks on a flat piece of iron (like the head of a nail [14.6] that is fixed in front of the table), then on a small hanging bell also fixed to the table.

The fasting monk faints at the scent of [15.6] relics; the smell in the sanctuary is a spiritual smell; at the great festivals.

---

[28] 30 November.

[29] St Pachomios (c.290–346) was the founder of coenobitic Christian monasticism. See H. Delehaye, 'Byzantine monasticism', *Byzantium: an introduction to east Roman civilization*, ed. N. Baynes and H. Moss (Oxford, 1962), 137.

[30] Silenus was a spirit of wild nature, like a satyr. He is associated with the god Dionysos and it is said he was his tutor. He had great wisdom. The first literary mention of Silenus appears in *Hymn. Aphr.* 262. See also W. Burkert, *Greek religion,* tr. J. Raffan (Oxford, 1987), 166, n. 42, and Ovid, *Metamorphoses*, XI.86–108.

[31] Vodena is the Bulgarian name for Edessa, a town built on the river Edessaios or Vodas (the latter meaning 'water' in Slavonic languages) and is known for its spectacular waterfalls. It is thought that Edessa is built on the site of the ancient town of Aigai. I am not sure about the connection of Silenus with this place, though some scholars believe that the first inhabitants were Thracians, who were known for the cult of Dionysos (see the preceding note).

Myrrh, Karavostasi.[32]

We must ask the doctor in the Lavra to show us [16.6] the copper icons that were brought down from Athos.

The grass-covered courtyard of Philotheou monastery. Our walk up there. Mist. Only the cypresses were visible. The bare chestnut [17.6] trees. The ivy. The whole grass-covered courtyard in the mist. The two cypresses inside the courtyard. An open corridor overlooking the courtyard of the monastery and the forest. A staircase [18.6] takes you to a wooden terrace (the roof of a house). The twin fountains in the mist; the arched windows. As he spoke, vapours came out of his mouth clouding his face like a breath of [19.6] incense. The horses steamed in the rain; in front of the cypresses, the mist moved invisibly like a breath.

The Divinity of the Glykophiloussa.[33] The monastery of Philotheou.

[20.6] The fragrance of the wood of the wild poplar is rising up, like secret myrrh, which, if it spread, would also raise our minds high.

[22.6] …The new-grown cypresses.

The three marvels we've seen up to now: The Portaïtissa, the Twelve-Year-Old Jesus, the Glykophilousa.

The Cretans' [23.6] cell.[34] The old man who has been talking to us about the Holy Mountain for years.

The blessing with holy water (Matins) (1 December) at Karakalou. On my forehead, the coolness of water [24.6] with rosemary.

As we sifted, the chaff went to the back, the stones, being heavy, to the front, and the divine grain stayed in the middle.

[25.6] …2 December. A delicate neck; laurel oil; [26.6] the strong acorn; the dewy shrubs.

---

[32] The Bay of the Standing Ship. According to tradition, after his release from the Arabs Peter the Athonite was sailing past Mt Athos when he realised that his ship was miraculously rooted in the sea off Karavostasi. He took this as a heavenly sign, so he left the ship and started climbing up the rock until he found a cave to rest. From there he watched his ship and its crew sailing away. G. Speake, *Mt Athos, renewal in paradise* (New Haven and London, 2002), 39.

[33] The sweetly-kissing Virgin, a type of icon representing the Virgin touching Jesus's face with her cheek. This particular icon must have moved the poet. The Virgin here has a calm beauty and her expression radiates tenderness and love. See Chrestou, *Το Άγιον Όρος*, 425.

[34] A place of isolation.

Falling down he slept like a lion and who would wake him up?

I must remember to ask for the icons [27.6] of the Byzantine musicians.

At the Great Lavra. The relics of St Basil the Great. The relics of Koukouzelis, the chanter.

The refectory of the Lavra. [28.6] Stone tables with grooves.

As we enter, above the door a votive; the ear of Atremis.

The virgin Daphne[35] escaping from Apollo's hands. Daphne took refuge on the Holy Mountain to save herself from [29.6] Apollo (her chastity). The crown of Nikephoros. The dalmatic.[36]

Antiphonetra.[37]

I said today, the day when the [30.6] grass that withered and the leaf that fell with the sun's kiss and with the holy sea breeze, rising to a higher life and tuning us in harmony with the universe, I said, this year I must realise a liturgical book, where, through traditional religious symbols, the whole of nature will come alive and divine, apocalyptically: like a dalmatic, like a kiss. [30.6a] In a higher sensual unity where the sense of life is a magnet that calls for an uninterrupted flight away from individual restrictions, above the snow (eternal spring, the daisies [1.7] the scent of the grass absorbing the sun etc. etc.) in and above springtime, at the hour when fruit and blossom meet.

On the slopes of Athos on the same day. Snow (on the top). Olive trees and cypresses, bare poplars, [2.7] daisies, and in the distance, the blue sea, a sleepless magnet. The cycle of my life completed as I stretched out with my manhood [3.7] to the grass; there all my life appeared to me as the highest good, above even its superior dancing, lifting the erotic pleasure as the humble bee lifts pollen on its legs. [4.7] The sudden breaths of wind that plough the warmth with a shivering, toss up a treasure of dry leaves, and stripping man of his past, leave him in eternal relationship with the uncreated source [5.7] of life.

---

[35] Apollo pursued Daphne, the mountain nymph, priestess of Mother Earth and daughter of the river Peneios in Thessaly. When he overtook her, she asked Mother Earth for help. Her prayer was answered: the goddess took her away and sent her to Crete but left a laurel tree in her place. See R. Graves, *The Greek myths*, 2 vols (Harmondsworth, 1984), I, 78; also Ovid, *Metamorphoses*, I.

[36] An imperial and ecclesiastical vestment. Generally an over-tunic reaching to the knees, perhaps of Dalmatian origin.

[37] The poet refers to one of the many historic icons of the Virgin. It is called Antiphonetra because, according to tradition, she forbade the empress Galla Placidia, daughter of Theodosios I, to enter the church (Chrestou, Το Άγιον Όρος, 422).

Get in tune with the universe. Every transitory emotion within me has vanished. I kneel down like an ox and grow wings like an archangel.

The magnet of the starlit sky; the night!

[6.7] Spruce trees; from the Lavra to Kerasia. A footpath on a cliff by the sea...
[7.7] ...Elevated to our original nature and strength. The snow we encountered. The mule was eating snow; we tasted it too.

> *The soul forgot itself in the green depths.* [8.7]
> *Like a star, the depths of the heart spoke*
> *As they glanced at the fir tree and the oak.*
> *On the strong acorns.*

Eagle-black (dark brown); eagle-black resin.

[11.7] ...The Skete[38] of Kausokalyvia, 6 Dec. [1]914. St Nicholas's day.

We visited the woodcarvers. The first one with grey eyes. The other, waking up from sleep, looked very [12.7] soft and very pale, with a beard like silk around his longish face and deep virginal eyes. His hand is as soft as wax, and as light as *antidoron*.[39] We then visited Arsenios, the woodcarver, who carved the [13.7] Second Coming on the enkolpion[40] of Karyes. He is self taught; he started with small, rough crosses. He worked on the Second Coming for 15 years and gave expression to every face. The glow of work is instilled on his countenance. [14.7] In his little room we can see all the tools of his craft. The beginning of a work *ébauche* ['rough draft']. His blackbird. It eats myrtle berries, ivy seed and dough out of the palm of the hand. Such faith in humans. It is black and shiny.

[15.7] At night, silence. On the veranda of the Joasaphs[41] I remembered Panselinos[42] again. I am deeply conscious of my moral elevation in a work where it is impossible to find any response. *Now all my work is well-grounded on willpower, as if on a rock, and eternal.*

---

[38] A small monastery, dependent on a greater one.
[39] Blessed but not consecrated bread distributed at the end of the Orthodox Liturgy.
[40] A reliquary worn on the breast.
[41] According to medieval legends, St Joasaph, the son of an Indian king, was converted to Christianity by the hermit Barlaam. Josaphat appears to be a corruption of 'Bodisatva', a title of the Buddha.
[42] The most important iconographer of the Macedonian school characterised by realism and vividness. His name is associated with paintings on Mt Athos. Archaeological and art-historical evidence suggests he lived between 1282 and 1328; he was mainly responsible for the original decoration of the church of Protaton at Karyes. See D.T. Rice, *Art of the Byzantine era* (London, 1986), 252ff.

[22.7] The Virgin Myrobletissa.[43]

The Mirror.[44]

St Paul's day; on the shore. The deep musical awareness of life among rocks and sea.

[23.7] The ocean has carved paths and so has the foam. The foam which vanishes with the recurring wave speaks to the rocks eternally, and my mind is listening like the mind of Proteus[45] – or of Glaucus. Circles, whirlpools, seaweed dragged along, fragrant girdles left by the Sea-nymphs, glide along the sides of the ship. Its latent power [24.7] can be seen in the yawning chasm, like the lion's shining teeth, the fiery throat down to the larynx below. The scattered islands, and in front of them the caiques passing through narrow channels as if through the mouths of dragons. The sea is bubbling up, like a squirming beast, and tosses up the miracle. [25.7] The pebbles, mixed with sea shells, are thundering. The head of Medusa (*motivo*) severed, the snakes move, bend whistle. Athena has assigned to the flute this final agony.

At the New Skete of St Paul. The gardens, the broad-leaved laurels; the olive trees, [26.7] lemon-trees (with fresh lemons like a virgin's breasts), orange-trees...[46] The Virgin Glykophiloussa in St Paul's Skete; with his little hand Jesus touches the Virgin's chin beneath [27.7] her lips. His other little hand rests on his tiny body, relaxed.

The icons that perspire. – The hand of St Nicholas, as if he had dipped it in the sea (says the monk).

[30.7] (If one moves forward in tune with nature, it is easy to stop. Yet, this very fact makes it more difficult to follow her.) The problem of *eros*.

---

[43] Myrrh-exuding. The celebrated icon of the Virgin in Dionysiou monastery. According to tradition, it was created by St Luke the Evangelist and it is the very icon that patriarch Sergios held in his hands during the siege of Constantinople by the Avars in 626. Therefore it is also called Akathistos. See Chrestou, *Τo Άγιον Όρος*, 424.

[44] In St Paul's monastery there is a remarkable icon of the Virgin. It is called the Mirror (*Kathreptes*) perhaps because its back is burnt. According to tradition it belonged to the empress Theodora, the wife of Theophilos. It shows the Virgin with the infant Jesus kissing her left cheek. See Chrestou, *Τo Άγιον Όρος*, 425.

[45] A minor sea-god endowed by Poseidon with the gift of prophecy and also the power to change his shape until firmly held (*Odyssey*, 4, 350ff).

[46] This ellipsis is part of the original text.

[31.7] At Dionysiou monastery. We climbed up from the *arsanas*[47].... A gorge. The wind, misty, rushed inside. We entered. The portico. Frescoes of the portico: the Apocalypse.

[1.8] At Dionysiou refectory. The Assembly of the Bodiless Host. A glowing dance. Jesus is in the middle: Twelve-years-old, a child. All with fire-red hair, [2.8] golden haloes, golden wings, golden stoles and belts. A sight more glowing than the harvest of wheat in a summer sunset. Their tunics are white, [3.8] but here and there slightly flame-coloured.

Above the golden swordblade of the sun as it sets over the ocean. A miracle.

[4.8] The face of Jesus in the Assembly of the Bodiless Host. Large, bright forehead, arched eyebrows, small face.

In the middle, the fireplace. Water is boiling in an amphora, for the older monks to warm [5.8] their wine.

The Dragon of the Deep.

The Holy Trinity in the Refectory at Dionysiou. The niche. Three angels [8.8][48] on the left; between the first angel and the middle one, Joseph, and between the middle and the third one (on the right) the Virgin's head.

[14.8] The bare rock (a pure expression of an innocent disposition on bare rock).

I am already reproducing the Dionysiou monastery. The graveyard. The grave of St Nephon. The [15.8] graves facing the sea. The gorge pours out wind like a river. Gales are beating the ocean below. Looking at the outside world from the Holy Mountain. The inner strength [16.8] becomes visible now. *L' esprit des matérialités.* (The ships below. A magnetic mountain. / I must read Tahilède again.) Compline at Dionysiou. The profound impression at Dionysiou.[49] The low, dark, icon-painted [17.8] corridors. Every colour is dark, heavy, discreet. Its tower.

---

[47] A landing place, with warehouses and buildings for workmen and seamen and a tower formerly used for defence against pirates. Every Athonite monastery has its own *arsanas*. See Cavarnos, *Anchored in God*, glossary.

[48] Editorial note: no omission here. There are no pages between 5.8 and 8.8. Presumably a leaf was torn out of the diary here (AMH).

[49] The Dionysiou monastery is quite imposing. It stands near the sea, on a precipitous rock and it rises to six storeys on the south side and four on the others. It was founded in 1355. Speake, *Mt Athos*, 76.

[18.8] Dometios's[50] coins (Dionysiou). The statuette of the pregnant woman. She has her left hand under her head (like a pillow) and her right under her heavy belly. Woman. The beauty of the pregnant woman. Deeply moved by this sacred condition of woman.

[20.8] Father Abraamios at Dionysiou told me: 'Since I saw you I felt peace.'

Here are almond trees in the moonlight. '*Bello fratello è il bosco Goringani, magnifica* [23.8][51] *la chiara notte lunare gli alberi danno in pieno fiore, pare che celesti profumi spirino intorno. Quale, o fratello Renato, può dare splendore al bosco Goringani.*'[52]

Kazantzakis's dream about the Holy Trinity at Dionysiou. The three [24.8] angels, the three streams that hold the seed of life, man's and woman's. I remembered Spiess.[53] *Physiologie. La vérité sur Nietzsche. L' âme et le corps.*

[28.8] The angel to St Pachomios: 'Only those who wish to live wholly in Christ will be clothed in this habit.'

She rubbed the apple on her apron, sparking off its fragrance. [29.8] She rubbed the citrus fruit with her hand.

At Gregoriou monastery. The Assembly of the Bodiless Host. It is reminiscent of Chinese art; the angel on the left looks like a Persian maiden.

---

[50] The poet is referring to one of those old monasteries which were founded between the tenth and fourteenth centuries when the number of monasteries on Athos was not controlled and restricted. Most of them functioned only for a while and then faded out. See Chrestou, *Το Άγιον Όρος*, 55–77.

[51] Editorial note: no omission here. The pages for 21.8 and 22.8 are blank. Presumably Sikelianos turned over two leaves by mistake (AMH).

[52] Source of the Italian quotation not identified.

[53] There are two writers by the name of Spiess who could have attracted Sikelianos' attention: (1) Henri Spiess (1876–1940), a Swiss poet, whose collection *Silence des heures* (1904) has placed him within the symbolist tradition; (2) Edmund Spiess, German scholar, doctor of Philosophy and Theology in the University of Jena, who wrote on eschatology, though his most important book was *Logos Spermaticos. Parallelstellen zum Neuen Testament aus den Schriften der Alten Griechen* (Leipzig, 1871), where he compared ancient Greek thought with the writings of New Testament. According to the Stoics, God, the *logos*, is a *logos spermatikos*, a seed-bearing word. The seeds of logos are active in the world and especially in human beings forming the central soul-force. See G.H. Rendall, *Marcus Aurelius Antoninus to himself*. (London, 1898), lii–lviii. In view of the context in which 'Spiess' appears, I believe that Sikelianos has the second author in mind.

[1.9] At Simonopetra monastery. Going out to the *arsanas*. The sea; suddenly the foam looks warm, as if a serenity of life is burning underneath. And, suddenly, I remember the warm hand of the [2.9] Magdalene, at Simonopetra.

The ascent to Simonopetra. Right and left the laurel tree is bursting forth, overshooting lavishly; a stream of laurel. Close by [3.9] a gorge where the withered trees are enveloped in dense ivy. We could hear the waves below, and above the sound of the water. A forest of laurel branches. Above [4.9] a semantron is calling joyfully, trembling like the hawk which, hovering over the precipice, moves around in circles. Do not forget this path; the Magdalene's divine warmth.

The whole body coming victorious out of the holy…[54]

[7.9] The day of the Magdalene.

Going uphill we met a snake which moved as if drugged and was basking in the heat. (Thursday 11 December). Further up, O warm miracle of perfume, we find wild violets. I placed them in the [8.9] case of St Dionysios's relics next to my father's letter.

You must ask Avyeris for Swinburne.

I kissed the Magdalene's hand three times.

[9.9] The Dark-Skinned Panagia. Byzantine. Like a child I leaned on her breast with the dark threshing floor around her nipple.[55] I felt I was her son. Towards April-May. [10.9] I look around me. Easter.

In my ears the roaring of the four rivers [11.9] flowing out of Paradise.[56]

I bridged Euphrates like Dionysos.[57]

[13.9] The quick speaking waters.

---

[54] Editorial note: this sentence was presumably concluded on the page for 5.9, but the pages for 5.9 and 6.9 are missing from the diary. Presumably another leaf that was torn out (AMH).

[55] Sikelianos has probably in mind the Virgin Galaktotrophousa, in the Simonopetra monastery. In this unusual icon the Virgin is portrayed enthroned giving suck to baby Jesus with her left breast.

[56] According to Genesis 2:10–14, God created four rivers that flowed from Eden towards the four cardinal points: Tigris, Euphrates, Pishon and Gihon. The last two have not been identified with real rivers.

[57] According to mythology Dionysos conquered India before Alexander the Great, bridging the Euphrates river with vine and ivy.

No. Like Daphne with Apollo. [14.9] You kept your virginity, but gave it away from the root to the bright seed.

[15.9] Travelling around Greece, like the priest who goes around the Church with a cross, I place you on the navel of Delphi. [16.9] Mother, here I come; naked before you, like Achilles before Thetis. Mother, I am your son. [17.9] And you are more boundless than the seas far as prayer and slumber reach.

[18.9] I saw the holy man, and he looked to me like Silenus when hunted in the woods by Midas. (When he caught him he was tasting the [19.9] honeycomb.) The haven of your joy etc.

> *The haven of your joy is like a summer shelter*
> *made from freshly cut branches, which*
> *the cattle, stopping by, pull out to graze on.*

The taming, inside and out, of nature.

Delphi.

32

Five imitations of Jenny Mastoraki

Sarah Ekdawi Brandt

The five texts presented here are not translations in a conventional sense, which is why I have elected to refer to them as imitations. My translator's manifesto can best be summed up as the attempt to produce an equal music, and not a literal rendering. Before presenting my versions, I shall provide brief details of the author, the collection from which these texts are drawn, and my translating strategies.

Jenny Mastoraki was born in Athens in 1949, and studied Byzantine and medieval Greek literature at Athens University. She has published four slim volumes of poetry, and the five 'imitations' that follow are all taken from the latest of these, *With a garland of light* (Athens, 1989). Since 1989, Jenny Mastoraki has not published any poetry.

With a garland of light was hailed by leading Greek critics as a masterpiece. The collection comprises thirty-four short lyric poems and two slightly more extended prose poems. The poems are untitled, and I have numbered them here in square brackets, in order to indicate their positions in the sequence. The poems of *With a garland of light* are oblique and elliptical, with no real narrative content and very little referential content. They follow a dreamlike logic of their own, associating images and scenes that do not share any obvious features. There are, however, themes running through the collection that connect the poems to each other, though diffusely.

The poems of *With a garland of light* make extensive use of allusion, chiefly to Mavilis and Solomos. I have replaced Mastoraki's allusions, where possible, with completely different allusions that belong to the target language and culture, rather than including numerous footnotes about nineteenth-century Greek poetry. Mastoraki's allusions would be instantly recognisable to her readers, and I have aimed at producing a comparable effect.

All the poems in this collection have a very dense sound-texture. The underlying rhythm throughout is iambic. There is also occasional rhyme and a certain amount of alliteration and assonance. For Mastoraki's understated iambics, I have drawn on the English tradition of iambic pentameter, though not too insistently. I have imitated Mastoraki in using occasional rhyme, but never in precisely the same places, since of course different words rhyme in different languages. I have also tried to reproduce, or rather approximate, the unsystematic alliteration and assonance of the originals, again in slightly different places.

The five texts presented here are representative of both the underlying themes and the shifts in tone of the whole collection.

[5]

There will come a time of lamentation,
enchantment, disbelief, regeneration,
kisses that don't betray, and hope corroding
our battered walls, our armour and our weapons.

And all the names of all the constellations
that watched our bitter wars will be forgotten.

There will come a time of understanding:
you will fall silent, so that you can hear me:
voice of a stranger, speaking in the darkness;
sigh of the battle-weary, now disarming.

And there will come a time of resolution:
an angel sailing near the rocks, in silence,
will count the risks of peace between old lovers.

[7]

Because the kissing-on-the-stairs, the parting,
the ships, the laughing waves, the devils dancing,
because the dizziness, the wicked girl,
white air, tossed sails, the madness of embarking,

scatter gold coins, let down your golden hair!

Because the recognition-scene again,
for it will come, and dawn will come again,
biting the world in two, revealing
love, miracles and rain.

Because the fear of love, the lover's touch,
the savage nakedness, transfixed and lost,
how like a grief, how very like a grief,
the happy ending.

[10]

Lovers transgressed, inflicting mortal wounds:
the pain of the betrayed does not recede;
an evil kiss will leave an evil mark
- madness of no-return, unspoken fear:
age-old attrition of the human heart.

Pain that recedes at dawn returns at night:
a jealous star will prick the eastern sky,
and shed its sickly light across the past;

pain, like a giant lizard creeping back
from mortal combat, with its body burnt
and head as pale as wax, regains its lair;
armed for attrition with betrayal, insult, evil kiss,
terror and sorcery, love will return.

[13]

Tender is sleep and everything it touches,
leaving no wound, no scar, no mark of entry;
covering voices, tracks, nocturnal bleeding;
scattering darkness.

Demonic rainstorm of a summer night:
a wild pursuit that breaks on river banks,
in sweet, harsh breathing; silence; splashing water.

And tenderly it circles, like a lover,
casting its nets across the quiet waters,
like heavy shadows on a moss-green landscape.

[32]

Now may drowned memories,
stagnating in dark pools,
come back to perjure, curse and bless,
come back;

their icy touch, their mouths,
the bruises left by pleading in the night
– the I-need-yous and I'll-be-theres –
come back; bring back remorseless love.

The pit is dug; the pools are dragged;
the menacing black net that opened closes:
demonic longing for things past.

ENVOI

33

'Use the middle – passive not used in Attic prose': a master's stimulus to a life of translation trials

Paul Tuffin

Although populated exclusively by males, the 'Athenaeum' at Sevenoaks School in the early to mid-1960s was no gentleman's club. Similarly, any exclusiveness that might be associated with its inhabitants had little to do with social standing but much to do with the limited numbers of sixth-formers who had elected to study classics (Greek, Latin and ancient history) up to 'A' Level. The Athenaeum was in fact a teaching room in the third-floor servants' quarters of the rather grand 'Manor House' that was part of Sevenoaks School's grounds on the outskirts of Knole Park in Kent and served as form room for the classics sixth. It contained a large dining table of some dark and ancient wood with various forms of chairs around it, bookshelves with a distinctly post-war look and loaded with battered Greek lexicons and Latin dictionaries, a blackboard of course, and, on any day of the school term, some seven, eight or nine 'boys' with varying abilities in their chosen subjects and varying degrees of commitment to improving these abilities.

On the day in question there was some excitement in this group of pupils: a new classics master had been appointed and was about to make his début before them. How would he compare with the existing ex-army major and the portly devotee of Beethoven? Memory of what that first class entailed has passed – whether it was Latin or Greek, Roman history or Greek history, but the image of a *young* man in a brown cord jacket, with a strong jaw, a slight west-country accent, and a broad smile that took little time to appear is readily available still. Mr Jordan (rapidly to become 'RHJ', 'Rob' or 'Bob Jordan' amongst the denizens of the Athenaeum – though never to the man himself) turned out not only to be a classics master and therewith master of deep mysteries such as those of Greek accentuation and versification, but also master of the offside rule in rugger (a winter-term three-times-a-week trial by ordeal for most Athenaeum dwellers), as augured by his later appearance on the games field, looking spruce and bewhistled in boots, shorts, and rugby shirt – a second image that survives.

The messages were numerous: despite the unquestionable depth and breadth of knowledge of his field that this classicist had, he could nevertheless be young, fit, and presentable – even by the standards of a child (well, sixteen-year old) of the sixties. The key message, however, was in the smile and its companion laughter, which told of the enjoyment to be found in the challenges of studying classics, including even those dread exercises in translation – unseens, prose composition, and verse composition. (This smile, it might be noted, was still able to present itself when a rather sheepish sixteen-year-old, who, on a fortnight's school excursion to Greece, had taken it upon himself to leave the main group of students and travel with a fellow rebel not to Crete but to Thessalonike – and then to spend the period of separation in a misery of concern for the consequences of this act – finally greeted his master on his return with apologies, fear, and great relief.)

The exercises in translation, discussion of what might be seen as correct and why this might be so, and advice on improvement continued for pupil and master throughout the sixth form, preparing the way for the pupil into similar activities at undergraduate level. Here he added modern, medieval, and Byzantine Greek to the mix for translation and attempted some larger pieces of literary translation. Professional life in Australia led the former pupil to the teaching of undergraduate (modern) Greek-English interpreters and translators for a decade or so, before returning his focus in more recent years to earlier Greek and the task of translating into English the work of Byzantine chronographers.

Physical remains from sixth-form classics days are scarce but in one surviving notebook there is preserved the pupil's attempt to translate into ancient Greek a passage taken from the writings of Sir Walter Raleigh. In the red ink of correction there is a masterly comment on an aorist passive verb form 'Use the middle – passive not used in Attic prose'. The pupil was being reminded (not for the first time) of the audience at whom the translation was being aimed – that group of well-educated and rather critical fifth-century Athenian citizens with an ear for rhetoric, whose only shortcoming as an audience was their blatant non-existence – and of the constraints on choice of language form that this implied.

This brief comment, one amongst a number of others, on a piece of Greek prose composition, itself only one amongst many others, that achieved a mark of only 'β- ?', nevertheless symbolises 'a master's stimulus to a life of translation trials'. The stimulus lies in its demand to consider carefully the choice of language form to be used to convey the translated meaning to the target audience and, implied in this, the criteria that are to be taken into account in making this choice – particularly, perhaps, the degree to which the translator will 'process' the meaning in order to make it accessible to the target group – the point where, in my experience, the 'trials' most especially lie.[1] Thus, for example, one of the attempts,

---

[1] Of course these are not the only cruces in the process of translating, as the body of work produced on translation theory evidences.

mentioned above, at 'larger pieces of literary translation' (a collection of literary critical essays), where the translated text tried to represent in English the difficult and sometimes involuted language and style of the original, was rejected for publication in the end as being insufficiently accessible for the intended readership, while interpreting and translating students were failed if they were tempted to include their own explanations of oblique original discourse, and a balance is hopefully being achieved latterly by learning to accompany translation into English from difficult Byzantine texts with copious paratextual assistance.[2]

'Use the middle – passive not used in Attic prose' – for the stimulus towards the life of translation trials, sincere thanks, RHJ – and, you know, despite their non-existence, that hard-to-please crowd of fifth-century Athenian citizens seems to be calling something out to you:

εὖγ' εὖγε νὴ Δί' εὖγε

---

[2] I have in mind here particularly what I learned through my collaboration with Professor William Adler of North Carolina State University on the translation of *The Chronography of George Synkellos* (Oxford, 2002).

Abbreviations

AASS: Acta Sanctorum (Brussels, 1643–)
AHG: Analecta hymnica graeca, XI: *Canones Iulii*, ed. I. Schirò (Rome, 1966–1983)
AnalBoll: Analecta Bollandiana (Paris, Brussels and Geneva, 1882–)
B: Byzantion (Paris and Brussels, 1924–)
BBTT: Belfast Byzantine Texts and Translations (Belfast, 1991–)
BHG: Bibliotheca Hagiographica Graeca, ed. F. Halkin (Brussels, 1957)
BMFD: Byzantine monastic foundation documents, ed. J. Thomas and A.C. Hero, 5 vols (DOS, 35, Washington, DC, 2000)
ByzIntCong: Proceedings of the International Byzantine Congress (various, 1920–)
BZ: Byzantinische Zeitschrift (Leipzig and Munich, 1892–)
CS: Cistercian Studies Series (Kalamazoo, 1969–)
CSCO: Corpus Scriptorum Christianorum Orientalium (Leuven, 1903–)
CSEL: Corpus Scriptorum Ecclesiasticorum Latinorum (Vienna, 1866–)
CSHB: Corpus Scriptorum Historiae Byzantinae, ed. B.G. Niebuhr (Bonn, 1828–)
DOP: Dumbarton Oaks Papers (Washington, DC, 1941–)
DOS: Dumbarton Oaks Studies (Washington, DC, 1951–)
EETS o.s.: Early English Text Society, original series (Oxford, 1864–)
EETS e.s.: Early English Text Society, extra series (Oxford, 1867–1921)
EHR: English Historical Review (Oxford, 1886–)
JÖB: Jahrbruch der österreichischen Byzantinistik (Vienna, 1950–)
OCP: Orientalia Christiana Periodica (Rome, 1935–)
ODB: Oxford Dictionary of Byzantium, ed. A.P. Kazhdan et al., 3 vols (New York and Oxford, 1991)
PG: Patrologiae cursus completus, Series graeca, ed. J.-P. Migne (161 vols, Paris, 1857–1866)
PO: Patrologia orientalis (Paris, 1897–)
ROC: Revue de l'Orient chrétien (Paris, 1896–1946)
SC: Sources Chrétiennes (Paris, 1955–)
SPBS: Publications of the Society for the Promotion of Byzantine Studies (Aldershot, 1992–)
SubsHag: SubsHag: Subsidia Hagiographica, Société des Bollandistes (Brussels, 1886–)
SynaxCP: Propylaeum ad Acta Sanctorum Novembris. Synaxarium Ecclesiae Constantinopolitanae e codice Sirmondiano, ed. H. Delehaye (Brussels, 1902)
TTH: Translated Texts for Historians (Liverpool, 1985–)
TU: Texte und Untersuchungen zur Geschichte der altchristlichen Literatur (Leipzig, 1883–)
WByzSt: Wiener byzantinistische Studien (Vienna, 1964–)

Index of authors, texts, translators and theorists

Ælfric of Eynsham, 8, n.17, 210–235
Akathistos hymnos, 35
Alexander the monk, 157–184
Alfonso X the Wise, 87
Allen, Pauline, 37
alto ex Olympi, 130
An ABC to the Virgin, 103–110
Anderson, Jeffrey, 12
Apophthegmata patrum, 34, 41
Apologus de Rustico et Hero, 120
Apology for Smectymnus, 117
Ars amatoria, 76
Archimedes, 87
Ascham, Roger, 116, 120
Aurora coelum purpurat, 136

Balsamon, Theodore, 40
Barkhuizen, Jan, 35
Barnstone, Willis, 95
Basil of Caesarea, 40
Basil of Seleucia, 143–156
Basnett-McGuire, Susan, 10
Ben Tibbon, 89
Benjamin, Walter, 101, 111
Blastares, Matthew, 40
Blemmydes, Nikephoros, 24, 25
Bridges, Robert, 137
Brinsley, 122–123
Brut, 91–102

Candea, Virgil, 6
Cavafy, C.P., 296–313
Chandler, John, 129
Chaucer, Geoffrey, 103–110
Choniates, Niketas, 25–26
Chrétien de Troyes, 72–82
Chrysostomides, Julian, 26

Cicero, 38
Cliges, 72–82
Comus, 113
Constas, Nicholas, 35, 37
Constantine Rhodios, 62–65
Copeland, Rita, 98
Coppola, Sylvia, 10
Cunningham, Mary, 6, 8
Cursor mundi, 106

Daniel de Morlei, 88, 90
Del Governo de' regni, 68
de Man, Paul, 101
Dendrinos, Charalambos, 26
Derrida, Jacques, 101
Dexios, Theodore, 24
Diadochos of Photike, 30
Dios, abbot, 57–61
Discovery of the True Cross, 157–184
Drummond, William, of
   Hawthornden, 129
Dryden, John, 10, 120
du Bellay, Joachim, 125
du Cange, Ch. 22
Dumas, Alexander, 289

Elytis, Odysseus, 289–290
Epitaphium Damonis, 114, 124
Erec et Enide, 72, 75
Eustathios of Thessalonike, 7, 25
Evagrios, 32

Featherstone, Jeffrey, 37
Festa, Nicolao, 24
Finlay, Patricia, 12
Friel, Brian, 10, 83

INDEX OF AUTHORS, TEXTS, TRANSLATORS AND THEORISTS

Gaimar, 92
Galen, 87
Gentzler, Edwin, 84, 85
Geoffrey of Monmouth, 91, 99, 100
Germanos, patriarch of Constantinople, 57–61
Gregory of Nazianzos, 38
Gregory of Nyssa, 58–61
Guillaume de Deguileville, 106–109

Herman of Carinthia, 89
Hippocrates, 87
Hirst, Anthony, 12
Historia regum Britanniae, 92
Hoccleve, Thomas, 104, 105, 109
Holy Mountain Journal, 314–331
Horace, 112, 118, 119, 121, 123, 126, 141–142, 287–288
Hörandner, Wolfram, 26
Hortus/The garden, 117
Hunain ben Ishaq, 89
Hypotyposis of Evergetis, 5, 267

Ibn al-Muqaffa', 66
Iser, Wolfgang, 95, 99, 100
Iusta Edovardo King, 113

Jam lucis orto sidere, 130
Jesu dulcis memoria, 130
Johnston, David, 11

Kalila wa-Dimna, 68
Kalosynas, Antonios, 23
Kamateros, John, 7
Kazantzakis, Nikos, 314
Keats, John, 15
Kelly, Stephen, 11
Kimchi, David, 16
King Mark and Iseut the fair, 76

Langtoft, Piers, 92

Lydgate, John, 104, 105, 107, 109
Layamon, 91
Le Chevalier au Lion, 72
Le Chevalier de la charette, 72, 75
Le conte du Graal, 72
L'estoire des Engleis, 92
Leo VI the Wise, 64
Life of Mary/Marinos, 37
Life of Matrona of Perge, 37, 37
Life of Moses, 58, 60
Limberis, Vassilike, 35–36
Liturgy of the Minor Blessing of the Water, 240–247
Lost in translation, 10
Lycidas, 113, 114

Mahabharata, 66
Maimonides, 89
Makres, Makarios, 23
Mango, Cyril, 28
Mannyng, Cyril Robert, 98
Mant, Richard, 128–137
Mantuan, 112, 118
Mark the deacon, 41
Marvell, Andrew, 118
Mastoraki, Jenny, 12, 332–335
Mayer, Wendy, 37
Metamorphoses, 76
Michael *ho tou Thessalonikes*, 7
Milton, John, 112–127
Moschos, John, 34, 196
Mullally, Evelyn, 11
Munitiz, Joseph, SJ, 6

Nathan ben Jehiel, 17
Neophytos of Cyprus, 12, 267–273

On Elijah, 143–156
On the presentation in the temple, 145
On the Resurrection, 1, 143
On the Nativity, 1, 143

On preaching the Holy Cross in England, 249–266
Ovid, 76, 120
Oracles of Leo the Wise, 24

Palamas, Kostis, 289
Palmer, G.E.H., 28
Pancatantra, 66
Papadiamandis, Alexandros, 289–294
Paul of Monemvasia, 12, 185–193
Pelerinage de la vie humaine, 106–108
Peltomaa, Leena Mari, 35–36
Philip of Oxford, 249
Philokalia, 28, 31–32
Pliny the younger, 38
Politian, 287
Procopius, 39, 45
Prodromos, Theodore, 7
Proklos, 35
Pseudo-Joshua the Stylite, 46
Pseudo-Kodinos, 22
Pseudo-Zachariah of Mitylene, 46
Ptolemy, 87

Quintilian, 38, 116

Raimundus, bishop of Toledo, 87
Rashi, 16
Rede, Richardus, 96–97
Richards, I.K.A., 84, 96
Robert of Chester (or Kent), 89
Roman breviary, 128–137
Roman de Brut, 92
Roman d'Eneas, 73
Roman de Thebes, 73
Roman de Troie, 73
Romanos the Melodist, 12, 143–156, 290
Ros/On a drop of dew, 117
Russell, Norman, 28
Paul of Monemvasia, 11, 15–21

Ricoeur, Paul, 101
Rutherford, Janet, 30–32

Salutis aeternae dator, 134
Speculum vitae, 98
Spiritual meadow, 34
Scott, Roger, 12
Seth, Symeon, 67
Ševčenko, Nancy, 12
Shelley, Percy Bysshe, 111
Sherrard, Philip, 28
Sikelianos, Angelos, 12, 314–331
Stabat mater dolorosa, 130
Steele, Richard, 141
Steiner, George, 12, 24, 30, 83, 89
Stephanites kai Ichnelates, 66–71
Stow, John, 109–110
Strategios, Antiochos, 42
Symeon the New Theologian, 12, 236–239
Symeon of Sinai, 274–286
Synaxarion of Evergetis, 28
Synesios of Cyrene, 43, 49

Te lucis ante terminum, 132
Te splendor et virtus patris, 135
Theodore II Laskaris, 24
Thompson, John, 11
Translations, 10, 83,
Trapp, Erich, 22
Treatise on the Old and New Testaments, 210–235
Tornikes, George, 7
Turner, John, 12
Typikon of Pakourianos, 5, 267
Typikon of Phoberou, 5, 267
Typikon of Kecharitomene, 5, 267
Typikon of Pantokrator, 5, 267
Typikon of St Sabas, 40
Twain, Mark, 289

Vegliante, Jean-Charles, 85
Venantius Fortunatus, 133–134